Black Baseball Out of Season

ALSO BY WILLIAM F. MCNEIL
AND FROM MCFARLAND

Red Sox Roll Call: 200 Memorable Players, 1901–2011 (2012)

*All-Stars for All Time: A Sabermetric Ranking
of the Major League Best, 1876–2007* (2009)

*Miracle in Chavez Ravine:
The Los Angeles Dodgers in 1988* (2008)

*Backstop: A History of the Catcher and
a Sabermetric Ranking of 50 All-Time Greats* (2006)

The Evolution of Pitching in Major League Baseball (2006)

*Gabby Hartnett: The Life and Times of the
Cubs' Greatest Catcher* (2004)

*The Single-Season Home Run Kings: Ruth, Maris,
McGwire, Sosa, and Bonds*, 2d ed. (2003)

*The California Winter League: America's First Integrated
Professional Baseball League* (2002; paperback 2008)

*Cool Papas and Double Duties: The All-Time Greats
of the Negro Leagues* (2001; paperback 2005)

*Baseball's Other All-Stars: The Greatest Players from the Negro Leagues,
the Japanese Leagues, the Mexican League, and the Pre–1960 Winter Leagues
in Cuba, Puerto Rico and the Dominican Republic* (2000)

Black Baseball Out of Season

Pay for Play Outside of the Negro Leagues

WILLIAM F. MCNEIL

McFarland & Company, Inc., Publishers
Jefferson, North Carolina, and London

The present work is a reprint of the illustrated case bound edition of Black Baseball Out of Season: Pay for Play Outside of the Negro Leagues, *first published in 2007 by McFarland.*

LIBRARY OF CONGRESS CATALOGUING-IN-PUBLICATION DATA

McNeil, William.
Black baseball out of season : pay for play
outside of the Negro leagues / William F. McNeil.
  p.   cm.
Includes bibliographical references and index.

ISBN 978-0-7864-6924-6
softcover : acid free paper ∞

1. Negro leagues—History.   2. Baseball—United States—History.
3. African American baseball players—History.
4. Discrimination in sports—United States—History.   I. Title.
GV875.N35M36   2012   796.357'08996073—dc22   2007010787

BRITISH LIBRARY CATALOGUING DATA ARE AVAILABLE

© 2007 William F. McNeil. All rights reserved

*No part of this book may be reproduced or transmitted in any form
or by any means, electronic or mechanical, including photocopying
or recording, or by any information storage and retrieval system,
without permission in writing from the publisher.*

Cover photograph: Two Royal Poinciana players practicing
their techniques in the early 1900s (courtesy Larry Lester)

Manufactured in the United States of America

*McFarland & Company, Inc., Publishers
Box 611, Jefferson, North Carolina 28640
www.mcfarlandpub.com*

Many deserving Negro League veterans have been inducted into the National Baseball Hall of Fame since 1972, 35 at last count, 17 in 2006. One hopes many more will follow in the years to come. It is unfortunate for the baseball community as a whole that most white fans never had the opportunity to see these legendary athletes in action because of the segregation that existed in organized baseball during the first half of the twentieth century.

This book is gratefully dedicated to the thousands of anonymous black professional baseball players whose talents were played out in the hazy world of the Negro leagues. Their efforts paved the way to the final integration of organized baseball.

Contents

Acknowledgments	ix
Introduction	1
1. All Roads Lead to Florida	5
2. Cuban Paradise	30
3. 25th Infantry Regiment Baseball Team	52
4. California, Here I Come	62
5. Barnstorming	89
6. Puerto Rican Winters	111
7. Dominican Republic Adventures	134
8. Far Away in Venezuela	156
9. Other Venues	186
10. Looking Back	205
Appendix: Negro League Player Statistics	209
Bibliography	223
Index	225

Acknowledgments

The following people were extremely helpful in the production of this book, and were generous with their time, as well as with their information, statistics, and photographs. Several of them also gave me their permission to quote from their books.

Thank you to:

Dick Clark and Larry Lester for permission to use their photographs and their statistics from *The Negro Leagues Book*.

Jorge S. Figueredo for permission to use information and statistics from his book *Cuban Baseball*.

Jorge S. Figueredo and Charles Monfort for permission to use the photo of Cristobal Torriente.

Emilio "Cuqui" Cordova for permission to use photographs from his book, *Historia De Los Leones Rojos Del Escogido*, and for providing me with a copy of his excellent book.

John Holway for permission to use his photographs and to quote from his many Negro League books.

Luis Alvelo for permission to use his photographs, and for the historical photocopies he sent me of newspaper articles regarding Puerto Rican baseball during the 1930s.

Larry Hogan for permission to use his photographs.

"Jim" Riley for permission to quote from his books *Dandy, Day, and the Devil* and *The Biographical Encyclopedia of the Negro Baseball Leagues*, and for permission to use his photographs.

Luis Munoz for permission to use his photographs.

Robert W. Peterson and Patricia D. Kelly, director of the photograph collection of the National Hall of Fame Library, for permission to use the Robert W. Peterson photographs.

Reid N. Poles for use of photographs from the 1913 Fe team in the Cuban League and photographs of Spottswood Poles.

Jerry Malloy for permission to use his photograph of the 25th Infantry Regiment baseball team.

Yuyo Ruiz for permission to use his photographs.

Jay Sanford for permission to use his photographs.

Debi Murray, director research/archives, The Historical Society of Palm Beach, and her staff of volunteers, for an outstanding research effort in recovering copies of the *Palm Beach Daily News* and *Palm Beach Life*, for the chapter on the Florida Hotel League.

David M. Waldstein, writer/research, The Historical Society of Palm Beach, for his assistance in copying pertinent articles from *Palm Beach Life*, for the chapter on the Florida Hotel League.

Introduction

Most Negro League baseball players, as well as most major league baseball players, had to work during the off-season in order to make ends meet during the first half of the twentieth century. Major league players earned about as much money as a typical blue-collar worker in the United States. Negro League players earned less. Many of the ballplayers, both black and white, formed teams and toured the country after the regular baseball season ended, playing each other in exhibition games from New York to California, and from Oregon to Florida. From the teens through the 1940s barnstorming was a popular attraction, particularly when all-star teams headed by Dizzy Dean, Bob Feller, or Satchel Paige were involved.

Baseball fans west of St. Louis and south of Washington, D.C., were unable to see their heroes in action during the regular season, and they flocked to the parks to see them in the fall, many of them for the first time. Legendary major league players like Lefty Grove, Jimmie Foxx, Joe DiMaggio, and Ted Williams, as well as Dean and Feller, showcased their talents in such far-away places as Des Moines, Iowa; Wichita, Kansas; Wilmington, Delaware; and Montgomery, Alabama. They were opposed by the cream of Negro League baseball, including Paige, "Bullet Joe" Rogan, Josh Gibson, and "Cool Papa" Bell.

This book chronicles the integrated exhibition games played between Negro League teams and their major league counterparts from the "Three-Finger" Brown game against the Leland Giants in Cubs Park in 1909 to the famous Satchel Paige–Bob Feller tour in 1947. But more than that, it also documents the organized winter baseball leagues that operated in the United States, in Florida and California, in a number of Caribbean Basin countries, and in Central and South American countries. It traces the development of the game in each location, from its inception to its final place in history, and it details the contributions of the Negro League players to the success of the endeavor.

For the black players who didn't want to enter the labor market but who chose not to participate in the barnstorming tours, the lure of exotic locations that sponsored winter league baseball enticed them to leave home for from three to six months over the winter. At first, it was Palm Beach, Florida, where the two most prestigious hotels in the state, the Breakers and the Royal Poinciana, fielded their own baseball teams, composed entirely of black players. The rivalry between the hotels began in the late 1890s and continued until 1931. Some of the great Negro League players who showcased their skills in Palm Beach were "Cyclone Joe" Williams, John Henry Lloyd, and "Spot" Poles, the "Black Ty Cobb."

Out in California, a man named Joe Pirrone organized an integrated professional winter baseball league in 1920. Usually a Negro League team from the east was matched against three white teams composed of major league players and Pacific Coast League players. It was the first integrated professional baseball league in the United States in the twentieth century, and it operated successfully until World War II. It gradually faded from the scene during the 1940s, disappearing completely after Jackie Robinson integrated organized baseball. The major league players who participated in the California Winter League included Bob Meusel of the New York Yankees, his brother Emil "Irish" Meusel of the Giants, Babe Herman of the Brooklyn Dodgers, and the traveling man, Buck Newsom. They were opposed by such black stars as Mule Suttles, Turkey Stearnes, Dobie Moore and "Bullet Joe" Rogan. Mule Suttles destroyed white pitching to the tune of .378 with 64 home runs in just 450 at-bats. He was ably assisted by Turkey Stearnes who tattooed the likes of Buck Newsom, Sloppy Thurston, and Larry French for a .373 batting average with 56 homers in 754 at-bats.

Some Negro League players traveled south, to Cuba and other environs. The first Cuban League was organized in 1878 when three teams vied for the supremacy of the baseball world from December 29, 1878, through February 16, 1879. Initially the Cuban League was a segregated league, but by 1900 it was fully integrated. Once again the Negro Leaguers crossed swords with major league players as well as with the top Cuban players, and they more than held their own in head-to-head competition. Jud Wilson, one of the game's most natural hitters and the top hitter in Negro League baseball with a career average of .354, paced the Cuban League as well with a career average of .372. He was followed by Oscar Charleston at .360 and Dobie Moore at .353. Cristobal Torriente, Cuba's Babe Ruth, slugged the ball at a .352 clip and Alejandro Oms compiled a career average of .345. Chuck Dressen of the Cincinnati Reds and Eddie Brown of the Brooklyn Dodgers both came in at .314.

Other countries, most notably Puerto Rico, the Dominican Republic, and Venezuela, formed amateur baseball leagues shortly after the turn of the century. Negro League players began wintering in Puerto Rico in the 1920s and when the Puerto Rican Winter League got underway in 1939, they played a major part in its success. Josh Gibson hit a stratospheric .480 in the 1941–42 season, Satchel Paige went 19–3 with 209 strikeouts in 205 innings in 1939–40, and Willard Brown, the man known as Ese Hombre (That Man), led the league in home runs four times while compiling the highest career batting average in Puerto Rican Winter League history, .350. Today, major league teams send their most promising minor leaguers to Puerto Rico to refine their skills.

The Dominican Republic relied on their homegrown talent during the formative years of the game in that country, but that changed in the 1937 presidential campaign, when each of the three presidential candidates supported a team in the Dominican League and canvassed the entire Western Hemisphere to find the best baseball players money could buy. Most of the talent in the Dominican League came from the Negro Leagues, with Satchel Paige, Josh Gibson, and "Cool Papa" Bell leading the parade. The league also recruited Perucho Cepeda from Puerto Rico and Martin Dihigo, "Cocaina" Garcia, and Silvio Garcia from Cuba. The cost of operating the league became so overwhelming that professional baseball in the country went on a 13-year hiatus, finally reappearing as a summer league in 1951. Four years later, the league converted to a winter league in order to serve as a training ground for promising minor league players. The Dominican Winter League is still active today and is one of the most respected winter leagues in the Western Hemisphere.

Venezuela entered the baseball picture early in the twentieth century and was basically an amateur league until the early 1930s when one of the teams, the Concordia, began recruiting players from other countries. It put together one of the most celebrated integrated baseball teams in the Western Hemisphere with its own Luis Aparicio, Sr., the father of the Chicago White Sox Hall of Fame shortstop; Perucho Cepeda, the father of the San Francisco Giants' Orlando Cepeda, from Puerto Rico; Tetelo Vargas from the Dominican Republic; Martin Dihigo from Cuba; Josh Gibson and Rap Dixon from the American Negro Leagues, and Jimmy Jordan of the Brooklyn Dodgers. It was truly an international group, called by many baseball experts the greatest baseball team of the twentieth century. Concordia not only competed in the Venezuelan League, but also toured in the Western Hemisphere several years, playing against the best teams in Cuba, the Dominican Republic, and Puerto Rico, winning many more than they lost. When the Venezuelan Winter League was inaugurated in 1946, it received immediate credibility thanks to the presence of such Negro League stars as Roy Campanella, Buck Leonard, and Sam Jethroe. Over the years, the Venezuelan Winter League has grown to become one of the top winter leagues in the hemisphere.

Not all players participated in winter baseball however. Some players stayed home and opted for various types of manual labor during the winter months. Satchel Paige, for instance, took time off one winter to write his memoirs. Others worked in construction, or on the docks like Buck Leonard, or became insurance men, but very few players could afford to just relax during the off-season. Ted Page was an exception. He had the best of all worlds one winter. He was both working and relaxing, all at the same time. When he played for the Pittsburgh Crawfords, the team was owned by Gus Greenlee, the area's most notorious numbers czar. Greenlee hired Page to act as lookout for his numbers headquarters. The operation was located on the second floor in an old vacant house in Hazlewood, Pennsylvania. The money taken in by the numbers racket was brought to the house, counted, and put away. All Page had to do was to sit in a chair outside the front door and look out for any suspicious people approaching. If he saw anything suspicious, he just pushed a buzzer to alert the people on the second floor so they could get rid of the money. And for that, he was paid $15 a week, enough money to live on.

Winter leagues also operated in Mexico, Panama, Colombia, and other countries. These leagues, unknown to the players at the time, would have far-reaching effects on the game over the years, particularly on organized baseball. While most of the owners and executives of major league baseball teams were adamantly opposed to permitting black players to enter the hallowed halls of their sacred precincts, there were a few forward-thinking men who admired the black players and who realized that they could significantly improve the level of play in the Big Show. John McGraw, for one, quickly saw the benefits of having players like Dobie Moore or Joe Rogan in his lineup. One year he sought to pass Negro League second baseman Charlie Grant off as an American Indian, calling him "Chief Tokahoma," but his ruse was exposed by Chicago White Sox owner Charles Comiskey, and he was forced to terminate his experiment. Casey Stengel was another booster of Negro League players but his recommendations to major league managers and club owners fell on deaf ears. Sadly some of baseball's greatest names failed in their responsibility to their fellow man. In addition to Comiskey, Connie Mack, Clark Griffith, and other big league owners prevented the integration of organized baseball for almost half a century. Still, thanks to the performances of Negro League players in integrated winter leagues throughout the Western Hemisphere, the skills of players like John Henry Lloyd, Josh Gibson, and Cyclone Joe Williams became well known in white professional baseball circles, if not by major league fans themselves. Owners like Griffith, Mack, and Comiskey, although refusing to accept Negro League players as the equal of the white players, were nevertheless happy to benefit monetarily from Negro League baseball by renting their ballparks out to Negro League teams when the major league team was on the road. These influential men were well aware of the talent that was being wasted in the shadowy world of Negro League baseball, but they didn't have the moral courage to force the issue. It was left up to Brooklyn Dodgers general manager Branch Rickey, and the new baseball commissioner, A.B. "Happy" Chandler, to once and for all destroy the cancer of segregation by allowing a Negro League shortstop named Jackie Robinson to sign a contract to play organized baseball with the Montreal Royals of the International League, the Dodgers' top farm club. Two years later, in 1947, Robinson joined the Brooklyn club and the end of the long struggle began.

1

All Roads Lead to Florida

Florida was a swampy, bug-infested wasteland until the mid–1800s. The only people living in the state were a handful of anti-social pioneers who set up housekeeping along the beaches of what is now Miami, and a few white and Indian families who inhabited northern areas around Jacksonville and St. Augustine.

Henry Morrison Flagler is generally recognized as the architect of modern day Florida, having had the foresight to see how an overgrown swampland teeming with wild animals and poisonous insects could be developed into America's finest and most popular winter resort and retirement community. Flagler, who was born in New York and became an oil millionaire after teaming with John D. Rockefeller to build the Standard Oil Company of Ohio, first visited Florida in 1883 when he and his wife, Ida Alice Shrouds, honeymooned in St. Augustine after a 90-hour train ride down the east coast of the United States from New York to Jacksonville, followed by a boat ride down the St. Johns River and a 15-mile train ride from Tocoi Junction. The astute businessman, realizing the need for better hotel accommodations in Florida, purchased land in St. Augustine and built the prestigious Ponce de Leon Hotel, a lavish four-story, 450 room hotel, at a cost of $2,500,000. The hotel, which opened on January 10, 1888, was the beginning of a life-long love affair between the oil magnate and the state of Florida. Within a short period of time, Flagler built the Alcazar Hotel in the same city, to serve people with more modest budgets. According to Kevin McCarthy, "He had Albert Spalding design a baseball field, which was built in 1889 and later used for spring training. That same year saw baseball games between the African-American employees of Flagler's hotels, including members of the famous Cuban Giants." The Giant players who wintered in St. Augustine included Frank Grant, George Stovey, Clarence Williams, and William Selden.

New York Giants manager John McGraw first visited Florida in 1890 as part of a touring minor league all-star team under the direction of Al Lawson, McGraw's manager at Wellsville. According to Frank Graham's biography on McGraw,

> Parts of Florida of that day were almost primitive. The roads were few and poor, and traveling wasn't easy. But he was young and eager to see as much of the world as possible. He didn't mind the jolting rides in the carriages or carryalls, or on the trains that puffed uncertainly along the undulating right of way that stretched across the sandy terrain. He saw all the towns that Lawson had promised, and many more that Lawson never heard of. And in the years to come, when he was traveling up or down or across the state, and the train would stop at some inland town, he would peer out the window and recognize the name on the station signboard, and he would say: "I played here once ... a long time ago. The ball park was right over there, about where those stores are now and...."

It was during this early period that Flagler realized the need for a better railroad system in the state, and he set about to rectify the situation as it existed in 1890 when McGraw was there. He purchased the Florida Railroad, improved the track between Jacksonville and St. Augustine, and eventually extended the system from Jacksonville down to Miami, laying the final section of track in 1896.

Henry Flagler had visited Palm Beach for the first time in 1891 and two years later he purchased 140 acres of land situated between the Atlantic Ocean and Lake Worth. He built a large mansion for himself and his wife on part of the land and constructed Palm Beach's first hotel, the Royal Poinciana, on Lake Worth. It was a large, prestigious seven-story structure with 1,060 rooms and 460 private baths, catering to the rich and famous of the northeast, people like the Cabots, the Whitneys, and the Vanderbilts. In 1894 the hotel opened its doors for the first time and Flagler's Florida East Coast Railway, now reaching Palm Beach, brought the first northern tourists to the area in style. In 1896 Flagler added a second hotel, the Palm Beach Inn, strategically located on the beach. Over the next few years, as guests requested rooms "down by the breakers," Flagler renamed the hotel The Breakers.

Henry Flagler built a golf course between the two hotels in 1897 and also built a baseball field that occasionally encroached upon one of the golf course's fairways. Flagler, in his search to provide diversions for his guests, formed two baseball teams, one from each hotel, and he set out to hire the best black players he could find, to entertain the guests with competitive and occasionally humorous baseball games. He hired only black players because he could put them to work as busboys or waiters when they weren't playing baseball. They slept in barracks near the hotel and were paid from $23 to $33 a month, with captains receiving $40 and headwaiters $75. The teams played two games a week from late January to mid–March, usually a 14-game schedule. Ed Andrews, a former major league player, was hired to run the baseball program. The games were well attended by the hotels guests and, as reported by Stuart McIver "Elegantly clad socialites, sipping tea or scotch in the Royal Poinciana and Breakers grandstands, cheered for—and bet heavily on—players who would have moved immediately into the Big Leagues if not for the racial barriers of the day."

The first recorded mention of baseball games between the Poinciana and the Breakers teams appeared in the *Palm Beach Daily News* on Thursday, January 27, 1898, with a simple announcement under "Amusements and Attractions" that "baseball games are played on the Royal Poinciana grounds, in the afternoon, three times a week." Two weeks later the *News* noted, "The game of baseball yesterday between the Inn and Poinciana teams, resulted in a score of 2 to 13 in favor of the Inn team." The baseball games were often part of day-long festivities that included such things as a "grand cake walk in the coconut grove," and track and field competitions including 100 and 220 yard dashes, a shoe race, a boxing match, a pie eating contest, and a three-legged race in the morning, a baseball game in the afternoon, and a grand ball in the Poinciana ballroom in the evening. On February 12, it was reported that the Inn team had once again defeated the Poinciana team, this time by the score of 8–2. Another full day of festivities reported on February 23 illuminated the racial bigotry that existed in the country at that time and continued in many states for decades, some in fact up to the present time. The *Palm Beach Daily News* noted, "The sports at the ballpark yesterday morning were attended by near fifteen hundred people, for whom ample seating accommodations were provided. The grounds are in most excellent condition and the participants in the sports afforded great amusement to the spectators. Kodaks and cameras were kept busy and many a funny picture will be the result. The three-legged race, pie eating contest and shoe race afforded a fund of amusement, but the most comical and ridiculous contest was the sand river diving. Four contestants entered, two withdrawing. The other two ebony hued divers rubbed their heads together in the flour and came up looking like two Dromios, their crinkly hair resembling a cotton ball and their faces a sight to behold. The successful finder of the hidden coin received $5 for his feat."

The newspaper coverage of baseball games between the Royal Poinciana hotel and the Breakers hotel was spotty during the early years of the century, for good reason. The games were intended as a pleasant diversion for the guests of the hotels, and the players were assumed to be simply waiters who had a working knowledge of the game of baseball. Neither the hotel guests nor the newspaper reporters were aware that they were watching professional baseball players in action, and certainly not players who were the equal of white major league players.

There were no reports of baseball games played between teams representing the two hotels between 1899 and 1902 although there were games played. The local press did cover games played between white teams representing hotels in Ormond, Mount Pleasant, and DeLand, but no mention of games between the Poinciana and Breakers hotels in Palm Beach. In 1903 games between the hotels were played on the Royal Poinciana diamond located on County Road. The February 11 edition of the *Palm Beach Daily News* reported the first shutout in the competition between the two hotels. Charles "Kid" Carter dazzled the Poinciana players, blanking them 8–0. As the *News* noted,

> The Breakers team played a game that would do credit to any college or professional nine in the country. Their fielding was brilliant and snappy, and their battery timely. The second and third basemen, [Sol] White and [John] Hill made some rattling good throws and stops. Hill figured in a brilliant double play, caught a difficult foul and made a three-base hit. The Breakers battery, Carter and [Clarence] Williams, was also very good. The pitcher had a manner of delivery that would win him first prize in a cakewalk every time. The ball came like a cannon shot, and his opponents didn't seem to see it very often. Williams, the big catcher, was another old Cuban Giant. A fair spectator, seeing the C.X.G. on his uniform, asked her escort what it meant. "Oh, I don't know," said he, "Guess it stands for Catching Xtra Garrulous." Both interpretations were singularly appropriate.

Later in 1903, the Breakers burned to the ground and was replaced by a more attractive building.

The next year, although no games were reported, the Poinciana roster was published.

Emmet "Scotty" Bowman	INF/OF/P/C
Rube Foster	P
G. "Home Run" Johnson	2B/SS
Pete Hill	2B
John Hill	SS
Sol White	INF/OF
Charlie Grant	INF
Bill Monroe	2B
"Big Bill" Smith	C
Dan McClellan	P
Mike Moore	3B

The powerful 1904 Royal Poinciana club boasted four future Hall of Famers: Pete Hill, Sol White, Charlie Grant, and Rube Foster. Standing (left to right): Emmett "Scotty" Bowman (INF/OF/PIC), unknown, Rube Foster (P), unknown, Grant "Homerun" Johnson (2B/SS). Sitting (left to right): Pete Hill (2B), John Hill (SS), Sol White (INF/OF), unknown, Charlie Grant (INF) (courtesy Jay Sanford).

As can be seen from the above roster, the Poinciana team had some of black baseball's finest players of the early part of the 20th century. Twenty-five-year-old Rube Foster, later called "the father of Negro League baseball," was in his prime as a pitcher in 1904. The 6'2", 200-pound right-hander was noted as a smart pitcher who had a full repertoire of pitches including a devastating screwball. Pete Hill, at 24, was recognized as a five-point player, who could hit for average, hit for power, run, field, and throw. Sol White, an outstanding second baseman in his day, was nearing the end of the trail in 1904 but could still show the youngsters a thing or two. Bill Monroe, at the age of 28, may have been the best second baseman, black or white, of his era. Grant "Home Run" Johnson was the top black shortstop at the turn of the century and the Negro League's first recognized slugger. Scotty Bowman enjoyed a twelve-year career in the Negro Leagues as a pitcher and a position player. And Charlie Grant was such a talented second baseman that John McGraw tried to sign him to a major league contract, passing him off as an Indian.

The Royal Poinciana team, with Rube Foster, took two out of three games from the Breakers Bulldogs with one tie in 1905. The games were well attended, especially by the ladies, as the *Royal Poinciana Daily Program* of February 7 noted. "There is an unusual interest in the baseball games this winter, and even the young women attending have become familiar with the star players of each team, and know which men to make their wagers on. 'Foster is in the box' or 'Foster is not pitching today' often means considerable, either way you put it, to those in the long green pavilion." No box scores were located, but the results were noted, and it is likely that Foster pitched in all four games, finishing with a record of 2–1.

Foster, Monroe, and Sol White, along with Charlie Grant, were back in Florida the following winter but no game accounts were located. However, the 1907 season proved to be one of the most interesting seasons in the history of the Florida Hotel League, or the Coconut League, as it was popularly known. Palm Beach, in addition to the Royal Poinciana and Breakers hotels, was also home to the Palm Beach Resort, and that hotel organized a baseball team composed entirely of white players from organized baseball, including major leaguers Malcolm "Kid" Eason of the Brooklyn Dodgers, Miller Huggins of the Cincinnati Reds, Clyde Engle of the Cleveland Indians, and Billy Maloney of the Chicago Cubs. Another resort team, in Miami, hired Tom Needham of the Boston Braves, Tom Doran of the Boston Red Sox, and Phil Lewis of the Brooklyn Dodgers. The Negro League players in town for the winter included Grant "Home Run" Johnson, Dan McClellan, Frank Earle, Bruce Petway, Bill Gatewood, Phil Bradley, and John Hill.

The Breakers and Poinciana teams engaged in a spirited rivalry that saw Poinciana defeat the Bulldogs three games to one. And the fans were often entertained prior to a game by Allen's brass band, a group of talented hotel waiters. According to Kevin McCarthy, one spectator at the games wrote in 1907,

> I went over to the baseball game and such sport I never had in my life. Both teams are colored and composed of employees of the Breakers and Poinciana hotels, who are hired because of their baseball ability and then incidentally given employment as waiters or porters. Many of them play on the Cuban Giants team during the summer so that the quality of baseball ranked with professional white teams. The greatest sport was in listening to the coaching and watching the antics of a full grandstand back of first base. Their sympathies were pretty evenly divided between the two teams so, accordingly, whenever either team would make a hit, then was the time to watch the bleachers. The crowd would yell themselves hoarse, stand up in their seats, bang each other over the head, and even the girls would go into a frenzy, as if they were in a Methodist camp meeting. The third baseman on the Poinciana team [probably John Hill] was a wonderful ballplayer and kept the whole crowd roaring with his horseplay and cakewalks up and down the sidelines.

Bill Monroe was also admired by the fans who called him the fastest man they had ever seen.

The Breakers-Poinciana games might have been the most entertaining games of the winter, with much merriment and fun, but the games had to be taken very seriously by the players because there was a considerable amount of money wagered on the outcome of the games by hotel guests and friends of both teams. The most interesting games however had to have been the encounters that matched a picked nine from the two hotels against the white major leaguers from the Palm Beach Resort and the Miami resort. It was an integrated professional baseball game, one of the first, if not the first contest of its kind in the United States. The Negro Leaguers won the series 4–2–1 but all the games were closely contested. In the opening game of the series, the Miami-Palm Beach lineup included Needham, Engle, Lewis, and Doran. The Royal Poinciana-Breakers contingent showcased the talents of "Home Run" Johnson, Bowman, Bradley, Mike Moore, Frank Earle, Pete Booker, and Bobby Winston. Earle faced off against a New York Giants farm-hand named Duggan as reported by *Palm Beach Life*.

> The most enthusiastic crowd of the season turned out to see the first game between the professional team and the picked nine from the Poinciana and Breakers colored teams. The grandstand was filled and the fans were on hand en-masse scattered everywhere about on the turf and there was some of the most prolonged rooting and cheering heard on the diamond this year.
>
> The work of Engle, Moore, and Schirm was magnificent, and won great applause from the spectators. A splendid showing was also made by the rest of the fellows, but there was something lacking which could not offset the great hits of Robinson, "Daddy" Moore, and Johnson, who never failed to land someway or other.
>
> There was no final score noted, but *Palm Beach Life* did say, "It was a victory for Poinciana that almost proved a walkover."

In game two, Moore, Miller, and Bowman all singled in the second inning and Gatewood brought them all home with a tremendous blast to right field, good for two bases. Bowman's sacrifice fly eventually scored Gatewood, giving the PB-B team a 4–0 lead. The white team was not ready to quit however, and eventually tied the score with a two-run rally in the eighth inning. The game was called after nine innings with the score still tied at 4–4.

The next game saw M-PB push over two runs in the bottom of the fourth for a 2–0 lead, but the lead was short lived as the black squad bounced back with four runs of their own to recapture the lead. Duggan and Needham ended a RP-B rally in the eighth inning with a magnificent double play, and Al Robinson was caught stealing in the same inning. The final score was Royal Poinciana-Breakers 5 and Miami-Palm Beach 2.

Game four saw the black team push over two runs in the bottom of the first and add another run in the second for a 3–0 lead. The eighth inning proved to be the most exciting inning of the game. Pete Hill and Bobby Winston both punched out singles, but Petway, Bowman, and William Binga were retired before a run could score. In the bottom half of the inning, James singled but was thrown out at the plate on Brown's double, and Brown was later thrown out at the plate on Donald's double. The Negro Leaguers prevailed 3–2.

The Miami-Palm Beach squad finally came to life in game 5. They jumped out to a 2–0 lead in the second inning, but saw the Poinciana boys knotted the score in the third. After Palm Beach recaptured the lead with single runs in the fourth and sixth innings, the black team fought back to tie the game one more time with a two-run rally in the seventh. Palm Beach pushed over the winning tally in the eighth to win the game 5–4.

The white boys repeated their success in game six, winning a hard-fought 5–3 battle, with Duggan out-pitching Bill Gatewood. Winston, Gatewood, and Booker excelled for the Poinciana-Breakers team while "Engle and Schirm, together with Duggan and Quiesser, saved the day several times with exceedingly clever work," according to *Palm Beach Life*.

The final game of the series was a fitting climax to a heated rivalry, as reported by *PBL*.

The game was witnessed by an even greater crowd than was the exhibition immediately preceding, and they came expecting something fast and furious, something aside from the ordinary, and they were not disappointed. It was the greatest game of the year, in which the mettle of every man in the fray was tried to the utmost from the time the game was called until the curtain fell on the scene. The first few innings were eventful periods in the game, Palm Beach registering one run on an error in the second and came very nearly getting in another had it not been for Booker's splendid catch. Engle's work was distinguished by the usual excellent performances in the third, as was that also of Duggan and Quiesser, the battery for Palm Beach.

Frank Earle homered in the third to give his team a 1–1 tie and, although both teams threatened over the next five innings, stout pitching and defense prevented further scoring. The score remained 1–1 into the ninth inning when the Negro Leaguers scored the game-winner. Scotty Bowman opened the bottom of the ninth by reaching first base on an error, Bradley also reached on an error, and Robinson's sacrifice moved both runners into scoring position. Frank Earle was walked intentionally to load the bases, and Big Bill Gatewood ended the tense struggle by singling in the winning run. *Palm Beach Life* reported that "Gatewood was picked up and carried bodily from the field by the frenzied fans, who shouted themselves hoarse, throwing hats, canes and what not into the air in demonstrations of enthusiasm for the victory for the waiters. It was the final appearance for the Palm Beach professionals and the multitude in the grandstand were with them to a man, but to no avail, the other fellows were too strong for them." This series was an eye-opener for many of the hotel guests and other fans who attended the games. Previously they had viewed the black players as a humorous diversion, but not as particularly skilled baseball players. Now, after watching them take the field against professional players, including many major leaguers, and coming away victorious, they finally realized that the Negro Leaguers were not waiters playing baseball but highly skilled professional ballplayers in their own right, who were forced to wait tables because of the Jim Crow laws that infected the country.

The 1908 season saw a new Negro League team enter the fray, the Tigers representing the Hotel Royal Palm in Miami. The roster of the Tigers included Brodie Francis, Scotty Bowman, Clarence Williams, and Bruce Petway. Poinciana had Harry Smith, Frank Earle, Phil Bradley, and Bill Monroe, while the Breakers countered with Dan McClellan, John Henry Lloyd making his Coconut League debut, Harry Buckner, and Chappie Johnson. The competition between the Poinciana nine and the Breakers Bulldogs was keen as usual, but the Miami team was outmatched. They were beaten in the opening game by Poinciana by the score of 7–4, although Brodie Francis of the Tigers created a sensation with his sparkling play around second base. The diminutive 5'5", 140-pound infielder made the play of the day, with a leaping catch of a line drive off the bat of "Big Bill" Smith and then whirling and throwing to third base to double up Al Robinson trying to advance. The Breakers Bulldogs walloped the Tigers in game two, scoring ten runs in the third inning en route to a 16–4 victory. Winning pitcher Dan McClellan was relieved by Harry Buckner in the sixth inning with the game well in hand. Scotty Bowman suffered the beating. In the finale of the series, the Breakers prevailed once again, although the Tigers made a game of it this time before succumbing 5–4. Later in the season, the Poinciana team met the Tigers in four more games, winning them all. The scores were 3–0, 8–3, 5–3, and 7–4.

Dan McClellan was one of the finest Negro League pitchers during the first decade of the twentieth century (courtesy Dick Clark).

The first Poinciana-Breakers game was won by Poinciana by the score of 3–1 behind the clever pitching of Frank Earle. The talented right-hander, who had gone a perfect 4–0 on the mound in 1907, was on his way to a 5–0 record this year. Earle played in the Negro Leagues for 14 years, starting out as a pitcher but, like Babe Ruth, he was converted to an outfielder to take advantage of his powerful bat. The two teams exchanged 6–2 victories with George Wright, the shortstop for the Poinciana team, dazzling the crowd with two sensational stops to begin double plays with Bill Monroe and Al Robinson participating. Two more games were split before the Breakers evened the series with an 8–6 win on Wednesday, February 12. The collapse of pitcher John Bright in the top of the seventh inning paved the way for an eight run Breaker rally, wiping out a 1–0 Poinciana lead. Harry Buckner protected the lead although a two-run uprising in the bottom of the ninth made it close. Poinciana regained the series lead two days later when Frank Earle handcuffed the Bulldogs, winning easily by an 8–2 count. Third baseman Sam Mongin of Poinciana made the fielding play of the day with a circus backhand catch of a fly ball. The next game ended in a 3–3 tie, but witnessed a history-making event. Harry Buckner, playing center field, stepped to the plate in the seventh inning with the Breakers clinging to a 3–2 lead and he promptly tied the score with a mammoth home run to left field, the first home run recorded in the Coconut League. The final game of the season saw the Poinciana nine shut out the Breakers 1–0 when Bruce Petway laced a triple to right field in the fifth inning and later came in to score the game's only run.

The Palm Beach fans were once again treated to a series matching the Negro League players from the Royal Poinciana and Breakers hotels against white teams, this time from Ormond and Seabreeze. The Ormond team was represented by minor league players, several of whom, like Mike Mitchell, Fred

Mitchell, and Tommy Madden, had brief trials with major league teams. The Palm Beach squad included John Henry Lloyd, Dan McClellan, Baumann, Buckner, Earle, and Petway. The first game of a two-game series was well played by both teams, with Earle out-pitching E. Dugan and the hotel squad plating the winning run in the 10th inning of a 3–2 game. The second game ended in a 3–3 tie as both Dugan and Buckner went all the way in the 12-inning game.

Ormond arrived in Palm Beach with a strong white contingent including major leaguers Tom Needham, Jim Delahanty, Jack Hoey, Matty McIntyre, Terry Turner, John Butler, and Fred Applegate. But if they thought they were going to intimidate the Negro Leaguers, they were sadly disappointed. Frank Earle kept the white team in check while his mates pounded the serves of Applegate to the tune of 8–2. In the getaway game, Buckner out-lasted O. Ritchie to win 9–7. A three-run rally in the bottom of the sixth inning overcame an early 5–4 Ormond lead, and Palm Beach added two more runs in the seventh for a comfortable 9–5 cushion.

Reporting of games remained spotty in 1909 and the only item of note appeared in the January 26 edition of *Palm Beach Life*. "The old baseball grounds have been absorbed into the new and improved golf course. The long green pavilion, which has for many seasons past served so admirably for the grandstand, has been moved over to the new grounds, which are near the Jungle tennis courts. The new grounds are just as easily accessible and conveniently arranged as was the old diamond."

In 1910, Negro League teams in their entirety began traveling to Florida, a practice that would continue, off and on, for the next two decades. Rube Foster and his Chicago Leland Giants represented the Royal Poinciana Hotel while the Royal Giants of New York City played under the banner of the Breakers Hotel. Poinciana took the season series five games to three with one tie. Rube Foster paced the Poinciana team, running up a perfect 3–0 record. He captured the season opener by a count of 4–1, striking out four men along the way. Frank Earle took the loss for the Breakers. A newspaper advertisement for the nearby Hotel Palm Beach noted suites with private bath starting at $3 per day. Dan McClellan gave the Breakers their first victory with a 6–1 win in game two. One of the more exciting games of the season was played on February 21, with Frank Wickware and Harry Buckner matching pitches for nine innings, although it took some dazzling defensive plays to give Poinciana a 1–1 tie. Pete Hill brought the crowd to its feet with a sensational, game-saving, running catch in right-center field in the ninth inning. Earlier, John Henry Lloyd and catcher Pete Booker had pulled off an electrifying double play to kill a Breaker rally. A good old-fashioned donnybrook sent the big crowd into a frenzy in game five. The Breakers knocked three pitchers out of the box in the fourth inning, scoring six runs before Rube Foster could stem the tide, but that was only the beginning of the excitement. Poinciana bounced back with a five spot of its own in the sixth inning to tie the score. John Henry Lloyd came up with the bases loaded and, with a count of no balls and two strikes, he sent a tremendous shot into the outfield, called the longest ball ever hit on the Poinciana diamond. Three runs scored and Lloyd would have had himself a grand-slam homer, but he slipped and fell rounding the bases and had to be content with a triple. Rube Foster's team added three runs in the seventh to give their manager a hard-fought 9–6 win, coming back from a 6–1 deficit to win it. The next game, a 6–4 victory for the Poinciana nine, produced the first triple play in Hotel League history. Pete Booker hit a line drive to right field with men on first and second. Both runners, thinking the ball was going to fall in for a hit, took off at the crack of the bat, and were hung out to dry when Phil Bradley made a nice running catch in right field. Bradley's throw to Robinson at first base recorded the second out and Robinson's throw to Mongin who relayed it back to Monroe completed the rare feat. The season ended on a fitting note. Poinciana clinched the series behind the shutout pitching of Rube Foster, the 30-year-old screwball artist from Calvert, Texas, who fanned six Bulldogs en route, a high number of strikeouts in those days. Pete Duncan was the defensive star of the game, making what the *Palm Beach Daily News* called "the greatest catch, with one hand, ever seen at Palm Beach. This was made after a long run, after which he fell among the wheels of a rolling chair, but held tight to the ball."

The 1911 Coconut League was a hard-fought series that saw the Breakers Bulldogs finally win a season series from the Royal Poinciana nine, eight games to six. The Bulldogs got off the mark quickly, winning the opener by an 8–6 score, but then they dropped three in a row before righting themselves with a 17–6 rout in game five, highlighted by a Pete Duncan home run. The Breakers won another one-sided game the next time out, winning 10–4 behind the tantalizing slants of Dan McClellan who fanned six Poinciana batters. Etheridge of Poinciana smashed a triple, losing his shoe as he rounded second base. Rube Foster, manager of the Breakers team, was reprimanded by the umpire and by the press for indulging in some "non-ethical" tactics during the game, including having his players attempt to spike the opponents. The furor succeeded in bringing the players under control, and good, clean games were the fashion of the day thereafter. And the competitive spirit demonstrated by the two teams brought the fans out in force. The remaining nine games were played before a packed grandstand.

One of the best games of the season was played on February 24 when Pop Andrews used his famous slowball to keep the Breakers' batters off balance all day. He struck out four men en route to a 3–0 shutout, his fifth consecutive victory. Bill Monroe slammed a three-base hit for the winners. The Breakers bounced back to win the next game by a 6–5 count as reported by the *Daily News*.

> Earl Thomas, prize cakewalker and leader of the rooting gang, started his fans to cheering and singing when the Poinciana team seemed to wake up and do some fine playing. Pierce, first base for the Breakers, made a home run, after a hard hit to left, which Earle muffed, allowing him to secure a homer. Handy made one of the most remarkable running catches and double plays ever seen here, running at least fifty yards to catch the ball six inches from the ground. Earle also made a very clever running overhand catch in deep left after a long run. [Big Bill] Smith, catcher for the Poinciana, came to bat at a needy time, when the score was 6–2, hitting the ball for the longest home run ever made here, and a clean one.

Pat Dougherty, the "big side-wheeler" who was the best left-handed pitcher in the Negro Leagues between 1909 and 1918, was the winning pitcher. Seven days later, the Breakers took the measure of the Poinciana nine again, this time by a 7–6 score. Three Breakers pitchers were called on to hold the Poinciana batters in check after they had raked Bill Lindsay for five runs in the top of the third. Rube Foster followed Lindsay to the mound and he was relieved by Dan McClellan, who finished the game. The Breakers scored in six of the last seven innings off Frank Earle, who went the distance. Second baseman Bill Handy walloped a triple for the winners. The victory gave the Breakers a 7 to 6 lead in games played, with one game remaining on the schedule. The Breakers won that game also, although no score was reported. *Palm Beach Life* reported on the entire season.

Baseball played an important part during the season in affording an attraction to the thousands of hotel guests and visitors who were here. Not only was the rivalry keen between the two teams, the Breakers and the Royal Poinciana, the teams being composed of the Negro employees of the two hotels, but there was also a strong enthusiasm on the part of the guests of each hotel for the team that represented their hotel. This made each baseball game an attraction and the crowds were present in the long green pavilion, while many others who could not get seats, contented themselves by standing three and four deep along the heavy ropes which kept them off the diamond. It is needless to say that the spacious bleachers, reserved for the help and employees, were always filled to their capacity. When the series of games was played, it ended with the victory for the Breakers, winning eight and Royal Poinciana winning six games. The Breakers in the beginning started out in the lead but the Royal Poinciana team soon caught up with them and passed them by leaving the Breakers, after the height of the season, with apparently small chance to catch up and make good. But this they did by capturing the last four games played.

The newspaper coverage of the Hotel League or Coconut League baseball games in 1912 remained pretty much the same as it had been at the turn of the century. The game summaries were much more complete, but there were still no box scores included in the

Two Royal Poinciana players (both unidentified) practicing their techniques in the early 1900s (courtesy Larry Lester).

write-ups, and the players were still not respected for their immense talents. Entire articles, discussing the exciting plays in the game, often did not include a single player's name. They were referred to simply as "the pitcher," "the third baseman," or the "left fielder." The hotel teams, however, had several new players in 1912. Poinciana had Specks Webster catching, Wes Pryor at shortstop, Jap Payne in right field, and Frank Wickware and Sam Crawford pitching. The Breakers added George Wright at shortstop, Billy Francis at third base, and Jude Gans in center field, in support of pitchers McClellan and Buckner. After a three-day rain delay, the season got underway with the Breakers edging the Royal Poinciana nine 5–4 in 10 innings. The two teams battled through seven scoreless innings before Poinciana plated the first run of the game on a stolen base and a bad throw that allowed the runner to circle the bases. They added three more runs in the 8th and looked like a sure winner until the Bulldogs broke loose with two runs in the bottom of the eighth and two more in the ninth to tie the score. The Breakers' left fielder, probably George Brown, slashed a bases loaded single between third and short to drive in the game-winner in the 10th. The second game was played in chilling weather, as noted by the *Palm Beach Daily News*. "Furs, sweaters, pole-coats, and mittens were in vogue at Palm Beach stadium where the society folk gathered to watch this second contest of the diamond." The Breakers Bulldogs routed the Royal Poinciana team 13–4 in a game called in the eighth inning because of the cold. Poinciana finally got on the board in game three behind the tantalizing serves of Pop Andrews who "slow-balled 'em to death," winning 4–2. The *News* reported,

> Taking the game as a whole, it was clean, snappy, and worth-while watching ... Earle, the new captain of the Poinciana team, seems to have a good influence over the team and they worked well for him yesterday.... Out in left field garden where Earle scooped up a long hit after a hard run, proved one of the life-savers in the game as it came at a critical time.... Big Al [Robinson], at first base, covered his bag in good shape and gathered up the miscellaneous throws that would have been hard for the average first baseman to collect...."Chappie" Johnson, the Breakers backstop, was a great bulwark for his team to lean against and depend upon, in the tight places that he controlled.... Andrews pitched a good game for the winners and "Specks" [Webster], the other half of the battery, held onto the fast ones and threw better than heretofor.

Walter Ball, one of the top pitchers in the Negro Leagues from 1903 to 1923, and newly married, arrived in Palm Beach with his wife, Rosetta, after pitching in the Cuban League, and pitched Poinciana to two victories, an 8–1 win over lefty Pat Dougherty, who was raked for all the runs in his seven innings of work, and a 1–0 shutout over Lee Wade. Pop Andrews also tossed a shutout, blanking the Bulldogs 3–0 on March 12, paced by Al Robinson's triple. The Poinciana team won the season series, eight games to six, leaving the Breakers with just one season victory since 1903. The highlight of the season was a tremendous home run to deep center field off the bat of Bennett. Other home runs were credited to Frank Earle, Bill Handy, and Al Robinson who also had a triple to his credit. One report stated that Louis Santop, the black Babe Ruth, hit a 485 foot home run in 1912, but no record of that hit has been located.

The outlook began to brighten for the Breakers team in 1913 when they held the Royal Poinciana team to a 7–7 draw in games. Then, beginning in 1914, they reeled off three consecutive Coconut League championships. Their success coincided with the arrival of "Cyclone Joe" Williams, the legendary right-handed flame-thrower out of Seguin,

Texas, who was at the peak of his legendary skills at 26 years of age. Over the three-year period from 1914 through 1916, the Breakers went 25–17–4, with Williams contributing 16 wins to their cause against just 3 losses. The 1914 race for the championship was not a cakewalk, however, thanks in part to the pitching of Dizzy Dismukes of Poinciana, who appeared in seven of the fourteen games played, and finished with a perfect 6–0 record. Dismukes' teammates included "Spot" Poles, often called "the black Ty Cobb," Jules Thomas, and Bill Pettus. Joe Williams was supported by a veritable who's-who of Negro League talent, including Pete Hill, John Henry Lloyd, Louis Santop, and Bruce Petway, three of whom, plus himself, are now members of the National Baseball Hall of Fame in Cooperstown, New York. The years between 1914 and 1918 were the Golden Age of Florida Hotel League baseball, with great players manning the rosters and detailed newspaper coverage complete with box scores. And finally, after almost twenty years of relative anonymity, the players were treated with a newfound respect for their enormous skills, as reported in the opening newspaper article introducing the players. "As we are informed that the men composing both teams are all stars, selected from the leading colored baseball aggregations of America, ripping good baseball should be presented by them to their patrons during the season of 1914." And, in order to give the two teams added incentive to play hard, it was agreed that the gate receipts would be split on a 60–40 basis, with the winning team sharing 60 percent of the gate and the losing team 40 percent. In the past, the gate receipts were split 50–50.

The opening game of the 1914 season, on January 27, lived up to all the pre-game hype with "Cyclone Joe" Williams out-pitching Frank "The Red Ant" Wickware by a 4–3 count. The game was scoreless for the first four innings. Then Poinciana touched Williams for a run in the fifth, only to have the Breakers push over

John Henry "Pop" Lloyd was the only batter to maintain a career batting average of more than .300 in the Coconut League (courtesy Noir Tech Research).

two runs in the top of the sixth for a 2–1 lead. The newspaper reported that the game probably should have been called in the seventh inning with the same 2–1 score because it grew so dark over the last two innings that the darkness contributed to the final four runs being scored. Billy Francis at third base and Louis Santop in left field were singled out for the sensational defensive play by the *Daily News*. "A low fly toward third was caught close to the grandstand after a long sprint by the sack artist [Francis] for the Breakers, and he got a splendid hand when he nailed the ball as it sailed over his shoulder. The fans had not finished applauding this catch when the left fielder [Santop] galloped over to the ropes and pulled down another difficult fly, when it looked impossible." Lloyd with two base hits and one run scored, and Santop with two hits and two runs scored, led the Breakers' attack. "Spot" Poles ripped "Cyclone Joe" Williams for three base hits while Bill Pettus chipped in with two, for the losers. The game coverage was also notable for including the first box score of a Hotel League game, sixteen years after the league began operations.

Breakers				**Poinciana**			
Player	R	H	E	*Player*	R	H	E
Petway	0	1	1	Poles	0	3	0
Hill	0	1	0	Payne	0	0	0
Gans	0	0	0	Webster	0	1	1
Lloyd	1	2	0	Thomas	1	1	0
Santop	2	2	0	Pettus	2	2	0
Grant	0	1	0	Barber	0	0	0
James	0	0	0	Handy	0	1	0
Williams	1	0	0	Pryor	0	1	0
Francis	0	1	1	Wickware	0	1	2
Totals	**4**	**8**	**2**		**3**	**10**	**3**

The next game was a 3–2 victory for Poinciana, and the game after that was a brilliant 1–0 shutout for the Breakers' Joe Williams over Poinciana's southpaw slinger, Frank Harvey. Noting the seriousness with which the players approached the games, Dizzy Dismukes reported in a 1929 edition of the *Pittsburgh Courier*, "Rivalry was so keen between the two teams that the headwaiters, Joe McClain of Poinciana and Evans, now deceased, of the Breakers, seldom spoke during the winter season. There was no fraternizing of the players of the two clubs. Yours truly, playing with Poinciana, was at Palm Beach two years before going into the Breakers quarters, which was only half a block away." Lee Wade tossed a three-hit shutout at the Poinciana nine on February 7, winning 3–0 thanks to some strong defensive work by Jude Gans, as reported in the *Daily News*. "Gans, in the left garden, deserves great credit for the showing he made and the four flies he pulled down. He had to show great speed to get under them in the first place and in all but one instance after he got his hands on the ball he landed in a heap. Twice he stumbled over the mounds near the tall coconut trees and the other time he came in from deep left and gathered in a short fly that many thought he did not catch."

One of the more interesting games of the year took place on the 14th, with Dizzy Dismukes giving the Royal Poinciana team a tie in the series against the Breakers by beating the Bulldogs and "Cyclone Joe" Williams 4–2. It was Williams' first loss of the year, but he bounced back in the next game to take the measure of Wickware and Harvey by a 3–1 score behind the slugging of John Henry Lloyd who laced three base hits. Unfortunately, "Cyclone Joe" ran into Dismukes again on the 28th and came out on the short end of a 1–0 score. "Spot" Poles stole home in the bottom of the ninth inning to seal the victory, after Dismukes had choked off a Breakers rally in the eighth inning by fanning Louis Santop with the bases loaded. Once again Joe Williams rescued his team, in the season finale. With the Breakers holding a lead in the series 7 games to 6, the big fireballer threw another shutout, this one by a 3–0 score over Frank Wickware.

Overall the 1914 season was a pitchers season, with Dizzy Dismukes posting a perfect 6–0 record, followed by Joe Williams at 6–2. Although "Spot" Poles led all hitters with a torrid .353 batting mark, only one other batter broke the magic .300 mark, John Henry Lloyd who hit an even .300. Louis Santop batted .294 with two doubles, but no other batter on either team hit more than .265.

The Breakers, under new manager John Henry Lloyd, won the 1915 championship seven games to five, with one tie, defeating Frank Earle's Poinciana nine. "Cyclone Joe" went 3–0 on the mound and he had the help of "Cannonball" Dick Redding who added a 2–0 mark to the Breakers' total. The Bulldogs captured the opener 5–4 behind Williams and never looked back. Ben Taylor carried the big bat for the losers, rapping out three base hits including a bases-loaded triple in the eighth inning that brought his team within one run, but "Spot" Poles ended any thoughts the Poinciana team might have had of upsetting Williams, as reported by the *Daily News*. "Poles' catch in the eighth inning following a long run across slippery ground, was the finest one ever made at Palm Beach and he became the hero of the game." The following week, the Breakers finally caught up with their nemesis, Dizzy Dismukes, knocking him out of the box in the first

"Spot" Poles led the Coconut League in batting twice between 1914 and 1916 (courtesy Reid N. Poles).

inning, scoring seven runs and putting the game on ice early. Leroy Grant paced the rally by slamming a three-run triple. Redding coasted to an easy 8–4 victory. "Spot" Poles (.417), Leroy Grant (.500), and John Henry Lloyd (.364) were the batting stars for the Breakers Bulldogs during the season, in support of Williams and Redding. Del Clark (.444), Bill Pierce (.417), Jules Thomas (.400), and Ben Taylor (.364) wielded big lumber for Poinciana.

It was a three-peat for the Breakers team in 1916 as they outlasted the Royal Poinciana nine 10–6–1. Once again "Cyclone Joe" Williams led his charges with a 5–1 record, including two shutouts, and he was backed up by Ad Langford at 5–2. "Spot" Poles led the hit parade with a .353 batting average and two doubles. He was the only Bulldog batter to hit over .300. For Poinciana, Ben Taylor hit .343, Joe Hewitt hit .333, Tod Allen came in at .313, and Ashby Dunbar posted an even .300 mark. Poinciana's hitting was good, but it could not offset the pitching lapses. Dismukes posted a 2–2 record, but John Donaldson could do no better than 1–5. He lost a heartbreaker to Williams in the opener, when an outfield error by Dunbar in the eighth inning allowed the only run of the game to cross the plate. Donaldson lost to Langford 4–2 in his next outing, and then was hammered 8–1 in a return match with "Cyclone Joe." Jules Thomas knocked in five runs for the Bulldogs on a bases loaded triple and a two-run single. And "Spot" Poles chipped in with three hits for the winners. Williams beat Donaldson again on February 4, this time by a 7–3 count. The Poinciana southpaw finally broke into the winner's circle with five innings of relief that brought him home a 2–1 winner when Joe Williams walked Dismukes with the bases loaded in the bottom of the ninth. One of the more interesting games of the season was played on March 3 when a hotel guest named Morton F. Plant put up a $100 purse to go to the winning team. Both the Poinciana nine and the Breakers nine went with their aces in an attempt to win the big prize, with "Cyclone Joe" Williams facing off against Dizzy Dismukes. And the game was worthy of the contestants, with neither team able to dent the plate through the first five innings. In the Breakers' half of the sixth inning, with one out, Bill Handy drew a base on balls, moved to second on an infield hit by Williams, advanced to third when "Spot" Poles was walked, and scored on a sacrifice fly by Felix Wallace. That would prove to be enough for Williams who, with dollar bills playing on his mind, mowed down the Poinciana batters with monotonous regularity. His only difficulty came in the eighth inning when his own error allowed Joe Hewitt to reach first base. Dunbar sacrificed Hewitt to second base, but when "Candy Jim" Taylor rifled a single to left field, Hewitt attempted to score and was cut down on a throw from Blainey Hall to Specks Webster. That was all Williams needed. He put the Poincianas away quietly in the ninth inning. Poinciana won the next-to-last game of the season with a 16–3 rout of the Bulldogs, but Joe Williams' team bounced back to take the season finale by a 7–1 score behind Langford.

Revenge is sweet as the Poinciana team discovered in 1917 when they finally broke the Breakers jinx by capturing the season series seven games to six, with two ties. The season was a groundbreaking one that saw the Royal Poinciana Hotel recruit Rube Foster to manage the team in hopes of wresting the league championship from the Breakers Bulldogs. He brought many of the top players from his Chicago American Giants team with him. The Breakers brought "Cyclone Joe" Williams back as manager, along with players from the New York Lincoln Giants. As it turned out, the year could have been called the year of "The Mule" as Luis "El Mulo" Padron, a strong, stubborn Cuban import, completely dominated the two-team competition. After going 1–2–1 in his first four games, the big southpaw swept his last four games, tossing two shutouts and yielding a total of just three runs. His slate for the season showed 9 games pitched including 8 starts, 8 complete games, three shutouts, 65 innings pitched, 5 wins against 2 losses, and a 1.52 total run average (TRA). One of the keys to his success was shutting down the Breakers' spark plug, "Spot" Poles. He held the speedy little leadoff man to a .182 batting average with just one extra-base hit in 33 at-bats. And, along the way, he defeated two of the best black pitchers ever to toe the rubber, "Cyclone Joe" Williams and "Cannonball" Dick Redding.

In the season's opener, on January 31, the crafty Padron and the tall, lanky right-hander matched pitch for pitch for ten innings before the game was called with the score deadlocked at 1–1, although Williams came within one out of throwing a shutout. The Breakers scored their only run in the third inning on two-out doubles by Poles and Hewitt. The Royal Poinciana nine, trailing 1–0 against "Cyclone Joe," pushed across the tying run in the bottom of the ninth on a single by Barber and a two-out double by Lloyd. The play of the game occurred in the second inning when Poinciana attempted a suicide squeeze play with Lloyd on third, Francis on second and DeMoss at the plate. DeMoss missed the attempted bunt, Santop, the Breakers' catcher, tagged Lloyd coming home and threw to Wallace at third to nab Francis trying to advance. In his next start against Williams, Padron had his change of pace working to perfection as he tossed a two-hitter to blank the Bulldogs 2–0. And in the final game of the season, he out-pitched Williams again, also by a 2–0 count. He also matched pitches with Redding twice, winning one and losing one. His other two victories and his second loss came against Andrew "Stringbean" Williams.

Pete Duncan took hitting honors for the season, batting .321 in fifteen games. John Henry Lloyd, the only other batter to hit above .222, came in at .309. For the Breakers, Blainey Hall hit .333 and Louis Santop hit .276, the only batters to finish above .175. On the mound, "Stringbean" Williams had a 4–2 mark, Redding was 2–2, and Joe Williams finished at 0–3–1.

The year 1918 was a war year with World War I in full bloom in Europe, and many of the Negro League players were away defending their country, with Redding and Poles both seeing action in France, and Lloyd assigned to an army quartermaster depot in Chicago. Redding was able to pitch four games for Rube Fosters' Poinciana team before leaving for military service, but the fire-balling right-hander could do no better than a 1–3 record. The season opened on February 6 and Tom Williams pitched Poinciana to a 5–3 victory over Padron and the Breakers Bulldogs. A sellout crowd of 1,200 hotel guests was entertained by the hotel band before the game with a rousing rendition of "Over There." The *Daily News* in reporting on the game said, "If the members of these two teams continue playing in the form they showed yesterday afternoon, there is no reason why any of the visitors should prefer the major league games, no matter by whom played nor the color of the players."

The most heralded pitching matchup of the year took place on February 5 when "Cyclone Joe" Williams faced his archenemy, "Cannonball" Dick Redding, in a battle of flamethrowers. The game, unlike most games of its type, more than matched the press notices. Unfortunately, many fans missed the classic because as the *Chicago Defender* reported, "The weather was so cold that the attendance was not up to the usual number, but those who braved the wintry blasts were well repaid." Both pitchers were in midseason form and the game was scoreless after four innings. In the top of the fifth, Jules Thomas lined a double to left-center field and scored on a sacrifice by Gonzalez. That was all the support that "Cyclone Joe" would need on this day as he set the Poincianas down with just three scattered singles.

Breakers

Name	Pos	R	H	E
Gans	1B	0	1	0
Chacon	SS	0	0	0
Wiley	RF	0	0	0
Hall	LF	0	2	0
Santop	C	0	1	0
Thomas	CF	1	2	0
Gonzalez	3B	0	0	0
Lundy	2B	0	0	1
J. Williams	P	0	0	0
Totals		**1**	**6**	**1**

Royal Poinciana

Name	Pos	R	H	E
Barber	RF	0	1	0
DeMoss	2B	0	0	0
Hill	CF	0	0	0
Duncan	LF	0	0	0
Petway	C	0	0	0
Francis	3B	0	0	0
Grant	1B	0	0	0
R. Williams	SS	0	1	1
Redding	P	0	1	0
		0	**3**	**1**

```
Breakers          0 0 0   0 1 0   0 0 0—1—6—1
Royal Poinciana   0 0 0   0 0 0   0 0 0—0—3—1
```

Two Base Hits: Thomas (2)
Strikeouts: J. Williams 9, Redding 3.

The season was marked by some brilliant pitching, particularly on the part of Richard "Big" Whitworth, a towering 6'4", 215 pound right-hander, whose blazing fastball sent numerous hitters back to the bench grumbling to themselves. Whitworth paced Foster's Poinciana squad with a perfect 5–0 record that included a 1–0 shutout of "Cyclone Joe" Williams. Frank "The Red Ant" Wickware complemented Whitworth's heroics by registering a 2–1 mark. Pete Duncan led all hitters with a .317 batting average, followed by Jess Barber at .273. Joe Williams of the Breakers came away victorious in two 1–0 pitching duels with Poinciana's best, but could do no better than 2–3 overall as his support failed him at crucial times. Blainey Hall put together another .300 season, powering the ball at a .309 clip, ably assisted by Beattie Brooks at .273 and Doc Wiley at .269. Dick Lundy, known affectionately as "King Richard," generally considered to be one of the four greatest shortstops in Negro League history, made his first visit to Palm Beach, but could do no better with the bat than .167 in 13 games.

By 1919 World War I was over and so was the Palm Beach coverage of the Coconut League. The only game reports coming out of Palm Beach after this time were those printed in the *Chicago Defender* and the *Pittsburgh Courier*, two of the country's most prominent black newspapers. Except for one item from the *Daily News* dated February 13, 1919, all was quiet on the eastern front. The league was still in existence, it still attracted the top players from the Negro Leagues, and it was still a popular diversion for the guests of the Royal Poinciana and Breakers hotels, but for some reason it was no longer considered newsworthy by the local media. An article titled "They Were Giants: Negro League Baseball in Florida, 1920's & 1930's" documented the popularity of the game during that period, as well as the social atmosphere that permeated everyday life.

> The teams competed each Tuesday and Friday afternoon at 3:00 P.M. The game was limited to seven innings so that the players could finish in time for their evening hotel duties. While

the players held servile jobs in the hotel and lived in segregated dormitories, they were truly athletic stars to the many wealthy northerners who spent their winters in Palm Beach. Palm Beach baseball expressed several contradictions. While employed in the lowest levels of hotel labor, the black men of baseball were cheered loudly by the nation's elites "wintering" in Palm Beach. Palm Beach was establishing a model for race and sport that would continue to the present: respecting the athletic achievement of African Americans yet continuing the social structures of racism.

No game reports have been located for either 1919 or 1920, but in 1921 the Chicago and Pittsburgh newspapers began publishing occasional stories and box scores. The league continued to be a haven for the outstanding Negro League players with manager Rube Foster, Ping Garder, Bingo DeMoss, Jimmie Lyons, Dave Malarcher, Rap Dixon, and Bobby Williams representing the Royal Poinciana Hotel and manager John Henry Lloyd, Jess Barber, Billy Francis, Louis Santop, Blainey Hall, Eddie Douglas, Chester Brooks, "Cyclone Joe" Williams, and Phil Cockrell wearing the colors of the Breakers Hotel. In one of the early games, right-hander Jack Marshall blanked Lloyd's troops 7–0 behind the timely hitting of Gardner, Lyons, Dixon, and Grant, each of whom pounded out two base hits. Lloyd accounted for two of the Breakers' four hits. The next game, on February 2, was an exciting affair that the Poinciana nine appeared to have locked up until the Breakers exploded for six runs in the last two innings. As the Bulldogs came to bat in the top of the eighth inning, they found themselves on the short end of a 4–0 score, with lefty Dave Brown tossing a two-hitter, but a double by Brooks, singles by Lee Miller and Joe Williams, and an error by Brown himself plated three runs to cut the lead to 4–3. After Rube Foster's cohorts added a run in the bottom of the inning, Douglas hit a one-out single off Brown in the ninth bringing Tom Williams, on his way to a sensational 15–7 season with the Chicago American Giants, into the game. But Williams was unable to halt the uprising before the Bulldogs added another three-spot to their total to take the lead 6–5. In the bottom of the ninth, with Roy Roberts on the mound in relief of Joe Williams, Malarcher and Dixon singled and Leroy Grant was hit with a pitch to load the bases. When Marshall hit into a force play at the plate and John Beckwith fanned, it looked like Roberts would weather the storm, but Bobby Williams spoiled the scenario by singling in the tying run. After DeMoss grounded out to end the inning, the game was called so the players could return to their duties for the evening meal in the dining room of the hotels. The box score below does not agree with the totals for the Poinciana nine, which was not unusual in the early days of the game.

Royal Poinciana

Name	Pos	R	H	E
Gardner	RF	1	1	0
Beckwith	RF	0	0	0
B. Williams	SS	0	2	0
DeMoss	2B	1	1	0
Lyons	LF	0	0	0
Warfield	CF	1	1	0
Malarcher	3B	1	2	0
Dixon	C	0	0	0
J. Brown	PH	0	0	0
Grant	1B	0	2	0

Breakers

Name	Pos	R	H	E
Gardner	RF-2B	0	1	0
Francis	3B-2B	0	0	1
Cockrell	RF	0	0	0
Santop	C	0	1	0
Hall	LF	0	0	0
Lloyd	SS	0	0	1
Douglas	1B	1	1	0
Brooks	CF	2	2	0
Thomas	2B	0	0	0
Miller	3B	2	2	0

Royal Poinciana					Breakers				
Name	Pos	R	H	E	Name	Pos	R	H	E
D. Brown	P	0	0	0	J. Williams	P	1	1	3
T. Williams	P	0	0	1	Roberts	P	0	1	0
Johnson	P	0	0	0					
Mirabal	P	0	0	0					
Totals		6	12	1			6	9	5

```
Poinciana    0 0 1   0 1 0   2 1 1—6—12—1
Breakers     0 0 0   0 0 0   0 3 3—6— 9—5
```

Two Base Hits: Barber, Brooks (2)
Three Base Hits: Roberts, Dixon.

Pitcher	IP	W	L	H	SO	BB
D. Brown	8⅓	0	0	6	7	1
T. Williams	⅓	0	0	3	1	0
Johnson	0	0	0	0	0	2
Mirabal	⅓	0	0	0	0	0
J. Williams	8	0	0	9	0	1
Roberts	1	0	0	3	1	0

There were only five other games reported in the dailies, with the Breakers winning three games by scores of 2–1, 4–0, and 3–0, and Poinciana winning the other two by scores of 1–0 and 5–2. In the first game, Santop singled in one run and the eventual game-winner crossed the plate on a single by Lloyd and a double by Douglas. Rap Dixon singled in the lone Poinciana run. Roy Roberts tossed a 4–0 shutout in the second game sparked by John Henry Lloyd who doubled and stole home in the second inning. The Breakers added three more runs in the fourth on base hits by Hall, Thomas, and Barber. Phil Cockrell limited Rube Foster's crew to two hits in his 3–0 gem. The Bulldogs knocked Tom Williams out of the box in the first inning, scoring two runs on singles by Barber and Lloyd and a double by Santop. The final run came across without benefit of a hit, three walks and an error doing the damage. Poinciana finally got on the board when they blanked the Bulldogs 1–0 before Johnson and Marshall combined on a 5–2 win over Roberts. The game was even after seven innings, but Foster's boys pushed across the tie-breaking run in the eighth and added two more in the ninth for good measure. The game took almost three hours to complete thanks to the nineteen bases on balls issued by the pitchers, with Roberts issuing ten of them.

There were no reported games in 1922 and the following year only two games were reported with each team winning one. The only score that was published was a 10–3 romp for the Breakers behind the pitching of George Washington Johnson. The *Pittsburgh Courier* noted, "The hitting of Capt. Lundy and Mason of the Ponces, and Raggs and G. Johnson of the Breakers were the features of the game."

The 1924 season passed unnoticed, but in 1925, coverage once again improved to the point that nine games were reported with the Royal Poinciana Hotel taking the Coconut League championship by winning seven games against two losses. The big story of the year was a perfect game thrown by Bob McClure of the Baltimore Black Sox against the Breakers Bulldogs. The big 6', 190-pound righty, coming off a 15-4 season in the Eastern Colored League, set down 27 batters in succession to win 2–0 but, as the *Courier* reported, he had his share of luck also. "He was backed up by superb fielding, several lightning plays turning hits into outs. Kenyon, the left fielder, made two sparkling catches in the outfield, robbing Chaney White and Phil Cockrell of hits. His bat also helped win the game when he tripled in the fourth inning and scored on an infield out." In another important game, according to the *Courier*, 39-year-old "Cyclone Joe" Williams, manager of Poinciana, "pitched in the same masterful form which has characterized his work on the mound for the past fourteen years, holding the Breakers to six hits. Three of these hits came in the seventh inning when, with the game safely tucked away, he eased up a bit, the Breakers escaping a shutout by scoring two runs in that stanza." The final score was 12–2.

Poinciana

Name	Pos	AB	R	H
W. Johnston	CF	4	1	0
G. Williams	SS	3	2	3
Smith	3B	2	1	0
Scales	2B	4	2	2
Thomas	RF	4	2	2
Cason	1B	2	2	1
Kenyon	LF	3	1	2
Gatewood	C	4	0	1
J. Williams	P	2	1	0
Totals		28	12	11

Breakers

Name	Pos	AB	R	H
B. Scott	LF	4	0	1
Downs	SS	3	0	0
Cockrell	RF-2B-P	3	0	0
White	CF	3	0	1
Eggleston	3B	3	0	1
Lewis	C	1	0	0
Lee	2B	2	1	1
B. White	2B-C	3	1	1
T. Allen	1B	3	0	1
Gardner	P	0	0	0
Flournoy	P	3	0	0
		28	2	6

Poinciana	0 2 3	7 0 0	0—12—11—2
Breakers	0 0 0	0 0 0	2— 2— 6—2

Two Base Hits: G. Williams, Kenyon
Struck Out: Williams 4, Gardner 2, Cockrell 2, Flournoy 2.
Bases On Balls: Gardner 3, Flournoy 2, Cockrell 1.

It was during this period that Joe Williams was first referred to in print as "Smokey Joe." The *Chicago Defender* continued to call him "Cyclone Joe," but the *Pittsburgh Courier* alternated between "Cyclone Joe" and "Smokey Joe."

Later in 1925, the Breakers Hotel burned to the ground for a second time, which, according to several sources, was started by one of those "new fangled" curling irons. The new Breakers Hotel, built at a cost of six million dollars, was called one of the finest resorts in the world.

The Coconut League could still boast of some great Negro League players during the 1920s, but the overall quality of the league decreased significantly as the decade progressed, particularly on the mound. Although many outstanding pitchers like Cockrell, Pud Flournoy, and Nip Winters (who tossed a three-hitter at Poinciana on February 13, winning 3–0) wintered in Palm Beach, pitching legends like Redding and Foster were often replaced by lesser names such as Otis Starks, Hubert Lockhart, and Chippy Britt. Even 39-year-old Joe Williams, no longer the "Cyclone" of his youth, was treated roughly more often than not, except for brief flashes of form as noted above.

The rosters for the two hotel teams showcased a number of new players in 1926, including Jap Washington, Vic Harris, and John Reese, plus journeymen Mike Brown,

Bob Saunders, Specs Clark, Ray Vaughn, Jack Wallace, Jimmy Reel, a player named W. Burton, and a Cuban pitcher named Panier. Some of the old reliables like Williams and Phil Cockrel returned, but for the most part it was a new cast of characters. The opening game of the Coconut League proved to be unlucky for manager Joe Williams of Poinciana. Even though his team won the game, he went down with a painful injury that kept him on the sidelines for a month. The big right-hander attempted to stop a line drive back through the box with his pitching hand, and the ball struck his hand, tearing off the nail and straining ligaments in his pitching arm. As fate would have it, in his first game back after the injury, Williams went down again, when Roy Roberts hit him with a pitch on the same hand he had injured previously.

The Royal Poinciana nine captured the championship with five victories against four losses and three ties. It was a hitters year in 1926, the first time in the long-running series that the hitters dominated the pitchers. Poinciana had no less than eight .300 hitters in the statistics that have been recovered. Jap Washington, who batted .346, also led the league with two home runs, the first time anyone ever hit more than one homer in a season. An unknown player by the name of W. Burton was crowned the batting champion with an average of .480.

The 1927 season saw George "Tank" Carr, the 32-year-old slugger of the Hilldale Daisies, covering third base for Joe Williams' Poinciana team. The Coconut League championship was hotly contested by the two hotel teams and, in the end, there was no winner as each team won six games with one game ending in a tie. The Breakers got off to a fast start in the title chase by winning three of the first four games. With the series tied at one game each, Sam Streeter of the Breakers, a left-handed spitball pitcher who toiled for the Birmingham Black Barons during the summer, bested Joe Williams 3–1 in a spirited pitching duel. His most troublesome inning was the sixth when the Poinciana team loaded the bases with no outs, but the tiny, chunky, southpaw escaped without damage by fanning the side. "Cyclone Joe," on the other hand, pitching with a sore arm, was touched up for a long home run to center field by catcher Charles Spearman that was the deciding hit. Anderson Pryor of Poinciana had three hits for the day, while Burlin White chipped in with two, giving him eight base hits in nine at-bats to start the season. The big guns for the Breakers were Spearman, Mitchell, and Streeter, all with two hits. Williams was knocked out of the box in the fourth game, a 5–5 tie that saw the two teams combine for 18 base hits. Vic Harris and Bobby Williams each punched out three hits for the Breakers, while Carl Perry and Jap Washington had two, as did John Jones of the Royal Poincianas. The Bulldogs extended their lead to three games to one with an 11–7 victory in game five. Anderson Pryor slammed a two-run homer in the first inning as the Poincianas raced to a 7–0 lead, but Joe Williams couldn't hold the lead as he was raked for 16 hits and issued five free passes.

Poinciana won the next three games to take the lead in the series, with pitcher Ping Gardner, called by Jim Riley "a little fellow with an underhand delivery," using his submarine delivery to good advantage on February 25, taking the measure of the Breakers Bulldogs by a 6–2 count. The *Courier* noted, "His fast one was hopping, his curve ball looked more like a horse shoe than anything else. In the Breakers third he opened with his beautiful breaking drop curve ball and was never in danger." In the Poinciana half of the inning, after Burton walked, Gardner drove a ball onto the golf course for a two-run homer. Joe Williams' team scored again in the fifth when Chance Cummings and

Chaney White pulled a perfect double steal, with Cummings sliding home while pitcher "Lefty" Gisentaner held the ball. After the Breakers cut the lead to 3–2 in the sixth inning, the Poinciana crew pounded Gisentaner for three more runs over the final three innings, one of them coming on a long home run off the bat of Jap Washington.

Poinciana					Breakers				
Name	Pos	AB	R	H	Name	Pos	AB	R	H
Harris	CF	4	1	2	C. Perry	2B	3	0	1
E. Pryor	SS	4	1	0	B. Williams	SS	4	0	1
Clark	2B	3	1	2	Streeter	CF	4	0	1
Carr	3B	2	1	1	Washington	1B	4	1	2
Cummings	1B	4	1	2	C. Spearman	C	2	1	1
B. White	C	2	0	1	Forbes	3B	2	0	0
Burton	RF	3	0	0	Gisentaner	P	3	0	1
Jones	LF	3	0	0	Vaughn	RF	3	0	0
Gardner	P	3	1	2	Reel	LF	2	0	1
Totals		28	6	10			27	2	8

Poinciana   0 0 2   0 1 0   2 1 x—6—10—0
Breakers   0 0 0   0 0 2   0 0 0—2— 8—1

Three Base Hit: B. White
Home Runs: Gardner, J. Washington.

The Breakers trailed the Royal Poincianas six games to four with just two games remaining in the season, but they rallied to take the final two contests and gain a tie for the league title. In game 12, a sloppy contest with numerous errors, Ping Gardner outlasted Joe Williams, who could have sued his teammates for non-support, by a count of 7–6. In the final game of the season, the Breakers evened the series with an 11–2 victory over Joe Williams' cohorts, driving 6'3", 225-pound right-hander Will Jackman from the mound in the process. The submarine pitcher proved to be no puzzle to the Bulldogs, who iced the game with seven runs in the opening stanza, sparked by Spearman's three-run homer to right field. Once again, the Poinciana defense fell apart, with shortstop Specs Clark booting four balls.

The year 1928, as McIver reported, "was a fateful one for Palm Beach hotel teams, starting the decline of black baseball at the resort. The St. Louis Browns of the American League had begun conducting spring training in West Palm Beach, and that fall a killer hurricane struck the coast, wrecking the Royal Poinciana, in its heyday the world's largest resort hotel, along with the baseball field's wooden bleachers." The hotel was eventually torn down between 1930 and 1935, and the league ceased operations in 1931 after struggling through three years following the disaster.

According to the recovered newspaper reports, the Breakers Bulldogs captured the Coconut League championship by winning five of the ten games played, with one tie. In the opening game of the season on February 2, the Breakers edged the Royal Poinciana nine 4–2, with Red Ryan besting Rube Chambers. The Bulldogs scored all their runs in the fourth inning when Ryan unloaded a grand-slam home run to right-center field. The game was a tragic farewell for Chambers, who was found dead in a boxcar five days later. The talented left-handed screwball pitcher was apparently shot by criminal elements who were never apprehended. John Holway interviewed Judy Johnson, who had wintered in Palm Beach that year. He said,

> The rivalry between the two hotels was intense, but it was the money-making that lured many of the players down there. The pay and tips were excellent. Beyond that, there were floating crap games and, for the really adventuresome, rum-running from nearby Cuba to the prohibitionist but thirsty mainland. Many a man could "hustle' himself a nice bit of cash in just a few months, as much as he could make in a whole year of playing ball back north. Judy didn't participate in these off-the-field enterprises, but he observed them—the rum was sometimes stacked against the wall of the dormitories, right up to the ceilings.

Back on the ballfield, "Lefty" Williams of the Breakers defeated Poinciana 5–1, giving his team a 4 to 2 lead in the series. Jap Washington hammered a two-run homer off Joe Williams in the first inning to put his team on the road to victory. After playing a 4–4 tie, the Breakers, behind "Lefty" Williams, defeated "Cyclone Joe" again, this time by a 1–0 score. Williams held the Breakers to just two base hits but unfortunately they both came in the fourth inning and led to the only run of the game. Three days later, the Breakers won again, this time by a 7–4 count. Vic Harris' two-run single in the sixth inning broke a 4-all tie and proved to be the difference in the game. Poinciana won the next two games to cut the margin to five games to four, but they were unable to overtake the Bulldogs. On March 8, "Cyclone Joe" Williams flashed his old form as he blanked the Breakers 7–0. Pud Flournoy pounded out two doubles for the Royal Poincianas. In the season finale, the two teams played to a 1–1 tie, with Joe Williams pitching another gem for the Poincianas, and Red Ryan matching the old master pitch for pitch.

The Coconut League was winding down rapidly as the decade of the twenties was coming to an end. No other box scores were discovered, and only brief mention of the 1929 to 1931 seasons were made in the *Pittsburgh Courier*. In 1929, the Breakers captured the opening game of the season by a 2–0 count, but the identity of the winning pitcher was not revealed. On February 19, the Breakers won again, but three days later the Poinciana nine won to even the series at four games each. Luther Farrell of Poinciana was involved in both decisions, and W. Gay gave him all the support he needed in his victory with three base hits. The last game reported was a 4–3 victory for Poinciana, giving them the title in games located. Ted Trent of the Breakers held a 3–1 lead over Luther Farrell in the seventh inning when the Poincianas came to life. W. Gay lined a two-run triple to the golf course, to tie the score, and brought home the game-winner on a single by Chaney White. Buck hit a two-run homer for the Bulldogs.

The 1930 pennant went to the Royal Poinciana nine, three games to one. "Cyclone Joe" Williams was the winning pitcher in a 5–3 Poinciana victory on February 4 after the Breakers had won the opening game of the season. Berry hit a home run for Poinciana and Williams had a run-scoring single, while Alonzo Mitchell had a double for the Breakers. Poinciana also won the third game 5–3 behind a pitcher named H. Grey. Many of the players who filled out the hotel rosters during the final years of the Coconut League, like Grey, W. Burton, L.E. Oliver, Pace, W. Gay, C. Jones, and Ken Robinson, were relative unknowns in the Negro leagues. They may have been local amateur players or they may have played in lower level professional Negro leagues. In the next encounter, the two teams battled to a 1–1 tie with Joe Williams on the mound for the Poinciana nine. Pace of the Breakers stole home for his team's only run. The last game reported was another victory for Joe Williams, as the old warrior, given a 6–0 cushion early in the game, held on to win 6–5. Another old veteran, Billy Francis, hit a home run for the Bulldogs. The *Courier* noted, "The pitching of Joe Williams featured the contest, and he pitched what might almost be called big league ball, striking out men at crucial stages of the game."

The 1931 season rang down the curtain on the Coconut League, at least as far as the newspaper coverage was concerned. The Poinciana nine won two of the three games reported to capture the last Coconut League championship. Joe Williams was still at the helm of the Royal Poinciana team in 1931 and Burlin White captained the Breakers Bulldogs. Some of the players reported to be in Florida included veterans Clint Thomas, Chance Cummings, Ed Stone, Tex Burnett, and Pud Flournoy, but most of the players, like Yunk Jones, "Lefty" Tom Glover, Cecil Johnson, Bill "Big C" Johnson, "Slim" Vaughn, an infielder named Galloway, and a catcher named Jones, were hardly household names. Manager "Cyclone Joe" Williams took the mound for the league opener on February 13, and he carried his team to a 3–2 victory over Flournoy and the Breakers. The game was closely contested for six innings, but in the seventh inning, Galloway booted two balls and the Poinciana team quickly capitalized on the miscues to score the winning runs. The last newspaper article concerning the Florida Hotel League appeared in the *Pittsburgh Courier* on February 21, 1931, reporting a 4–0 victory for the Breakers Bulldogs over the Poinciana team. The pitcher throwing the whitewash at the Royal Poincianas was not identified, but the losing pitcher was Ping Gardner. Poinciana won the final game reported by a score of 4–3 with Joe Williams chalking up the last two outs with the tying run on third base. It was only fitting that Williams was the winning pitcher in the last Coconut League baseball game ever reported.

The Coconut League, particularly during the first two decades of the twentieth century, was one of the strongest professional baseball competitions in the United States. There were all-stars at every position, and that was never more evident than on the mound where some of the country's greatest pitchers held court. It is well known that good pitching will stop good hitting every time, and the Coconut League had an excess of pitching talent, where the likes of Rube Foster, "Cyclone Joe" Williams, "Cannonball" Dick Redding, Frank Earle, Dizzy Dismukes, Frank "The Red Ant" Wickware, and Luis "Mulo" Padron kept the batters on the defensive week after week. Since the teams played only two games a week, it was possible for one pitcher to pitch in 50 percent or more of his team's games. In 1914 for instance, Joe Williams pitched in ten of the Breaker's fourteen games, including three in relief.

Pitchers had another advantage in Palm Beach. They could keep their arms limber during their off-field hours and still pitch with more-than-adequate speed during the two-games-a-week league schedule. But hitting required much more practice, and that was hard to come by for waiters who were kept busy from sunup till sundown serving the hotel guests breakfast, lunch, and dinner, while also cleaning the dining room and setting up the tables again between meals. It is a testimonial to John Henry Lloyd's superior plate discipline that he was able to compile a .309 batting average against such dominant pitchers. He was the only hitter with a minimum of 100 at-bats to boast of a .300 or better batting average. The only other batters to hit over .231 were "Spot" Poles at .285 and Blainey Hall at .282. Pete Duncan stung the ball at a .320 clip in 97 at-bats. Louis Santop could do no better than .231, Pete Hill struggled at .214, and Jimmie Lyons was bogged down at .181.

2

Cuban Paradise

Cuba was the second country in the Western Hemisphere to embrace baseball as a popular national sport, trailing only the United States. The U.S., in fact, played a major part in introducing baseball to the Cuban people. There are a number of different stories about how baseball first reached the island, but all of them probably contributed to the success of the sport. Nemesio Guillo, a young Cuban student, supposedly brought the game back to Cuba with him in the summer of 1864. Guillo had been sent to Mobile, Alabama, by his parents eight years earlier at the age of 11. He and two friends studied at Spring Hill College before returning to Cuba with a baseball bat and ball in tow. Coincidentally, the same year, sailors from a ship loading sugar for the American market at the port of Matanzas, "The Athens of Cuba," organized a baseball game against Cuban longshoremen, but that experience was probably incidental, and did not contribute significantly to the growth of the game. It was more likely the experiences of Guillo and his countryman, Esteban Bellan, that brought the game to Cuba. Bellan, a student at Fordham University in New York City, was so infatuated with baseball that he stayed in the States during the summer of 1869 and played baseball with the Troy Haymakers. He was a member of the squad that carved out a 17–17 tie against the mighty Cincinnati Red Stockings, the only blemish on the Red Stockings' undefeated season that included 57 victories. Bellan went on to play three years for Troy after they became members of the first major league in the U.S., the National Association of Professional Base Ball Players. He held down the hot corner for the Haymakers during his three-year career, batting a modest .251, but he had one memorable day with the bat when he punched out five base hits in five trips to the plate against future Hall-of-Fame pitcher Al Spalding.

Returning to Cuba, Bellan helped organize the Havana Club in 1872, and he participated in the country's first organized baseball game against the Matanzas Club at Palmar del Junco in Matanzas on December 27, 1874. Both pitchers were allowed to "throw" the ball instead of "pitching" it, meaning they could throw hard instead of tossing it gently over the plate. The result was that Havana thrashed Matanzas 51–9 as pitcher Ricardo Mora dazzled the Matanzas batters with his blinding speed. Bellan, who caught the game, crushed three home runs and scored seven runs and Mora chipped in with a home run of his own. Matanzas had a spotty history in the Cuban League down through the years, but many outstanding black baseball players originated in the area as a result of the Afro-Cuban population of the city. Matanzas was initially the center of the sugar-growing region in Cuba, becoming home to thousands of former slaves who had worked the sugar cane fields. Over the years, the city produced some of Cuba's greatest players, many of them wearing the names of their slave owners, such as Jose Mendez, Martin Dihigo, Valentin Dreke, and Minnie Minoso.

As baseball began to take hold in Cuba, however, it was still at the bottom of the priority list for most of the populace. Civil strife permeated the country as the 300-year reign of Spanish domination was drawing to a close. During the early 1800s, Spain had transported more than 200,000 black slaves from Africa to Cuba to work the sugar and tobacco plantations and the iron mines. The Spanish governing body tried to instill a Spanish way of life into the country, including elevating the Caucasian race to a master-race status and reducing non-Caucasoid races, such as the Negro and Indian races, to a position of subservience. In Spanish Cuba, government appointees, landowners, and businessmen were all white. Blacks and Indians were either slaves or freed laborers. That situation didn't sit too well with the populace at hand since the white aristocrats were in the minority in the country. In fact, more and more of the population were becoming mulatto, or mixed race. By 1943 approximately 25 percent of the population was black or mulatto, and by the end of the 20th century, mulattos would account for 51 percent of the population, with 37 percent white, and 11 percent black. Throughout the colonial period, Cubans opposed the Spanish authority and resisted Spanish activities and entertainment at every opportunity. As early as 1830, anti-Spanish demonstrations and riots dominated Cuban political life. In October 1868, Carlos Manuel de Cespedes led an uprising to demand implementation of the reforms that had been promised to them over the years but had never been carried out. After ten years of guerrilla warfare, hostilities ceased on October 10, 1878, with the submission of the insurrectionists and concessions by the Spanish government. The treaty guaranteed to abolish slavery and to cease the importation of cheap labor from China. Three years later, the equal civil rights status of both blacks and whites was guaranteed. That civil rights proclamation, coming 82 years before the United States would begin to address the issue, was one of the most important social changes in Cuba in the 19th century. And it would lead, in the next twenty years, to the establishment of the hemisphere's first integrated professional baseball league. During the Ten Years War, many Cuban nationalists were deported to distant Spanish colonies like Morocco. Other revolutionaries fled the country to the Dominican Republic, Venezuela, and Colombia and, wherever they went, they brought baseball with them. They, along with the Americans, were the missionaries of baseball, carrying the sport to the far ends of the Western Hemisphere.

The peace that resulted from the treaty of 1878 lasted for only 17 years, at which time the people rose up once again in opposition to the oppressive policies of the Spanish government. This time the Cuban rebels were eventually joined by the United States, which entered the fray after the battleship *Maine* was blown up in Havana Harbor on February 15, 1898. The war lasted less than four months after the *Maine* incident as the United States destroyed the Spanish fleet in Manila Harbor in the Philippine Islands, and the Spanish forces were defeated in Cuba in the famous charge up San Juan Hill in Santiago. By the terms of the treaty, Spain ceded the Philippines, Guam, Puerto Rico, and all the Spanish West India possessions to the U.S., and Cuba was recognized as an independent territory under the protection of the United States.

Even as war enveloped Cuba in the late 1800s, and the relationship between the people and the Spanish government disintegrated, baseball marched on. Baseball and politics were closely intertwined. The Cuban people disliked the Spanish authorities, and they disliked the Spanish sports of bullfighting and cockfighting. They loved the American sport of baseball, which infuriated the Spanish authorities who considered it to be a form of protest against Spain. The first Cuban professional league was formed in 1878-79, with Havana edging Almendares 21-20 in the opener. Esteban Bellan, along with Cuban hero Emilio Sabourin, paced Havana to the league championship. Interestingly, an American was one of the stars of the second Cuban League season, and a victim of national discrimination. Pitcher George McCuller of Colon, one of two Americans in the league, fanned 21 Havana batters on November 23, 1879, establishing a strikeout record that has never been broken. He also hit the first home run in Cuban League history in a 13-8 victory over Havana, but his fame was short lived as his presence brought protests from the other teams in the league and, when the league upheld the protests, Colon withdrew from the league and the American players went home.

Esteban Bellan was generally recognized as the best player of his era in Cuba, and he led the Havana Club to four league championships in five years, playing every position except pitcher, and also serving as manager. Cuban League baseball was initially a game for white, upper class Cubans, similar to the situation that existed in the United States. Social change was on its way in the country, however, beginning with the actual abolishment of slavery in 1886 that freed thousands of blacks from the heinous bondage that had imprisoned them for more than two centuries. But freedom in 1886 still did not extend to the baseball diamond. The teams in the first Cuban League were sponsored by elite white social clubs, and those clubs excluded blacks from their membership. Team photos of the league champions reflected the tenor of the times. The greatest players, all white, were Antonio "El Ingles" Garcia, arguably the greatest Cuban player of the 19th century; outfielder Alfredo Arcano, the game's first home run leader; and pitchers Adolfo Lujan and Juan Pastoriza. Blacks were relegated to playing baseball on the sandlots or on black amateur teams that could play only other black teams.

Blacks may also have played with and against whites on sugar mill teams. And as noted in *The Pride of Havana*, "In the period between the Ten-Year War and the War of 1895, Cuban black players were coveted by emerging Mexican teams in the Yucatan area. Cuban families who emigrated from Cuba to that region—La Emigracion, which, as we saw, also included Florida and New York—took baseball to Mexico. Cuban blacks such as the famed Quince y Medio, so known for his having gone around the bases in fifteen and a half seconds, were stars in the early stages of Mexican baseball."

Civil unrest exploded again in 1895 when Maximo Gomez y Baez led a popular insurrection against Spanish oppression. Baseball was banned by the authorities on May 19, 1895, as an evil American sport, further alienating the people from their Spanish conquerors. At this same time, Emilio Sabourin, one of Cuban baseball's pioneers and organizers, was arrested for revolutionary activities and was sent to Spain where he died in a Spanish prison in 1897. The government permitted baseball to resume on December 12, 1897, even though the insurrection was still alive. Three teams, Feista, Havanista, and Almendarista, played a ten-game schedule in 1897-98 and a 12-game schedule in 1899. Social change had come slowly in Cuba, but the elimination of racial discrimination, at least in the world of baseball, was brought to a head in 1900 when the Liga Nacional de Base Ball was dissolved, for what was reported to be "reasons of a social nature." The reasons were, in fact, due to the admission of two new teams to the league, San Francisco, an all-black team, and Cubano, an integrated team. Severino T. Soloso, the owner of the original Cuba team, rather than participate in an integrated league, gave his ownership position in the team to Augustin "Tinti" Molina, who had once hit a home run in an exhibition game against an American team, and Jose Poyo. According to Roberto Gonzalez, Soloso gave Molina and Poyo the team's uniforms, but insisted that they had to add a "no" after Cuba because Soloso didn't want an integrated team playing under his team's name, and the addition of "no" after Cuba, that now read Cuba no, meant "This is not team Cuba." Many upper class whites left the new league, called the Cuban League, at this time and played for their social clubs as amateurs. But the Cuban League flourished with the two new teams plus the all-white teams, Havana and Almendarista. And, fittingly, the all-black San Francisco team walked off with the 1900 pennant, beating Havana by 3 games. With the introduction of one black team and one mixed-race team, the Cuban League became the first integrated professional baseball league in the world, except for brief interludes of integrated play in the American minor leagues. The 1910-11 California Winter League, with the black Leland Giants, would be the game's second integrated professional league.

Julian Castillo, Cuba's first black superstar, made his appearance in the Cuban League in 1901. The powerful right-handed batter, standing 6', 2" tall and weighing a muscular 240 pounds, was one of the greatest hitters in Cuban baseball history, a slugger in the mold

Julian Castillo, one of the first blacks to play in the Cuban League, was its most devastating slugger during the first decade of the twentieth century (courtesy Yuyo Ruiz).

of Frank Thomas and David Ortiz. He was born in Havana on January 31, 1881, and he hardened his body cutting sugar cane during the hot summer months, and spent the winters playing baseball. Castillo began his Cuban League career with San Francisco, and immediately created a reputation for himself as a formidable slugger by rapping the ball at a league-leading .454 clip, still the all-time Cuban League single season batting record. He also set the pace in base hits and doubles that year. The class of the league however was Havana, who captured the title with a 16–3 record. On February 3, 1901, the two teams met and Havana emerged victorious behind the pitching of the legendary Carlos "Bebe" Royer, who was the league's top pitcher at 12–3. There were no American Negro League players in the Cuban League in 1901 as they hadn't yet made their presence felt south of the border, but several of the Cuban players eventually made their way north to compete in the Negro leagues during the summer hiatus, including Castillo, Luis "Mulo" Padron, and Emilio Palomino.

San Francisco					**Havana**				
Name	*Pos*	*AB*	*R*	*H*	*Name*	*Pos*	*AB*	*R*	*H*
P. Benevides	RF	4	0	0	M. Lopez	LF	4	0	1
C. Moran	3B	4	1	0	R. Calzadilla	C	5	1	1
A. Baro	LF	4	0	0	L. Padron	3B	5	1	1
J. Castillo	CF	5	1	2	V. Gonzalez	2B	4	2	3
F. Moran	SS	4	0	3	A. Arcano	CF	3	1	1
E. Palomino	P	5	0	0	R. Valdes	SS	4	0	1
S. Jimenez	2B	3	0	0	C. Royer	P	3	0	1
P. Silveiro	C	4	0	1	J. Zubillaga	RF	3	1	1
E. Fontanalis	1B	2	0	0	J. Castener	1B	4	1	2
Totals		35	2	6			35	7	12

After a lukewarm sophomore season, the right-handed-hitting Castillo paced his new team, Havana, to the league championship by leading the league in base hits, triples, home runs, and batting average. Havana won the title again in 1904, with Castillo hitting .358 with a league-leading 5 triples in 67 at-bats. The powerfully built first baseman was just an average fielder and base runner, but his slugging prowess set him apart from the other players. Over the course of his 13-year Cuban league career, Julian Castillo hit a solid .310, the seventh highest batting average in Cuban league history, and he averaged five home runs for every 550 at-bats in the dead ball era. It was predicted that he would have been a .300 hitter in the major leagues, and could have averaged 31 home runs a year in the lively ball era. He won four batting titles during his Cuban League career. He also led the league in hits, doubles, and triples four times each, and in home runs three times. He was elected to the Cuban Hall of Fame in 1943.

One of the most famous visitors to Cuba over the years was John McGraw, the fiery third baseman of the Baltimore Orioles during the 1890s and the manager of the New York Giants from 1902 to 1932. McGraw made his first visit to the island nation in 1890 as a member of a minor league all-star team led by his manager at Wellsville, Al Lawson. As Frank Graham reported in his biography of McGraw, "The Havana that McGraw saw for the first time was very different from the Havana he was to know in later years. The Spanish-American War was still eight years away, and the city was filled with Spanish soldiers, there to hold in check the restless subjects of their king. It was crowded, dirty, and noisome. The hotel at which the players were quartered was old and moldy. The food was not to their liking. But they managed to enjoy themselves. They were delighted with the interest that the Cubans took in baseball." The games themselves were all one-sided, with the Americans routing the Cubans in five games. They blanked Havana 17–0, whipped Fe 11–4, beat Havana again by a count of 10–1, whitewashed Almendares 14–0, and defeated a Cuban all-star team 14–3.

The first decade of the 20th century was probably the most important period in Cuban baseball history. The new racial freedom that resulted in the integration of the Cuban League led directly to visits to the island by all-black teams from the United States and eventually to the addition of Negro League players to Cuban League rosters. It also encouraged major league all-star teams to travel to Cuba for exhibition games. A historic event took place in Cuba in 1900, at least as far as Negro League baseball players were concerned. The first all-black team from the U.S., the Cuban X-Giants, played 15 games on the island against local teams, winning twelve games and losing only three. This tour gave American black players their first opportunity to play baseball during the winter months outside the continental United States, and it represented the first time a black team traveled outside the country. The X-Giants' squad included Charlie Grant, Grant "Home Run" Johnson, Clarence Williams, Sol White, and Rube Foster. The X-Giants returned to the island in 1903, but struggled, going 2–7–1 despite having many of the same players. There were two shutouts in the series. Bernardo Carillo blanked McClellan 4–0 and Rube Foster and George Wilson tossed goose eggs at Jose Munoz by the same score.

The Cuban X-Giants were back again in 1904, with "Home Run" Johnson, Dan McClellan, Scotty Bowman, and Harry Buckner. Hill, Foster, and Grant did not play, but the Giants won 7 of 9 games without them. McClellan, Buckner, and Bowman threw shutouts at their Cuban opponents, with Buckner out-pitching Jose Munoz 4–0, McClellan besting Munoz by the same score, and Bowman taking the measure of Munoz by a 12–0 count. Bowman topped all pitchers with a 3–0 record and a 4.00 total run average (TRA). Buckner went 2–2 with a 3.00 TRA, and McClellan went 2–0 with a 3.50 TRA. The Cuban X-Giants outscored their Cuban opponents in the series by a count of 48–31.

The winter of 1904-05 was a busy time for baseball in Cuba as four other all-star teams invaded the country, including two teams with major league players on their roster. A group of minor leaguers from Lynn, Massachusetts, were first on the scene, and they went down to defeat five times in eight games, with two wins and a tie. Next came the All-Nationals with two bona fide major league players, "Dutch" Jordan of Brooklyn and Shad Barry of the Cubs, plus a gaggle of minor leaguers. The Cubans, behind Jose Munoz and Luis "Mulo" Padron, won four of five. Another minor league contingent from Tampa, Florida, made the trek south to challenge the Cubans, and they came up short, losing four of six. Finally, the All-Americans, a major league all-star team, arrived for a twelve game series against Havana and Azul. The American team, including Hall-of-Fame shortstop George Davis and a group of non-entities, took the Cubans to task seven times in 12 games with one tie. Luis Munoz won all four games for the Cubans, with two shutouts.

In 1905 the Cuban X-Giants, with Pete Hill and Rube Foster back once again, won five games and lost four. The following year, the X-Giants, with Bruce Petway and Pete Hill in tow, played an 11-game series against the Havana and Almendares clubs. In closely contested games, the X-Giants won 7 and lost 4. Luis Munoz went 1–1 for Almendares, tossing a 6–0 shutout at the Negro Leaguers, then losing 4–3.

Having watched the Negro Leaguers in action for four consecutive years, the powers that be in the Cuban League decided it was time to recruit some of the talented Americans to play in the Cuban League. And the Negro Leaguers were happy to join the league. Playing baseball in Cuba offered many advantages to them. They were more or less on a working vacation, where they could earn a decent salary during the off-season, bring their wives along if they wished, relax in the balmy climate, and be treated like equals. By the 1930s they were earning $600 and more a month during the four-month season, and living like kings. As Bruce Chadwick noted, "The Cienfuegos team near Havana, put its Negro Leaguers up in a luxury apartment house in the richest section of the city. Each apartment had a kitchen, dining room, living room, study, balcony, two bedrooms, and its own maid." The team clubhouse, according to Chadwick, had a laundry service for uniforms and street clothes, a shoeshine boy, and a small lounge. And the playing schedule offered an added incentive, if one was needed. They played only three games a week, a night game on Thursday and a doubleheader on Sunday. The rest of the time they were on their own, free to travel, enjoy the beach, visit the racetrack, the jai alai fronton, the casino, or just lounge around their apartment. They also escaped, even if temporarily, the indignities of their Negro League existence in the States, where they practically lived on a bus, traveling from city to city and playing as many as three games a day, and sometimes four games. They often slept on the bus between cities, hung their sweaty uniforms out the window to dry, and ate cold sandwiches on the run.

In January 1907, no less than nine black players from the north joined the Cuban League, including Harry Buckner, Charlie Grant, Grant "Home Run" Johnson, Bill Monroe, Pete Hill, Rube Foster, Chappie Johnson, Dan McClellan, and Ray Wilson. Almendares, with an all-Cuban cast with the exception of Buckner, won the league championship by one game over Fe in a season that ended on April 14. But a few of the American blacks excelled in their first full year in Cuba. Rube Foster, with his screwball darting to and fro, compiled a record of 10–5. Grant Johnson hit Cuban pitching to the tune of .348 and Bill Monroe produced a solid .346 average. But Pete Hill could do no better than .264, and Charlie Grant, Ray Wilson, and Chappie Johnson fell below the Mendoza line with averages of .186, .194, and .192 respectively. Harry Buckner went 1–2 on the mound and Dan McClellan lost both his decisions.

Another Negro League touring group, the Philadelphia Giants, arrived late in the year of 1907 and actually participated in two tours of duty, one in October and another one in December. The roster for the American team this time included John Henry Lloyd, who might have been the greatest shortstop in Negro League history, as well as "Home Run" Johnson, Bill Holland, and Bill Gatewood. The Giants went 5–7–1 in October, and then split the ten games in December. Their opponents in the two series, the Almendares Blues, went on to win the 1908 league championship with a dominating performance, winning 37 games against just 8 losses. Jose Munoz had a banner season, winning 13 games against a single loss, and leading the league with five shutouts. His compatriot, Jose Mendez, known as "El Diamante Negro" or the "Black Diamond," went a perfect 9–0 in his rookie season. Pete Hill, settling in as a force to be reckoned with, hit a resounding .343, and led the league with 5 triples in 175 at-bats. Hill also led the league in runs scored and base hits. "Home Run" Johnson finished with a .310 batting average and Bill Monroe came in at .319. John Henry Lloyd's visit to Havana was the beginning of a 22-year love affair with Cuba. The big shortstop, who joined the Havana club in the fall of 1908, was called "El Cuchara" (the shovel) because he scooped balls out of the dirt like a shovel, often ending up with as much dirt in his glove as ball. Lloyd played 13 seasons in Cuba and, in addition to his outstanding defensive skills, he also batted .329 in 1,327 at-bats.

The following season, the Brooklyn Royal Giants descended on Havana again and managed to win 7 of the 13 games played. Mendez went 1–1 against the invaders, while Munoz lost both his decisions. In November, the Cincinnati Reds, who finished fifth in the recent National League pennant race, tangled with the tough Cubans in a ten-game series. The teams split the ten games, but the highlight of the series was the pitching of 21-year-old Jose Mendez, who was fresh off his rookie season in the American Negro leagues where he went 3–0. The slightly built righthander, who stood 5', 8" tall and weighed a feathery 160 pounds, threw smoke, and had a sharp-breaking curveball to match. Mendez mesmerized the Reds in his first start, tossing a one-hitter and winning 1–0, with nine strikeouts. Miller Huggins spoiled Mendez's bid for a no-hitter with a two-out infield single in the ninth inning. Two weeks later, Mendez blanked the Reds for seven innings in relief and, four days after that exhibition, he pitched another complete game, winning 3–0, with 8 strikeouts and no walks. El Diamante Negro's performance was phenomenal, tossing 25 consecutive scoreless innings against a formidable major league team.

When Rube Foster's Leland Giants visited Cuba in the fall of 1910, they went 5-4-1, defeating Havana five straight, but falling to the Almendares Blues 0-4-1. They lost to "Bombin'" Pedroso twice and Jose Mendez twice. Mendez bested Pat Dougherty 1–0 in a closely contested pitching duel. Rube Foster pitched the best game of the series for Leland, blanking Luis Munoz and Havana 7–0. During the regular 1910-11 Cuban League season, several Negro Leaguers participated,

Jose Mendez, a wiry right-hander with blazing speed, was one of Cuba's greatest pitchers (courtesy Robert W. Peterson Collection, National Baseball Hall of Fame).

including Pete Hill, "Spot" Poles, John Henry Lloyd, Bruce Petway, Grant Johnson, Walter Ball, Clarence Williams, and Jesse Barbour. Hill walked off with the batting championship, stinging the ball at a .365 clip with a league-leading 5 triples in 96 at-bats. Poles was a close second with an average of .360. The other North Americans did not fare as well, with Ball going 2–8 on the mound, and Petway (.193), Barbour (.214), and "Home Run" Johnson (.245) struggling with the bat.

In 1911 the first Cuban players appeared in the major leagues. Armando Marsans and Rafael Almeida were both white, but their dark complexion caused them to be viewed with suspicion by race-conscious American baseball fans around the National League circuit. Even Cincinnati president Garry Herrman was suspicious, according to Bjarkman, stating, "We will not pay any Honus Wagner price for a pair of dark-skinned islanders." Finally, in an effort to dispel the fears of the fans that a black player might have sneaked into the major leagues, Cincinnati management sent to Cuba for official documents confirming that the two players had, in fact, a Castilian, or Spanish, heritage. Rafael Almeida and Armando Marsans debuted with the Cincinnati Reds on July 4, 1911, at Chicago's West Side Grounds. Almeida would play just three years, hitting .270 in 285 at-bats, while Marsans would hang around for eight years as a utilityman, batting .269 in 2,273 at-bats. Both players were in the 5', 10", 160-pound range and exhibited little power, but both were good fielders, Almeida at third base and Marsans in the outfield. In addition to their major league experience, both players played in Cuba for more than 20 years and in the Negro leagues for two years.

John McGraw had enjoyed Cuba so much on his first trip in 1890 that he visited the island paradise again in November 1911 for a series of exhibition game against the top Cuban teams, after his New York Giants had dropped the World's Series to Connie Mack's Philadelphia Athletics. As Graham recounted, "The years between had wrought many changes in him and, of course, in Havana. He, who had been there as an unknown kid ballplayer out of Wellsville, N.Y., trouping with a shabby lot of minor leaguers, returned now as the famous manager of the Giants, champions of the National League. In place of a dirty overrun city in which Spanish troops were garrisoned and Cuban patriots rotted in the dungeons of Morro Castle or died before firing squads, he found a bright, gay capital of a fledgling republic, in which baseball, not bull fighting, was the principal sport." Although the trip was a vacation for McGraw and his team, he still took the baseball games seriously and, when his team dropped a couple of early games to the Havana Reds and the Almendares Blues, the feisty manager read them the riot act as reported in his biography, *McGraw of the Giants*. "You've been beaten because you haven't taken these games seriously, and I'm not going to stand for it any longer! There will be morning practice until you pull yourselves together—and there will be less knocking around the bars at night." He went on to say, "You'll be out there or you won't play at all. That means you'll take the next boat home—or stay here at your own expense." The speech apparently worked because the Giants won the next game 4–0 when Christy Mathewson out-dueled Jose Mendez, and went on to take eight out of the last nine games.

McGraw brought the Giants back again in 1920, and he himself returned on vacation almost every year after the baseball season ended, to enjoy the balmy weather and to participate in his two favorite activities, jai alai and horse racing. He even purchased the Oriental Horse Racing Track in Marianao in partnership with Giants owner Charles A. Stoneham, and spent much of his free time trying to beat the gambling line on the two sports, as well as the games of chance at the casino. Graham described one of McGraw's visits to Cuba in the fall of 1921: "Behind him lay a pleasant winter in Havana: watching the horses run ... and having a good bet on many a winner; hearing the pleasant whir of the wheels and the dice clicking in the casino; strolling in the sun on the beach at La Playa; giving ... or attending ... parties at the Biltmore or Nacional or the Country Club."

The November 16, 1912, edition of the *Chicago Defender* reported on the visit of the Philadelphia Athletics to Cuba. "Last year the Philadelphia Americans were beaten nine out of twelve games, but so far they have had little difficulty in defeating the Islanders with the aid of Umpire Owens who seems to be giving the major leaguers the benefit of all close decisions, thereby enraging the fans and the Havana press. The situation grew so intense that Owens has been escorted to and from the field with a police escort, while the editors of the press advocated running him out of Havana." Notice of the limited success that American League teams had experienced in Cuba reached the ears of American League president Ban Johnson, who took immediate action. Feeling that the exhibition games were embarrassing his league, he issued an ultimatum decreeing that trips to Cuba by American League teams were banned. Johnson was quoted by Burgos as saying, "We want no makeshift club calling themselves the Athletics to go to Cuba to be beaten by colored teams."

Martin Dihigo, the man known as "El Immortal" in Cuba, began playing in the Cuban League as an outfielder-infielder in 1922 at the age of 16. He began pitching when he was 18, an age when he also posted a .300 batting average for the first time. The 1920s were perhaps the most exciting time in Cuban League baseball, with some of Cuba's legendary players, like Dihigo, Torriente,

Cristobal Torriente, one of baseball's great hitters, batted .336 in the Negro Leagues and .353 in the Cuban League (courtesy Jorge S. Figueredo and Charles Monfort).

Luque, and Baro, in their prime, and facing off against the top Negro Leaguers like Oscar Charleston, Lloyd, Dobie Moore, and Jud Wilson, and major league stars like Eddie Brown, Charlie Dressen, Jesse Petty, and Johnny Allen. The 1923-24 Santa Clara Leopards have been called the greatest professional baseball team ever assembled. They fielded one of the most sensational outfields of all time with the legendary Charleston flanked by Cuban heroes Pablo "Champion" Mesa and Alejandro Oms. The Leopards went 36–11 on the season to take the league title by 11½ games over Havana. A typical game, played on February 11, 1924, matched Santa Clara against Almendares. It was a hotly contested game with the Leopards' Rube Currie edging Jesse Petty by a score of 5–4. Oliver "The Ghost" Marcelle and Estaban Montalvo provided most of the fireworks with home runs. Currie was presented with a 5–2 lead in the sixth inning but Jose Mendez had to be rushed into the game in the eighth inning to preserve the victory.

Jud Wilson posted the highest career batting average in the Cuban League (.372) and was #2 in the Negro Leagues (.354) (courtesy John Holway).

Almendares

Name	Pos	AB	R	H
Herrera	2B	5	0	2
Dreke	LF	4	0	0
Dressen	3B	4	1	1
Torriente	CF	3	1	1
Lundy	SS	4	1	3
E. Brown	CF	4	0	0
Henry	1B	4	0	1
Krueger	C	4	1	3
Petty	P	2	0	0
Boada	P	1	0	0
Winters	PH	1	0	0
Totals		36	4	11

Santa Clara

Name	Pos	AB	R	H
Warfield	2B	5	1	1
Marcelle	3B	5	1	2
Charleston	CF	2	0	0
Oms	LF	1	0	1
Moore	SS	4	1	3
E. Douglas	1B	4	1	0
Montalvo	RF	3	1	1
Rojo	C	4	0	1
Currie	P	4	0	0
Mesa	LF	3	0	0
Mendez	P	0	0	0
Totals		34	5	9

Almendares Blues	2 0 0	0 0 0	1 1 0—4—11—0		
Santa Clara Leopards	1 0 0	0 1 3	0 0 x—5— 9—0		

Two Base Hits: Dressen, Torriente, Lundy, Rojo, Krueger.
Three Base Hits: Moore, Henry
Home Runs: Marcelle, Montalvo

Pitcher	IP	W	L	H	SO	BB
J. Petty	6	0	1		4	2
Boada	2	0	0		1	1
R. Currie	7 2/3	1	0		2	1
J. Mendez	1 1/3	0	0		1	0

The season averages for some of the top players in the 1923-24 Cuban League reflect the skills of the black players when measured against their white major league counterparts.

Name	Pos	AB	R	H	D	T	HR	BA
Oliver Marcelle	3B	178	42	70	5	5	3	.393
Dobie Moore	SS	184	28	71	9	6	1	.386
Alejandro Oms	LF	139	33	53	7	4	2	.381
Oscar Charleston	CF	176	59	66	9	5	3	.375
Pablo Mesa	RF	186	29	61	12	3	1	.328
Charlie Dressen	3B	164	20	59	15	2	0	.360
Eddie Brown	CF	167	27	54	10	3	2	.323

Pitcher	G	CG	W	L	Pct.
Bill Holland	13	8	10	2	.833
Adolfo Luque	11	5	7	2	.778
Jesse Petty	18	7	7	6	.538

"Bullet Joe" Rogan wintered in Cuba during 1924-25 and pitched for the pennant-winning Almendares Blues, compiling a 9–4 record. In one game against Santa Clara, as told to John Holway by Chet Brewer, Rogan demonstrated the confidence he had in his pitching repertoire.

Rogan was winning 2–1 in the ninth, Brewer said, with the bases loaded and a great Cuban hitter named Alejandro Oms up. Everybody in Cuba knew Oms could hit the curve ball. So Biz Mackey, probably the greatest catcher in blackball history, wagged one finger for a fastball. Rogan shook him off. Mackey called time and went out to the mound.

"Bullet," he said. "You know this man can hit a curve ball."

"He can't hit mine," Rogan replied.

"You have to be crazy," Mackey muttered.

"You do the catching," Rogan said, "I'll do the pitching."

Mackey squatted back down behind the plate and flashed the sign for a fastball again. Again Rogan shook him off. This time Mackey trotted over to Luque in the dugout.

"This man out there must be crazy," he said. "He wants to throw a curveball."

"Well," Luque shrugged, "It's his money just like it's ours, and he's doing the pitching. I guess we'll have to go along with it."

Said Brewer: "Rogan threw Oms a drop ball, an overhand breaking ball. Oms left the ground. His cap came off, swinging at it. Rogan threw him two more and walked away. Oh, he could throw that ball."

Jelly Gardner and Turkey Stearnes were also in Cuba in 1924, and with the unbearable heat that often settled over the ballpark, Gardner had a habit of feigning heat exhaustion in the middle of the game so he would be replaced, usually by Stearnes. One day, as Gardner pretended to be overcome by the heat, Stearnes, on the bench, thought to himself, "Oh, no you don't. Not this time," and he collapsed in a faint in the dugout, leaving Gardner to recover and continue playing.

"Cool Papa" Bell made his first trip to Cuba in 1928. By that time, he was already a six-year veteran of the Negro leagues. He was introduced to the Negro leagues by his brother Fred who arranged for him to try out with the St. Louis Stars in 1922. The 19-year-old Bell was a southpaw pitcher at that time, and when he was preparing for his first start, his placid countenance caused one of his teammates to note what a cool character he was. Another player tabbed him with the nickname that would become his trademark, but first added Papa to give it more color. When "Cool Papa" Bell arrived in Cuba, he had his new wife, Clara, with him. It was their honeymoon and they spent a blissful winter absorbing the sights and sounds of the beautiful southern city of Cienfuegos, known as "The Pearl of the South." And "Cool Papa" enjoyed playing baseball in Cuba because, as reported by the McKissacks, "Everybody was the same down there. We could go in any restaurant, stay in hotels, and oh, the fans? They loved us."

According to Bell, there were a lot of white players from the southern states who played winter ball in Cuba. At first, when the whites realized there were black players in the league, they refused to play with or against them. But the Cubans told them that anyone could play in their league. It didn't make any difference what color a player was. The white players eventually gave in, and played in the league, and it was a good learning experience for them. They got to know the black players on a personal level and many of them became close friends.

On January 1, 1929, "Cool Papa" Bell, playing in spacious Aida Park in Cienfuegos, held his own new years celebration by smashing three inside-the-park home runs, the last one in the eighth inning off the legendary Martin Dihigo, as the Elephants outlasted the Havana Lions 15–11.

Havana					Cienfuegos				
Name	Pos	AB	H	E	Name	Pos	AB	H	E
J. Olivares	SS	6	1	2	C.P. Bell	CF	5	3	0
A. Bejerano	LF	6	1	0	B. Russell	RF	4	1	0
A. Oms	CF	5	2	0	W. Wells	SS	4	2	0
J. Wilson	1B	5	4	0	C. White	LF	4	2	0
C. Smith	RF	5	2	0	F. Duncan	C	4	0	0
J. Rojo	C	3	1	0	N. Joseph	3B	4	2	0
M. Dihigo	1B, P	5	4	0	A. Cortez	1B	3	0	0
R. Herrera	2B	5	3	0	Celada	2B	5	2	0
O. Levis	P	1	1	0	L. Tiant	P	1	0	0
C. Bell	P	1	1	0	C. Williams	P	4	3	0
A. Alfonso	3B	2	0	0					
M.A. Gonzalez	C	1	0	0					
Totals		45	20	2	Totals		38	15	0

Havana Reds   3 1 3   0 1 0   0 1 2—11—20—2
Cienfuegos   2 0 0   5 1 4   0 3 x—15—15—0

D—Smith (3), Dihigo (2), Williams, Herrera
T—Wilson (2), Levis, Wells,
HR—C.P. Bell (3)

The following year, according to Bell, he was leading the batting race with two weeks to play, but because his team was out of contention for the pennant, management sent the American players home to save their salaries. And the move cost "Cool Papa" a chance at the batting title and the $500 prize given to the champion, because he didn't have enough at-bats to qualify.

George "Mule" Suttles played in Cuba three years between 1928 and 1939. When he arrived in Cuba to play for Cienfuegos, he was in the prime of his career at age 27, having just hit .372 with 19 home runs in 275 at-bats for the St. Louis Stars in the Negro National League. Buck Leonard, who played against Suttles in the Negro leagues, tried to caution Cuban pitcher Jose Acosta against throwing Suttles a low curveball. Suttles was murder on low curveballs but, like many pitchers, Acosta didn't think Suttles could hit his curveball. As Acosta watched his pitch to Suttles disappear over the left field fence some 500 feet from home plate, he just shook his head and said, "I've never seen a ball hit that far in my life." Suttles went on to punish many Cuban League pitchers during the year, finishing the season with a .314 batting average and a league leading 7 home runs in 175 at-bats, pretty good power in a park with a 500 foot left-field fence and a 400 foot right-field fence.

A new, modern baseball stadium opened its doors on October 10, 1930. La Tropical Stadium was a pitcher's dream, with outfield distances from home plate of 498 feet, 505 feet, and 398 feet, left to right. The huge park, with a seating capacity of more than 20,000, hosted a major league all-star game on the 10th, with Larry French pitching Jewel Ens' All-Stars to a 2–0 victory over Carl Hubbell and the Dave Bancroft All-Stars. The nine game series also matched major league all-star squads against Cuban teams. Hubbell edged Cuban ace, Ramon Bragana 2–1 in game 5, but the Cubans gained a measure of revenge by knocking off Bob Smith of the Boston Braves 5–2.

Unfortunately for the baseball fans of the island nation, the regular season didn't last much longer than the exhibition series. The country had suffered through an economic crisis in the 1920s caused by foreign domination of finance, agriculture, and industry, particularly American companies' control of the sugar industry and, by 1930, the situation had reached epic proportions, with numerous riots and acts of violence. Anti-American feelings that had festered in some areas for years suddenly surfaced. The situation even affected baseball, as noted in the *Chicago Defender*.

> The bottom fell out of the Cuban winter baseball league completely here after 22 playing days. Internal strife among the Cuban people is one of the factors that contributed to the downfall of the league. Because of frequent rioting and ill feeling between rival parties here, the baseball fans were afraid to come out to the games and the gate receipts were seriously lowered on that account. Old time baseball men, with years of playing in the Cuban circuit, are saying that it will be bad business for American players of color here as long as present conditions continue.

The Negro League exodus, led by John Henry Lloyd, included "Cool Papa" Bell, Dink Mothell, Oscar Charleston, Chino Smith, and Dick Lundy.

Manager Wilbert Robinson took his Brooklyn Dodgers to Cuba for spring training in 1931, after the political situation had stabilized, and they entertained the fans by playing five intra-squad games in La Tropical Park before leaving the island. Adolfo Luque, who was winding down a memorable 20-year major league career, won two games for the Robins team over the Dodgers team by scores of 2–1 and 4–3.

The Negro League presence during the 1930s was almost as good as in the '20s. Some of the more talented visitors to the island nation included Willie Wells, Ray Dandridge, Josh Gibson, Buck Leonard, Ray Brown, and Hilton Smith. Wells, in particular, was popular with the Cuban fans, as reported in the *Chicago Defender* on December 28, 1935: "Willie Wells, best of shortstops in colored baseball circles in the States, is playing bang-up ball in the Cuban winter baseball league as a member of the Santa Clara team. The magnificent performances of Wells on the short field, his heavy hitting and his skillful base-running have captured such a throng of fans that they become wild with joy as they see 'Scrappy's' humanity on the field."

Raymond "Jabao" Brown played in the Cuban League for thirteen years, from 1936 to 1948, and his first year was sensational. Pitching for the Santa Clara Leopards, Brown allowed just three walks in tossing a 7–0 no-hitter against the Havana Lions in Santa Clara's Boulanger Park on November 7, 1936. Less than six weeks later, on December 16, 1936, he pitched a doubleheader against Havana at home, dropping a tough 1–0 decision to Louis Tiant Sr. in eleven innings in the opener, and then coming back to capture the nightcap 2–0 with a masterful five-hitter. The Lions scored the only run of the first game when Couto singled, went to second on a sacrifice by Tiant, and came around to score on a two-out base hit by Pedro Arango. In game two, the Leopards' runs were driven in by Carlos Blanco and Brown. Overall, Ray Brown finished the day with a split in the two games, yielding just 12 base hits in 20 innings, with 4 strikeouts and 4 bases on balls. For the season, Brown compiled an outstanding 21–4 won-loss record

Chino Smith hit a fantastic .434 during five years in the Negro Leagues and .335 in Cuba before his death from yellow fever in Cuba in 1931 at the age of 27 (courtesy Jay Sanford).

and led the league in victories, in winning percentage (.840), and in complete games (23). He also managed a .311 batting average with 27 runs batted in, in 132 at-bats.

Buck Leonard was in Cuba that year also, playing first base for the Marianao Tigers. Martin "El Immortal" Dihigo was the manager and, as Leonard noted, the teams top home-run hitter and top pitcher. Dihigo batted .323 for the season with 4 home runs, and finished with a 14–10 record on the mound. Buck Leonard hit .304 with 1 home run. The pennant race that year was sensational with Marianao sweeping the last three games of the season from the Santa Clara Leopards to tie the Leopards for first place. Dihigo won two of the games by scores of 7–2 and 3–0 on consecutive days. A three-game playoff ensued with Ray Brown beating Dihigo 6–1 in the opener, but the Tigers roared back once again and took the crown by winning games two and three by scores of 4–2 and 7–3. Silvio Garcia won game 2 and "El Immortal" took Ray Brown to task in the finale.

Buck Leonard noted in his biography,

> That might have been the year that I got thrown out of a game in Cuba. The umpire called a runner safe at first base on a double play and I thought he was out. And I got to arguing with the Cuban umpire. He couldn't understand what I was saying and I couldn't understand what he was saying. He put me out of the ball game and said that I called him a name and I had to pay ten dollars before I could play the next day. I *did* call him a couple of names. I learned to speak Spanish a little bit, but I was talking in English. That's why I was telling him that. I thought he couldn't understand what I was saying, but maybe he did understand *some* English! At least he made a good guess about what I was saying. He looked at that expression on my face and could tell I wasn't saying nothing good.

Martin Dihigo, arguably the greatest all-around player in the Western Hemisphere during the first half of the twentieth century, presently resides in the baseball halls of fame in four countries.

In 1937, 24-year-old Ray "Hooks" Dandridge made his first visit to the island of Cuba. The flashy fielding third baseman, playing for Almendares, hit a respectable .289 and led the Cuban League with 11 stolen bases in 57 games. Dandridge came to love playing baseball in Cuba. The ballparks were the most modern he had ever played in, the people were friendly and were knowledgeable about the game. The men would congregate in the square in Havana and argue baseball all day long. They knew all the players, and they knew each player's strengths and weaknesses. And the weather was perfect. Dandridge, who was called Talua in Cuba, after a character in a radio program, played winter baseball in Cuba for 12 seasons, compiling a fine .282 career batting average. One of the most historic games that Dandridge participated in was played in La Tropical Stadium on December 7, 1937. It was Cuba's first night baseball game, matching Almendares against Marianao. Actually, lighting problems and other considerations made this game a one-shot experiment. No other night games would be played in the league until the mid-forties. In this game, the Tigers of Marianao edged the Almendares Blues 6–5 with a run in the bottom of the eighth inning. Martin Dihigo, in relief of Hilton Smith, was the winning pitcher and Silvino Ruiz, in relief of Leon Day, was the loser. Tacho Santaella drove in three runs and Azucena Perez drove in two for the winners while Ray Dandridge drove in two for the losers.

Almendares

Name	Pos	A	R	H
A. Bejerano	LF	4	1	1
R. Dandridge	3B	5	1	2
W. Wells	SS	4	0	1
R. Linares	CF	5	0	0
F. Correa	2B	4	0	1
R. Estalella	RF	4	0	0
F. Duncan	C	3	1	1
C. Blanco	1B	4	1	1
L. Day	P	2	0	0
J. Abreu	PH	1	1	1
S. Ruiz	P	1	0	0
Totals		37	5	8

Marianao

Name	Pos	AB	R	H
A. Santaella	2B	4	1	2
S. Garcia	SS	4	0	1
C. Spearman	RF	5	0	0
E. Stone	CF	1	1	0
B. Brown	LF	4	1	1
J. Perez	3B	4	1	2
F. Guerra	C	4	2	2
F. Barradas	1B	3	0	1
H. Smith	P	3	0	0
M. Dihigo	P	1	0	0
		33	6	9

Almendares   0 0 0   0 0 2   3 0 0—5—8—0
Marianao   0 3 0   0 0 2   0 1 x—6—9—0

Two Base Hits: Wells, Brown, Santaella
Three Base Hit: Dandridge
Home Run: J. Perez

Pitcher	IP	W	L	H	SO	BB
L. Day	6	0	0	5	7	4
S. Ruiz	2	0	1	4	0	1
H. Smith	6	0	0	6	3	2
M. Dihigo	3	1	0	2	1	1

After the conclusion of the regular 1938 Negro League season, an all-star team invaded Cuba, with Buck Leonard, Felton Snow, and Sammy T. Hughes. Other players, like Josh Gibson, Willie Wells, and Ray Brown, were in the country to play in the winter league. Brown took his wife with him and Wells arrived with a pretty young lady from Jacksonville, Florida, that he introduced as his hairdresser. Leonard's wife often traveled with him when school was out, or visited him over the Christmas holidays. The Negro Leaguers had a big year in the winter league. The Santa Clara Leopards, who were loaded to the gills with the likes of Josh Gibson, Sam Bankhead, Lazaro Salazar, and "Cocaina" Garcia, swept to the league title by five games. Gibson destroyed Cuban League pitching, batting a torrid .356 and leading the league with 11 home runs in 163 at-bats, and

50 runs scored. Garcia at 11–4, Brown at 11–7, and Salazar at 6–2, anchored a pitching staff that also included Johnny Taylor and Leroy Matlock. Martin Dihigo of Havana was the league's top pitcher with a record of 14–2, but he couldn't carry the Lions to the title by himself. Other Negro League visitors that year included Ray Dandridge (.319), Willie Wells (.278), "Double Duty" Radcliffe (5–8 on the mound), and Theolic Smith (5–9).

Radcliffe reversed his fortunes the next year, pacing the Almendares Blues to the title with a 7–3 record. He was ably supported on the mound by Rodolfo Fernandez at 7–4 and Adrian Zabala at 7–5. Willie Wells played a sensational shortstop for the Blues and stung the ball at a .328 clip. John Washington hit .307 and Henry Kimbro batted .294, but it was the pitching that saved the day. One unfortunate incident marred an otherwise pleasant winter. Early Wynn, a 19-year-old right-handed pitcher with Havana, who had just finished his rookie season with the Washington Senators in the American League, walked into a cabaret in Havana one afternoon, and spied Wells sitting with Bill Dunlap formerly of the Boston Braves. Dunlap invited Wynn to sit with them, but Wynn, from Alabama, just snarled and said, "I don't drink with niggers." One word led to another and pretty soon Dunlap got up, said "I don't have to take that," and laid a hurt on the big pitcher that put him out of action for the rest of the year.

The 1943–44 Cuban League pennant, won by the Havana Reds, was something of a redemption for the team after having lost the last two pennants to the Almendares Blues by a total of six games. This time, they beat the Blues by six games. The season was also a personal triumph for the ace of their pitching staff, "Cocaina" Garcia, who was a one-man wrecking crew, leading the league with 12 wins against just 4 losses, and pacing his team at the plate with a .431 average. And to top it off, he threw the first no-hitter in La Tropical Stadium history, blanking the Marianao Tigers 5–0, on December 11, 1943.

Two Cuban entrepreneurs, Bobby Maduro and Miguel Suarez, built a new baseball stadium in El Cerro, central Havana, in 1946. Gran Stadium, popularly known as El Cerro, with a price tag of $2,000,000, was a beautiful ballpark with a seating capacity of 34,000 people, and more hitter-friendly distances of 324 feet, 410 feet, and 340 feet, left to right. The

"Cocaina" Garcia starred in the Cuban League from 1926 to 1948 (courtesy Yuyo Ruiz).

inaugural game, played before a packed house of wild, screaming fanaticos on October 26, 1946, matched Adolfo Luque's Almendares Blues against Martin Dihigo's Cienfuegos Elephants. The lineups were liberally sprinkled with more than a half-dozen former and future major league players like Alex Carrasquel, Danny Gardella, and George Hausmann, and an equal number of Negro League players, including Lazaro Salazar, Luis Tiant, Sr., and Ducky Davenport. The Blues had all the better of the game, romping to a 9–1 decision behind Jorge Comellas. Every player on the Blues team had at least one hit, with shortstop Avelino Canizares pounding out three singles and Angel Fleitas hitting a single and a double. Roberto Ortiz hit the only home run of the contest.

Almendares

Name	Pos	AB	H
Canizares	SS	5	3
Hausman	2B	5	1
Davenport	CF	4	1
Salazar	1B	4	1
R. Ortiz	RF	4	1
Fleitas	C	5	2
S. Amaro	LF	5	1
Rodriguez	3B	4	1
Comellas	P	4	1
L. Tiant, Sr.	P	0	0
A. Crespo	PH	1	0
Gibson	P	0	0
A. Zabala	P	0	0
Totals		40	12

Cienfuegos

Name	Pos	AB	H
Pages	CF	4	0
C. Perez	3B	2	1
N. Reyes	SS	4	1
R. Gladu	RF	4	0
D. Gardella	1B	4	1
Heredia	2B	4	2
A. Mesa	LF	4	1
R. Noble	C	4	1
A. Carrasquel	P	2	0
		33	7

Almenadres 000 304 2 0 0—9—12—0
Cienfuegos 001 000 0 0 0—1—7—0

WP—Comellas
LP—Carrasquel

Doubles—Fleitas, Hausman, Canizares
Triples—C. Perez
Home Runs—R. Ortiz

Adolfo Luque was not only a great pitcher. He was also an outstanding manager, compiling a record of 705-641 for a .524 winning percentage. He led his team to 11 league championships in 30 years, including 1946-47. The all-star team that year was a mixture of Cuban, Negro League, and major league stars. At a time when segregation still ruled in the United States, blacks, whites, and Latinos, played together, lived together, and socialized together in Havana, Santiago, and other cities around the island nation. Negro League pitcher Max Manning noted that Brooklyn Dodgers farmhand Carl Erskine taught him how to throw a change of pace that couldn't be detected by opposing coaches. And catcher Clint Courtney studied Negro League catcher Bill Cash's foot movements and throwing technique, trying to improve his own defense. Bruce Chadwick noted, "Old photos show groups of five and six players, half white and half black, laughing at a joke in the dugout together, an astoundingly integrated scene just ninety miles from Florida, where blacks were still lynched."

The international flavor of the 1946-47 Cuban League all-star team can be seen in the following lineup.

C Andres Fleitas. He batted .316 en route to a career average of .274 in 13 years. He played 15 games for the Washington Senators in 1948.
P Agapito Mayor. He went 10–4 on the mound. He compiled a 68–64 career record in Cuba between 1938 and 1953. And he was 98–76 over an eight-year career in Mexico.
P "Cocaina" Garcia. He led the league with a .769 winning percentage based on a 10–3 record. His career mark was 91–60, and he also went 96–68 in Mexico.
1B Lennie Pearson. He led league with 45 RBIs in 265 at-bats. The Negro League star batted .263 over five years in Cuba while leading the league in RBIs three times. He averaged .316 with 16 home runs for every 550 at-bats over a 15-year Negro League career.
2B Roberto Avila. The Mexican native batted .323 with 13 doubles and 4 triples. After two years in Cuba, Avila went on to an excellent 11-year major league career, batting .281 with 1296 base hits. He sparked the Cleveland Indians to the 1954 American League pennant with a league leading .341 batting average. He also played six years in Mexico, averaging .329.
SS Hank Thompson. He led league in triples with 6 in 225 at-bats. Thompson was a six-year veteran of the Negro Leagues (.343) who enjoyed a nine-year major league career between 1947 and 1956, batting .267. He batted .263 with 26 home runs with the New York Giants in 1954 and then hit a torrid .364 in the World Series as the Giants captured the world championship.
3B Lou Klein. He led the league in batting at .330, and compiled a career record of .281 over five years. He batted .259 during his five-year major league career.
OF Santos Amaro. He batted .289 en route to a fine .294 average over 13 years. His son Ruben and grandson Ruben Jr. both played major league baseball.
OF Pedro Pages. He batted just .247 but he was an outstanding defensive player. His career average in Cuba was .260 over 15 years, and he was elected to the Cuban Hall of Fame in Miami in 1997. Pages also played in Mexico for eight years, hitting a respectable .313.
OF Roberto Ortiz. He led the league in home runs with 11 in 234 at-bats. Ortiz had a successful 14-year career in Cuba, batting .280. He led the league in batting twice, with a .337 average in 1943-44 and a .311 average in 1947-48. He also batted .304 during 7 years in Mexico, and .255 during a 6-year hiatus in the major leagues.

As integration gained a foothold in organized baseball in the United States, the Negro leagues began their slow decent into oblivion, and former Negro League players were rapidly becoming scarce. The Cuban League was still a popular training ground for aspiring young Americans, and it still drew many black players as well as white players from North America, but now most of them were members of organized baseball. Even the Cuban players approached the game with a new resolve now that the "color problem" had disappeared. The 1947-48 Cuban League season, the first season after Jackie Robinson had invaded the major leagues, was the beginning of a new era in baseball, where all players could be measured by their skills and not by the color of their skin.

Over the winter of 1947-48, a rival winter league was organized by Cuban players.

It was called the Players Federation, and Ray Dandridge was quick to accept the big money offered to him to jump to the new league. The league operated from October 30, 1947, through March 10, 1948, and it employed most of the major league players who were in Cuba, like Sal Maglie, Max Lanier, and Danny Gardella, and many of the Negro League players like Dandridge, Ray Brown, and Bus Clarkson, but it didn't run as smoothly as expected. The owners of the teams in the established Cuban League didn't look with favor on the jumpers and, as Dandridge told Jim Riley,

> During that time I thought everything was going along smooth and things were alright. Then they started taking the ballplayers who jumped from one club to another to the jail. They ganged them all up and took them down to the police headquarters. The entire team was arrested. It happened that I was out that day, and when I come back I asked, "Where are all the guys?" And he said, "Well they done got all of them and took them down to the police headquarters." So then I took a trip to the jail. I got a taxi and went down there, and I went to the police headquarters and said, "You all looking for me?" And they said, "Yeah, Talua, where you been? We been looking all over Havana for you."
>
> After they got out, the new league only lasted about six weeks and when it broke up, the team folded and all the ballplayers who went over to that league were barred from the regular league in Cuba. And then I went from Cuba to Sonora, Mexico, and I played there for a season.

Baseball was a slightly different game in Cuba compared to the game played in the United States. It was more personal and more intense. Adolfo Luque, possessor of a violent temper, kept a loaded pistol in his desk and often carried it with him in the clubhouse to intimidate players. One time, the Negro League players on one of Luque's teams demanded more money before they would take the field for a game. The enraged manager stormed around the clubhouse waving his pistol and threatening any player that refused to play that day. The crisis was finally settled amicably, but not before the players witnessed the scary side of Adolfo Luque. In another incident, recounted by Jim Riley,

> Luque, regarded as a tough hombre, was known to carry a gun to enforce discipline on his team and on more than one occasion he fired it to emphasize a point. Once Luque told Terris McDuffie to go into a game to pitch with only two days rest and McDuffie refused. Luque took him into his office, reached into a drawer and pulled out a pistol and asked McDuffie again if he was ready to pitch. This time McDuffie saw the wisdom of his manager's request and said, "Gimme the ball," and went out and pitched a two-hitter.
>
> All ballplayers, black and white, knew that Luque was not a man to mess with. "Luque was a hot-tempered Cuban," agrees Willie [Wells]. On one occasion, while playing for Luque's team, he saved another player from being shot by the volatile manager."

Apparently Luque had gotten into an argument with "Double Duty" Radcliffe, and was threatening Radcliffe with his gun, but Wells stepped between the two men and convinced Luque to holster his weapon.

The late 1940s and early 1950s brought many more minor league players to Cuba to refine their skills, particularly from the Brooklyn Dodgers. Their contingent included such minor league stars as Johnny and Chris Van Cuyk, Chuck Connors (later a television star as *The Rifleman*), Bill Antonello, and Harry Taylor. The winter league remained strong through the 1950s, until the new Cuban dictator, Fidel Castro, eliminated all professional sports in the country in 1962. During the last two decades of professional baseball in Cuba, the country had made significant progress in promoting the game. In addition to their outstanding winter league, the country joined organized baseball in 1946, and participated in the new Caribbean World Series from 1949 to 1960.

After World War II ended, organized baseball began to return to normal. New leagues were formed and some existing leagues were expanded. It was a boon to Cuba because they were invited to join the Class C Florida International League. On the evening of April 18, 1946, the Havana Cubans defeated Miami Beach before 12,000 excited fans who crowded into La Tropical Stadium to witness Cuba's first game as a member of organized baseball. Eight years later, Cuban pride increased even more when the Sugar Kings were admitted into the AAA International League, competing against such minor league powerhouses as the Montreal Royals and the Syracuse Chiefs. The Sugar Kings roster included such players as Ken Raffensberger, Carlos Pascual, Johnny Lipon, Clint Hartung, Pedro Formental, and Emilio Cueche. The team finished a respectable fourth in the eight-team league, but lost their opportunity to participate in the playoffs when they were beaten in their final game by the Chiefs. Emilio Cueche, the veteran right-hander, was hammered for five runs in the first inning as the Chiefs coasted to a 13–4 victory. Cuba finished third in 1955 and third again in 1959, their best showings in the International League. On July 13, 1960, as international tensions between Fidel Castro's government and the government of the United States increased to the breaking point, the International League revoked Cuba's franchise, and the franchise was awarded to Jersey City. The era of professional baseball in Cuba was over after more than 80 years.

3

25th Infantry Regiment Baseball Team

The famous 25th Infantry Regiment was the all-black company popularly known as the Buffalo Soldiers. The regiment was formed in 1869 and saw service in the United States, Hawaii, the Philippine Islands, and Mexico. Its baseball tradition had its beginnings in Missoula, Montana, where the first team was formed in 1894 by Master Sergeant Dalbert P. Green, who was instructed to form a regimental team after an informal baseball game between an interracial infantry team and an all-black cavalry team created such interest and enthusiasm that Colonel Andrew S. Burt believed that organized teams would be good for morale and would relieve the boredom that existed during periods of peace and quiet on the frontier. Green, who was named team captain, noted that "Players generally furnished their own uniforms and shoes; these consisted of canton flannel drawers (altered by company tailors), a dark blue flannel shirt, and a pair of barrack shoes (heels cut off), stockings, and caps purchased by the players. Practice was held in the evening after retreat, games being played on Sundays and Holidays. The 'Old Timers' didn't take to the game as they do at the present time. An athlete, to be considered, had also to show soldierly qualities of the very highest type." He considered the 25th Infantry Regiment teams that were stationed in Hawaii between 1914 and 1918 to be among the greatest teams he was ever associated with. As he said, "During my connection with the team it has played against players in different parts of the United States and foreign possessions, and who have become famous in both the National and American Leagues, not mentioning the minor leagues at all."

The 25th Infantry Regiment was part of the invasion force that confronted the Spanish army in Cuba during the Spanish-American War. But, as reported by Nankivell, all the enemies weren't wearing Spanish uniforms. "Segregation and inequality marked the eight-day crossing from Tampa to Santiago, Cuba. The Twentieth-Fifth Infantry and other black regiments were assigned to six transport ships with white soldiers. In most instances, the black soldiers lived and slept on the lower decks. On his transport vessel, the *Concho*, according to Twenty-Fifth Infantry Sgt. Maj. Frank W. Pullen, black and white troops were vertically separated, white troops on the port side, black soldiers on the starboard side. The brigade commander ordered that the black and white soldiers on board should not intermingle," and the white troops "should make coffee first, all the time." "God knows," recalled Pullen, "how ... we lived through those ... days on that miserable vessel."

However bad the discrimination was, though, the 25th Infantry distinguished themselves admirably on the battlefield. They, like their white counterparts, were severely hampered by the heat, humidity, and incessant rain in Cuba, especially wearing those

The 25th Infantry Regiment baseball team. Back (left to right): unknown, unknown, unknown, Bob Fagan, Andy Cooper, Hurley McNair, unknown. Front (left to right): Dobie Moore, Joe Rogan, Lem Hawkins, unknown, "Heavy" Johnson (courtesy Jerry Malloy).

heavy blue flannel uniforms. Within one month of landing, more than half of the 25th was stricken with malaria, a common illness under those conditions. On July 1, three weeks after arriving in Cuba, the 25th and other regiments totaling 6,600 men, attacked the Spanish fort at El Caney. Other black regiments participated in the famous charge up San Juan Hill with Teddy Roosevelt, bringing the war to a quick and decisive conclusion. The 25th was back in Long Island by August 22, ready for reassignment.

After short stints in western outposts like Fort Logan, Colorado, Sergeant Green and his 25th Infantry teammates were sent to the Philippines on February 6, 1899, where they fought insurgents, suffering some casualties including 10 men killed. Still, the baseball team continued to practice and play games when they had the opportunity. According to Jerry Malloy, "In 1901, when the 25th was sent to Manila for a month, the team issued a challenge in the *Manila Times* to play anyone—'For money, marbles, or chalk, money being preferred.' This braggadocio nearly came to a ruinous conclusion. The team entered a five-game competition with $500 at stake to win at least three—and lost their first two games. But, as Green informs us, they came back and won the last three."

Between 1901 and 1914, the 25th Infantry served with honor in such places as Kansas, Nebraska, Texas, the Philippines, and Hawaii. According to James A. Riley, Oscar Charleston ran away from home in 1911 when he was fifteen years old and served with the 24th Infantry Regiment in the Philippines. While there Charleston was a member of the regiment's track team, and was recorded as running the 220-yard dash in 23 seconds. He was also the only black player on the baseball team. He apparently left the army by 1915 when he joined the Indianapolis ABCs as a pitcher-outfielder.

The 25th Infantry baseball team rose to prominence after it was stationed at Schofield Barracks in Hawaii. They established themselves as the best team on the island of Oahu, and began to compete against college teams, and teams from the high classification Pacific Coast League. Baseball was serious business to the men of the 25th Infantry, as noted in Nankivell's book.

> The Regiment arrived at Schofield Barracks on January 15, 1913. Lieutenants O.H. Saunders and R. P. Harbold, 25th Infantry, Regimental Baseball and Athletic Officers respectively, quickly assembled the baseball material for the organizing of a Regimental team. Company teams were organized, and Battalion teams were formed; the winner of each Battalion team was pitted against winners of the others, and then Battalions series were played, the best players being picked and a regimental baseball squad formed.
>
> In this squad there was a Plan and Strategy Board and after each game its defense and offense were carefully gone over to the edification of all. The team and the regiment were greatly encouraged by the unstinted aid and encouragement that was extended to them by its devoted and lovable commander Colonel Lyman W.V. Kennon, 25th Infantry (now deceased), who gave all that he had in encouragement and loyalty, and was joined by the entire commissioned and enlisted personnel in rendering their unexcelled support.
>
> An array of young players having joined the regiment at this time a strenuous tryout was given to all that sought positions on the team and such stars as [Lem] Hawkins, Company A; Aulston, Company C; Crafton, [Bob] Fagan, and [Oscar] Johnson, Company K, soon added their names to the regimental book of fame. A Post League was organized consisting of the 1st and 25th Infantries, 4th Cavalry, and the 1st Field Artillery and a regular league schedule was arranged and played, the championship being won by the 25th Infantry. A City League was also formed in the city of Honolulu, consisting of the All-Chinese, Portugese, Asian's, and the Champion 25th Infantry from Schofield Barracks. A regular league schedule was played for the championship of the Island of Oahu and in which the 25th Infantry won the championship. Great credit is due the two great veterans, Sergeant Collins, Company I, and Sergeant Swinton, Company K, and also Sergeant Jasper, Company A. This trio played consistent ball, and kept the youngsters going at top speed. As the champions of the Island of Oahu, the 25th Infantry team had to defend its crown against all foreign invaders; the main offenders were teams picked from the stars of both Major Leagues and also the Pacific Coast League who generally sojourned in Hawaii during their off seasons in California.

The leader of the team was Wilbur Rogan, better known as "Cap," short for Captain, to his fellow soldiers because of his leadership qualities, not only on the baseball field, but also in army matters. William "Big C" Johnson told John Holway, "Charleston was everything—but Rogan was more. Rogan could do everything, everywhere. When I first met him he was a catcher, he and "Heavy" Johnson. Whenever they needed a pitcher, Rogan would go on in there ... Rogan looked like a soldier, his deportment, his carriage. [When he went to Honolulu on leave], he put his Sunday clothes on. He was dressed." Joe Taylor, another member of the 25th, added, "Rogan was very gentlemanfied. [He was] easy going, a jolly good fellow.... His greatest pitch was his fast ball. They called him "Bullet" even then. You were also allowed to throw the spitball in those days. Rogan used to chew slippery elm, and that made the saliva slippery."

Rogan, who was born on July 28, 1893, in Oklahoma City, Oklahoma, enlisted in the army on October 19, 1911, and served three years with the 24th Infantry in the Philippine Islands where he established himself as both a leader and an outstanding catcher on the baseball team. Oscar Charleston, arguably the greatest player in Negro League history, was his teammate for two years in the Philippines and, like Rogan and Dobie Moore after him, was also a member of the army track team. Cap Rogan was discharged in 1914, but after a very brief stint as a civilian, he re-enlisted and found himself in Hawaii as a member of the 25th Infantry. The period from 1914 to 1920 is generally recognized as the most glorious period in the history of the 25th Infantry Regiment baseball team, and it coincided, not coincidentally, with the tenure of Cap Rogan. The man who would become famous in the Negro leagues as "Bullet Joe," was a one man team. He was a catcher and second baseman, and one of the best, if not *the* best, pitcher, black or white in the game. He had a no-nonsense, no-windup delivery, and he possessed a blinding fastball, an equally fast curveball, and a devastating change-up palm ball. He took the mound for the most important games, but also caught, played second base, and cavorted in the outfield when he wasn't pitching. He was also the team's best hitter, and the fans in the grandstand would often shout, "Touch 'em all, Cap, touch 'em all," when he stepped to the plate.

Rogan seemed to carry the 25th on his back for much of the decade, but he did have help. His teammates from 1916 to 1920 included four players who would later follow him to the Kansas City Monarchs of the Negro National League—Dobie Moore, Lem Hawkins, Bob Fagan, and Oscar "Heavy" Johnson—plus Fred Goliath, who would play with the Chicago Giants in 1920, and William "Big C" Johnson, who would join the Dayton Marcos in 1920. Andy Cooper and Hurley McNair

Wilber "Bullet Joe" Rogan, known as "Cap" in the army, was the spearhead of the 25th Wreckers attack (courtesy R.W. Peterson Collection National Baseball Hall of Fame).

Dobie Moore entered the army in 1916 at the age of 21, serving four years before leaving to play baseball for the Kansas City Monarchs (courtesy R.W. Peterson Collection National Baseball Hall of Fame).

who played for the 25th around 1919 and 1920 joined the Detroit Stars and the Kansas City Monarchs respectively in 1920. Moore, from Atlanta, Georgia, joined the 25th Infantry in 1916 at the age of 21, and matured as both a soldier and a baseball player over the next four years, when he and several other teammates bought their way out of the army for $150. After he joined the Kansas City Monarchs in 1920, Dobie Moore developed into one of the greatest Negro League shortstops ever, a superior defensive player with wide range and a powerful throwing arm, and a dangerous long ball threat who averaged 35 doubles, 15 triples, and 16 home runs for every 550 at-bats, to go along with a .355 batting average, the highest batting average for any hitter with more than 1750 career at-bats. Lem Hawkins played in the California Winter League before joining the army in 1918 and then enjoyed an eight-year career in the Negro leagues between 1921 and 1928. Bob Fagan played second base for the Kansas City Monarchs from 1920 to 1923. Oscar "Heavy" Johnson, a bulky 6', 250-pound outfielder, had a 12-year career in the Negro Leagues, where he earned a reputation as a powerful hitter who averaged .350 during his career with 15 home runs for every 550 at-bats. Hurley McNair compiled a .322 career average in the Negro leagues between 1911 and 1937, with a short interruption for military service.

During the early Rogan years, before Moore and several others joined the team, the 25th had already established a reputation for itself on the island. In 1912 they went 33–1, capturing the Hawaiian Island Championship. The next year, with Oscar Johnson, Hawkins, and Fagan in tow, they compiled a record of 20–1, losing only to a major league–PCL all-star team managed by Willie "Happy" Hogan, formerly of the St. Louis Browns, and led by "Death Valley" Jim Scott, who was on his way to a 20–21 season with the Chicago White Sox. Nankivell reported on the game. "A holiday was declared for this great event, and a parade with both of the teams in line led by the 25th Infantry Band, preceded the game; the whole garrison turned out to do honors to both teams. Corporal Willis, Company L, was pitted against ... Scott ...

and although we lost, we had the satisfaction of seeing Willis pitch one of his best games." John McGraw, who saw the 25th in action during his visit to the islands on a world tour by a major league all-star team, said that Rogan would be a great major league pitcher if he was white.

In 1914 the 25th won 11 and lost only 1. By this time, the team known as the "Wreckers" was the dominant team outside the United States. The Spalding Company, noting the reputation of the regiment, offered to sponsor the club on a tour of the west coast, but the request was denied because it served no military purpose. In February of that year, as reported by Phil Dixon, "Each February, from 1914 to 1918, the United States Army participated in general track and field meets during week long celebrations of George Washington's birthday. The Washington birthday celebrations, which were also called the Mid-Pacific Carnival, were held in Honolulu, Hawaii. At the Mid-Pacific Carnival of 1914, the entire regiment of over 1,100 enlisted men proceeded to the city by rail, marching through Honolulu's most populated business districts. Curious onlookers lined the streets in record numbers to cast an eye at the great Negro soldiers. It was during one of these Mid-Pacific Carnivals that Rogan was timed running the 100-yard dash in less than eleven seconds."

By 1915, the baseball exploits of the 25th Infantry Wreckers were being carried by the most popular black newspapers in the United States. One early article reported on a game between the 25th and the 1st U.S. Infantry, won by the Wreckers on a home run by Oscar "Heavy" Johnson. Another newspaper report from the *Indianapolis Freeman*, discovered by Phil Dixon, told of a Johnson home run that traveled so far that "he hurtled around the diamond, sat down, fanned himself, and had drunk a bottle of soda water before the ball had been found and thrown to the home plate." The *Chicago Defender*, in an article dated March 18, 1916, reported that the 25th defeated a team called the Travelers by a 7–2 count in Honolulu. Rogan was the catcher that day, and batted second in the lineup, behind second baseman Bob Fagan. First baseman Hawkins batted seventh and third baseman Dobie Moore, in his first season on the team, batted eighth. Fagan led the Wreckers' attack with four hits including a double. Rogan chipped in with two hits and Moore garnered one.

Cap Rogan stole the headlines on November 24 when he pitched the Wreckers to a 7–3 victory over the All-Stars at Athletic Park in Honolulu. The stocky right-hander fanned the first nine men he faced, but he weakened in the fourth and the All-Stars crossed the plate three times, breaking his string of 52 consecutive scoreless innings. That was all the offense the All-Stars could muster however, as Rogan kept them under control over the final five innings, while compiling 18 strikeouts in a route-going effort. Fred Goliath was the hitting star for the Wreckers, slamming a double and a home run in four at-bats. Moore and Rogan each had one of the 25th's six hits. The Wreckers dominated the Post League that consisted of four white teams and the 25th. They blanked the Artillery Brigade 6–0 on January 27, 1917, sparked by the brilliant defensive play of third baseman Dobie Moore, who saved his pitcher, Jasper, on several occasions. On one play, with a runner on third base, Moore raced back into left field to make a spectacular over-the-shoulder catch and then wheeled and threw the runner out attempting to score from third base. The crowd cheered his play wildly according to the newspaper. Rogan's triple and Fagan's double led the 25th's attack. The Wreckers went on to take three straight from the white 32nd Regiment in the championship series, winning the finale 3–2 with a two-run rally in the bottom of the ninth.

With the conclusion of the Post League, the Wreckers set their sights on bigger game. They hosted the Portland Beavers of the Pacific Coast League twice, once in February according to John Holway, and again in March. Portland had a strong team at that time, including seven past and future major leaguers. Bill Rodgers had played for the Cincinnati Reds in 1915 and 1916, Bill Stumph toiled for the New York Highlanders in 1912 and 1913, Gus Fisher batted .261 for the Cleveland Indians in 1911, and "Gloomy Gus" Williams played for the St. Louis Browns from 1911 to 1915. Babe Pinelli and Charlie Hollocher would both begin major league careers in 1918, and Dink O'Brien would see limited service with the Philadelphia Phillies in 1923. The Wreckers were not impressed by all the talent on the Beavers and showed the pros how the game should be played. In the February game, Cap Rogan blanked the Beavers 3–0 on a two-hitter and fanned 13 men. He also cracked a double in three at-bats. On March 2, Rogan and Dobie Moore shared game honors, with Rogan keeping the Beavers under control for eight innings and Moore saving the game in the ninth. In the fateful 9th, with the 25th protecting a 4-1 lead, Portland loaded the bases against Rogan, bringing pinch hitter Gus Fisher to the plate. As the *Chicago Defender* reported,

> Moore, the big third sacker of the Wrecking Crew, placed one of his lunch hooks on the spheroid at Schofield after Gus Fisher had hit one on the nose which looked like a three-ply swat, and the eminent catcher walked back to the bench, and Portland was downed by a score of 4–1. The Wreckers had a safe lead up to the ninth canto, when Rogan began to shake, and three Beavers were quietly waiting on the hassocks when Mr. Fisher perambulated up to the rubber and thereupon hit one of Rogan's shoots a mile a minute down the third base line. Moore, the guardian of the difficult corner, who boasts a pair of hands which are somewhat smaller than an elephant's ear, reached for the ball as it shot out toward the left field. He gathered it in to his asbestos glove, and the crowd journeyed home.

Portland Beavers

Name	Pos	AB	R	H
Willie	RF	4	0	0
Hollocher	SS	4	0	0
Rodgers	2B	4	0	1
Williams	CF	3	1	1
Stumpf	1B	3	0	1
Wolfer	LF	3	0	1
Pinelli	3B	3	0	0
O'Brien	C	3	0	0
Higbee	P	1	0	0
Schatzlein	P	1	0	0
Penner	P	1	0	0
Starbria	PH	1	0	0
Plaker	PH	1	0	0
Totals		32	1	4

25th Infantry Regiment

Name	Pos	AB	R	H
Smith	SS	4	0	0
Swinton	CF	2	1	0
Rogan	P	3	1	1
Johnson	C	2	1	1
Goliath	RF	2	1	1
Crafton	LF	4	0	1
Hawkins	1B	2	0	0
Moore	3B	2	0	1
Fagan	2B	2	0	0
		23	4	5

```
Portland Beavers         0 1 0   0 0 0   0 0 0—1—4—3
25th Infantry Regiment   0 2 0   0 2 0   0 0 x—4—5—2
```

Strikeouts: Higbee 2, Rogan 7.
Bases on balls: Higbee 3, Schatzlein 2, Rogan 3.

In another game, Oscar "Heavy" Johnson crushed a tremendous home run in the bottom of the 9th inning to defeat the Olympic club of California.

Cap Rogan took a furlough from the army for about three months in 1917, between April and June, to play for J.L Wilkinson's All-Nation team, touring the Midwest and playing the top semi-pro teams and black teams. He apparently played more than a dozen games for the All-Nations, in Kansas, Missouri, and Iowa. He played left field in a game against the Nebraska Indians, recording a triple and a steal of home in his team's victory. In another game, in Topeka, Kansas, Rogan smashed a long two-run homer over the left field fence. And in Pleasanton, Kansas, he added three base hits, including a double, to his resume. Back in Hawaii during his absence, the 25th continued winning, beating the All-Stars 8–1 in the opening game of the Oahu-Service League on May 6, as the *Defender's* headlines noted, "They Don't Miss Rogan At All; 25th Infantry Beats All-Stars." A crowd of 1,500 fans jammed onto the field at Fort Armstrong, Honolulu, to see the two teams in action. The *Chicago Defender* reported,

> The formal opening of the league was one of the best seen in Honolulu. It was on par with the opening of the Pacific [Coast] League on Saturday. Following out the military spirit of the occasion, the All-Stars and Twenty-fifth Infantry teams marched around the diamond while the band played. It was a big feature that was heartily applauded by the large number of fans who gathered to watch the team in action. If there is any baseball fan around Honolulu who believes that the Twenty-fifth Infantry cannot play ball without one Wilbur Rogan, then they were not among the many who saw the Wreckers in action yesterday afternoon at Moihili. The Wreckers didn't miss Wilbur one particle and defeated the All-Stars to the tune of 8 to 1. "Honolulu" Johnnie Williams, who had pitched for the Detroit Tigers in 1914, was scorched for all eight runs during his five-inning tenure on the mound for the All-Stars. Lem Hawkins led the Wreckers' attack with three base hits.

Cap Rogan was back in harness on July 1, as reported by the *Defender*.

> The post baseball park was the mecca for the fans this afternoon, the Twenty-fifth and Thirty-second Infantry nines being billed to battle and 3,000 of the faithful turned out and witnessed the Wreckers down the Infants by the one-sided score of 9–3. It was a wild and woolly exhibition of the national pastime, abounding in several instances with strenuous kicking of the umpiring by the athletes representing the baby regiment and at one time it appeared the chief umpire, Thompson, would forfeit the game to the Wreckers. Mr. Thompson appeared very much off today in his decisions on balls and strikes. Rogan again appeared in the lineup of the Twenty-fifth Infantry and celebrated his return by cracking out two hits, one of which was a long home run drive out of the lot via center field.

Chief Waterhouse started the game for the 25th, pitching $4\frac{2}{3}$ innings before running into trouble in the top of the fifth. He was relieved by Jasper with the score tied at 2–2 and the bases loaded, and Jasper nailed down the final out and shut the 32nd out the rest of the way. Swinton and Fagan had two hits apiece for the Wreckers and Dobie Moore and Fred Goliath chipped in with home runs. Lem Hawkins and "Heavy" Johnson were the defensive standouts for the Wreckers.

The following month, the Wreckers defeated a picked team from the 32nd and 1st Infantry Regiments 11–2. Goliath punched out three base hits for the 25th, Rogan and Smith had two each, and Johnson contributed a triple. Jacques Jasper tossed a four-hitter for the win, with six strikeouts and two bases on balls. The Wreckers continued to wreak havoc on their Hawaiian Island opponents as noted by the *Chicago Defender* regarding the game of November 22, 1917: "Whoever gave the Ninth Field Artillery [white] license to play 25th Infantry Wreckers is something that 1,511 fans want to know. A big reputation that came down from Schofield Barracks was shattered, and badly at that. At Moihili Field in the drop-curtain game of this day, 'Lefty' Moore was sadly bumped by the sluggers known as Wreckers and was retired from the mound at the close of the fourth terrible spasm. During his unfortunate reign, the 25th walloped him for seven hits and scored six runs. Likins, who also came into town with some rep, returned to Leilehua a sadder but wiser man. During his five cantos on the hill, the Wreckers pasted him for ten hits, scoring the second batch of half a dozen runs." The final score was 12–1 with Chief Waterhouse tossing a masterful game, limiting the 9th Field Artillery to three hits. Cap Rogan led the Wreckers' attack with four hits including a homer and two triples. "Heavy" Johnson had a single and a homer, Dobie Moore chipped in with a triple, Bob Fagan had three singles, and Lem Hawkins contributed two singles to the barrage.

Ninth Field Artillery					25th Infantry Regiment				
Name	*Pos*	*AB*	*R*	*H*	*Name*	*Pos*	*AB*	*R*	*H*
Miller	RF	4	0	0	Hawkins	1B	5	2	2
Donaldson	2B	3	0	0	Smith	SS	6	2	2
Moore	P-CF	1	0	0	Rogan	CF	5	5	4
Venema	CF	2	0	0	Johnson	C	4	1	2
Likins	CF-P	4	0	0	Swinton	C	1	0	0
Mulkern	1B	3	0	0	Goliath	RF	4	0	1
Schulde	SS	2	0	1	Moore	3B	4	1	1
Zitland	LF	3	0	1	Crafton	LF	4	0	1
Johns	2B	2	0	0	Fagan	2B	4	1	3
Schulze	C	2	0	0	Waterhouse	P	5	1	2
Fleetwood	PH	1	1	1					
Totals		27	1	3			42	12	18

9th Field Artillery   0 0 0   0 0 0   0 0 1— 1— 3—3
25th Infantry Regiment   1 0 2   2 4 0   3 0 x—12—18—2

Three Base Hits—Rogan 2, Moore (25th)
Home Runs—Johnson, Rogan.

That was the last recorded baseball game played by the 25th Infantry Regiment baseball team in Hawaii. They were transferred to Camp Stephen D. Little on the Arizona-Mexico border in 1918, and settled down to life in the southwest. But their baseball exploits in Hawaii would be discussed for years to come, not only by the natives of the island, where they captured the Hawaiian Islands Championship every year between 1914 and 1918, but also by members of the United States Army and by the black community in the States. In Arizona, the men of the 25th continued to play baseball, when the opportunity arose, but their primary job was patrolling the border and protecting settlers from Mexican bandits. The nearby town of Nogales was an international town, one-half being on the Mexican side of the border and the other half on the American side, with a wire fence, running east and west separating the two countries. A few days before the arrival of the 25th Infantry in Nogales, a bloody battle ensued between American troops and Mexican troops and civilians spurred on by German agents. The fight was a serious one, resulting in the deaths of 7 Americans and 129 Mexicans. Peace was restored in short order, and the 25th was assigned the job of making sure it remained quiet. Within months of their arrival in Nogales, the World War ended, and life became more peaceful along the border, giving men the time to participate in baseball and in track and field competitions. In one such track meet in July 1919, Dobie Moore competed in both the running broad jump and the 440-yard relay. As for their soldiering, Cap Rogan, a member of the machine gun squad, was army all the way. He looked like a solder and acted like a soldier and when he left the base for town, he was all spit and polish. Dobie Moore was regarded as a good, but not outstanding, soldier who was often assigned to duty as an orderly. Oscar "Heavy" Johnson, on the other hand, was the regiment misfit, who was in the guardhouse as often as he was out of it. If an important baseball game happened to coincide with his sentence, however, the colonel would order Johnson's release and, if Johnson played well in the game, the colonel would let him stay out of the guardhouse—until his next offense.

The regiment's baseball activity in Arizona was beginning to wind down in 1918 due to travel restrictions during World War I. There were almost no games reported in 1918, and just a few the following year. There was one game of note in 1919 however. Casey Stengel, on a barnstorming tour through the southwest with an all-star team, was greatly impressed with Cap Rogan and Dobie Moore, whom he described as "as good as any major leaguers." Stengel told John Holway, "I first saw Rogan down below Albuquerque. We were down near the Mexican border, and the army brought these buglers and made all the soldiers line up and march across the field like this and pick up pebbles and rocks so we could play." He also said that Rogan was one of the best, if not the best, pitcher that ever pitched. When Casey returned to Kansas City after the tour, he alerted J.L. Wilkinson to the bevy of talent wasting away under the hot Arizona sun. And Wilkinson, having already seen what Rogan could do when he was with the All-Nation team, recruited Cap and four of his teammates to play for the Monarchs in 1920. Rogan was transferred to Jefferson Barracks in St. Louis, Missouri, sometime prior to January 1920, and, according to Jerry Malloy, "On June 29, 1920, Sergeant Rogan, service number AT3 349 211, was honorably discharged from the 25th Infantry Regiment's machine-gun company. Just three days later he shut out Rube Foster's Chicago American Giants on one hit in Kansas City in his Negro League debut. "Bullet" Rogan was on his way to glory. By midseason, Moore, McNair, Johnson, Hawkins, and Fagan, Rogan's teammates with the Wreckers, had joined the Monarchs." Moore probably joined Rogan in St. Louis between February and June, was discharged about the same time, and also became a member of the Monarchs around July 1.

The 25th Infantry Regiment baseball team that represented Fort Huachuca in 1918 and 1919 was one of the strongest professional baseball teams in the country at that time, including the major league teams. A lineup that included "Big C" Johnson behind the plate, "Chief" Waterhouse, Jacques Jasper, and Cap Rogan on the mound, an infield of Hawkins, Fagan, Smith, and Moore, and an outfield of "Heavy" Johnson, Goliath, and either Crafton or Swinton, could hold its own with anyone. Smith, the shortstop, may have been Cleo Smith who played in the Negro leagues for ten years, from 1922 to 1931, with the Baltimore Black Sox, New York Lincoln Giants, and others. The statistics for the ten games uncovered for the future Negro League players, during their time with the 25th Regiment, can be found in the appendix. No statistics were located for either Andy Cooper or Hurley McNair who joined the regiment in Arizona.

Jasper and Waterhouse were two of the best pitchers on the 25th Infantry staff, going back to at least 1912. One newspaper reported that Cap Rogan's complete pitching record for the 25th Infantry Regiment between 1914 and 1920 was 58-2.

4

California, Here I Come

The history of the state of California is fascinating, and is recommended reading to anyone interested in the development and growth of the United States. A brief summary of that history is recounted here to provide a background for understanding the treatment of blacks in Southern California during the late 19th and early 20th centuries. Baja California was discovered by Hernando Cortez in 1530, and the northern area around San Francisco was discovered by Sebastian Vizcaino in 1602. The name California was given to the area by explorer Francisco de Ulloa, after a mythical country described in a romantic Spanish novel written about 1510. From its discovery until the mid-18th century, there was little activity in the region, but beginning with the founding of the Mission San Diego in 1769, the exploration of the San Francisco Bay area in 1772, and the founding of the Mission of San Francisco de Asis in 1776, the wheels of progress began to turn, slowly at first, and then at an ever increasing rate.

Los Angeles was first viewed by an expeditionary party that was developing a trail from San Diego to San Francisco in 1769, as recorded by Father Juan Crespi, a member of the party: "After traveling about a league and a half through a pass between low hills we entered a very spacious valley, well grown with cottonwoods and alders, among which ran a beautiful river from north-northwest, and then, doubling the point of a steep hill, it went afterward to the south." Several years later, the governor of California, Felip de Neve, was instructed to establish a pueblo, or town, in that location. The pueblo, containing a plaza, fields, pastures, and royal lands, welcomed the first settlers from Mexico, 11 men, 11 women, and 22 children, on September 4, 1781. More than half, twenty-six of the 44 original settlers, identified themselves as mulatto or black. Of the 11 men, two were Spaniards, four were Indians, one was a mestizo, two were black, and two were mulatto. By 1800, the town had grown to 70 households and 315 people. San Francisco had a population of 867 people at that time.

The development of the state moved more rapidly in the 19th century. Mexico declared its independence from Spain in 1821, and extended its authority into the territory of California. Other important dates:

Mexico abolished slavery in 1829.
Los Angeles became a city in 1835 with a population of 1250.
The United States declared war on Mexico in 1846.

The Treaty of Guadalupe Hidalgo in 1848 ended the Mexican-American War. California became a territory of the United States as a term of the treaty, and entered the Union as a free (non-slave) state, by the compromise of 1850. Although California had four black governors before 1850, the decision to enter the Union as a free state was not universally popular. Many of the early settlers of Los Angeles were Spanish landowners from Mexico who had been slaveholders before the practice was abolished there, and who were hoping to resurrect it in Southern California. They supported the Confederacy and, at one time, wanted Southern California to become an independent state, and enter the Union as a slave state.

California's population began to explode when gold was discovered at Sutter's Mill, on the south fork of the American River, near San Francisco, on January 24, 1848. Word of the discovery spread like wildfire and soon adventurers, fortune hunters, businessmen, bankers, shopkeepers, con men, prostitutes, gamblers, and other shady types that typically follow boomtowns, began to descend on Northern California by ship, horse, and wagon train. Ships carrying the adventuresome reached the west coast by sailing around Cape Horn, while wagon trains carried other immigrants through Indian territory to reach the "promised land," or challenged the dangerous Oregon Trail in the north. The steamer *California* was the first ship to arrive in San Francisco, carrying 365 passengers. The population of the state, which had been 15,000 (not counting Indians) in 1848, skyrocketed to 115,000 by 1850, with most of the increase occurring in the north. San Francisco, home to just 500 people in 1848, exploded to a raucous city of 25,000 in just one year. Los Angeles, which had a population of just 2,228 people in the 1836 census, including 603 men, 421 women, 651 children, and 553 "domesticated Indians," remained stable into the 1850s.

California became the nation's 31st state in 1850, and Los Angeles was incorporated as an American city. The population of 1,610 included 15 blacks and 8 Jews. Peter Biggs, a barber and escaped slave, was the first African American to settle in Los Angeles. As I had reported in another book, "By 1860, the population of San Francisco had grown to an unwieldy 149,000. The heavy influx of people even affected the Los Angeles area 400 miles away as the inhabitants of the north quickly exhausted their supply of foodstuffs. Beef, particularly, was in great demand, so Southern California responded to the crisis, and soon became a major supplier of meat, vegetables, and other provisions, to the populous north. Cattle ranches sprang up all over the valley around the Los Angeles River, and cattle drives soon became a common sight, as they wound their way north to the gold fields."

The 2,228 people in Los Angeles in 1836 became 4,385 people in 1860 and 11,183 people by 1880. Then, five years later, the Santa Fe Railroad began service between Chicago and Los Angeles, opening up the west coast to settlers from the east, eager to enjoy the balmy year-round climate of the west coast, and the population of the City of Angels went crazy. It more than quadrupled to 50,395 people in 1890, and rose to 102,479 people in 1900. In 1880, San Francisco had 233,959 residents compared to L.A.'s 11,183, but over the years, Los Angeles would gain the upper hand over its northern neighbor, finally realizing a population advantage in 1920 with 576,673 citizens compared to 506,676 citizens in San Francisco. The 1990 census had Los Angeles at 3,485,398 people, while San Francisco trailed far behind at 723,959.

Baseball was a late arrival on the west coast, making its first appearance in the San Francisco area, when well to do bankers and other businessmen familiar with the game from their days in the northeast formed teams all over the Bay area. The first baseball team was organized in 1859, and the first game in California was played in San Francisco the following January, with the San Franciscos and the Red Rovers playing to a 33–33 tie in nine innings. The game continued to grow from that point until, in 1886, the first organized league made its appearance as the California League. The league operated, off and on, until 1915 when it was sent into oblivion by the Pacific Coast League.

Los Angeles made its first appearance in a professional baseball league in 1892 when it joined the California League, and it surprised its opponents by walking off with the pennant. After finishing second to San Jose in the first half of the season, the Angels, as they were called, finished three games ahead of Oakland in the second half and then took the measure of San Jose in the championship series, winning five games and losing one. The following year, the Angels won the first half of the schedule, but then disbanded before the season ended. They would resurface ten years later as members of the Pacific Coast League.

The first winter league operated in 1897 with four teams, Los Angeles, San Jose, Oakland, and San Francisco. It disbanded after just one month, but another winter league surfaced in Northern California the following year, while the denizens of the south contented themselves with non-league competition. Amateur baseball thrived around the Los Angeles area during the late 1880s and early '90s. According to Larry Zuckerman, as noted by me previously, "Athletic Park (1891–96) was the first L.A. park to be used in organized baseball." It also hosted numerous town ball games involving not only two white teams, but white teams vs. black teams, as well. Zuckerman noted, "Local black clubs and winter black all-star teams regularly played at Fiesta Park (1897–1900), and the three Pacific Coast League parks in Southern California: Chutes Park/Washington Gardens (1901–1910), and its successor, Washington Park (1911–1925), and Vernon Park/Southside Park (1909–1915)."

California was home to racists just like the east coast, but they weren't as obvious, probably because there weren't as many minorities in California. As Beck and Williams reported, "Historically, blacks have suffered least from racial discrimination in California because of their small numbers." That may have been true, but the stench of bigotry permeated the landscape nevertheless, even to the highest levels of government. Peter H. Burnett was elected governor of the state in 1849 but, less than one year later, after proposing in his annual message that blacks be barred from California, he resigned his position. But the prejudice continued. In 1851 Indians and Negroes were prohibited from being witnesses in cases involving white men. And, according to the LAC *African American*, "After statehood, no blacks were elected to the state legislature until 1918 when the white candidate, whose campaign slogan was 'My opponent is a Nigger,' was narrowly defeated."

And the bigotry did not exclude the National Pastime. John E. Spalding noted several examples of racial intolerance in the northern part of the state with regard to the game of baseball.

> Robinson surprised the crowd at Haight Street Grounds when he sent a black man on the field as the team's mascot. "It was undignified and tended to make a burlesque of the game," the *Tribune* said.
>
> Members of racial minorities were not seen in great numbers in San Francisco in the 19th and early 20th Century and the few who lived in the region were often victims of racial discrimination. As late as 1910, less then 4 percent of San Francisco's population was Oriental and only a small fraction of 1 percent was black. Baseball crowds were so white, in fact, that

one newspaper felt it necessary to report that three "Chinamen" bought tickets to the Haight Street Grounds bleachers one Sunday in 1889.

Superstitious ball players thought the presence of a black brought them good luck. Albert G. Spalding's traveling Chicago team had brought black mascot Clarence Duval along when it appeared in San Francisco on the round-the-world tour the previous winter. At the dinner celebrating the teams' pending departure for Hawaii, the players persuaded Duval to dance for the crowd. Everyone enjoyed the performance. It was not reported whether the young man was allowed to eat dinner with the rest of the Spalding entourage.

Ten years later, the California League's Santa Cruz team had a young black mascot, Edward Purse. As he grew older, Purse became a good baseball player, and one observer recalled years later that "it broke his heart that he couldn't play for the team."

As the 20th century began, winter baseball was flourishing up and down the west coast, with the Southern California Winter League, later called just the California Winter League, entertaining the residents of Los Angeles County. Segregation was still the name of the game in the south, as far as team rosters were concerned, but white teams played black teams in independent games, although the organized winter league was still an all-white league. The independent games, matching a white team against a black team, were more than just baseball games. They were all-out wars to prove who were the best ballplayers, the whites or the blacks. Emotions ran high when the two races met on the field of battle. In 1902, for instance, the Trilbys were one of Los Angeles' best black teams, and they often matched bats with the best local white teams along the coast, including Long Beach, Santa Ana, and San Pedro. On March 16, 1902, the Trilbys walloped the San Pedro team by the score of 15–3. The following week, they were beaten by the Santa Ana team, 12–4. A rematch with Santa Ana ended in a dispute, as reported by a Santa Ana correspondent for the *Los Angeles Times*: "The ballgame Sunday afternoon on the local diamond between the Trilbys of Los Angeles and the local club, was witnessed by a large and enthusiastic crowd of spectators. Both clubs put up a good game from the start, and the spectators consequently got their moneys worth. In the first half of the ninth inning, with the local club at the bat, and the score standing 5 to 4 in their favor, a splendid fly let in two more runners. The umpire declared the ball 'fair,' but the visitors insisted it was 'foul.' The umpire was firm and the Trilbys quit, gathering up their paraphernalia, and hiking across lots to the Santa Fe depot." The next day, after some of the Santa Ana players had made disparaging remarks about the lack of sportsmanship of the black players, the *Times* reported that "The Trilby team is worked up to a white heat over some statements made about it by the Santa Ana club, and offers to play that club a match for any sum up to $100, either in Santa Ana or Los Angeles." There were no further articles in the newspapers regarding a possible rematch between the two clubs, but it is known that they remained popular opponents over the years.

The impression left with the residents of Southern California that black teams were unruly and not very talented changed dramatically on October 18, 1908, when Walter Johnson, the 20-year-old pitching sensation for the Washington Senators, fresh off a 14–14 season with the seventh place American League team, took the mound for the Olives of Los Angeles against the black L.A. Giants. Johnson pitched his usual strong game, fanning 20 Giants in 11 innings, but was beaten 6–5. The victory gave the black team instant respect and visibility around the L.A. area, and their drawing power in subsequent games against white teams didn't go unnoticed either. But as their popularity increased, biased media coverage surfaced. Local newspaper reports of games between black teams and white teams often presented a sarcastic caricature of the black players and their fans, such as the one that appeared in the *Los Angeles Times* on November 11, 1908, describing a game between the L.A. Giants and the Los Angeles Angels of the Pacific Coast League. It read in part, "There was a large, fat, dark cloud hanging over the southeastern part of the city yesterday afternoon, but shortly after 3 o'clock, the sky brightened a little and at 4 o'clock it looked like the coffee you got in restaurants. Hundreds of people did not know before that there was so much darkness in Los Angeles, but it was out in Joy Park yesterday all right and represented the flowers and the weeds of the colored population that rushed out to the dinky little ball yard to see the 'champion' colored Giants baseball team trim the Los Angeles champions of the Pacific Coast League." The article continued in the same vein for two long paragraphs as the writer gleefully recounted the Angels' 14–2 victory over the Giants. The win by the Angels was a foregone conclusion, as their team included a host of players with major league experience, such as pitcher Dolly Gray, as well as George Stovall at second, Rube Ellis in left, Pop Dillon at first, Roy Brashear in right, Curt Bernard in center, Jud Smith at third, and Jess Orndorff behind the plate.

The Giants persisted, however, defeating most of the amateur teams around the Los Angeles area and, as a result of the demonstrated skills of many of the black players coupled with their attractive drawing power, the league admitted a black team to the 1909-10 winter league season. The integration of the California Winter League coincided with the emergence of one of the most colorful and influential characters in the history of black baseball. His name was Andrew "Rube" Foster, and he was the most outstanding pitcher of his day, a superb manager and baseball owner, the founding father of the Negro National League, and a contributing factor to the eventual integration of organized baseball. Foster had a vision of making Negro League baseball a viable and self-sufficient operation, and he explored all avenues to exploit the skills of the black players and to maximize their visibility. The period from 1909 to about 1918 was probably the most important period in the history of the California Winter League, and Foster played a major role in the drama.

Rube Foster traveled the length and breadth of the land from the early 1900s to the late teens, constantly working to increase the visibility of the black players. In 1904, the great right-handed pitcher was a member of the Royal Poinciana team in the so-called Coconut League in Palm Beach, Florida, a two-team league that also included the Breakers Hotel. Three years later, he was among the first black players to play in the Cuban League, going 10–5 with the Fe Club. And, in 1909, he brought his Leland Giants from Chicago to Los Angeles, giving them the distinction of being the first black team to participate in the California Winter League. The modern integrated California Winter League, with one Negro League team playing in its own park, against three or more white teams, made its bow in 1920, but the actual beginning of an integrated California Winter League can be traced back to the 1909-10 season. Over the next eight years, from 1909 through 1918, the astute baseball entrepreneur divided his winters between Cuba, California, and Florida, and he usually ended his winter sojourn by scheduling a series of exhibition games along the Pacific Northwest with Pacific Coast League teams like San Francisco, Seattle, Oakland, Tacoma, and Portland, and then playing games on the return route home to Chicago through Idaho, Montana, Colorado, Kansas, and Missouri. He even provided his team with their own railroad coach so they could travel across the country in style. When the California Winter League became untenable, as will be discussed shortly, he concentrated his talents on forming the Negro National League, a dream of his that became a reality in 1920.

Rube Foster first brought his Leland Giants to California in full force the fall of 1909, with Cyclone Joe Williams, Ad Langford, Chappie Johnson, Bill Pettus, George Wright, Mike Moore, Bill Gatewood, Bobby Winston, and Walter Ball. The Leland team was more comparable to a Pacific Coast League club than it was to the old L.A. Giants, and it made its presence felt in the winter league, holding its own against teams that carried such major league players as Fred Snodgrass, Tillie Shafer, Walter Johnson, Gavvy Cravath, and Chief Meyers. On January 27, 1910, Cyclone Joe Williams defeated the San Diego Bears by the count of 5–2 in a California Winter League game. The *San Diego Union* said of the game, "It is doubtful if the Bears could have won as their opponents appeared to have them outclassed in several departments of the game. Williams, a 'dark horse,' long and slender, heaved balls across the plate that appeared about as small as shot, which some of the locals are in the habit of flinging at the unsuspecting. Johnson's good work behind the bat also helped the Giants put the game on their side." Williams held the Bears to six base hits, while striking out four and walking three, and he also contributed a two-base hit to the L.A. attack.

The Giants failed to win any winter league pennants between 1909 and 1914, but they were always in the thick of the pennant race, usually battling the San Diego Bears for the crown. And, they generated some of the most exciting memories over the years, many of them compliments of Cyclone Joe Williams. The tall, lanky right-hander tossed an 11-inning three-hitter at the Doyles team on December 18, 1910, winning 1–0 and sending 14 Doyles hitters back to the bench dragging their bats behind them. But Cyclone Joe was just getting warmed up. On January 7, 1911, he struck out 19 Doyles batters in a 7–0 rout of the local club, fanning the side in the second, third, and fifth innings. According to the L.A. *Times*, "Williams did not seem to have much at that, but it is always these 'have nothing' heavers that do the business. He shot most of them right over the plate, but he varied his speed with a floater and flung many high balls which ball players generally like, but could not use yesterday." Mike Moore, Bill Pettus, George Wright, and Williams all had two base hits. San Diego captured the 1910-11 winter league pennant with the Leland Giants a close second. Bobby Winston, a speedy outfielder and base stealer, led the Giants at bat with a .345 batting average. Williams, the team's top pitcher at 4-1, led the league in games (7), complete games (6), innings pitched (60), strikeouts (78), bases on balls (16), and shutouts (2). He also chipped in with the lumber, batting .381 in 6 games. And more important than the winning or losing of a pennant was the impression the black players were leaving with the fans around the L.A. area. Gone was the open hostility that erupted between the white and black teams on a regular basis six or eight years previous. There was a new respect between the races on the ball field, and an appreciation for the skills of the black players. Even the media began treating the black teams more fairly in their columns, reporting on the game as a contest between two equal teams, rather than resorting to caricatures to describe the efforts of the black team.

Two years later, Rube Foster returned to Los Angeles with his strongest team yet. He had Bill Lindsay, Dicta Johnson, and Bill Gatewood on the mound, backed by such stalwarts as Pete Hill, called by Cum Posey the most consistent hitter who ever lived; Bill Monroe, a magician around the keystone sack; and Bruce Petway, one of the best black catchers of all time. In another epic showdown with the Bears, the Chicago American Giants once again gave the San Diego contingent a battle before finally finishing in second place. C.J. Taylor led his team at bat with a robust .407 average. Bill Monroe chipped in with a .314 mark, and Jess Barbour hit .300. Tom Johnson went 3–0 on the mound, and Bill Lindsay compiled a 3–2 slate.

The Chicago American Giants did not participate in the 1913-14 California Winter League, but Rube Foster took them on his annual tour of the northwest preparatory to beginning their regular summer season in Chicago and, in one of the few newspaper accounts of their trip, they were reported to have defeated the Portland Beavers of the Pacific Coast League twice over the Easter weekend, with a lineup that included Hall-of-Fame players Cyclone Joe Williams, John Henry Lloyd, and Pete Hill, in addition to possible future Hall-of-Fame member Bill Monroe. The Negro League teams were becoming comfortable with the winter league competition by this time, and were significantly enlarging their fan base when their world collapsed. In a copy of the *Chicago Defender* dated April 11, 1914, as the Chicago American Giants were about to embark on their barnstorming tour of the Pacific Northwest, Allen T. Baum, president of the Pacific Coast League, dropped a bombshell when he "insisted the color line be drawn" and forbade PCL teams from playing black teams and from allowing black teams to use their parks. "Oakland and San Francisco heartily agreed, and refused to play. Walter McCredie of the champion Portland team thought otherwise and spoke so. Not only did he do this, but he played the Giants and the Portland team won a few games and lost a few more than they won.

"Joe Williams handed them a no-hit, no-run game, yet the coast fans rallied to the defense of McCredie, who has been the only man to disregard the color question and has gained a host of admirers by so doing." Unfortunately for the Giants, McCredie and his Portland Beavers were in the minority. As the *Defender* reported, "On Wednesday, the 1st of April, they arrived in Medford, Ore., and were turned down by every hotel and restaurant in town. They threatened to strike. Through a misunderstanding, no arrangements were made for feeding the men, and at a Japanese restaurant, where no color line is drawn, it was announced there would be nothing served until noon. After considerable argument, the proprietor secured cheese and crackers and these comprised the Giants breakfast."

The color barrier worsened with time, but it still took several years for the ballpark ban to be enforced by all the PCL teams. By 1916 however, there were no ballparks available to black teams that were large enough to make a game economically feasible. The Giants competed in the 1915-16 winter league but, because of the PCL ballpark ban, they were forced to play their home games in Athletic Park in San Diego, a park that, although it had just been built in 1902, was deemed to be unacceptable for use in the PCL one year later when San Diego applied for admission to the league. In 1916 Rube Foster was recruited by the Poinciana Hotel in Palm Beach, Florida, to bring his team there for the winter season to compete in the Hotel or Coconut League against Joe Williams and his Lincoln Giants team. He would winter in Florida for the next five years, leaving the California Winter League devoid of a talented Negro League team. A few black players like George Carr and John Donaldson appeared in a few games during the 1916-17 season, and they were joined by Dave Malarcher and Jose Mendez the following year, but the bulk of the White Sox roster was composed of local talent. And to further complicate matters, the U.S. involvement in World War I further decimated the player base and restricted travel while an outbreak of influenza drove fans away from the ballparks in record numbers.

The flu epidemic that hit the country with full force in the fall of 1918 caused serious problems for the baseball teams as recorded in the *Los Angeles Times* on January 27, 1919: "With players and spectators alike wearing influenza masks, a baseball game was played here [Pasadena] this afternoon between the Pasadena Merchants and Standard-Murphys. Several policemen were on hand to see that the masks were kept in place. No arrests were made. Even when sliding for their bases the runners managed to keep the cheesecloth over their noses and mouth." Long Beach prohibited all public gatherings and closed their schools to prevent the spread of the disease. And the U.S. government even halted the military draft.

Baseball on the west coast was sporadic at best during 1918 and 1919 as a result of the war and the flu epidemic, and the future of the winter league was in serious doubt. That's when two local businessmen, Doc Anderson and Joe Pirrone, stepped front and center to save the day. They realized that, in order for the winter league to survive, it would be necessary to have a strong Negro League entrant that would essentially double the fan base. Pirrone, who is known as "the father of the Winter League," was a well known semi-pro and professional baseball pitcher who had played in the winter league during the 1916-17 season. He was also a wheeler-dealer who knew a good business opportunity when he saw one. He knew that a winter league that included a Negro League team could be highly profitable, but he also knew that the Negro League team would have to have its own ballpark with adequate seating capacity for several thousand people. And that's where Anderson came in. Pirrone convinced Doc Anderson, a local contractor who had made a fortune selling well-water to townsfolk in Iditarod, Alaska, around 1910, to build a ballpark exclusively for the use of black winter league teams. And Pirrone promised Anderson that most of the winter league games would be played there. The new Negro League ballpark, called Anderson Park, or White Sox Park, opened for business on April 25, 1920. It was an enclosed park with a ten-foot high board fence. It had box seats, and grandstands down both foul lines, with a reported seating capacity of 2,800 people, although the field would occasionally accommodate a standing-room-only crowd of more than 4,000 people for key games, with fans standing ten deep around the outfield. The L.A. *Times* noted, "The big opening day game of the Los Angeles White Sox ball team and the Cline-Cline club will be held tomorrow at the new $8,000 Anderson's Park, located at East Fourth and Anderson Streets, just across the Los Angeles River. A big parade with a thirty-five piece band will precede the game, which will start at 2:30 P.M. Toots Schultz will pitch for Cline-Cline and Wood for the White Sox." No report of the game was found in the local papers, but many games were played throughout the summer leading up to the winter league season that began in October.

Joe Pirrone and his brother John, determined to give the fans the best baseball they could provide, and to attract the large black population in the city, had traveled east during the summer and recruited many of the Kansas City Monarchs, including "Bullet Joe" Rogan, Dobie Moore, "Tank" Carr, and Hurley McNair, to come to the coast for the inaugural winter league season. The first winter league game that was covered by the media matched Blue's All-Stars against the L.A. White Sox on October 24, with the All-Stars coming out on the long end of the score as reported in the *Times*.

> The Blue All-Star baseball club composed of Coast League and major league stars, nosed out the White Sox team (colored) in a riotous game at the Sox park yesterday afternoon. The final score was 5-4. The Sox had the tying run on third and the winning run on second in the last half of the ninth with none out.
>
> None of the next three batters was equal to the occasion, [Lem] Hawkins and Baker being easy infield outs and Kyle striking out.
>
> The All-Stars scored one run in the second inning, but a rally in the third frame netted four markers and salted the game away.
>
> Rogan quenched the All-Stars for the rest of the game, allowing them only two hits in the remaining six innings.
>
> Carr and Moore provided the fielding features with one-handed stabs of liners. A large crowd of wild-eyed fans witnessed the festivities.

Blue's All-Stars

Name	Pos	AB	R	H
Elliott	SS	3	0	1
Westerzil	3B	4	0	0
Blue	1B	3	1	1
Eddington	RF	4	2	1
Haley	2B	3	1	0
Rose	LF	3	0	1
Hannah	C	3	0	0
Oldham	P	1	0	0
Shellenback	P	1	0	1
Sarnis	CF	1	0	0
Baker	C	2	0	0
Totals		29	5	6

L.A. White Sox

Name	Pos	AB	R	H
Woods	CF	4	0	0
Fagan	2B	4	0	0
Carr	3B	3	1	1
McNair	LF	4	2	2
Rogan	p	4	0	2
Moore	SS	4	1	2
Hawkins	1B	4	0	0
A. Kyle	LF	4	0	0
Shorrs	C	0	0	0
W. Kyle	PH	0	0	0
		33	4	7

Blue's All-Stars   0 1 4   0 0 0   0 0 0—5—6—2
L.A. White Sox   0 2 0   0 0 0   0 0 2—4—7—2

Pitcher	IP	W	L	SO	BB
Oldham		1	0	7	2
Shellenback		0	0	2	0
Rogan	9	0	1	10	9

Doubles: McNair, Shellenback, Rogan

Pirrone, in an effort to make the league even more respectable, formed his own team, Pirrone's All-Stars, and manned it with some of the major league's finest players, including Bob Meusel, who had batted .320 for the New York Yankees in 1920, his brother Emil "Irish" Meusel (.309 for the Philadelphia Phillies), Tony Boeckel (.268 for the Boston Braves), and Max Carey (.289 with a league-leading 52 stolen bases for the Pittsburgh Pirates), as well as pitchers Duster Mails (7–0 with Cleveland and 1–0 in the World's Series), Speed Martin (4–15 with the Chicago Cubs), and Specs Meadows (18–14 with the Philadelphia Phillies). The 1920-21 California Winter League season was a smashing success. The White Sox captured the pennant with a 22–15 record, sparked by the pitching duo of "Bullet Joe" Rogan (8–8) and Rube Currie (12–4). Rogan, who also played center field when not pitching, paced the league's batters with a .368 average and 5 home runs. Pirrone's All-Stars were worthy opponents, however, winning the season series against the White Sox, 11 games to 10, but their big bats were relatively silent, with Bob Meusel checking in at .286 and his brother "Irish" mired in a .235 slump. Only Art Griggs at .350 finished above the magic .300 mark.

Joe Pirrone and Doc Anderson had saved the integrated league from extinction, beginning a period of unparalleled success that would last for more than twenty years. The Golden Age of the California Winter League, between 1920 and 1940, witnessed a parade of Negro League legends and major league stars that was almost endless. Rogan, "Cool Papa" Bell, Mule Suttles, Satchel Paige, and Willie Wells matched wits and bats with the likes of the Meusel brothers, "Irish" and Bob, Babe Herman, Heinie Manush, and Bobo Newsom. The Negro Leaguers won more than 60 percent of the games played, but in fairness to the white teams, it was not a level playing field. The Negro League teams faced pitching that, in spite of the presence of men like Newsom, Larry French, and Bob Feller, was on the average at AA level or below, while the white teams faced Negro League pitching that was at AAA level or slightly higher.

Some of the Negro League's greatest players wintered in Southern California during the 1920s and 1930s. The 1921-22 Negro League entry was called the Colored All-Stars, although it had essentially the same personnel as the 1920 Los Angeles White Sox. Oscar Charleston, considered by many people to have been the greatest player ever produced by the Negro Leagues, captained the All-Stars to the pennant. He also pounded the ball at a .405 clip, tying his teammate Henry Blackman for team honors in that category. Bob Meusel of Meusel's All-Stars captured the winter league batting title with an average of .425. Blackman, Biz Mackey, and "Tank" Carr tied for the home run lead with 3 each. Jim Jeffries of Charleston's Bear Cats went 9–5 on the mound, leading the league in victories, games pitched (14), and complete games (11). His teammate, John Taylor, led the league's pitchers in strikeouts (54) and innings pitched (100).

One of the most exciting series of the season took place on the weekend of January 14–15, 1922, when "Irish" Meusel's All-Stars tangled with the Colored All-Stars, before the largest crowds ever to see games at White Sox Park, standing-room-only crowds estimated to be 4,000 people. Meusel's team was one of the strongest white teams ever to play in the California Winter League, with seven outstanding major leaguers on the squad, including:

Bob Meusel, who hit .318 with the New York Yankees in 1921.
"Irish" Meusel, who hit .343 with the New York Giants in 1921.
Tony Boeckel, who hit .313 with the Boston Braves in 1921.
Lu Blue, who hit .308 with the Detroit Tigers in 1921.
Johnny Rawlings, who hit .278 with the New York Giants in 1921.
Johnny Bassler, who hit .307 with the Detroit Tigers in 1921.
And pitcher Bill Pertica, who went 14–10 with the St. Louis Browns in 1921.
They were opposed by Oscar Charleston's crack Bear Cats with:
Charleston, a career .340 hitter in the Negro leagues, who hit .437 with 17 home runs in 240 at-bats in 1921.
Dobie Moore, a career .355 hitter in the Negro leagues, who hit .372 with 11 home runs in 242 at-bats in 1921. He is considered by many to be the greatest all-around shortstop in Negro League history.

Biz Mackey, a career .322 hitter in the Negro leagues, who hit .317 with 13 home runs in 286 at-bats in 1921. He is considered to be the greatest defensive catcher in Negro League history, and arguably the league's greatest all-around catcher, the man who taught Roy Campanella the fine art of catching.

Henry Blackman, one of the top third basemen of his era and a dependable .300 hitter.

George "Tank" Carr, a career .310 hitter in the Negro leagues, who hit .330 with 15 home runs in 393 at-bats in 1921.

Hurley McNair, a career .322 hitter in the Negro leagues.

Jose Mendez, one of Cuba's greatest pitchers, and a slick-fielding shortstop in the Negro leagues.

The Colored All-Stars took the opener of the series on Saturday 3–2 with a three run rally in the bottom of the ninth inning before a huge crowd that ringed the outfield. Meusel's team, although held to just three hits by southpaw Jim Jeffries, held a 2–0 lead entering the bottom of the ninth inning. Then the roof caved in. Lem Hawkins' two-run double followed by a single to center field by Hurley McNair brought home the winning runs. Oscar Charleston, with a double and two singles, and Hawkins, with a similar production, paced the offense. Dobie Moore turned in the fielding gem of the game with a scintillating one-hand grab of Bob Meusel's line drive over shortstop that was ticketed for three bases. In the Sunday game, Meusel's team evened the score with a 7–6 victory. Lu Blue led off the game with a home run over the right-field fence off the slants of John Taylor, one of the famous Taylor brothers that included Ben, C.I., and Candy Jim. Two innings later, Bob Meusel duplicated the feat, this time with a shot over the left-field fence with two men on base, giving his team a comfortable 4–1 lead. The Bear Cats fought back, cutting the margin to 6–3 after seven innings, but Meusel's boys pushed over two more runs in the top of the eighth, stretching their lead to 7–3. In the bottom half of the inning, Carr and Charleston cracked doubles, and Mackey and Blackman followed with singles, but the rally fell one run short, with Meusel's All-Stars coming out on top, 7–6.

Biz Mackey is generally regarded as the greatest all-around catcher in Negro League history. He played 26 years in the California Winter League (courtesy John B. Holway).

Meusel's All-Stars					Colored All-Stars				
Name	Pos	AB	R	H	Name	Pos	AB	R	H
Blue	1B	4	1	1	McNair	LF	5	1	1
Rawlings	SS	3	2	1	Carr	RF	4	1	1
I. Meusel	LF	4	1	1	Charleston	CF	4	1	3
B. Meusel	RF	5	1	2	Mackey	C	3	1	1
Boeckel	3B	4	1	2	Blackman	3B	4	1	1
Sawyer	2B	4	1	1	Fagan	2B	4	0	1
Pirrone	CF	2	0	0	Hawkins	1B	3	0	1
Bassler	C	3	0	1	Mendez	SS-P	4	0	0
Pertica	P	4	0	0	Taylor	P	1	0	0
					Moore	SS	3	1	1
					Jeffries	P	0	0	0

```
Meusel's All-Stars      1 0 3    0 1 0    0 2 0—7— 9—2
Colored All-Stars       1 0 0    1 1 0    0 3 0—6—10—1
```

Doubles—Rawlings, Boeckel, Carr, Charleston (2)
Triples—Sawyer, McNair
Home Runs—Blue, B. Meusel.

Pitcher	IP	W	L	R	H	SO	BB
W. Pertica	9	1	0	6	9	2	0
Taylor	2⅓	0	1	4		2	1
J. Mendez	5⅔	0	0	3		1	3
Jeffries	1	0	0	0		0	1

In all, the two teams met eleven times during the season, with the Colored All-Stars coming out victorious seven times.

In the fall of 1924, Joe Pirrone built a new home for the black teams in the California Winter League, replacing ramshackle Anderson's Park at East Fourth and Anderson Streets. The new park, to be called Pirrone Park, or White Sox Park II, located at Thirty-Eighth and Compton Avenues, opened for business on October 25 with a game between two white teams, Sawyer's Stars and Joe Pirrone's All-Stars, with Pirrone's team on the long end of a 9–5 score. Ken Williams, the St. Louis Browns' slugger, "hit one nine miles over the right-field fence, for the circuit," according to the *Los Angeles Times*. "Williams clout was one of the longest ever hit in Los Angeles, the ball clearing Ascot Avenue, while it was still rising. Dod Murphy and Johnny Bassler also slammed out circuit clouts."

The new park changed the game dramatically, turning what used to be a pitchers game into a hitters game. Anderson Park, or White Sox Park I, measured 348 feet to left field, a barely visible 546 feet to center field, and 394 feet down the right field foul line. By comparison, Pirrone Park, or White Sox Park II, was 356 feet, 385 feet, and 235 feet, left to right. It was still a good poke for right-handed batters, but nothing more than a friendly chip shot for left-handed batters as long as they could uppercut the ball. There was an 80-foot high screen from the right field foul line to center field that turned line-drive home runs into singles.

The official winter league season opened on November 2, with Pirrone's All-Stars edging the Los Angeles White Sox 6–5. The *California Eagle* reported on the game. "With McNair, Hawkins, and Bell of the Kansas City Monarchs, Neal Pullen of the Baltimore

Black Sox, and Evans, Fagan, Savage, Foote, Munion, and Butcher in the lineup, the L.A. White Sox opened their new park Sunday.

"Their opponents were Pirrone's All-Stars, and sad to say, Pirrone and his leaguers won by a 6–5 score." Babe Herman homered in support of winning pitcher Pug Cavet.

Pirrone's All-Stars

Name	Pos.	AB	R	H
Smith	SS	4	2	2
Pirrone	CF	4	0	0
Brown	3B	4	1	1
Herman	1B	5	2	2
Bodie	LF	5	1	2
Sawyer	2B	4	0	1
Lapan	RF	0	0	0
Bachant	C	4	0	0
Cavet	P	4	0	1
McGraw	RF	4	0	0
Totals		38	6	9

L.A. White Sox

Name	Pos.	AB	R	H
Hawkins	SS	5	1	2
Fagan	2B	5	0	1
Evans	1B	5	0	1
McNair	CF	5	1	1
Pullen	C	4	0	3
Butcher	LF	4	2	1
Savage	RF	4	1	2
Foote	3B	4	0	1
Munion	P	1	0	0
Bell	P	2	0	0
		39	5	12

Pirrone's All-Stars   0 0 3   0 2 1   0 0 0—6— 9—3
L.A. White Sox   0 0 0   2 1 0   0 2 0—5—12—3

Doubles—Bodie (2), Hawkins
Triples—Foote
Home Runs—Herman

Pitcher	IP	W	L	SO	BB
Cavet	9	1	0	7	0
Munion	4⅓	0	1	4	1
Bell, "Cherry"	4⅔	0	0	7	4

That same fall, 18-year-old Willie Wells sneaked out of his house in Austin, Texas, against his mother's wishes and traveled to California to play for the St. Louis Giants in the California Winter League. It proved to be a valuable experience for the fledgling infielder. He lived with his manager in the Dunbar Hotel on Central Avenue, and sent most of his money home to his mother to help offset her disappointment at his leaving. And he learned to hit the curveball that had been confusing him for several years. Hurley McNair, a Negro League veteran with the Kansas City Monarchs of the Negro National League, who had a career average of .322, taught Wells how to hit the curve by tying his ankle to home plate during practice so he couldn't back away from the pitch. McNair then threw Wells curveballs for hours on end until he had mastered the art of hitting the breaking stuff, according to Jim Riley.

The decade of the '20s was a growing period for the California Winter League, and the quality of play increased each year. It was an important time for the Negro League players for several reasons. First, it confirmed Joe Pirrone's theory that the winter league could be a profitable enterprise if it included at least one Negro League entry. Large crowds attended every game, one game on Saturday and two on Sunday, with more than half of the fan base being black. Second, it proved to the Negro Leaguers and to the white players and fans that the black players could compete on an equal basis with Pacific Coast League players and with major league players. And third, it brought respect to the

Negro League players from their opponents and the white fans. Even the local newspapers began to report the games with a serious tone, instead of making sarcastic comments about blacks.

But just when it seemed that progress was being made in the race relations arena, the esteemed baseball commissioner, Kenesaw Mountain Landis, threw a monkey wrench into the winter league season on October 13, 1927, by issuing an edict that prohibited players in organized baseball from playing winter ball after October 31, an obvious attempt to destroy the integrated California Winter League. Joe Pirrone quickly adjusted the league's schedule to provide two weeks of action prior to the edict taking effect. As a result, when the season opened on October 15, there were several major league players in the lineup including Bob Meusel, Fred Haney, Jigger Statz, and Babe Herman. And even after the ban went into effect, some of the white players, such as "Irish" Meusel and Fred Haney, continued playing the entire season that ended in February.

In spite of Landis' brazen attack on the integrated California Winter League, the league prospered throughout the '20s and '30s, giving the west coast fans some of the best baseball in the country. The quality of the players continued to increase. Beginning with Dobie Moore and Joe Rogan in 1920, the California fans saw Negro League legends like Oscar Charleston, Jose Mendez, Biz Mackey, "Cool Papa" Bell, Willie Wells, Turkey Stearnes, Willie Foster, Chet Brewer, Jud Wilson, Mule Suttles, and Satchel Paige. For the record, as of 2006 there are 30 former Negro League players enshrined in baseball's Hall of Fame in Cooperstown, New York, and twelve of them, Paige, Stearnes, Bell, Wells, Rogan, Mackey, Suttles, Willie Foster, Joe Williams, Jud Wilson, Dandridge, and Lloyd, are California alumni. And John Beckwith and Dobie Moore, two of the Negro League's top three career hitters, should join their teammates in that hallowed hall in the near future.

The Negro Leaguers fielded some of the most powerful professional baseball teams, black or white, in the late '20s and early '30s. One of the strongest Negro League entrants was the 1926-27 team that included Turkey Stearnes, who batted .387 and led the league with 8 home runs in 106 at-bats; Joe Rogan, who went 6–2 on the mound with a .328 batting average; Willie Foster, who was a perfect 6–0 on the mound; Biz Mackey, who batted .316; and Willie Wells. Their 26–11 record gave them a 5½ game lead over the Shell Oilers. The 1928-29 team was just as strong, going 30–13 and winning the pennant by 9 full games over Shell. The roster that year included John Beckwith, who batted .485 and led the league with 14 home runs in just 101 at-bats; Biz Mackey, who scorched the ball at a .459 clip; Joe Rogan, who hit .406; Turkey Stearnes, who hit .372; Newt Allen, who hit .365; and Rap Dixon, who hit .360. Chet Brewer led the league in victories with 14 against just 4 losses, and Joe Rogan finished with a 9–1 record.

In the early '30s, the White Sox turned night into day, as announced by the *Pittsburgh Courier* on October 1, 1931: "The White Sox Park have put in lights for the coming season, and from all indications, things look very bright. Joe and John Pirrone, owners of the park, have spent something like $7,000 improving the grounds. The schedule will call for five games [a week] this season instead of the regular three games." The 1931 season opened under the lights on October 23, with Tom Wilson's Philadelphia Royal Giants defeating Joe Pirrone's Stars by the score of 8-1, behind the sensational right-handed fireball pitcher, Leroy "Satchel" Paige. As the *Los Angeles Times* reported, "Babe Herman of the Brooklyn Dodgers was in the All-Stars lineup and struck out four times in four trips to the plate. [Paige] struck out 11 men and allowed but five hits.... In the first two innings, Paige showed the fans some great pitching when he sent five batters that faced him to the bench on strikeouts."

The talent on the Negro League teams had improved to such an extent in the decade between 1924 and 1934, and the disparity in talent between the Negro League teams and the white teams had grown so large by the middle '30s, that the *Los Angeles Times* seemed almost bored to report the results of the Negro Leaguers' games. As Lyle K. Wilson noted, "The Royal Giants had gone on such a tear during the '33-34 winter league, that the *Times* preceded a report of another doubleheader sweep, with the following: 'Ho-hum! Life is so monotonous for those Royal Colored Giants. About all they have to do these days is to swing their mighty clubs, come Sunday, and make monkeys out of clubs composed of big-shot ballplayers. Yesterday was no exception. Joe Pirrone's All-Stars essayed the task of humbling the potent Giants at White Sox Park and were roundly spanked for a double trimming, 3–1 and 17–5.'"

The 1933-34 team might have been the strongest team ever to represent the Negro Leagues in the California Winter League. The Giants finished the season with a record of 34-8, leaving Pirrone's All-Stars a distant 22½ games in arrears. "Cool Papa" Bell led the league in batting with a .362 average, and in triples with 4 in 163 at-bats. Willie Wells hit .355, and Wild Bill Wright hit .351. No Giants batter hit less than .322. And Satchel Paige, who went 16–2, led the league in every pitching category, victories, games pitched (20), complete games (18), innings pitched (171), strikeouts (244), bases on balls (47), and shutouts (7). One of the Giants' opponents that year was Buck Newsome, an avowed racist, who was quoted as saying, "I'm not going up to the major leagues until I beat these niggers," to which "Cool Papa" Bell smiled and said, "Let's make him stay out here about two years." Buck did beat the Negro Leaguers three times over the winter, but he also lost five games. And he did make the majors that year, going 16–20 for the lowly St. Louis Browns.

The following year, the Giants were 34-5, a full 20 games better than the All-Stars. And their roster during those years included five Hall-of-Fame players—"Cool Papa" Bell, Willie Wells, Turkey Stearnes, Mule Suttles, and Satchel Paige. The opening series of the year was a microcosm of the entire season. The *Los Angeles Times* covered the event. "Thomas Wilson's Elite Giants opened the winter league season at White Sox Park by defeating the Pirrone's All-Stars two out of three games played. A mammoth street parade formed at 12th and Central Avenue, marched south on Central to Vernon Avenue, then to the park. One hundred and fifty cars and three bands were in the line of march. This was the greatest winter league opening ever staged here. With ['Spoon'] Carter pitching, the Giants won the game Saturday by the score of 14–5. Features of the game were the pitching of Carter, the hitting of Stearnes, Snow, Wells, Williams, Suttles, and Carter, the all-round playing of the Giants."

Pirrone's All-Stars					Wilson's Elite Giants				
Name	Pos	AB	R	H	Name	Pos	AB	R	H
Haney	3B	4	1	0	J. Bell	CF	5	1	1
Carlyle	CF	5	0	2	Hughes	1B	3	1	0
M. Almada	LF	4	1	1	Wells	SS	4	3	3
Demaree	RF	4	1	2	Stearnes	LF	5	3	4

Pirrone's All-Stars

Name	Pos	AB	R	H
Oglesby	1B	3	1	2
Knickerbocker	2B	4	1	1
Strange	SS	4	0	1
McMullen	C	3	0	0
Dorr	C	1	0	1
McDonald	P	2	0	0
Stine	P	1	0	0
Garland	P	0	0	0
V. Bell	P	1	0	0
Totals		36	5	10

Wilson's Elite Giants

Name	Pos	AB	R	H
Suttles	RF	5	3	2
Williams	2B	4	1	2
Snow	3B	5	1	4
Brown	C	4	0	0
Carter	P	5	1	2
		40	14	18

Pirrone's All-Stars   1 0 0   1 0 2   0 1 0— 5—10—?
Wilson's Elite Giants   3 0 0   3 0 3   5 0 x—14—14—?

Doubles: Wells, Dorr, Williams.
Three base hits: Wells.
Home Runs: M. Almada, Oglesby, Carter, Suttles, Knickerbocker.

On October 26, 1934, the love bug finally got to old Satch as reported by John Holway. "Greenlee threw a big party at his grill to celebrate the marriage of his star pitcher, Satchel Paige, to Janet Howard. Bojangles Robinson was best man. "We had to lock the door to keep the fans out," Paige wrote. "There was a bunch of fine looking girls out there with the fans," he sighed. He wished he had a tranquilizer to get through the ceremony, "but they hadn't been invented yet."

The newlyweds honeymooned in sunny California, where Paige pitched for Wilson's Elite Giants. Apparently his new domestic arrangement didn't affect his throwing in the least. He dominated Pirrone's All-Stars in his first start, winning 7–1 with 14 strikeouts, and he went on from there to log a perfect 8–0 mark, with 104 strikeouts in 69 innings, to pace his team to the pennant. Paige was beginning to get big headlines at this time, and his west coast legend would continue to

Turkey Stearnes was a five-point player in the mold of Willie Mays (courtesy John Outland).

grow over the years, bringing him to the attention of the professional baseball establishment all across the country.

The most exciting day of the season was January 27, 1935, when the Elite Giants matched weapons with Pirrone's All-Stars in White Sox Park. And it turned out to be Turkey Stearnes' day. The powerful left fielder for the Giants lit up the afternoon sky with his pyrotechnics, cracking four home runs and a single in six times at bat. He crushed two homers in the first inning, one with two men on base and another with the sacks loaded. He put another ball into orbit with Willie Wells on base in the fifth, and hit his fourth of the day with two men on in the sixth. In all, he drove in 12 runs for the day, including seven in the Giants 11-run first. "Pullman" Porter coasted to a comfortable 20–8 victory. Hughes and Wells chipped in with four hits apiece, and Wright and Brown each collected three as the Giants unloaded on three major league pitchers, Hank McDonald, Syl Johnson, and Larry French.

Pirrone's All-Stars

Name	Pos	AB	R	H
Colburn	3B	5	1	2
Sawyer	2B	4	2	2
Powers	1B	3	2	1
Arlington	CF	4	2	1
F. Bell	LF	4	1	2
Berkowitz	SS	4	0	0
Ograin	RF	4	0	0
McMullen	C	1	0	0
Dorr	C	3	0	0
McDonald	P	1	0	0
Johnson	P	1	0	0
French	P	2	1	1
Totals		36	9	9

Wilson's Elite Giants

Name	Pos	AB	R	H
J. Bell	CF	6	1	1
Hughes	2B	6	4	4
Wells	SS	6	4	4
Stearnes	lf	6	4	5
Suttles	1B	6	1	2
Wright	RF	5	2	3
Snow	3B	4	3	2
Brown	C	5	1	3
Porter	P	5	0	1
		49	20	25

Pirrone's All-Stars   0 0 0   0 0 2   6 0 1— 9— 9–0
Wilson's Elite Giants   1 1 1 0   0 4 3   1 0 x—20—25–0

Pitcher	IP	W	L	SO	BB
McDonald		0	1	2	1
Johnson		0	0	1	0
French		0	0	2	1
Porter	9	1	0	0	4

Doubles: F. Bell, Sawyer, Suttles (2), J. Bell, Porter.
Home Runs: Powers, F. Bell, Stearnes (4), Hughes.

The Negro League players had, by this time, gained the respect of the west coast fans and the local newspapers. Where the local papers presented the games of the black teams in just two lines between 1900 and 1920, the *Los Angeles Times* and the *Examiner* gave the Negro League teams banner headlines like these in the late '20s and '30s.

"Kings And Giants In Sox Park Double Bill."
"Paige Again Master, 7–1."
"Satchel Whiffs 17 Soapsters, Nine In A Row."
"It Was 'Turkey' Day, Stearnes Clouts Four Home Runs."

"Mule Kicks For Giants. Suttles Poles Two Homers As Colored Nine Takes Pair From Pirrones."

"Dizzy vs. Satchel In Mound Battle Tonight."

"Paige Attracts Throng Of 10,800; Great 'Satch' Invincible During Five-Inning Stint."

As can be seen from the above headlines, as Satchel Paige's legend grew during the 1930s, he commanded more and bigger headlines. And his reputation brought mammoth crowds into the ballpark to watch the strikeout ace in action.

The Giants continued to win winter league pennants through the end of the decade, with stars like Mackey, Bell, Suttles, Chet Brewer, Sammy T. Hughes, and "Wild Bill" Wright but, by the beginning of the forties, the sun was beginning to set on America's most important winter league. And World War II put the final nail in the coffin. With many of the players in military service and travel restrictions limiting the potential talent pool, the California Winter League struggled through the war years. Buck Leonard went to California in 1942 to play in the winter league, but after playing a couple of exhibition games against a major league all-star team, he went back home to Rocky Mount, S.C., and worked at the railroad station loading boxcars. He did return to California the next, year however, and played for the Baltimore Elite Giants in the winter league. The Giants were opposed by Pirrone's All-Stars, with Buck Newsome, Peanuts Lowrey, George "Catfish" Metkovich, Andy Pafko, Al Zarilla, and Jerry Priddy. The two teams played every Sunday from November through January. Baltimore won 7 of the 12 games played, and Leonard ripped the ball at a torrid .355 pace, with 2 triples in 31 at-bats. Tommy Sampson led the league in batting with a .433 average and Satchel Paige was the top pitcher at 3–1. Rip Russell of the Chicago Cubs hit the only home run of the series. There was some question about the effort put out by the two teams occasionally after someone said that the following week's crowd would be bigger if the two teams split the Sunday doubleheader. If one team swept both games, the crowd would be smaller because the fans would figure the winning team didn't have much competition. According to Buck Leonard, the twin bills were always split, coincidentally or not. At one point, Buck said, "We weren't so sure they were putting out 100 percent against us in exhibitions. But I think they were. We won some and they won some. We won a few more than they did because we were playing harder. We needed money and they were just passing the time. We made two hundred dollars every Sunday until Judge Landis stopped them from playing us."

The 1943 winter league season got off to a rousing start with the *Los Angeles Times*, so different from the atmosphere of twenty or thirty years ago, trumpeting the appearance of Satchel Paige in its October 25 edition with the headline "Paige Attracts Throng of 10,800." The story under the headline noted,

> The box office magic of Leroy (Satchel) Paige, greatest of all Negro baseball players, was plainly demonstrated yesterday when 10,800 fans jammed Gilmore Field to see him pitch for the Baltimore Colored Giants against Joe Pirrone's all-star array of major and coast leaguers.
>
> The teams broke even, the Stars capturing the opener, 8–2, and the Giants the finale, 4–1, but the games themselves were merely incidental.
>
> It was Paige whom the people came out to watch and, although he displayed his talents for only five innings of the opener before deciding to call it a day, he kept the crowd in an uproar with the wizardry of his slants.
>
> When he retired to rest his aging but still highly valuable bones, he held a 2–0 lead. He

had permitted only two hits and he had whiffed five. And the opposition was nothing to be sneezed at either, for it included seven gents fresh out of big league competition.

All-Stars				Colored Giants			
Name	*Pos*	*AB*	*H*	*Name*	*Pos*	*AB*	*H*
Lowrey	2B	5	4	Hyde	RF	4	0
English	3B	5	2	Bell	LF	3	0
Metkovich	RF	4	2	Spearman	RF	4	1
Pafko	CF	5	0	Leonard	1B	3	1
Dahlgren	SS	4	0	Easterling	3B	4	0
Novikoff	LF	4	1	Sampson	2B	4	3
Barton	1B	4	2	Radcliffe	C	4	2
Partee	C	3	0	Walker	SS	4	1
Kimball	P	2	0	Paige	P	2	1
Gullic	PH	1	1	McDaniels	P	1	0
Kress	P	1	0	Markham	P	1	0
Totals		**38**	**12**			**34**	**9**

All-Stars   0 0 0   0 0 1   4 1 2—8—12—3
Colored Giants   0 0 0   1 1 0   0 0 0—2— 9—3

Doubles—Novikoff, Lowrey (2), Metkovich, Barton (2)

Pitcher	*IP*	*W*	*L*	*H*	*SO*	*BB*
N. Kimball	6	1	0	8	2	2
Kress	3	0	0	1	0	0
Paige	5	0	0	2	5	1
McDaniels	2	0	1	6	1	1
Markham	2	0	0	4	2	1

The season moved along at a brisk pace for six weeks with Pirrone's All-Stars and the Colored Giants meeting 13 times, with the Giants coming out on top in 7 games, and the All-Stars in 5, with one game ending in a tie. Paige pitched in six of the games with one complete game, while compiling a record of 3–1, with 39 strikeouts in 36 innings. Chet Brewer's Kansas City Royals were also active in the winter league, with a lineup that included Ray Dandridge, "Cool Papa" Bell, Bill Wright, Willard Brown, and Biz Mackey, but they didn't fare as well as Paige's team, losing four of the seven games played. Then, just when things looked the brightest, Commissioner Landis struck again, as reported in the *Pittsburgh Courier*, under the headline, "Landis Clamps Down On Winter Leaguers." The article went on to say,

> Judge K.M. Landis, commissioner of organized baseball, last week ordered all major leaguers to desist further from pastiming in the Southern California Winter League. He further indicated they were liable to fines for having violated the rule prohibiting participation 10 days after the major league season closed. As yet, no fines have been levied with the players status still being under investigation. With the boom of war plus the personal appearance of Satchel Paige, this season's winter loop has been the most prosperous of the last decade. Crowds of seven and eight thousand have been common. Among the major league stars whose actions are under the scrutiny of Landis are [Peanuts] Lowrey, Skeet Newsome, Buck Newsom, Vern Stephens, and John Lindell.

In a follow-up story on November 18, the *Los Angeles Times* reported, "[Secretary to the commissioner Leslie M.] O'Connor disclosed that Johnny Lindell of the world's championship New York Yankees, whose cut of the World's Series pie amounted to $6139, reported to Commissioner Landis that he got only $3 a game. O'Connor expressed surprise at the smallness of the fee. 'Can you imagine a World's Series player playing for that kind of money?' he asked."

The *Pittsburgh Courier* kept abreast of the story in its December 4 edition.

> Commissioner K.M. Landis' "big stick" is being swung out here [Los Angeles] as well as in the vicinity of Philadelphia. Landis is now conducting an investigation of the California Winter League, in which 19 major league players have been playing. Most of the games in which these players have played have been against Negro teams. The big leaguers have played most of their games against Satchel Paige and his Kansas City Giants, which includes players from the Negro American and National Leagues. The games between Paige's team and the big leaguers have been used as a yardstick by baseball critics, If Landis cracks down, which he is likely to do, he will wipe out the sole means of measuring the abilities of Negro players with major leaguers. In 10 games played out here in the past five weeks, Paige and his mates won four games, the big leaguers won five, and one was a tie.

Landis' actions could have delayed the integration of organized baseball for another generation, but fate stepped in and took a hand. Sadly for the Landis family, but fortunately for the sport of baseball, the commissioner passed away in 1944. His successor, Albert Benjamin "Happy" Chandler, supported the integration of organized baseball by Jackie Robinson in 1946, giving black players equal opportunity to play alongside white players in the major leagues. As often happens in the name of progress, some things suffered as a result of integration. The Negro leagues, a social experience for thousands of black fans in the eastern sector of the country, slowly passed into legend, finally giving up the ghost in 1960. And the California Winter League expired during the decade of the '40s. By 1947 it was only a memory. But at least one of the winter league's greatest players was able to experience the major league atmosphere before he retired. Old Satchel Paige, age 42, was signed by the Cleveland Indians during their pennant struggle in 1948, and he produced as promised. In fact, the ageless one pitched two shutouts against the Chicago White Sox in one seven day period en route to an impressive 6–1 record in 21 games, as Cleveland nipped the Boston Red Sox in a playoff for the American League pennant. Satch enjoyed a five-year major league career, and continued to pitch in the high minors until he was 55 years old. And he capped his fantastic career with the Kansas City Athletics, tossing three shutout innings at the Boston Red Sox in 1965 at the age of 59.

Some old ballplayers who played against him remembered him as being much older, which says something about the memories of us senior citizens. Dutch Ruether, who pitched for the Brooklyn Dodgers in the 1920s, insisted in a *Los Angeles Times* article in 1954, "Paige can't be less than 51. I hit against him at Joe Pirrone's old White Sox Park in 1924. That was 30 years ago and Satch wasn't exactly a Boy Scout then. He was smart, fast, and had great control. When I was managing Seattle in 1935, we played Paige's barnstorming team. Before the game I made a bet with one of my players that Satch would strike out 18 men in nine innings. I was wrong, but I won the bet. Satch struck out 21."

Another old time ballplayer, Carl Sawyer, who played with the Washington Senators in 1915, and was a member of the California Winter League for more than 20 years beginning in 1916, had his own memories of Paige and the Negro League teams of the early years, as reported in the *Times*. "Well, you can draw your own conclusions, but in 1914 down in Alabama, I played against Paige." The *Times* went on to say, "Some of you old timers around here will remember Paige's mates in the days of Winter League ball.... Turkey Stearnes, Mule Suttles, "Bullet" Rogan, "Cool Papa" Bell, "Big Boy" Griffin, and Beautiful Snow, to name a few. "The Giants were terrific," recalled Carl. "They usually had only 11 or 12 men on their team and we always played double-headers every Sunday. It was an exception when we beat 'em at all."

Some of the most outstanding players in Negro League history showcased their talents in the California Winter League, including the following.

"Cool Papa" Bell may have been the fastest man ever to play in the Negro leagues. As one fanciful story went, "He could turn off the light switch on the wall and be in bed before the lights went out." In any case, he was the premier base stealer of his day. He also covered two-thirds of the outfield from his vantage point in center field. "Cool Papa" was a .328 hitter in the Negro leagues, with 29 doubles, 10 triples, and 8 home runs for every 550 at-bats. On the coast, he hit a blistering .368 over 12 years, with 28 doubles, 11 triples, and 15 home runs for every 550 at-bats. He led the winter league in batting twice, in 1924-25 with an average of .400, and in 1933-34 with an average of .362. That season, he also led the league in base hits (59), and triples (4). Bell had a field day with active major league pitchers, tattooing them to the tune of .354, with 12 doubles, 2 triples, and 3 home runs in 130 at-bats. His favorite targets were Sloppy Thurston (.429), Lee Stine (.382), and Buck Newsom (.321).

George "Tank" Carr was a Los Angeles resident who became an 18-year Negro League star, batting .310 with 10 home runs a year. The big 6', 2", 220-pound switch hitter was also a star in the California Winter League. During his ten-year CWL career, he stroked the ball at a .336 clip, with 21 home runs a year. In 1925-26, Carr hit .342 and led the league with 16 doubles and 8 home runs in 146 at-bats. And he played no favorites. He hit the major league pitchers for a .317 average, including .389 against Charlie Root, a 201-game winner in the major leagues.

Raleigh "Biz" Mackey was a versatile player who played several positions in California, including pitcher and shortstop, and he did an exceptional job at each. But he was best known for his catching skills, being rated by many baseball experts as the greatest all-around catcher in Negro League history. And with good reason. On defense, he had no weakness. He was death on bunts and pop fouls, a block of granite blocking the plate, and the sworn enemy of would-be base stealers. His chest protector was even imprinted with the slogan "Thou Shalt Not Steal." Mackey's California Winter League career began in 1920 and ended 25 years later, the longest tenure of any Negro League player. And, as usual, he excelled, batting .366 in 957 at-bats with 36 doubles, 10 triples, and 16 home runs a year. He hit .336 against active major league pitchers, including .419 against Sloppy Thurston, .375 against Red Oldham, and a sizzling .556 against Lou Koupal.

Walter "Dobie" Moore was arguably the greatest all-around shortstop in Negro League history. He was noted for his big hands, quick reflexes, wide range, and rifle arm on defense, and for his potent bat on offense. The powerful 5', 11", 200-pound right-handed slugger was one of the top hitters wherever he played. His .355 Negro League career batting average was the highest batting average for any player with more than 1,750 at-bats. And he supplemented that output with 35 doubles, 15 triples, and 16 home runs for every 550 at-bats. In the Cuban League, Moore pounded the ball at a .353 clip, number 3 all-time behind Jud Wilson (.372) and Oscar Charleston (.360). And in California he led all hitters with a career average of .385, with 41 doubles, 19 triples, and 19 home runs. Moore, who arrived in Los Angeles with the nickname "Home Run" Moore, starred for the pennant-winning Los Angeles White Sox in the league's inaugural season of 1920, batting .331 and leading the league with 46 base hits and 6 triples. Four years later, he single-handedly destroyed opposing pitching staffs, leading the league in most offensive categories, including batting average (.487 in 158 at-bats), doubles (17), triples (4), and home runs (12). And he played no favorites, batting a healthy .362 against active major league pitchers.

Wilbur "Bullet Joe" Rogan is recognized as one of the three greatest pitchers in Negro League history, along with Satchel Paige and Cyclone Joe Williams. In addition to having a blazing fastball and a sharp-breaking curve, the stocky 5', 7", 180-pound right-handed pitcher was also considered to be the best fielding pitcher in Negro League history. "Bullet Joe" could do it all. When he wasn't pitching, he was holding down center field or second base, with equal dexterity. And he had one additional advantage over his two rivals. He batted cleanup! He compiled a won-loss record of 42–14 on the coast, trailing only Chet Brewer, who won 43 games, and Satchel Paige, who won 56 games. Rogan's best year in the California Winter League was 1925-26, when he ran up a record of 14–2, leading the league in victories, games pitched (18), complete games (16), innings pitched (153), strikeouts (82), and bases on balls (52). He also stroked the ball at a .326 clip that year as the Philadelphia Royal Giants raced to the pennant by a 3½ game margin over the White King Soapsters. "Bullet Joe" also fared well against active major league players, out-pitching the likes of Duster Mails, Archie Campbell, and Bill Piercy, while compiling a 7–2 record against them, and slugging the ball at a .386 pace, with 6 home runs in 115 at-bats. He batted .417 against Campbell, and lit up Lou Koupal to the tune of .706.

Norman "Turkey" Stearnes was a superstar in the image of the Giants' Willie Mays. He hit for average, hit for distance, and could run, field, and throw. Stearnes was a graceful 6' tall, 175-pound gazelle who practically covered the outfield from foul line to foul line. He was noted for his great range, his dependable glove, and his outstanding throwing arm. And at the plate, he had few equals. He batted a solid .373 during an illustrious nine-year career on the coast with 28 doubles, 12 triples, and 41 home runs for every 550 at-bats. He was also a dangerous base runner whose blazing speed and aggressive nature boded ill for any infielder bold enough to try to tag the hard sliding Stearnes. His .373 batting average is the 4th highest average in California Winter League history. He is also #4 in doubles, #3 in triples, and #2 in home runs. He was even more successful against major league pitchers, hammering them at a .389 pace. His favorite targets were Charlie Root (.555), Wheezer Dell (.471), and Ray Keating (.357). And consistency was his forte. He never hit less than .324 in any California Winter League season. His greatest year was 1930-31 when he paced the Nashville Elite Giants to the pennant with a league-leading .387 batting average and a league-leading 5 home runs. His greatest day on the coast occurred on January 27, 1935, when he slugged four home runs and a single, and drove in 12 runs, in a 20–9 rout of Pirrone's All-Stars. Norman "Turkey" Stearnes is one of the 30 Negro League players who presently reside in the Baseball Hall of Fame in Cooperstown, New York.

Josh Gibson is generally regarded as the Negro League's answer to Babe Ruth, but George "Mule" Suttles has to be a close second. The big 6', 3", 215-pound right-handed hitter holds the record for the most lifetime home runs in the Negro leagues, with 234, 13 more than Gibson. And his season average of 40 home runs per 550 at-bats, trails only Gibson. On the west coast, he was #1 all the way, smashing 64 home runs in 450 at-bats, an average of 78 home runs for every 550 at-bats. He led the league in homers six times in eight years, with a high of 16 homers in 96 at-bats in 1934-35. He also led the league in batting twice, with an average of .474 (in just 38 at-bats) in 1930-31 and .586 (in 29 at-bats) the following year. During his California Winter League career, Suttles batted .378, including a .326 slate against active major league pitchers. He hit .345 with 2 homers in 29 at-bats against Buck Newsom, and .385 with 4 homers in 13 at-bats against Larry French.

Willie Wells is regarded as one of the four greatest shortstops in Negro League history, along with Dobie Moore, John Henry Lloyd, and Dick Lundy. He was a solid all-around player with wide range and a sure glove. He didn't have a strong throwing arm, but he was always in the right position to make a play. As a batter he hit consistently

Mule Suttles was the foremost slugger in the California Winter League, averaging 78 home runs for every 550 at-bats (courtesy Dr. Lawrence D. Hogan).

with surprising power for a little man who stood only 5', 8" tall and weighed a scant 160 pounds. His eight-year California career resulted in a .301 batting average with 40 doubles, 6 triples, and 11 home runs in 528 at-bats. He was even better against active major league hitters, raking them for a sizzling .376 average. He hit .345 against Buck Newsom, .471 against Sloppy Thurston, and .600 against Larry French.

Burnis "Wild Bill" Wright was called the greatest Negro League hitter ever to appear in California by many west coast baseball writers. His 11-year winter league career produced a .375 batting average, #3 all-time, with 26 doubles, 11 triples, and 15 home runs, in 416 at-bats. He hit a lusty .351 against major league pitchers, including .476 against Sloppy Thurston, and .364 against Larry French.

Chet Brewer played in the California Winter League for 12 years, winning 43 games against just 13 losses. His victory totals were surpassed only by Satchel Paige's 56. He was 2nd in career games pitched (72), 4th in complete games (42), and 3rd in innings pitched (402). His best year was 1928-29 when he led the Cleveland Giants to the pennant by 9 games over the Shell Oil Club. He dominated most of the league's pitching categories that year, including victories (14 against 4 losses), games pitched (18), complete games (14), innings pitched (146), and strikeouts (73).

William "Willie" Foster was one of the Negro League's five greatest pitchers. And in California he was almost perfect, winning 24 games in his three-year career against a single loss. Needless to say, his team, the Philadelphia Royals Giants, rode his coattails to pennants every year he pitched. And the tall, lanky southpaw was poetry in motion, going 6–0 in 1926-27, 9–0 in 30–31, and 9–1 in 31–32. His only loss came at the hands of Lou Koupal of Pirrone's All-Stars when the Stars erupted for 6 runs in the eighth inning erasing a 4–1 Giants lead. Foster's .960 winning percentage is the best winning percentage in winter league history by a wide margin.

"Wild Bill" Wright was called the most dangerous hitter in the California Winter League by many west coast baseball experts (courtesy James A. Riley).

Willie Foster may have been the greatest left-handed pitcher in the annals of Negro League baseball (courtesy John B. Holway).

Leroy "Satchel" Paige was arguably the Negro League's greatest pitcher. He certainly was their most outspoken supporter and drawing card. Wherever and whenever Satchel pitched, the fans came out in droves to watch the 6', 4", 180-pound right-handed fireballer in action. And he never disappointed his fans. His Negro League record was 147–92 for a .630 winning percentage. In California, it was much better. He was almost unbeatable on the coast, winning 56 games in 9 years against 7 losses, for a .889 winning percentage. During his first five years out west, he was 50–2, with 16 shutouts. His best year was 1933-34 when he led the league in most pitching categories, including games pitched (20), complete games (18), victories (16 against 2 losses), innings pitched (172), strikeouts (245), strikeouts per game (12.8), and shutouts (7). His career numbers are just as dominating as he led the league in games pitched (80), innings pitched (572), victories (56), strikeouts (766), and shutouts (17).

The California Winter League got off to a slow start in the early 1900s, held back by the lack of a dedicated Negro League entry each year, and by the Coast League park ban imposed on the teams by the president of the PCL in 1914. But it was resurrected in 1920 thanks to the efforts of Joe Pirrone and Doc Anderson. By the mid-'20s, the Negro League teams in the winter league had gained the respect of the baseball fans as well as the newspapers on the west coast. Instead of caricaturing the black players and their fans, publications like the *Los Angeles Times* were praising their skills, as well they should have. The rosters of the Negro League teams became more impressive each year, as noted earlier. From "Bullet Joe" Rogan, "Tank" Carr, and Dobie Moore in 1920, the mid-'20s showcased such talents as "Cool Papa" Bell, Willie Wells, Newt Allen, and Biz Mackey, the late '20s added Turkey Stearnes, Willie Foster, and Chet Brewer, and the early '30s introduced Mule Suttles, Jud Wilson, John Beckwith, and Satchel Paige. Essentially most of the greatest players in Negro League history, from 1900 to 1940, with the exception of Josh Gibson and Chino Smith, played in the California Winter League, crossing swords with the best pitchers the major leagues and the Pacific Coast Leagues could offer, and more than held their own. Moore, Wilson and Beckwith were three of the top four hitters in Negro League history, while Stearnes and Suttles were two of the three most prolific sluggers ever produced by the Negro leagues.

The California Winter League has faded from the memories of most old timers, and most people today don't know it ever existed. But it was an important league in its day. It was the first truly integrated professional baseball league in the United States. And it showcased such legendary ballplayers as "Cyclone Joe" Williams, "Bullet Joe" Rogan, Oscar Charleston, and Satchel Paige. It changed the attitude of a generation of people toward the black race. Instead of denigrating blacks, people on the west coast learned to accept them as equals and to respect their immense skills on the ball field. And the white players who competed against the Negro leaguers during the winter months brought their memories of the blacks back east with them. The California Winter League gave the black players tremendous visibility, and may have been one of the most important

John Beckwith compiled a career batting average of .352 in the Negro Leagues, #3 all-time. He batted .413 in California (courtesy Noir Tech Sports, Inc).

factors leading up to the integration of organized baseball. Certainly their sensational success in California proved they could compete on an equal basis with major league players. Ted Williams was particularly outspoken about the absence of Negro League players in the National Baseball Hall of Fame. In his speech at the Hall of Fame in 1972, Williams decried the fact that no former Negro League players were yet members of that respected institution. He knew first hand how talented the black players were, having played against blacks as a youth in California, and having played against some of the great Negro League players, like Satchel Paige, "Wild Bill" Wright, and "Cool Papa" Bell, in the California Winter League in the late 1930s.

The complete history of the California Winter League, along with the career batting and pitching statistics of its most prominent players, can be found in another McFarland publication, *The California Winter League*.

5

Barnstorming

Barnstorming was an easy and enjoyable way for professional baseball players to make ends meet during the off-season. As is well known, professional ballplayers, black and white, were not well paid for their efforts during the first half of the 20th century, so very few of them could just rest and relax between seasons. They still had to earn a living, by whatever means they had at their disposal. Many players worked in construction. Some worked on the docks, loading and unloading ships. And others worked as salesmen, selling everything from insurance to refrigerators. Carl Furillo of the Brooklyn Dodgers helped build the New York Trade Center as an employee of the Otis Elevator Company, and due to travel restrictions during World War II, Buck Leonard stayed home and worked at the railroad station loading and unloading boxcars, admittedly hard work. Other players continued to play baseball by barnstorming. In the interest of reaching a common goal, major league players and Negro League players often met in exhibition games after their regular seasons ended, traveling as far west as California and as far north as Canada, in October and November. Some ingenious players, like Satchel Paige, Dizzy Dean, and Bob Feller, formed their own all-star teams, and they often paired up and traveled together, playing each other night after night, and week after week, until the cold winter weather arrived.

One of the first recorded exhibition games matching a major league team against a Negro League team was a game between the Chicago Cubs and the Leland Giants in Cubs Park, Chicago, on September 22, 1909, with Mordecai "Three-Finger" Brown toeing the rubber for the Cubs and Pat Dougherty on the hill for the Giants. Brown was coming off the best year of his 14-year major league career. He had led the National League in victories (27), games pitched (50), complete games (32 in 34 starts), shutouts (7), and innings pitched (343). Dougherty, a left-handed sidearmer, was in the first year of his 10-year Negro League career, and had just won two games in the post-season playoff against the St. Paul Gophers. The game was a pitchers battle all the way, with Brown eking out a 1–0 decision on a 6th inning double by Joe Tinker, a sacrifice, and a sacrifice fly. Brown yielded four hits, one more than Dougherty, each pitcher fanned six batters, and Dougherty issued the only base on balls. The game was called on account of darkness after seven innings. Brown defeated the Lelands on two other occasions, including a stirring duel with Rube Foster.

Chicago Cubs				Leland Giants			
Name	Pos	R	H	Name	Pos	R	H
Zimmerman	2B	0	1	Wallace	3B	0	0
Sheckard	LF	0	0	Harris	2B	0	0
Schulte	RF	0	0	Hill	CF	0	1
Howard	1B	0	0	Payne	LF	0	0
Stanley	3B	0	0	Strothers	1B	0	0
Archer	CF	0	0	Wright	SS	0	1
Tinker	SS	1	2	Booker	C	0	0
Moran	C	0	0	Ball	RF	0	1
Brown	P	0	0	Dougherty	P	0	1
Total		1	3			0	4

Chicago Cubs   0 0 0   0 0 1   0 0 0—1—3—2
Leland Giants   0 0 0   0 0 0   0 0 0—0—4—1

Pitcher	IP	R	H	SO	BB	W	L
M. Brown	9	0	4	6	0	1	0
P. Dougherty	9	1	3	6	1	0	1

Doubles—Tinker (2), Zimmerman

Negro League teams didn't play just major league teams in their traveling exhibitions however. They played everyone and anyone, wherever and whenever they could make a buck. One memorable exhibition game against a minor league opponent matched "Cannonball" Dick Redding against the Jersey City Giants of the Eastern League in Olympic Park in New York City in 1912. Redding, facing the likes of "Turkey Mike" Donlin, who was still active in the major leagues, future major leaguer Al Schacht, and former major leaguer Ducky Holmes, had a career day, fanning 19 batters and tossing a perfect game. The Lincoln Giants pushed across the only run of the game in the bottom of the eighth inning on a double by "Spot" Poles and a single by John Henry Lloyd.

The Negro Leaguers often crossed the country by automobile or by bus, playing as many as five or six games a week, 50 weeks a year. Or, as in the case of Rube Foster's Chicago American Giants, they traveled in the comfort of their own custom designed railroad coach. In addition to exhibition games in the East and the Midwest, Foster's team visited cities across the United States during the second decade of the century, playing many local semi-pro and amateur clubs before challenging the teams of the Pacific Coast League. They routinely played series against the Portland Beavers, the Tacoma Tigers, and Seattle, as well as against various college teams. The series were evenly balanced, but the Giants captured the majority of the contests. In 1913, the American Giants established a record that will probably last forever, as reported in the *Chicago Defender*.

> Sunday the American Giants set a record when they defeated the Logan Squares, 9–3. This was their two-hundredth game. This is a record that has never been established before by any team. They started on the Pacific coast and played there and up through Vancouver and British Columbia, returning home by way of Butte, Mont., and St. Louis. Here they made a record that any team would be proud of, notwithstanding the fact that they lost to the Lincoln Giants in their series.
>
> Mr. Foster has given us a club within walking distance and has given us games where there has been more inside baseball played than in the World Series.

Score of Sunday's game:

American Giants	0 2 0 1 3 0 1 2 *—9—13—2
Logan Squares	2 0 0 0 0 1 0 0 0—3— 8—1

Two years later, two Negro League players were carted off to jail in the middle of an exhibition game. On October 29, in Federal League Park, Indianapolis, the ABCs faced off against Ownie Bush's All-Stars. In the top of the fifth inning, with the game tied at 1-1, Bush singled and then stole second. ABC second baseman Bingo DeMoss took exception to the call and charged umpire Jimmy Scanlon, who put up his fists to defend himself. Then, as reported in the *Defender*, "Charleston came to Demoss' aid and landed one on the ump's face, causing an ugly wound and letting him take the count. Spectators swarmed on the field, causing the police to take quick action. The two players were sent to jail where they were bailed out. The game resumed. The excitement was too much for the ABC's and the Stars won as they pleased." The final score was 5-1 in favor of Bush's All-Stars.

The Detroit Tigers met the St. Louis Stars in St. Louis in a three game series on October 2, 3, and 4, 1922. The Stars won the first two games by scores of 5-4 and 8-7. The result of the third game has not been found. The absence of Ty Cobb in the series was conspicuous as the great Detroit outfielder, after having been humiliated by black players in Cuba in 1909, vowed never to play against blacks again. And he never did. The Tigers could have used him in this series as the Stars dominated the action. In the first game, St. Louis pushed over a single run in the first inning, and added three more in the second on a triple by Charlie Blackwell, a single by Branch Russell, a hit batter, and a base on balls. After Detroit tied the score with four runs in the top of the eighth, the Stars got the game-winner in the bottom of the frame on a daring steal of home by Frank Warfield.

St. Louis Stars

Name	Pos	AB	H
Russell	3B	4	2
Warfield	2B	4	1
Charleston	CF	4	2
Kennard	C	4	1
Blackwell	RF	4	2
McAdoo	1B	3	1
Hewitt	LF	3	1
Riggins	SS	3	0
Meyers	P	3	1
Manion	PH	1	0
Totals		32	11

Detroit Americans

Name	Pos	AB	H
Haney	LF	4	1
Cutshaw	2B	3	2
Blue	1B	2	1
Veach	CF	4	1
Jones	3B	4	1
Moore	RF	4	0
Rigney	SS	4	0
Woodall	C	4	1
Ehmke	P	3	0
		33	7

Detroit Americans	0 0 0	0 0 0	0 4 0—4— 7—?
St. Louis Stars	1 3 0	0 0 0	0 1 x—5—11—?

Overall, the exhibition games between major league all-star teams and Negro League teams was pretty even. In other series that year, the O'Neil All-Stars led by Joe Sewell and George Uhle, who was 22-16 with Cleveland in the season just completed, took two games from the Negro League Tate Stars, led by "Candy Jim" Taylor and Rev Cannady.

Uhle beat the Tates 5–2 in the opener of the series and came back to complete the sweep by outlasting the Stars 9–7 in the finale. In another exhibition game, the ABC's and the Cleveland Indians played to a 7–7 tie. The following year, Rube Foster's Chicago American Giants and the Detroit Tigers went 1-1-1 in a three-game series. The first game was called after nine innings with the game tied at 5–5. In game two, "Old Folks" Pillette (14–19) beat Tom Williams handily by a score of 7–1. Heinie Manush with two singles and a double provided the fireworks for Detroit. In the finale of the series, the Giants gained a measure of revenge when George Harney gained the decision over Hooks Dauss (21–13 for Detroit in 1923) 8–6. Harney was his own best offense as he accounted for four of his team's 11 base hits, one of which was a double. On October 21, "Bullet Joe" Rogan, pitching for the Kansas City Monarchs, defeated a major league all-star team by the score of 7–5. The Monarchs ace fanned 11 major leaguers and paced his team at the plate with a single, double, and triple. Zack Wheat and Hooks Cotter had three hits each for the All-Stars.

In 1926, one of baseball's legendary pitchers first crossed swords with Negro League players and his experience left him happy that the major leagues were not integrated at the time. The Hilldale Daisies, one of the top black clubs in the east, met Earl Mack's All-Stars in a two game series. In the first game, played in Wilmington, Delaware. On October 1, Phil Cockrell, a tiny right-handed spitballer, edged the Macks 3–2 on John Beckwith's long two-run homer in the eighth inning following a single by Biz Mackey. The next day, in Shibe Park, Lefty Grove, who had just completed his second season with the Philadelphia Athletics in the American League, faced Nip Winters, a big 6', 5", 225-pound southpaw who mesmerized batters with his sharp-breaking curveballs, and who was coming off a scintillating 23–4 season in the Eastern Colored League. Grove had just gone 13–13 for the A's after putting up a 10–12 record in his rookie season, but he would experience his breakout season in 1927, with a 20–13 mark after curbing his wildness, and reducing his bases-on-balls from 6 a game to 3 a game. In this game, although Grove walked only one man, he couldn't match pitches with Winters, who scattered seven base hits in a 6–1 victory. Otto Briggs, a speedy little outfielder, punched out three base hits, including a double, to pace the Hilldale attack. Winters, a .300 hitter himself, banged a single and a double, and Oscar Charleston made his only hit count as he hooked a Grove fastball into the right field stands in the 5th inning.

Hilldale Daisies

Name	Pos	AB	R	H
Briggs	RF	5	1	3
Warfield	2B	5	0	1
Mackey	C	4	0	1
Beckwith	SS	5	0	1
Charleston	CF	4	0	1
Johnson	3B	3	1	0
Thomas	LF	4	0	0
Carr	1B	3	2	1
Winters	P	4	1	2
Totals		37	6	10

Mack's All-Stars

Name	POS	AB	R	H
Dykes	3B	3	0	0
Padgett	SS	4	0	1
Manush	CF	4	0	1
Burns	1B	4	0	1
Miller	RF	4	0	1
Schang	C	3	0	1
Heimach	LF	4	0	1
McCann	2B	4	1	1
Grove	P	3	0	0
Perkins	PH	1	0	0
		34	1	7

5. Barnstorming

Hilldale Daisies	1 2 0	2 1 0	0 0 0—6—10—1
Mack's All-Stars	0 0 1	0 0 0	0 0 0—1—7—2

Doubles—Briggs, Winters, Beckwith, Carr
Home Run—Charleston

The American Giants met an old friend at Schorling Park on Labor Day weekend 1927 when they crossed swords with the Hammond nine, led by former Chicago White Sox third baseman, Buck Weaver, an unfortunate victim of the infamous Black Sox scandal in 1919. Weaver was banned from organized baseball for life by Commissioner Kenesaw Mountain Landis for knowing about the World's Series conspiracy and not notifying anyone about it. The *Defender* had this to say. "Sunday the local fans celebrated Buck Weaver day. [He] came with Billy Nelson's Hammond nine and received a warm welcome from the crowd.

"Buck handled seven chances in fine fashion, knocking down three hot drives that were labeled hits and throwing his man out at first."

Weaver had one hit in three at-bats, but his team was defeated by Willie Foster's club 5–3.

One month later, the Giants tangled with the Duffy Florals of the Windy City at Schorling Park on Saturday and at the Florals home ground, St. Rita's Field, on Sunday. And a familiar face was stationed at third base. Buck Weaver was brought in by the Florals to add another healthy bat to their lineup. The 5', 10", 170-pound right-handed hitter went 2 for 4 and scored a run in the weekend opener

Oscar Charleston, a .340 hitter in the Negro Leagues, is often called the greatest all-around player in Negro League history (author's collection).

as the Florals triumphed 8–5. The next day he had one hit in three at-bats as the Giants got even by the score of 7–5.

The Homestead Grays defeated the All-Stars in Fairmont, West Virginia, 9–5, in October 1928, with "Lefty" Williams beating George Uhle. And on the 28th, forty-two-year-old "Smokey Joe" Williams out-pitched Rube Walberg (17–12) in Sharon, Pennsylvania, before a crowd of 3500 as the Grays defeated the All-Stars by the score of 8–4. The Grays team included John Beckwith and Martin Dihigo, while the All-Stars were represented by Jimmie Foxx (.327) and Harry "The Horse" Heilmann (.328). As can be seen in the lineup below, every member of the all-star team was an active major league player. There is an obvious error in the box score for the number of runs scored by the Grays. The individual runs scored total 9 but the inning-by-inning score shows only 8.

All-Stars

Name	Pos	AB	R	H
Sweeney	1B	5	1	3
Hassler	SS	3	0	1
Foxx	3B	4	0	1
Heilmann	LF	4	0	0
Miller	CF	4	1	1
Uhle	RF	4	1	2
Woodall	2B	4	1	1
O'Neil	C	4	0	1
Walberg	P	4	0	0
Totals		36	4	10

Homestead Grays

Name	Pos	AB	R	H
Gardner	3B	4	3	2
Cannady	2B	4	2	3
Dihigo	CF	3	0	2
Beckwith	SS	5	1	1
Washington	1B	5	1	2
V. Harris	LF	4	0	1
Graham	RF	4	1	1
J. Williams	P	4	0	0
Ewing	C	4	1	1
		37	9	13

All-Stars   0 0 1   0 0 0   0 0 3—4—10—1
Homestead Grays   1 0 3   1 0 0   1 2 x—8—13—0

Doubles—Sweeney, Gardner, Hassler, Cannady, Washington, Dihigo, Uhle.
Triples—Beckwith, Ewing
Home Runs—Woodall

Pitcher	IP	W	L	H	SO	BB
Walberg	8	0	1	13	10	1
J. Williams	9	1	0	10	3	1

Six other games were scheduled in the series, but the results of those games have not been located. Other exhibition games saw the Hilldales defeat the major league Stars and 36-year-old Joe Bush 9–5, and the Black Sox beat the Philadelphia All-Stars and Lefty Grove 9–3. The Sox battered Grove, who had led the American League with 24 victories in 1928, for 11 base hits, including doubles by Rap Dixon, Frank Warfield, and Jud Wilson and a home run by Dixon. Grove, who once told John Holway that he had never played against blacks, hated to lose to a Negro League team, and was known to tear the clubhouse apart, board-by-board, after such a loss.

Joe Williams faced major league opposition more than two dozen times during his storied career, winning more than 70 percent of them. Some of his appearances against major league teams are listed here.

5. Barnstorming

Date	Williams' team	Score	Opposing team	Score	Comments
10/27/12	Lincoln Giants	6 (W)	Philadelphia Nationals	0	JW SO 9
11/ /12	" "	6 (W)	Chases All-Stars	0	
/12	" "	2 (W)	New York Giants	0	Hooks Wiltse LP
10/11/13	" "	9 (W)	Philadelphia Nationals	2	G.C. Alexander LP, SO 9 JW SO 6
10/25/13	" "	0 (L)	Philadelphia Nationals	1	JW SO 13
11/15/13	" "	2 (W)	Benders All-Stars	1	Al Schacht LP
10/11/14	" "	10 (W)	Philadelphia Nationals	4	
10/18/14	" "	1 (T)	New York Giants	1	Rube Marquard pitched for N.Y.
10/09/15	" "	3 (W)	Buffalo Feds	0	Schulz LP JW SO 9
10/16/15	" "	2 (L)	New York Giants	4	Jeff Tesreau (19–16) WP, SO 17 JW SO 6
10/17/15	" "	9 (W)	New York Giants	2	Pol Perritt (12–16) LP
10/06/17	Hilldale Daisies	6 (W)	All Americans	2	"Bullet" Joe Bush LP
10/27/17	American Giants	9 (W)	All-Stars	3	JW 6 IP, SO 1, W 2
11/03/17	Lincoln Giants	11 (W)	Benders Leaguers	1	Chief Bender LP, JW SO 6
10/04/26	Homestead Grays	6 (W)	All-Stars	5	Rube Walberg LP
10/ /28	Homested Grays	8 (W)	All-Stars	4	Rube Walberg LP
9/08/32	Pitts. Crawfords	8 (L)	Stengels All-Stars	20	Roy Parmelee WP JW 47 years old

There are also several oral traditions for games pitched by "Smokey Joe" Williams, although no box scores have yet been located. Two of these games are shown here.

1917	Lincoln Giants	1 (W)	All-Stars	0	Walter Johnson LP
1917	" "	0 (L–10 innings)	New York Giants	1	Williams pitched a no-hitter, striking out 20 men , but lost the game in the 10th on an error.

"Smokey Joe" Williams record in the above listed games shows 14 victories against 4 losses and one tie.

Williams also pitched against minor league teams and semi-pro teams many times over the years. In one game, on April 3, 1924, Smokey Joe, pitching for the Royal Giants, fanned 25 Brooklyn Bushwick players in 10⅔ innings before losing the game by a 4–3 count in the 12th. The 39-year-old legend relieved Pud Flournoy with two men out in the first inning after the Bushwicks had scored two runs and had the bases loaded. He fanned former Brooklyn Dodger outfielder Jimmy Hickman to end the inning, and proceeded to blank the Brooklyn team over the next 10 innings while registering 23 more strikeouts. But in the 12th inning, after the Royal Giants had taken a one-run lead in the top of the inning, the aging Williams ran out of gas, and the Bushwicks jumped on him for two doubles and a single, sending him down to a 4–3 defeat. The Bushwicks were one of the strongest semi-pro teams in the country during that period and routinely used Brooklyn Dodgers players, both active and inactive. "Brickyard" Kennedy, the Brooklyn Dodgers' greatest pitcher around the turn of the century, frequently made his services available to the Bushwicks to earn extra money, much to the chagrin of his major league manager.

In mid-October 1929, the Chicago American Giants engaged in a knock-down, drag-out, seven game series with a major league all-star team that included Charlie Gehringer, Heinie Manush, and Harry Heilmann. The Giants were loaded also, with Mule Suttles, Willie Wells, and "Cool Papa" Bell, and that cast was good enough as they took the All-Stars to task, three games to one. In the Saturday, October 12 opener, the pitchers on both sides, Huck Rile for the Giants and Willis Hudlin (17–15 for the Cleveland Indians in 1929), were battered from pillar to post, with the Giants scoring three runs in the bottom of the eighth inning to win the game 12–11. The batting stars were too numerous to count. Harry Heilmann banged out four base hits in five at-bats, Art "The Great" Shires had three including a double, and Charlie Gehringer had two hits including the only home run of the series. For the victorious Giants, Mule Suttles pounded out three hits including two booming triples, and "Steel Arm" Davis chipped in with two singles and a double, while a mixed-race crowd of 4,700 screamed with delight. The *Chicago Defender* reported on the exciting climax to the three-run Giants rally in the 8th inning. "Wells tripled to the right field fence and Gardner scored with the tying run, Wells sliding under the throw to third safely. A moment later, Wells electrified the crowd by stealing home with the winning run, kicking the ball out of Schang's hand." The next day, the Giants won again, 10–1, and once again Willie Wells sent the fans into a frenzy by rifling a triple to right field

"Smokey Joe" Williams compiled a record of 14 wins and 4 losses in exhibition games against major league opponents (courtesy John B. Holway).

"Cool Papa" Bell was a sensational center fielder, an outstanding hitter, and the premier base stealer of his day in the Negro Leagues (author's collection).

and then stealing home again, this time against Steve O'Neil. Willie Foster tossed a three-hitter for Chicago and struck out nine major leaguers along the way. Earl Whitehill (14–15 with Detroit) temporarily stopped the bleeding for the All-Stars on Monday by throwing a 1–0 shutout at the Giants, edging Frog Holsey (10–4 during the season). "Cool Papa" Bell said Whitehill was the toughest big league pitcher he ever faced. Wally Schang had three hits for the winners. The Chicago American Giants bounced back to take a 3 games to 1 lead in the series with a close 7–6 win in game four. The batting stars in the game were Gehringer and Sweeney for the All-Stars and Suttles and Wells for the Giants. Sweeney had three singles and a double, and Gehringer pounded out three singles and a long home run for the All-Stars. Willie Wells had two singles and a double, and Mule Suttles chipped in with a single, triple, and home run for the Giants. The winning run was scored in the bottom of the ninth on a single by Gardner, a stolen base, a passed ball, and a single by the omnipresent Wells. The fifth game of the series was won by the All-Stars 2–0 as George Uhle scattered five hits and Heinie Manush clubbed a home run. Willie Foster took the loss. The last two games of the series, scheduled for the following weekend, were not found. That same week, on October 13, the Lincoln Giants defeated Lou Gehrig's All-Stars at the Protectory Oval in the Bronx, New York, 6–3, before 8,000 baseball fans. Gehrig's lineup included "Baby Doll" Jacobson, George Kelly, and Andy Cohen, while the Giants had John Henry Lloyd, Bill Yancey, Orville Riggins, and Bill Holland. Holland outpitched Murphy for the win. In game two, Gehrig, who had once pitched for Columbia University, took the mound and defeated Red Ryan in a pitchers' duel by a count of 3–2. Bill Skiff knocked in all three runs with a bases-loaded single in the 1st inning. The Giants' two scores came on a double by Yancey.

A year later, the Chicago American Giants were taking three out of four from a major league all-star team at Giants Park in Chicago between October 3 and October 6. The Giants captured the opener 6–5 in 10 innings. Oscar Charleston's third hit of the night brought in the winning run. George Harney, in relief of Webster McDonald picked up the victory, while Earl Whitehill took the loss in a complete game effort. The All-Stars won game two 14–3 behind a non-major league pitcher named Streuss. Art Shires rapped five hits in six at-bats for the winners. Game 3 went to the Chicago team 6–1 as Willie Foster spaced nine base hits and fanned five. The game was highlighted by Putt Powell's four base hits including a double, Jim Brown's three base hits, and a double steal by Rap Dixon and "Steel Arm" Davis, with Dixon stealing home. Art Shires and Davis reportedly kept the stands in an uproar with their clowning antics throughout the contest. In the finale, a five-run rally by the All-Stars fell just short as the Giants prevailed 7–6. A minor leaguer named Cohen went the distance for the All-Stars while Satchel Paige hurled into the ninth inning for the Giants. The tall, lanky Negro League legend attempted a complete game effort himself but he was driven from the mound in the All-Stars 9th inning uprising. Rap Dixon paced the Giants with three base hits.

On October 4, 1931, the Homestead Grays humiliated O'Neil's All-Stars, led by George Uhle and Steve O'Neil, by a score of 18–0 before a crowd of 18,000 in Cleveland Stadium. Sam Streeter tossed a shutout at the big leaguers, while his teammates battered Uhle and Dutch Henry at will. "The feature of the game," according to the *Defender*, "was the pitching of Sam Streeter, the base running of Evans and Page, and the hitting of Dixon." Josh Gibson, the Negro League's 19-year-old slugging sensation, smashed two homers to pace the Grays' attack.

The same day, in Muehlebach Field in Kansas City, Missouri, more than 7,500 spectators watched the Monarchs, with Willie Foster on the mound, edge Cot Tierney's All-Stars, and Heinie Meine, by a 4–3 score. The Monarchs scored in the 3rd on a single by Newt Joseph and an error. They pushed over another marker in the 5th on singles by Joseph and Nat Rogers and a sacrifice fly. The All-Stars tied the game in the 6th on a double by Lloyd Waner, a walk to Kuhel and a single by Paul Waner, then took a 3–2 lead in the 8th on Lloyd's single and Paul's double. The game looked secure for Tierney's boys at that point, but fate stepped in in the bottom of the inning to change the ending. Dink Mothell doubled to get the inning underway but, after two men had been retired, Newt Allen hit a lazy fly ball to Lloyd Waner in center field for what should have been the game-ending out. It wasn't. Waner dropped the ball as a chorus of gasps escaped from the crowd. Mothell came around to score on the play, evening the match at 3–3. Then Tom Young ended the misery by singling through short to plate Allen with the game-winner.

One of the more famous exhibition games between major leaguers and Negro Leaguers took place in St. Louis, Missouri, three days later. The St. Louis Stars tangled with Carey's All-Stars, with Ted Trent, a 6', 3", 185-pound right-handed pitcher with a big curveball and a tantalizing slider, facing Heine Meine, who had just led the National League in victories in 1931 while compiling a 19–13 slate for the Pittsburgh Pirates. Trent came away the winner in a 10–8 slugfest as Meine was roughed up by the Stars, being raked for 10 runs on 12 base hits, including three runs in the first inning and three more in the third. The St. Louis pitcher held a comfortable 8–1 lead after seven innings, but tired down the stretch after throwing more than 130 pitches. He struck out a total of 13 big leaguers in the game, including the New York Giants slugger Bill Terry four times. Terry had batted .349 in the season just ended after leading the National League with a .401 mark in 1930, the Senior Circuit's last .400 hitter. Paul Waner (.322) and Babe Herman (.313) fanned twice each. In fact, every member of the All-Star team struck out at least once with the exception of Lloyd Waner, who fanned only once in every 45 at-bats during his major league career.

St. Louis Stars

Name	Pos	AB	R	H
Bell	CF	2	3	1
Giles	3B	5	2	2
Wells	SS	5	1	0
Suttles	LF	4	1	2
Zoumps	2B	4	2	2
Redus	RF	3	0	2
Creacy	3B	4	1	1
Barnes	C	4	0	2
Trent	P	4	0	0
Totals		36	10	12

Carey's All-Stars

Name	Pos	AB	R	H
L. Waner	2B	4	2	2
P. Waner	Cf	5	2	2
Herman	RF	5	0	1
Terry	1B	4	0	0
Walker	LF	4	0	0
Seimer	C	3	0	0
Peters	3B	3	1	2
Williams	SS	4	1	0
Meine	P	3	2	2
		35	8	9

```
Carey's All-Stars     000   010   0 3 4—  8— 9—?
St. Louis Stars       303   100   1 2 x—10—12—?
```

In 1932, the Major League All-Stars met the Pittsburgh Crawfords in a seven game series, much to their dismay. The Crawfords pummeled them five games to two. The major leaguers showcased such stars as Hack Wilson (.297), Woody English (.272), Johnny Frederick (.299 with a record six pinch-hit home runs), and Danny Taylor (.324), while the Steel City contingent included Josh Gibson (.303), Oscar Charleston (.313), Jud Wilson (.256), and Satchel Paige (21–9). As noted in the *Pittsburgh Courier*, "The series started at York, the Craws winning 11 to 2, with Swift and French losing to Bell; at Greenlee Field on Sept. 28, Joe Williams and Gisentaner lost to Parmelee and Frankhouse 20 to 8; at Altoona, Radcliffe and Bell beat French and Frankhouse 4 to 2; on Saturday, Satchel Paige beat Parmelee of the Nationals, 10 to 2 in the first game and Swift and French got revenge on Bell, Gisentaner, Tincannon, and Radcliffe, by winning 9–8." Paige, just coming into his own at the age of 26, embarrassed the major leaguers, holding them to six hits and striking out 15. Johnny Frederick of Brooklyn, and Woody English of the Chicago Cubs, each with a single and a double, had four of the Stars' six hits. Al Todd of the Phillies and Rabbit Warstler of the Red Sox had the other two. Other members of the All-Stars included Hack Wilson, Danny Taylor, Chick Fullis, and Tom Padden. Josh Gibson pounded out four base hits for the Crawfords, while Ted Page and Bill Perkins chipped in with two each. A doubleheader in Cleveland on October 6 brought the series to a climax, and brought the Craws two more victories. They took the first game 6 to 4 in 10 innings, and then completed the sweep with a 4–2 win in the nightcap before a crowd estimated to be 5,000.

Satchel Paige was the greatest showman, black or white, in the annals of professional baseball (author's collection).

Two years later, Chet Brewer pitched against a major league all-star team in Jamestown, North Dakota. The Big Leaguers had Jimmie Foxx, Heinie Manush, Doc Cramer, and Pinky Higgins. Brewer was opposed on the mound by Ted Lyons, who had just completed a respectable 11–13 season with the last place Chicago White Sox. Foxx had had his usual sensational season, hitting .334 with 44 home runs; Manush batted .349 with 42 doubles, 11 triples, and 11 home runs; Cramer batted .311; and Higgins came in at .330. Yet with all that firepower, Brewer short-circuited them on three hits, winning 11–0.

Satchel Paige toured with more major league all-star teams and faced more major league batters than any other Negro League pitcher. He also matched pitches with many of the Pacific Coast League teams over the years. On November 27, 1933, while pitching for Wilson's Elite Giants in the California Winter League, he pitched against Johnny Babich and the barnstorming Portland Beavers in White Sox Park, Los Angeles, and came away a 1–0 winner on a 4th inning home run over the center field fence by Willie Wells. The game featured brilliant fielding plays by the Negro Leaguers, including a sensational running catch by Bill Wright. Other players on the Elite Giants were "Cool Papa" Bell, Jim "Cannonball" Willis, Felton Snow, Turkey Stearnes, and Mule Suttles. Paige was touched up for five base hits, but fanned 13 Beaver batters. Babich, the unlucky loser, yielded only two hits, a single by Sam Bankhead and Wells' homer.

On February 7, 1936, Paige pitched for a local black all-star team in Oakland, California, against a major league all-star team loaded with the likes of "Rowdy" Dick Bartell, Gus Suhr, Chick Hafey, Augie Galan, and a 21-year-old outfielder for the San Francisco Seals by the name of Joe DiMaggio. Joe D., who was coming off a .398 season with the Seals, would tyrannize the American League a little more than two months down the road, on his way to a rookie season in which he would lead the American League in triples with 15 while batting .323 with 44 doubles and 29 home runs. It was a historic game, with Satch facing Brooklyn Dodgers right-hander Johnny Babich. The two pitchers matched each other strike for strike for nine innings. Then, with the game tied at 1–1 in the bottom of the 10th, Satchel was touched up for a two-out single by Dick Bartell, the first all-star hit in 6⅔ innings. After Bartell stole second base and went to third on a passed ball, DiMaggio beat out an infield hit scoring Bartell with the winning run. Later, Joe D. was quoted as saying, "I think I'm ready for the majors now. I got a hit off Satchel Paige." Paige held the All-Stars to five base hits, struck out 12 and hit three.

Several years during the '30s, Negro Leaguers and Dizzy Dean's All-Stars traveled together across the country, north and south, east and west, playing exhibition games and socializing far into the night, downing a few beers and swapping tall tales about baseball and other worthy pursuits. The games weren't exactly played on a level playing field however, since Diz and his brother Paul often teamed up with a bunch of local players to play against the powerful Kansas City Monarchs lineup. But they packed them in wherever they went, with Diz and Satch pitching three innings each, and Diz, who was probably the greatest major league pitcher of his era, was the main attraction. One game had to be called in the fifth inning because people were all over the outfield and getting closer to the infield, trying to get a look at "The Great One." Newt Allen said the crowd went home happy after seeing Diz up close, and the players pocketed $1200 apiece. Dizzy Dean was a regular guy as far as the Negro League players were concerned, but his brother Paul was a quieter individual who didn't mix in easily. In the mid-1930s, both Dizzy and Satchel were in their prime, both in their mid to late 20s. Dizzy ran up a record of 30–7 in the National League in 1934, and 28–12 the following year. Satchel was beating everyone he met. From 1934 to '36, he went 21–0 in the California Winter League, 20–5 in the 1934 Negro League, and 28–2 in Bismarck, North Dakota, for a total mark of 69–7.

In another game, Old Diz picked on a Satchel Paige hummer and lined it over first base and down the right field line for three bases. As Diz stood on third base grinning from ear to ear, the fans behind third screamed and yelled for several minutes. Finally Satch ambled over to third base and whispered to Diz, "I hope your friends brought a lot of food, Diz, because if they expect to see you score, they're going to be here until after dark." Then he turned, walked back to the mound, and fanned the next three batters.

Dizzy Dean was a backwoods boy from Arkansas and he used a lot of derogatory terms when referring to blacks, such as coon and nigger, but he never said them in a mean-spirited way. Dizzy didn't have a mean bone in his entire body. He was just being Dizzy. It was the way he was brought up and, unfortunately, it was common practice in the United States during the first sixty or seventy years of the 20th century to use derogatory terms when talking about other races and nationalities, but with no ill-feelings intended. Names like kike, frog, wop, polack, chink, cracker, harp, and pope-lover were nonchalantly thrown around by all races and nationalities. There were no innocent parties.

Dizzy Dean, in fact, admired the black players, particularly Satchel Paige, and he often complimented them. One time he said Satch was one of the greatest pitchers who ever lived, behind him and Carl Hubbell. Another time, he told reporters that if Satch pitched for the Cardinals, they would wrap up the pennant by July and go fishing the rest of the year.

In his biography, Buck Leonard remembered many games he played against Dizzy Dean. "I never got to know Dizzy and never talked to him. Neither he nor his brother Paul ever talked to us. I don't think they were prejudiced as far as that goes. They were there for the money and didn't care about anything else. They didn't care who they were playing. Both of us were just there for the money."

Willie Wells remembered playing against major league all-star teams in California in the 1930s, and he admired many of them. As he told Jim Riley, "Dizzy

Buck Leonard compiled a career batting average of .335 in the Negro Leagues with 15 home runs for every 550 at-bats (author's collection).

Dean and Lefty Grove, they were tough. I admired the way they could play." As Riley reported, "His admiration also encompassed the Detroit Tigers' great second baseman, Charlie Gehringer. 'Hot damn, he could play!' Willie says with respectful emphasis. Charlie Gehringer was beautiful. Newt Allen was about the closest one to him in the Negro leagues." Gehringer also got high marks from other Negro League players. George Giles said he was the best major league ballplayer he ever saw. He made everything look easy. The worst thing about the exhibition games, according to Giles, was the traveling. The major leaguers traveled in style during the 1939 tour, stayed in the best hotels, and ate in the best restaurants. The Negro Leaguers often changed clothes in the bus, while they traveled all night to the next town. They couldn't take a bath, and ate sandwiches much of the time. Finally Giles couldn't take it any more. He quit in the middle of the tour, and went home to be with his family.

John Holway's summary of Dizzy Dean's traveling show of 1934 uncovered 12 games between the Dean All-Stars and various Negro League teams, including the Monarchs, the Pittsburgh Crawfords, the Philadelphia Stars, and the Black Yankees, between October 7 and October 23. On October 21 in Cleveland, in a game won by the Craws over the Deans, Satchel struck out 13 of the 18 men he faced, probably all semi-professional players. On the 23rd in Pittsburgh, the game, which was won by the Craws 4–3, was interrupted by a free-for-all, initiated by Vic Harris who, upset by a ball and strike call, pulled the umpire's mask out and let it snap back on his face. Then all hell broke loose as catcher George Susce and several fans took dead aim on Harris. Oscar Charleston and Josh Gibson were in the center of the action that was finally brought to a conclusion by the intervention of Dizzy and Ted Page. And the game continued. In 1935, Diz and Satch squared off in Kansas City, with Diz winning 1–0. Actually, Dean pitched only three innings. He was followed by brother Paul, Mike Ryba, and Mort Cooper. Satch pitched a complete game.

The next year, Satch and Diz squared off in York, Pennsylvania, but Diz didn't have it on that day. The Negro Leaguers ripped him for four runs in the first inning on a grand slam by Josh Gibson, who put one of Dean's fastballs into orbit over the center field fence. Dean reluctantly turned the pitching chores over to someone else and went to the outfield. His team lost 11–0.

In 1937, Satchel's All-Stars played a ten-game series against Rogers Hornsby's All-Stars. Hornsby was 41 years old at the time, and had just played his last game in a memorable 23-year major league career, but he could still swing a dangerous bat, having hit .321 in his big league farewell. And Satchel felt the need to challenge him. When Hornsby came up to bat in the first game, in Davenport, Iowa, Satch blew him away with fastballs that old Rogers couldn't catch up to. He repeated the feat in Hornsby's second at-bat, and then "Pullman" Porter added insult to injury by fanning the baseball legend twice more although, in fairness to Hornsby, it should be noted that the game was played under the lights and the field was smothered in fog. The major leaguers finally persisted however, and won the game 2–1 on a fly ball by Johnny Mize that got lost in the fog. The Negro Leaguers won in Des Moines 5–3, although 18-year-old Bob Feller held them to one hit over the first three innings. They also captured a doubleheader from the major leaguers in Denver, and won again in Des Moines. The rest of the tour was cancelled. Hilton Smith pitched in three of the games for a total of 18 innings, and was never scored on.

In 1942, as Leonard told it, Satch's All-Stars met Dizzy Dean's All-Stars in Griffith

Stadium in Washington, D.C., with 22,000 fans jamming the park to see their heroes in action. Satch's team won going away but, as Buck noted, Dizzy was over the hill at that point in his life and hadn't pitched in the major leagues for several years. One thing that stuck in Leonard's memory was that in the exhibition games, black fans could sit anywhere they wanted to in the stands, compared to the regular season major league games where they could sit only in the black section. In exhibition games, if a black fan bought a box seat ticket, he could sit in the box seat, perhaps next to a white person. Integrated barnstorming games like these were the first steps toward an integrated society. They were, as Neil Armstrong said when he stepped on the moon, "One small step for man. One giant leap for mankind.'

In another game in 1942, Dizzy pitched against the Negro Leaguers in Wrigley Field, Los Angeles. His team included Zeke Bonura, Cecil Travis, and Buddy Lewis. Bonura was a big, hard hitting first baseman, but not much of a fielder. He averaged 19 homers for every 550 at-bats during his major league career. Travis, a .314 career hitter, was a potential Hall-of-Fame shortstop whose career was cut short by World War II. And Buddy Lewis was another .300 hitter who lost four years to military service in WWII. The three of them were in the service at the time, but were given permission by their commanding officer to play in the game. Dean pitched three innings in the game, and Satchel went five. Hilton Smith entered the game with the score tied at 1–1, and came away the 3–1 winner.

Bob Feller and Satch toured together in the late 1930s and 1940s. According to Feller, the two mound legends faced each other more than 20 times during their careers, and the outcome was usually a toss-up. Their first meeting probably took place in Des Moines, Iowa, on October 7, 1936, when the 17-year-old farm boy, having just completed his junior year in high school, tangled with the 30-year-old battle scarred veteran of ten Negro League campaigns. Five thousand fans packed the little park to see the legendary Paige in action. They were not disappointed. He held the Major League All-Stars to one hit in three innings and sent seven of them back to the dugout on strikes. And the fuzzy-cheeked Feller was just as impressive. He struck out eight batters and also yielded only one hit. The big leaguers finally won the game by a 4–2 score with Mike Ryba decisioning "Pullman" Porter.

On October 5, 1941, Feller out-pointed Paige 4–1 in St. Louis, but as was their habit, both pitchers departed after three innings. In another game, Feller's All-Stars hit Satchel hard and beat the Paiges 4–3. Hilton smith came in and quieted the big leaguer's bats, but it was too late. Feller pitched three innings and then Ken Heintzelman came on and shut the Negro Leaguers down for six innings. Four years later, with Bob Feller fresh out of the service, he and Satchel Paige resumed their post-season exhibition series, with two games in Los Angeles. Feller's team won both games, by scores of 4–2 and 2–1. The two aces pitched five innings in game one with Paige leading 1–0 when they departed. A festive crowd of 23,000 raised the rafters as "Pullman" Porter and Chet Brewer were treated harshly by the major leaguers. In game two, with 14,000 people looking on, the two gladiators went seven innings each, and this time the game was all knotted up at 1–1 when Feller and Paige hit the showers. Rapid Robert fanned 13 men in his seven-inning outing, while Satch countered with 8. Feller's All-Stars won the game 2–1 in 10 innings.

The next year, Feller and Paige assembled teams of the best players available from the Negro Leagues and the major leagues and traveled cross-country, playing a schedule of 12 games from New York to Los Angeles. Feller's team included Stan Musial, Charlie Keller, Phil Rizzuto, and Ken Keltner, and Paige countered with players like Hilton Smith, Hank Thompson, and Johnny Davis. The tour ran from September 29 to October 17, with Feller and Paige normally starting the games and pitching three innings each. Feller's All-Stars won the series 7 games to 5, and the two aces finished with identical records of 1–1. Johnny Sain went 2–0 for the Fellers and Mickey Vernon led the hitters with an average of .375. Buck O'Neil batted .333 for the Paiges and three different pitchers, including Smith, finished with 1–0 records. On October 5, before a crowd of 27,462 fans in Yankee Stadium, Paige hurled five innings, fanning four, and his all-stars blanked the major leaguers 4–0. Hank Thompson was the batting star with a double and a home run to right field off Rapid Robert. One week later, in Blues Stadium, Kansas City, Feller's All-Stars were leading Satch's Negro League All-Stars 2–0 with two runners on base, in the bottom of the ninth inning, when "Cherokee Johnny" Davis stepped to the plate to face Spud Chandler, on his way to a 20–8 season with the New York Yankees. Davis, a big 6', 2", 200-pound right-handed hitter, who would lead the Negro League with 8 home runs in 159 at-bats in '46, while batting a solid .340, put Chandler's fastball over the left field fence. On his way around the bases, Davis picked up Yankee shortstop Phil Rizzuto and carried him piggyback to third base. Then both men raced home and slid across the plate together.

In 1945, a Negro League all-star team called Mackey's All-Stars played a five-game series against Dressen's All-Stars, a major league team that included Ralph Branca, Virgil "Fire" Trucks, Red Barrett, Eddie Stanky, Frank McCormick, Tommy Holmes, Whitey Kurowski, Buddy Kerr, and Clyde Kluttz. Don Newcombe, on his way to the Brooklyn Dodger farm club at Nashua, New Hampshire, pitched for Mackey's team, as did Roy Partlow, and Bill Byrd. Other members of the Negro League team were future major leaguers Monte Irvin and Roy Campanella, plus Johnny Davis, Willie Wells, and Ed Stone. Newk and Partlow stymied Dressen's team for seven innings in the opener of a doubleheader in Ebbets Field on October 7, leaving with a 4–2 lead, but wildness on the part of Byrd allowed the major leaguers to score two runs in the eighth to tie the game, and Stanky's single in the ninth won it. Lennie Hooker, a right-handed knuckleball pitcher, out-pitched Branca in a five-inning abbreviated game in Newark, New Jersey, on the 12th. The final score was 2–1. Branca came back two days later to win a laugher, 10–2, backed by Kurowski's three base hits and Kluttz's three-run dinger. The series closed out with another doubleheader in Ebebts Field on October 14. Fire Trucks shut down the Negro Leaguers on four hits in the opener to win 3–1. Kerr banged a two-run triple in the bottom of the eighth inning to beak a one-all tie. The nightcap, called on account of darkness after five innings, ended up in a scoreless tie. Leafwich and Barret were the pitchers. Frank McCormick led all hitters with a .545 average. He and Willie Wells, who hit .400, were the only batters with 10 or more at-bats to hit over .300.

The next year, Satchel Paige's All-Stars traveled with Bob Feller's All-Stars, on a cross-country exhibition tour. Paige's team included Sam Jethroe, Hank Thompson, Quincy Trouppe, and Buck O'Neil. Their team was weakened when Jackie Robinson formed his own all-star team and hired a number of top Negro League players. Feller's team had Bob Lemon, Charlie Keller, Mickey Vernon, and Phil Rizzuto. The tour began in Pittsburgh, traveled through Ohio, Illinois, Iowa, Kansas, and ended in New York. Hilton Smith pitched two complete games on the tour, edging Bob Feller 3–2 and then losing 6–3. The two teams were evenly matched and played to overflow crowds wherever they went. Bob Feller's All-Stars beat the Paige team by a count of 6–5 in Chicago on the trip home on October 2. Both Feller and Paige pitched three innings. Gentry Jessup bested Johnny Sain in Baltimore 7–4 four days later. Then, on Sunday, October 13, 1946, Satch beat Feller 4–0. Both pitchers went five innings, with Satch leading 1–0. The Negro Leaguers added another run in the sixth off Spud Chandler, and raked the Yankees ace for two more runs in the eighth on a triple by Buck O'Neil. Hank Thompson's tape-measure home run in the fifth inning off Feller was the play of the day. A crowd of 27,402 fans crowded into Yankee Stadium to see the two baseball legends in action. It was a lucrative tour as well. Ken Keltner, who earned $12,000 playing for the Cleveland Indians during the regular season, picked up $6,000 for the tour, before Baseball Commissioner Kenesaw Mountain Landis ordered the tour ended.

Paige's All-Stars

Name	Pos	AB	R	H
Wilson	SS	3	1	2
Thompson	3B	3	1	2
Jethroe	CF	4	0	0
Davis	LF	4	0	0
Troupe	C	2	2	1
Easterling	2B	4	1	2
Benson	RF	4	0	1
O'Neil	1B	3	0	1
Paige	P	2	0	1
Stanley	P	2	0	0
Totals		**35**	**4**	**9**

Bob Feller's All-Stars

Name	Pos	AB	R	H
Rizzuto	SS	3	0	0
Berardino	2B	3	0	1
Vernon	1B	4	0	1
Keller	LF	4	0	1
Heath	RF	4	0	1
Chapman	CF	4	0	1
Keltner	3B	4	0	0
Chandler	P	1	0	1
Hegan	C	2	0	1
Hayes	PH-C	3	0	0
Feller	P	1	0	0
		33	**0**	**7**

```
Paige's All-Stars        0 1 0   0 1 0   0 2 0—4—9—1
Bob Feller's All-Stars   0 0 0   0 0 0   0 0 0—0—7—0
```

Doubles—Chandler, Thompson
Triples—Easterling
Home Runs—Thompson

Pitcher	IP	W	L	R	H	SO	BB
Paige	5	1	0	0	3	4	1
Stanley	4	0	0	0	4	5	1
Feller	5	0	1	1	4	0	4
Chandler	4	0	0	3	5	3	0

In 1947, Feller and Paige were at it again, but this time the Negro League team was called Brewer's All-Stars and the major league team went under the name of the Feller-Blackwell All-Stars. Brewer's Stars took the series, 3 out of 5. Feller and Paige started the opener, and Paige left after five innings, trailing 1–0. His team eventually lost 2–1 and he was tagged with the loss. The Fellers took game 2 by the same 2–1 score. Then in game 3, Satch pitched four innings, fanning nine men to go along with the eight he fanned in game 1, but this time he had a 2–0 lead when he departed. In the finale of the series, on November 3, the two adversaries locked horns in a challenge match, with

Feller challenging Paige to a 9-inning duel. The contest was one-sided with the Negro League legend winning easily 8–0 and sending 15 of Feller's men back to the bench dragging their bats behind them. Feller pitched 8 innings with 5 strikeouts. Overall, Satch went 1–1 in the series, and struck out an amazing 39 batters in 22 innings, an average of 16 batters for every 9 innings pitched. His opponent, Bob Feller, also went 1–1, but his strikeout totals have been lost, although he did fan 12 in 17 innings over one three-game stretch.

A partial summary of the Paige-Feller competition follows.

Date	Location	Winner	Paige Summary IP W L SO BB ER	Feller Summary IP W L SO BB ER
10/05/41	Sportsman's Park, St. Louis	Feller's AS, 4–1	4 0 1 4	4 1 0 1
10/02/45	Wrigley Field, L.A.	Feller's AS, 4–2	5 0 0 8 0	5 0 0 6 1
10/06/45	San Diego, CA.	K. C. Royals, 6–0	5 1 0 0	0 0 1
10/27/45	Wrigley Field, L.A.	Feller's AS, 3–2 (10)	7 0 0 8 1	7 0 0 13 1
09/29/46	Forbes Field, Pitts.	Feller's AS, 3–0	0 0 1	1 0
10/05/46	Yankee Stadium, N.Y.	Paige's AS, 4–0	5 1 0 4 1 0	5 0 1 0 4 2
10/07/46	Columbus, OH.	Paige's AS, 4–3	0 0	3 0 0 5 0
10/08/46	Dayton, OH.	Feller's AS, 7–6	3 0 0 5	3 0 0 1
10/09/46	Comiskey Park, Chicago	Feller's AS, 6–5	3 0 0 3 0 0	3 0 0 1 2 0
10/12/46	Kansas City, MO.	Paige's AS, 3–2	5 0 0 0	5 0 0 0
10/13/46	Wichita, KS	Feller's AS, 5–3		
10/16/46	Wrigley Field, Chicago	Feller's AS, 4–3	5 0 1 7 4 4	5 1 0 7 2 3
10/17/46	San Diego, CA.	Feller's AS, 2–0	5 0 1 2	5 1 0 2 0
10/18/47	Wrigley Field, L.A.	Feller's AS, 2–1	5 0 0 8 1 0	5 0 0 5 1 1
10/24/47	Wrigley Field, L.A.	Feller's AS, 2–1	4 0 1 7 1 1	4 1 0 2 1 0
11/30/47	Wrigley Field, L.A.	Royal Giants, 8–0	9 1 0 15 4 0	8 0 1 5 1 5
Totals			63 3 5 60 17 17	62 5 3 46 15 15

The pitching matchups are summarized below, on a per-game basis, using the above statistics.

Name	IP	SO	BB	ERA
Satchel Paige	9	13	3	2.35
Bob Feller	9	8	3	2.18

Some years, particularly in the 1920s and '30s, Negro League teams played exhibition games outside the geographical limits of the United States, in other countries of the Western Hemisphere and elsewhere. Several years they traveled more than 6,000 miles to the Far East, entertaining fans in Japan and other Asian countries, and conducting baseball clinics for the local ballplayers. They were among the United States' best good-will ambassadors in the early part of the century. The Philadelphia Royal Giants, with "Tank" Carr and Biz Mackey, left San Pedro, California, in February 1927 for a 19-day trip to Yokohama, Japan, on the *La Plata Maru*. During their two-month stay in Japan, the Giants played local teams in many cities, including Tokyo, Yokohama, Nagasaki, Kobe, Kyoto, and Osaka. They ran roughshod over the Japanese teams, running up a 23–0–1 record but, much to their credit, they tried to keep the score as close as possible so as not to embarrass their opponents. The Japanese appreciated that because they knew the Giants could win by almost any margin they wanted. One of the Japanese players said the Royals were real gentlemen, both on and off the field, unlike the major leaguers who visited the country several times during the '30s. Players like Babe Ruth and Al Simmons made a mockery of the game and humiliated the Japanese by their antics, both on and off the field. Ruth once carried an umbrella on the field at first base, Lou Gehrig played in galoshes, and Al Simmons laid down in the outfield, insinuating that no Japanese player could hit the ball that far. And off the field, the major leaguers, with Ruth leading the way, were a rowdy group while the Negro Leaguers were well behaved.

The Negro League players found the Japanese players to be fast runners and good fielders, but weak hitters and just average pitchers. The Japanese, on the other hand, were mesmerized by the skills of the Americans, who were much bigger, and more athletic, than the Japanese. According to one Japanese player, the Giants throws were "like arrows." The Japanese were also fascinated by catcher Biz Mackey firing the ball to second base like a bullet, while still in a crouch. And, of course, the power of the Philadelphia contingent amazed them also. Mackey, in fact, hit the first home run ever hit in Jingu Stadium in Tokyo, a park that had opened the previous year. In addition to the games, the Philadelphia players impressed their hosts by conducting clinics for Japanese players, concentrating on base running and throwing the ball.

In 1932-33, the Philadelphia Royal Giants returned to the Pacific area on a six-month exhibition tour, visiting the Philippines, Korea, and China as well as Japan. They compiled a record of 47–2–1, losing one game in Japan by a 4–3 count in 10 innings. William Ross won 16 straight games at one point, threw five straight shutouts, and fanned 63 men over his last five games. Mackey, who often played shortstop and pitched on the tour, in addition to his catching duties, led his team at the plate with an average of .388. He was followed by second baseman Javier Perez and left fielder Martin at .362 each, "Tank" Carr at .355, and Andy Cooper at .342. The Royal Giants set sail from Manila on December 1 to Los Angeles, where they were entered in the California Winter League.

The next year, the Giants had another successful junket to the Far East, once again visiting Japan, China, the Philippines, and Hawaii. The four-month tour included about 35 games against local opposition. The Giants visited Yokohama before leaving Japan, and were awarded a hero's welcome, with a parade and a banquet. William Ross, manager of the Giants, gave a lecture on baseball, after which he received one of the greatest ovations ever given to a ballplayer. The Japanese fans, who enjoyed the games as well as the instructional clinics conducted by the Royal Giants, were sorry to see the Negro Leaguers leave. On January 13, the Giants defeated the All-Filipinos in Manila by a score of 8–2, with Andy Cooper scattering seven hits for the victory. Cooper went 3 for 4 at the plate, including a double, to pace his team at bat. Mackey punched out 3 base hits in 5 times at bat.

In 1935, the Philippine fans first saw a major league all-star team, with Babe Ruth, Lou Gehrig, and Lefty Gomez, pound their heroes in three games. Then they watched in admiration as the Royal Giants put on a show for them. Chet Brewer, one of the Negro League's greatest pitchers, dazzled the fans with his finesse, his fine control, and his moving fastball. In five games against local all-star teams, Brewer tossed three shutouts and was touched up for single runs in the other two games. He allowed a grand total of seven base hits while striking out 42 men in 45 innings. According to the Manila newspaper, the consensus of opinion was that Brewer was a better pitcher than Lefty Gomez, who yielded three runs on seven hits in his only start. And Biz Mackey was rated much higher than the Philadelphia A's catcher, Frankie Hayes.

Over the years, statisticians, digging through musty newspaper files, uncovered more than 450 box scores of exhibition games played between Negro League teams and major league teams, and the results showed that the Negro Leaguers won between 60 percent and 70 percent of the encounters. With that scenario, imagine what the major league scene would have looked like if the leagues had been integrated over the entire history of major league baseball. Pitching won-loss records would probably be the same, but ERAs and strikeouts would be much different, with ERAs higher and strikeouts lower. Most batting statistics, however, would have changed dramatically, including batting averages, doubles, triples, home runs, runs batted in, runs scored, strikeouts, and bases-on-balls, which would all have been reduced significantly by the influx of Negro League pitching talent, with the exception of strikeouts, of course, which would have increased.

A review of the oft-quoted statistics, however, revealed that they were somewhat misleading. Competitions between Negro League all-star teams and major league all-star teams were common occurrences during the first half of the twentieth century and, for the first three decades, they were hard-fought battles by two groups with something to prove. Negro League players went all-out during the games to prove to the white players and their fans that they were as talented as the major league players. And the white players also played hard because, in that era, blacks were considered to be inferior to whites, both physically and mentally, and white players, particularly from the south, were humiliated when they lost games to black teams. As noted earlier, Ty Cobb, from Georgia, refused to play against blacks after being embarrassed by them in Cuba, Lefty Grove, from Maryland, who was beaten by Negro Leaguers several times in exhibition games, denied in interviews that he had ever played against them, and Buck Newsom, from South Carolina, said he couldn't go up the big leagues until he could beat "those niggers" in the California Winter League.

That attitude changed significantly during the 1930s and '40s. The Negro League players had the same mindset as before but the white players were beginning to appreciate the skills of the black players, and many friendships blossomed between blacks and whites as a result of the competitions. Many of the white players now looked on the games as an easy way to make a few extra dollars, they enjoyed the post-game socializing, and they didn't particularly care if they won the games or not. In addition, major league all-star teams were often headed by one high-visibility superstar like Dizzy Dean or Bob Feller, who were often supported by a group of minor leaguers or local amateurs. As a result, many of the statistics noted above were unreliable. Still, the Negro Leaguers did prove their point because in those games where a Negro League all-star team battled a true major league all-star team the Negro Leaguers held their own. John Holway, in his groundbreaking book, *The Complete Book of Baseball's Negro Leagues: The Other Half of Baseball History*, reported that he located 158 post-season games between Negro League teams and white major league all-star teams, defined by Holway as having at least five major leaguers including the pitcher in the lineup, and in those games the Negro Leaguers won 57 percent of the encounters. It was not a perfect solution, but it was close enough to be able to evaluate the skills of the Negro League players.

In the decades following the integration of organized baseball, the careers of Negro

League players have been reviewed in greater detail, and white baseball fans across the country have made a painful discovery. They missed seeing some of the greatest baseball players in history because of the major league's despicable segregation policy. They never had the opportunity to see players like Josh Gibson, Oscar Charleston, "Cyclone Joe" Williams, "Bullet Joe" Rogan or "Cool Papa" Bell, in action. And their loss is America's loss. Hopefully, that kind of situation will never occur again.

6

Puerto Rican Winters

Baseball came to Puerto Rico in the 1890s, brought to the country by the sons and nephews of a Spanish Army officer who was transferred from Havana to San Juan in 1890. As the game took hold on the Spanish-held island, political upheaval once again reared its ugly head. The Spanish-American War, that began in February 1898, brought American Marines to the island within months, and resulted in Puerto Rico being made an American protectorate. According to Jose A. Crescioni Benitez, the first recorded baseball game in the country was played on June 14, 1896, Borinquen defeating Almendares by a score of 22–11. The batteries for the inaugural game were Amos Iglesias and Jesus Cabanas for Borinquen and Caballero and Leon for Almendares. Ticket prices ran from ten cents for bleacher seats to forty cents for reserved seats in the shade. Two years later, on January 9, 1898, the two teams met again, this time on the San Juan Bicycle Course. Crescioni Benitez reported that the game actually took three weeks to complete. The first attempt was rained out after three innings and the second attempt was rained out after four innings. Finally, on January 30, the game was completed, but the result was the same as the first game with Borinquen defeating Almendares, this time by a score of 9–3.

As the new century approached, baseball teams began sprouting up in every village and town on the island, and soon professional teams were competing in tournaments on Sundays and holidays. The first Puerto Rican League was organized in 1901 with six teams, with players initially sharing gate receipts, and then playing for an agreed upon salary. In 1902, the Cuban Stars, the champions of the Negro Leagues, visited the island. By 1910, as reported by Crescioni Benitez, there were many new teams on the island including Savarona, Colectiva, Trolley, and Plata of Cayey and, as they traveled around the island displaying their talents before their rabid fans, they became Puerto Rico's first baseball heroes, with names like Ciqui and Fabito Farbell, William Guzman, Manuel Mutis, and Cholo Garcia.

In 1913, Leon Cadore, a member of the Detroit Tigers organization, accompanied a group of minor leaguers to Puerto Rico. Three years later, three foreign professional baseball teams converged on San Juan, two from Cuba and one from the United States. The Brooklyn Royal Giants met the Havana Stars and the Cuban Stars in a series of exhibition games, much to the enjoyment of the fans who flocked to the parade grounds at El Morro Castle, the Spanish fortification that dated back to 1539, to witness the professionals in action. Some of the most outstanding black players of the first half of the 20th century performed for the Puerto Rican fans in integrated games, including Luis "Mulo" Padron, one of Cuba's top pitchers as well as one of her top sluggers. Padron compiled a record of 39–23 on the mound during his Cuban League career, and he also led the league in home runs six times. Other black players of note included Strike Gonzalez, one of Cuba's all-time greatest catchers; Eustaquio "Bombin'" Pedroso, a Cuban legend who had tossed an 11-inning no-hitter at the Detroit Tigers in 1909; Jose Mendez, another Cuban pitching legend; Cristobal Torriente, Cuba's Babe Ruth; Louis Santop, one of the Negro League's greatest catchers; and "Cannonball" Dick Redding, another famous Negro League pitcher, as well as the white Cuban, Adolfo Luque, who would go on to win 194 games in the major leagues.

The Borinquen Stars traveled to Venezuela in 1918 for an exhibition tour. The team included Pedro Miguel Caratini, "Millito" Navarro, Ramon "Moncho El Brujo" Blondet, Chechon Vega, Tingo Daviu, and Benito "Juey" Torrens, recognized as the "Father of Venezuelan Baseball." After World War I more and more teams from the United States and Cuba visited Puerto Rico during their off-season. Among the best-known players to exhibit their talents on the island were white major leaguers Leon Cadore and Heinie Zimmerman, and black Cuban Leaguers Martin Dihigo and Alejandro Oms. Cadore, who won 68 major league games between 1915 and 1924, is best remembered as the Brooklyn Dodgers' pitcher in the longest major league game ever played, a 1–1 tie with the Boston Braves. Cadore pitched the entire 26 innings, yielding 15 base hits while striking out seven men and walking five. Zimmerman enjoyed a 13-year major league career as the third baseman in the famous Tinker to Evers to Chance infield. He led the National League in home runs in 1914 with 14. Dihigo, a Cuban legend, played baseball all over the Western Hemisphere between 1922 and 1947. Most of his career was spent in Cuba, Mexico, and the American Negro leagues, with brief stops in the Dominican Republic and Venezuela, and exhibition game visits to Puerto Rico. Oms' career spanned the years from 1917 to 1946, primarily in Cuba and the Negro leagues. Tetelo Vargas, arguably the greatest player from the Dominican Republic prior to 1950, was a regular in Puerto Rico from the late '20s until 1950, posting a career PRWL average of .320 for 16 seasons. In fact, after nine years in the winter league, the 41-year-old Vargas owned a career average of .368, all compiled after the age of 32. He went on to play seven more years in Puerto Rico as his skills gradually declined. Some of the legendary Puerto Rican players of the early period included Jacinto "Jayase" Hernandez, Monchile Concepcion, and Jose "Pepe" Santana.

The year 1918 was an important year in the history of Puerto Rican baseball. The most prominent men in the game met in San Juan and formed the Puerto Rico Baseball Association, combining the Insular League and the San Juan Baseball Association. George Villard, the director of the American Railroad Company, was elected the first president. Teams included Army, Fisk, the Mayaguez Cardinals, Pope, and the Ponce Lions.

Pedro Miguel Caratini, a great shortstop, was a noted home run hitter in Puerto Rico in the 1920s, but he is better known as a baseball pioneer, who traveled to the Dominican Republic as a mathematics teacher, and stayed around to play baseball and teach the game to the natives of the island during the '20s and '30s. Luis Alvelo, one of Puerto Rico's foremost historians, provided information about the early players. "Jayase" Hernandez played with the Humacao Stars and All-Borinquen from the mid-'20s until 1938–39. "He was a big, strong, colored outfielder who stood 6', 2" tall. He traveled to Santo Domingo with the Ponce Lions for a short series one year." Hernandez was one of Puerto Rico's first home run hitters, banging out home runs against the Cuban Stars and the Lincoln Giants. Monchile Concepcion played both the infield and the outfield during the 1930s. Although his records are unavailable, Concepcion was known as an excellent hitter. "Pepe" Santana, well known as "El Bambino," was tall and strong like "Jayase." He played first base in the mid–'20s and finished his career with San Juan in the early '40s. He played against some of the most famous teams of his time including Almendares, Ramirez Stars, Black Yankees, Cuban Stars, General Trujillo's famous 1937 Los Dragones, and the Havana Giants, as well as most of the American minor league teams that visited the country during the '20s and '30s such as York, Camden, and Newark. Another of the pioneers was "Millito" Navarro, an outstanding second baseman during the 1920s, '30s, and early '40s. He was the first Puerto Rican native to play in the Negro leagues, handling the keystone duties for the Cuban Stars in 1928 and 1929. The speedy, 5', 5", 160-pound Navarro was also a track and field star in his country, specializing in the hurdles and the sprints. He played six years in the Puerto Rican Winter League, retiring at the age of 37, following the 1943-44 season.

One of the greatest teams ever assembled, as reported by Eduardo Valero in *Puerto Rico's Winter League*, "was the *Concordia* from Venezuela, with Hall of Famers Josh Gibson, Satchel Paige, and Martin Dihigo, among other Latin stars like Tetelo Vargas from the Dominican Republic and 'Frank' Coimbre and Emilio Navarro from Puerto Rico." Many minor league teams visited Puerto Rico during the '20s and '30s to do battle with the locals, and their rosters included future major leaguers like Johnny Mize, Wally Moses, Paul Richards, and George McQuinn. Visiting teams from the Negro leagues included the Brooklyn Eagles, New York Black Yankees, and the New York Lincoln Giants, and they boasted some of the game's greatest players like Josh Gibson, Buck Leonard, Ray Dandridge, Leon Day, and Satchel Paige. George Scales was one of the first Negro Leaguers to visit Puerto Rico, spending the winter there with the Lincoln Giants in 1926. The Giants traveled the island playing exhibition games against Puerto Rico's finest teams including San Juan and Ponce with the great "Pancho" Coimbre.

In an effort to attract more foreign baseball teams to Puerto Rico, the government built a new stadium in San Juan in 1930, the Sixto Escobar Stadium, called the most beautiful stadium south of Washington, D.C. The park had a seating capacity of more than 13,000 people and was located near the beach. The new stadium attracted many foreign baseball teams including Almendares, Concordia, Licey, Ramirez Stars, and Azteca. Some of the game's greatest talents, such as Rodolfo Fernandez, Alejandro Oms, Martin Dihigo, Lazaro Salazar, "Cocaina" Garcia, Tetelo Vargas, and Ramon Bragana, showcased their skills on the grass of Sixto Escobar. In addition, many minor league teams took a working vacation to the land of sunshine. These included York, Richmond, Hazelton, Asheville, Akron, Camden, and Newark. Josh Gibson played with the Ramirez All-Stars in 1932. There is one newspaper account of a doubleheader played between the Ramirez team and the Brooklyn Royals, another touring Negro League team. The two teams split a doubleheader with the All-Stars out-slugging the Royals in the opener by a count of 9–6. The winning pitcher was Harry Salmon of the Homestead Grays, but he had to be bailed out by Harry Richardson and John "Neck" Stanley as the Royals fought back from a 9–1 deficit to make a contest of it. Brooklyn bounced back to take the nightcap 8–4 behind the pitching of Frank "Big Red" Blake and a 15 hit attack. Josh Gibson caught both games for the All-Stars, but there were no box scores identifying who delivered the big base hits. John Hayes caught both games for Brooklyn. Gibson made a habit of wintering in Puerto Rico during the '30s and early '40s. He loved the people, the weather, the money, and the facilities, and he went back year after year from 1932 to 1945 except for two years he spent in Cuba. He even brought his girlfriend Hattie Jones to Puerto Rico some years. The big slugger became a legend on the island in a relatively short period of time. His prodigious home run blasts were the talk of the country. And they were long—so long in fact that signs were nailed to trees to record his longest shots. One homer, perhaps his longest, was said to have traveled 600 feet or more, over the left field fence at Sixto Escobar Stadium, finally coming to rest near the beach. That homer was witnessed by Johnny Mize who said, "He was at second base when the ball cleared the fence."

On February 16, 1933, the Black Yankees and manager George Scales set sail on the Puerto Rico Line, headed for San Juan where they were conducting their spring training. As the *Pittsburgh Courier* reported, "They will stay until the first week of April playing exhibition games throughout the island just as soon as the boys round into shape. They are very much pleased with all the conditions they have encountered down there, and are already planning another invasion of the island in 1934." The players who made the trip with the Black Yankees included Jesse Hubbard, Ted Trent, Bill Holland, Clint Thomas, Crush Holloway, Connie Rector, Luther Farrell, Rev Cannady, Chester Williams, Dave Thomas, and Tex Burnett. Holloway was an early casualty, as he sprained his ankle in an early game and had to leave the lineup.

Another *Courier* article from Puerto Rico, dated December 16, 1933, was a letter from J. Francis Edwards, sports editor of *El Imparcial*, the noted San Juan newspaper, in which he told about the baseball season down there, and

> about the colored players from the "States" who are dazzling the natives with their ability. Among the colored boys are Tex Burnett, George Carr, Dick Lundy, Joe Dunn, Lefty Jones, Bill Holland, and John B. Johnson's Brooklyn Giants. Many white players of minor leagues are on the "Hazelton" club which is managed by George Hockette, star pitcher from the New York–Pennsylvania League. Lundy and his pals play on the San Juan White Stars, which also includes native players. Johnson's team is used intact.
>
> Games are played on Saturday and Sunday afternoons and on Sunday mornings. Lundy is the outstanding shortstop of all the clubs and leads in fielding percentages.
>
> The Escambron ball park, seat of all the games, was opened a year ago. It is located in the heart of San Juan, the capital. A quarter-mile running track encircles the playing field and track meets are held there by the various schools. The nearest fence is 380 feet from home plate.
>
> The Islanders take their baseball seriously and even the amateur teams attract thousands to their games. Trophies are awarded and a pretty girl is always named "Empress of the Baseball Season." With the closing of the leagues in the United States in the fall, the professional season begins.
>
> Different teams have been invited and have played series of games on the island in recent years. Last winter, you may recall, the Black Yanks went down for several weeks. The Concordias, Martin Dihigo's club in Venezuela, visited there for a series, as did the Almendares outfit from Havana.
>
> "Shine" Smith, one of the Bolden Stars staff last year, is back from San Juan. He was with Johnson's Brooklyn Giants, and other players on the team included Spearman, Capers, Ellis, Blake, Dunn, Bianchi, Paul Dixon, Jackson, Roach, Bergen, and Tom Dixon.

George "Tank" Carr played with the Santurce Crabbers during the winter, before returning to the States to play with the Philadelphia Stars. Another Philadelphia player in Puerto Rico that year was Slim Jones, one of the most promising pitchers of his era, but one whose problems with alcohol caused his career to end prematurely, with his tragic death from pneumonia at the tender age of 25. The 6', 6", 185-pound fireballer was credited with 210 strikeouts over the winter of 1933-34, but his total, although the highest total ever recorded in Puerto Rico, has not been recognized because at that time there were no official leagues, mostly weekly games and tournaments. During the '34 Negro League season, Jones ran up a record of 21–7, stuck out 112 batters, and compiled a total run average of 2.23.

Most of the Negro League players in Puerto Rico, as well as the visiting major leaguers, appreciated the rewards for playing baseball in the country while escaping the northern winters. As Van Hyning noted, "The U.S. players commented on the hospitality of the Puerto Ricans, the tasty food, the tropical weather and the beaches and recreational activities. They had fun while earning extra money during their off-season. Players had plenty of time for fishing, socializing in town plazas, and dinner at the homes of teammates, fans, and team officials. It was a common sight to see players mingling with fans in restaurants, bars, and movie theatres."

In the fall of 1934, Josh Gibson accompanied the Brooklyn Eagles to the island, along with Rap Dixon and Dick Seay. As Donn Rogosin wrote it, "The emotionalism of the Latin fans shocked even the Negro leaguers." "They were fanatics," laughed Dick Seay. "They'd throw oranges or lemons at us depending on whether they liked us or disliked us." Seay became so infatuated with the country and the people and the absence of discrimination that he made Puerto Rico his home after he retired from the game.

Luis Alvelo had a warm spot in his heart for the Negro League players who held baseball clinics for the youngsters in San Juan, visited the people in their homes, and brought toys to the children in the hospitals. Shortly after the 1934 visit by the Brooklyn Eagles, a new amateur league was formed with teams in Ponce, Caguas, San Juan, Aguadilla, and Santurce. Alvelo remembered the first game he attended in his hometown of Ponce. Willard Brown, who was known in Puerto Rico as "Our Babe Ruth," hit a tremendous home run over the left field fence that landed near the beach. In the same game, Puerto Rican legend "Pancho" Coimbre lashed out two singles and two doubles in four at-bats. The fans greeted the Negro League players after the game, with smiles and handshakes for Wilmer Fields, Bob Thurman, Bus Clarkson, Raymond Brown, and many more. Luis Alvelo also remembered that he had one of his first beers, an India. "That day it was like my birthday, beautiful day, good music, good memories, and a nice cold beer."

In the fall of 1935, Ray Dandridge led a Negro League all-star team, organized by Abe Manley, back to the island. His teammates included Buck Leonard, Ray Brown, Vic Harris, who managed the team, Ed Stone, Dick Seay, Frank Duncan, Slim Jones, and Leon Day. The team played games every weekend and on holidays through the winter, against teams like Ponce, and visiting teams such as Azteca from Mexico, and Almendares from Cuba. In early March the Eagles met the Cincinnati Reds, managed by Chuck Dressen, who were training in Puerto Rico. The Reds, with Paul Derringer, George McQuinn, and Kiki Cuyler, managed just one victory in four games against the Negro League club. Martin Dihigo, often called the greatest all-around player in Negro League

The Negro League all-star team before leaving for Puerto Rico in 1936. Back (left to right): Ed Stone, Slim Jones, Ray Brown, Rufus Lewis, Terris McDuffie, Buck Leonard, Johnny Hayes. Front row (left to right): Ray Dandridge, Dick Seay, Bill Sadler, Leon Day, Frank Duncan, Vic Harris (courtesy Dr. Lawrence Hogan).

history, handcuffed the Reds on three hits on March 5, winning 5–1. Cincinnati used four pitchers, including 19-game winner Paul Derringer, in a futile attempt to halt the Eagles barrage. Rodolfo Fernandez defeated Derringer 2–1 on a four-hitter in game 2. Afterward, he said, "You know how much I get for that game? Fifteen dollar." Hi Bithorn stepped in against the Reds on March 9, and blanked them over the first four innings while the Eagles built a four-run lead. The *Pittsburgh Courier* reported, "The Eagles leaped ahead in the first inning when Brown knocked a triple to center field, bringing home [Vic] Harris and Tetelo [Vargas]. In the third, Stone singled, bringing home Tetelo, and Brown, who had walked, took advantage of Myers' error to make the fourth run." The Reds pushed over a marker in the fifth on a triple by Calvin Chapman, and then netted three more in the eighth on base hits by McQuinn, Byrd, Myers, and Peacock, sending Bithorn to an early shower. The score was still tied at 4–4 in the bottom of the ninth inning when the Eagles plated the game-winner on a single by Veach that scored Dick Seay.

Cincinnati Reds

Name	Pos	AB	R	H
Chapman	RF	5	1	1
Riggs	3B	5	0	0
Cuyler	LF	5	0	1
McQuinn	1B	5	1	1
Campbell	C	5	0	1
Byrd	CF	5	1	1

Brooklyn Eagles

Name	Pos	AB	R	H
Harris	LF	5	1	0
Tetelo	SS	2	1	0
Leonard	1B	3	0	0
Brown	CF	3	1	1
Stone	RF	4	0	2
Dandridge	3B	4	0	0

Cincinnati Reds					**Brooklyn Eagles**				
Name	*Pos*	*AB*	*R*	*H*	*Name*	*Pos*	*AB*	*R*	*H*
Myers	SS	4	1	1	Duncan	C	3	0	0
Kampuris	2B	3	0	1	Seay	2B	4	1	2
Styne	P	0	0	0	Bithorn	P	2	0	0
Herrmann	P	0	0	0	Veach	P	1	0	1
Schott	P	0	0	0					
Hunt		1	0	0					
Scarcia		1	0	0					
Peacock		1	0	1					
Totals		40	4	8			28	5	6

```
Cincinnati Reds      0 0 0   0 1 0   0 3 0—4—8—3
Brooklyn Eagles      2 0 2   0 0 0   0 0 1—5—6—2
```

Doubles—McQuinn
Triples—Brown, Chapman

The Reds finally salvaged one game in the series when they beat the Eagles 3–2 on an error by Buck Leonard.

In the fall, the Negro Leaguers were back again, this time with Satchel Paige, Josh Gibson, Buck Leonard, and Jimmie Crutchfield. Leonard liked to winter in Puerto Rico because he could work on his game, and improve those areas he was weak in. As he noted, "That's another thing about winter baseball, you can practice whatever you're weak on. They'll send somebody out to the ballpark with you in the morning and you can hit for two hours if you want to. You can field for hours if you want to, and the local boys will help you out. They'll send two or three of them out there and they'll pitch to you just as long as you want to hit, or they'll hit ground balls to you just as long as you want to field. That is really how to improve your baseball skills, by playing winter baseball. Because at that time, they only played games on Saturday evening Sunday morning, and Sunday evening. All the rest of the time you could practice if you wanted to."

The official professional Puerto Rican Winter League was organized in 1938-39, and it has become the longest continually-running winter league in the Western Hemisphere. The owners of the six original teams, the San Juan Senators, the Ponce Lions, the Caguas Criollos, the Mayaguez Indians, the Humacao Oriental Grays, and the Guyama Witches, were determined to win the all-important inaugural winter league championship, and they set about to staff their rosters with the best players they could find. There was a flurry of activity over the summer of 1938 as the owners went on a recruiting campaign from New York to Caracas, with briefcases full of money. Negro League players were in the most demand, having showcased their talents in Puerto Rico as far back as 1913 as members of such touring teams as the Brooklyn Royal Giants, the Black Yankees, and the Lincoln Giants. In 1938 however, the owners discovered there was serious competition for the services of the Negro League players, particularly from Cuba where Negro Leaguers had been wintering since 1907. And the two greatest Negro League players were unavailable in 1938, as Satchel Paige was still recovering from a sore arm he had suffered in the rarefied air of Mexico the previous year, and Josh Gibson was committed to playing in Cuba. Still, the owners were able to attract several Negro Leaguers to their first season, including George Scales, Dick Seay, Jimmie Crutchfield, Jim Starks, and Eddie

Stone. And they recruited Raymond Brown from Cuba after he had pitched his Santa Clara team to the Cuban League pennant with an 11–7 record. The league also attracted celebrated players from other countries, like Alejandro Oms from Cuba and Tetelo Vargas from the Dominican Republic, and it showcased the great Puerto Rican stars Perucho Cepeda, Luis Olmo, and "Pancho" Coimbre. The season had many exciting games, including an 18-inning battle between the San Juan Senators and the Humacao Oriental Grays. Carmelito Fernandez of Humacao and Gerardo Rodriguez of San Juan matched each other pitch for pitch until the 18th when Humacao pushed over the deciding tally in a 2–1 victory.

The pennant race was close for a time, but Guyama's overall balance of pitching and hitting proved to be too much for their opponents to overcome and the Witches won the pennant by 5½ games over Humacao. Perucho Cepeda was voted the Most Valuable Player in the league after leading his team to the league championship. He led the league in batting, runs batted in, and base hits. Cepeda's teammate, Tetelo Vargas, the "Dominican Deer," led the league in runs scored and triples. Rafaelito Ortiz was Guyama's top pitcher with an 11–3 record, while Cefo Conde chipped in with 7 wins against 4 losses. The Witches went on to claim the world's semi-pro championship when they defeated the Duncan Cementers from the United States in a September playoff series. Rafaelito Lopez tossed two shutouts at the American champions, one of them a six-inning no-hitter called because of rain, and Guyama took the series four games to two.

Other Negro Leaguers made their marks in the statistics race in Puerto Rico's inaugural season. Dick Seay showed the way in stolen bases with 33 in 163 at-bats, Raymond Brown was the top pitcher (7–0) and the ERA leader, and Eddie Stone was the home run leader with 9 in 148 at-bats.

Perucho Cepeda and "Pancho" Coimbre, both Hall-of-Fame caliber players, were in their sunset years when the Puerto Rican professional league began. Roberto Clemente once said that Coimbre was a better player than he was, and would have been one of the best major league players ever if he had had the opportunity to play in the majors. Pancho hit .337 in 13 seasons in the PRWL although he was already 30 years old when the league was organized. He also hit .377 in the Negro leagues in 616 at-bats, and .346 in 356 at-bats in Mexico. The happy-go-lucky Coimbre just loved playing baseball, and he was once quoted as saying, "Baseball is in the heart of all Latin people. They feel in baseball. They think in baseball." And he thought baseball all the time. In the 1942-43 season, he won the batting title with an average of .342, and two years later, at the age of 35, he captured his second batting title, hitting .425 in 109 at-bats. The secret of "Pancho" Coimbre's success with the bat may lie in the fact that he had one of the best batting eyes of any player in history, striking out only 20 times in 1750 at-bats, an average of just 6 strikeouts for every 550 at-bats. At the same time, he walked 99 times for every 550 at-bats. In Mexico, he fanned just 12 times for every 550 at-bats, with 48 bases on balls.

Perucho Cepeda, the father of major league star Orlando Cepeda, was 32 years old in 1938, yet he batted .325 for eleven seasons in the PRWL. In fact, he was an even more prolific hitter than the record shows. During his first four years in the league he averaged .411. If he had enjoyed the benefit of a long career beginning when he was in his early 20s, he probably would have compiled a career batting average in the .350 range. The long-ball hitting shortstop, appropriately enough, won the first two PRWL batting championships, with averages of .465 and .386, while pacing the Guyama Witches to the league championship both years, with records of 27–12 and 39–17 respectively. He also led in RBIs and base hits both years, and in triples in 1939-40.

The Guyama Witches of the early years of the winter league were one of the best teams in Puerto Rican Winter League history. In addition to Perucho Cepeda, they also had Tetelo Vargas and Alejandro Oms in the outfield and Cefo Conde and Rafaelito Ortiz on the mound. Vargas blistered the ball at a .415 clip in 1938-39 and .363 in 1939-40, and he led the league in triples in 1938-39 with 9, and in runs scored both years. Ortiz paced the league's pitchers with 11 victories in 1938-39. The next year, the Witches had the benefit of Satchel Paige, and he didn't disappoint. The Negro League legend won the league's MVP award by going 19–3 on the mound with 208 strikeouts in 205 innings, setting all-time Puerto Rican League records in victories, strikeouts, and innings pitched. He endeared himself to the fans in his first game when he blanked the Santurce Crabbers by the score of 23–0. In another game, Paige fanned 17 Mayaguez batters in a 1–0 victory over Bud Barbee. Tetelo Vargas scored the game's only run. Paige

Francisco "Pancho" Coimbre was one of the greatest hitters and outfielders in Puerto Rican baseball history. He hit a solid .337 (#2 all-time) over a 14-year Puerto Rican Winter League career (courtesy Yuyo Ruiz).

didn't return to Puerto Rico for eight years after his record-setting performances, preferring to stay in the United States and barnstorm with major league all-star teams. Buck Leonard told John Holway about one incident that took place when he played for the Mayaguez Indians.

> We had three men on base in the first inning, two out, and Bus Clarkson, the shortstop, came to bat. Satchel told the catcher to get out from behind the plate, he was going to walk him. The catcher said, "No, you can't walk him, three men on base, you're gonna walk a run home." Satchel said, "Well, I'd rather walk a run home than have him hit three or four home, so let's walk him." The manager came running out: "No, no, don't walk him, don't walk him." Satchel said, "I know what I'm doing." So the catcher stepped out to the side and Satchel threw four balls and the run scored. Satchel said, "Now, that's all you're gonna get today." And that's the only run we did get. He beat us about 8–1 or something.

Raymond Brown was another of the great Negro League pitchers who would have made outstanding major leaguers if they hadn't been denied the opportunity by the heinous organized baseball segregation agreement. Brown, a 6', 1", 195-pound right-handed pitcher was a noted curveball pitcher, but he also owned a live fastball as well as a sinker and a slider. The Dayton, Ohio, native, a 2006 Baseball Hall of Fame inductee, starred not only in the Negro Leagues and Puerto Rico, but also in Mexico and Cuba. His career won-loss records included 46–20 in Cuba, 51–36 in Mexico, 116–34 in the Negro leagues, and 12–10 in the U.S. minor leagues when he was 43 years old. Raymond Brown pitched for San Juan in the Puerto Rican Winter League in both 1938–39 and 1939–40, going a perfect 7–0 both years. He led the PRWL in earned run average the second year with a miniscule 1.05. Brown's overall record in 1938–39 was one for the ages. In addition to going 11–7 in Cuba and 7–0 in Puerto Rico, the husky right-hander pitched the Homestead Grays to the Negro National League pennant with a 15–0 record during the summer of 1938, giving him an overall record of 33–7. In 1941-42, pitching for the pennant winning Ponce Lions, Brown earned his $500 salary, a figure that was much higher than the average salary commanded by the American players. He went 12–4 on the mound and once again led the league in ERA, this time at 1.80. He also played the outfield when not pitching and stole 12 bases. Five years later, the crafty sinker ball specialist was credited with a victory over the New York Yankees as Ponce jumped all over Yankees pitching for 12 big runs sending 5000 fans in Sixto Escobar Stadium into a frenzy. Brown held the Bronx Bombers in check until the 8th inning when he turned the reins over to Jose Santiago. The final score was 12–8. Ray Brown's PRWL career totals for six years show 40 victories against 20 losses and a 2.16 ERA for 496 innings pitched. Partial statistics credit him with a .292 batting average. His career pitching record in all leagues was 277 wins against 129 losses for an outstanding .682 winning percentage.

The 1939-40 season was much more successful from a recruiting standpoint, as the owners attracted even more foreign players to their winter league. The Negro League contingent included, in addition to Satchel Paige and Raymond Brown, Leon Day, Silvio Garcia, Josh Gibson, Bill Byrd, Dick Seay, Clarence Palm, Ed Stone, Roy Partlow, Gene Benson, and Bill Perkins, Paige's favorite catcher.

Leon Day pitched for Aguadilla during the 1939-40 season, recording a 12–11 won-loss record for a team that could win only 21 of 55 games. Day racked up 186 strikeouts in 207 innings, while registering a 2.17 ERA. In addition to his pitching, he batted a cool .330. And he was impressive from the very beginning. On opening day, in October, he blanked the Santurce Crabbers 6–0. On January 7, 1940, he faced Bill Byrd of Santurce in one of the great pitching duels in Puerto Rican Winter League history. Aguadilla scored on the spitball ace in the first inning, but they would get no more. The Santurce Crabbers tied the score at 1–1 in the fourth, and Byrd and Day settled down to a long Sunday afternoon in the sun. The goose eggs piled up inning after inning, until the sun set in the west and the umpire called the game on account of darkness. The final score of the 18-inning game was 1–1, and Leon Day had struck out 19 batters over the course of the day.

Silvio Garcia pitched for Ponce that same year, going 10–6 with a league-leading 1.32 ERA. He also hit .298 with 24 RBIs in 124 at-bats. That was his only season in Puerto Rico. He spent the remainder of his winter league career in his Cuban homeland. Garcia was a world-class shortstop who played all over the Western Hemisphere for 17 years, compiling a .284 batting average and covering the infield like a blanket. His limited pitching record included three full seasons, one each in Puerto Rico, Cuba, and Mexico, and his won-loss records of 10–6, 10–2, and 10–2 respectively support his reputation as an outstanding all-around player.

Josh Gibson was player-manager of the Santurce Crabbers in 1939. The big slugger who hit .380 with a league-leading six home runs in 150 at-bats was an imposing figure to opposing players according to Van Hyning: "Mayaguez infielder Nica Bayron recalls rounding third, trying for an inside the park homer, and seeing Gibson set to crouch, 'He looked like a monument to me. I sort of stopped, and got a close look at him. He was so impressive.'" "Millito" Navarro, a third baseman for Ponce, admitted, "I was trembling when Josh Gibson came up. I hoped and prayed he wouldn't hit one towards me. Those shots of his were rockets. Luckily, none were hit in my direction." One of Gibson's moon-shots, the famous 600-foot wallop, landed in the ocean beyond the left field fence.

The Guyama Witches raced to the pennant once again, as noted above, with Cepeda, Oms, and Vargas supplying the power, and Paige, Conde, and Ortiz, pro-

Josh Gibson was selected as the league's Most Valuable Player in 1941-42 after hitting .480 with 13 home runs in 123 at-bats. Luis Rosario, Jr., sports director of the newspaper El Imparcial, hands Gibson his trophy (courtesy Luis Alvelo).

viding the pitching punch. The triumph wasn't that easy, however, as the San Juan Senators with Raymond Brown, Roy Partlow, Clarence Palm, and Gene Benson challenged them every step of the way. The final standings showed Guyama with a 39–17 record and San Juan just one game behind at 38–18. Ponce was another five games in arrears.

In the fall of 1940, the Negro League exodus to Puerto Rico was more impressive, and the quality of play got even higher. Buck Leonard, often called the Negro League's Lou Gehrig; Roy Campanella, the Baltimore Elite's 19-year-old catching sensation; Bus Clarkson, a power hitting shortstop; Monte Irvin, who would later star with the New York Giants; Dave Barnhill; Lenny Pearson; and Ted Young; plus Partlow, Palm, and Byrd, all joined the winter festivities in Puerto Rico.

Roy Campanella remembered those days in his autobiography.

> I got an offer to play ball with the Caguas club in the Puerto Rican Winter League. I was interested. Not only would I be working at my trade, I'd be paid a lot more than anything I might be doing around home. I went down there with a couple of teammates, Lennie Pearson and Bill Byrd. It was my first trip across water, and I sure enjoyed it. Down there with

the fences way off, nobody was hitting those home runs so easy. I hit eight that winter to beat out Buck Leonard, a veteran Negro League first baseman built like a wrestler. Before that, the most homers hit in one season was six, by Josh Gibson.

I learned to speak some Spanish in Puerto Rico. Not so much for social as for baseball purposes. Few of those Latin-American pitchers spoke English. So I had to learn their lingo to understand how they thought.

That winter set the blueprint of my life for the next seven years. Baseball in the United States each summer, baseball in the tropics each winter. I was playing the game fifty of fifty-two weeks.

In his free time, Campanella was drawn to the water. "I enjoyed being a beach boy. There's no prettier blue and green water anywhere than the Caribbean. Another thing we used to do a lot in Puerto Rico was fish. Not only off a pier for pan fish, but deep-sea fishing too. Many's the time I caught dolphin that weighed better than forty pounds, and sharks too. But I never did tie into a tuna or a sail."

Campy played for the pennant-winning Caguas team that finished with a 27–15 record. He batted a respectable .263 and led the league with 8 home runs in 171 at-bats. The Criollos, the first-half winner, met Santurce, the second-half winner, in the postseason playoffs to determine the league champion. Caguas was down three games to two in the series, and Santurce was leading 2–1 in the fifth inning of the crucial sixth game, when Campanella came to bat with the bases loaded. The roly-poly backstop took a Luis Cabrera curve ball downtown, sending it over the left field fence to give his team a 5–2 lead. After he crossed the plate his teammates hoisted him on their shoulders and carried him back to the dugout while the fans stuffed money through the fence, as was the custom at that time. Campy's hit was the beginning of a 14-run rally that gave his team the momentum they needed and they went on to take the series, four games to three.

Several other Negro League players had successful seasons also. Bus Clarkson played for Mayaguez and led the league with 48 runs scored in 148 at-bats. Monte Irvin played shortstop for the San Juan Senators, and rapped the ball at a torrid .371 clip in 159 at-bats. Buck Leonard, with Mayaguez, batted .390 with a league-leading 17 doubles and 8 home runs in 118 at-bats. And Leon Day, pitching for Aguadilla, a team with a 19–22 record, went 10–6.

The 1941-42 season saw another bevy of Negro League stars descend on Puerto Rico. Roy Campanella was back again, and he was joined by Ray Dandridge, Willard Brown—who would electrify the Puerto Rican fans with his long home runs, earning him the sobriquet "Our Babe Ruth"—"Wild Bill" Wright, Willie Wells, Dan Bankhead, Dan's brother Sam Bankhead, Barney Brown, Ray Brown, Monte Irvin, Bus Clarkson, Leon Day, Lenny Pearson, Quincy Trouppe, Billy Byrd, and Terris McDuffie. The addition of such talented players as the preceding group, in support of the already outstanding array of native stars such as Perucho Cepeda, "Pancho" Coimbre, Cefo Conde, Rafaelito Ortiz, Jorge Tirado, and Luis Olmo, plus the "Dominican Deer," increased the level of play in the Puerto Rican Winter League to a near–AAA level. The reputation of the league continued to increase over the next decade to the point where, after Jackie Robinson integrated organized baseball, major league teams would begin sending their most promising rookies and their top farmhands to the league to perfect their craft.

My book *Baseball's Other All-Stars* reported, "Puerto Rican baseball historian Luis Alvelo called the '40s the 'Golden Age' of baseball in Puerto Rico. Perhaps from a fans-player relationship standpoint, Alvelo is correct. Certainly the Negro League players endeared themselves to the people of the island. As Alvelo noted, 'They filled the park with music and unforgettable moments.' They played major league quality baseball, and they took time to instruct the youngsters in the finer points of the game, visited fans in their homes, and brought toys and good cheer to the children in the hospitals. Just as in Japan, the Negro League players were some of America's most effective goodwill ambassadors."

Ray Dandridge spent the winter of 1941-42 romping around the infield for the Santurce Crabbers, exciting the crowds with his dazzling fielding and daring base running. He had a good season, but the team did not. He stung the ball at a .288 clip in 104 at-bats, but Santurce could do no better than tie for fifth place with a 21–23 record. Dandridge spent most of the next decade in Cuba, but returned to Puerto Rico in 1953-54 to take the place of Bus Clarkson, who had been suspended for spitting at an umpire. The forty-year-old Dandridge still covered the infield superbly, but his bat had declined to the point where he could do no better than a .232 batting average. Still Ray had fond memories of the island. "I remember the oceans, the way the sun used to do this little dance off it, and how beautiful they treated us. No money."

One of the highlights of the 1941-42 season was the All-Star doubleheader between the Northeast All-Stars and the Southeast All-Stars. The Northeast team included Roy Campanella, Josh Gibson, Monte Irvin, Ray Dandridge, Willard Brown, and Billy Byrd. Manolo Garcia, an outfielder on the Northeast team, remembered the performance of Josh Gibson that day, as reported by Tom Van Hyning: "Garcia still remembers Gibson's two homers in the afternoon game off Leon Day and Barney Brown. 'After Gibson hit the one off Day, he just laughed as he rounded the bases. Later in the game, I got a hit off Barney Brown. Gibson hits another one, and keeps laughing.'"

Many of the Negro League players, including Leon Day, Willie Wells, Josh Gibson, Bill Wright, Roy Campanella, and Monte Irvin, found themselves stranded in Puerto Rico after the Japanese bombed Pearl Harbor on December 7, 1941. They were refused permission to fly home at the end of the season, and sea travel was dangerous because the Germans were torpedoing ships all over the Atlantic Ocean, but Wright and Campanella booked passage on a ship anyway, according to Van Hyning: "'For eight days we were on that boat, only had cold lunch food,' Wright later recalled. 'One day Campanella said we ought to put all our money in a bottle and throw it overboard—since we weren't going to make it anyway. But we did get to Newport News.'"

Josh Gibson, who played for Santurce, had a career season in Puerto Rico in 1941-42, leading the league with a stratospheric .480 batting average, 13 home runs in 123 at-bats, and a .957 slugging average. His .480 batting average and .957 slugging average are all-time records for the league. The batting race that year had one of the most fantastic finishes in the annals of professional baseball. According to Alvelo, "On January 12, 1942, [Willard Brown] was leading the league with .441; Gibson trailed in ninth place with .355. 'Heh, Trouppe,' Gibson said. 'I'm not going to try to hit any home runs. I'm just going to try to bat .500.' A week later Josh had moved into third place with .412 to Willard's .456. By February 9 Josh had shot into first place, .460 to .402 for Brown. 'You know what he ended up batting?' Trouppe demanded. 'Four seventy-nine! He was hitting screamers through the infield.' Josh's record still stands, having withstood the challenges of such great latter-day hitters as Willie Mays, Roberto Clemente, Tony Oliva, and

Orlando Cepeda." The 30-year slugger was at the peak of his legendary career at this time, and he was voted the league's Most Valuable Player, receiving his trophy from Luis Rosario, Jr., the sports director of El Imparcial newspaper at a banquet at the end of the season. During the following 1942 Negro League season, he hit .323 with a league-leading 11 home runs in 121 at-bats, and the next season he absolutely destroyed Negro League pitching. He led the league with 190 at-bats, 99 base hits, 32 doubles, 8 triples, 14 home runs, a .995 slugging percentage, and a .521 batting average.

Sam Bankhead, who played with the pennant winning Ponce Lions, managed by George Scales, batted .351 with 16 doubles in 168 at-bats. The hard-hitting shortstop returned to the island twice more, compiling a career batting average of .311. Raymond Brown was the ace of the Ponce pitching staff, posting a 12–4 record and leading the league in ERA at 1.80. The Ponce team also had the benefit of Howard Easterling, but for the most part they were a Puerto Rican team, and they went on to win four successive pennants between 1941-42 and 1944-45. In the 1941-42 season, "Pancho" Coimbre batted .372 with a league-leading 46 runs scored. He went on to lead the league in batting in 1942-43 with an average of .342 and repeated the feat again in 1944-45 with an average of .425. In 1943-44 he was second with an average of .376. He also led the league with 27 RBIs and 20 stolen bases in 1943-44. Cefo Conde led the league in victories with 10 in 1942-43 and Tomas Quinones was second with 8. Rafaelito Ortiz ran up a perfect 15–0 slate in 1943-44, and Quinones came back with a 16–3 mark a year later. Ponce was awarded the league championship in 1941-42, 1943-44, and 1944-45 without a playoff. They defeated Santurce 4 games to 1 in the 1942-43 final, thereby claiming four straight league championships. After finishing in second place in 1945-46, the Indians rebounded in 1946-47 to take yet another league championship, defeating Caguas 4 games to 3 in the final series. They were led by three Puerto Rican pitchers, Juan Guilbe (5–4), Tomas Quinones (9–4), and Jose "Pantalones" Santiago (8–2).

Leon Day went 12–9 with Aguadilla in 1941-42, with a league-leading 168 strikeouts in 199 innings and a 2.93 ERA. He also hit a sizzling .351 and, in the process, ducked many bean balls thrown at him by opposing pitchers, particularly other Negro League pitchers. As Day related it to "Jim" Riley, "Me and old Chet Brewer got in a knockdown duel. Chet Brewer threw hard, and he was knocking my men down ... boom! boom! boom! I said, 'That's alright,' and I went out there and started knocking them suckers down ... boom! boom! boom! I'd knock them down. So the next inning, he'd knock us down. And I'd knock them down. So I came to bat and I said, 'I know Chet ain't going to throw at me because I'm pitching.' You know, that sucker almost hit me in the *head*! I just did get out of the way! 'You had to have guts if you were going to play,' his Newark buddy, Ray Dandridge says of their style of play."

Twenty-seven-year-old Quincy Trouppe, a catcher with Guyama, led the league with 10 triples and 57 RBIs. Monte Irvin of San Juan showed the way in doubles with 18 in 158 at-bats. Bus Clarkson of Mayaguez was the stolen base leader with 18 in 156 at-bats. "Wild Bill" Wright, with San Juan, batted .280 in 157 at-bats. It was Wright's only season in Puerto Rico. He lived and played in Mexico most of his career after 1940, although he did venture north occasionally to play in the California Winter League until 1945. Barney Brown led the league's pitchers with 16 victories in a 16–6 season for the Guyama Witches, but it wasn't enough for his team to overtake the pennant-winning Ponce Lions. Willie Wells scorched the ball at a torrid .378 clip in 106 at-bats. Roy Campanella, who had been taught the fine points of catching from the Negro League's greatest defensive catcher, Biz Mackey, had an outstanding season behind the plate for Caguas, and he batted .295. His home run total was down from his league-leading performance the previous year but in one game he crushed two home runs in the same inning, both off Dave Barnhill. Francisco "Pancho" Coimbre, the pride of Ponce, led the league in runs scored with 46 in 164 at-bats.

Many Puerto Rican players had sensational seasons in 1941-42. Perucho Cepeda slugged the ball to the tune of .377, while Jorge Tirado began a catching streak that has not been duplicated. He caught every game for the Ponce Lions from 1941-42 through 1944-45. The pitchers were led by Juan Guilbe who went 11–2. Rafael Ortiz was 8-4, and Cefo Conde was 8–8.

Organized baseball was beginning to take notice of the Latino players as the 1940s got underway, and several Puerto Rican baseball players joined the major leagues during the next decade. The first Puerto Rican native to play in the major leagues was Hiram Bithorn who pitched for the Chicago Cubs between 1942 and 1947, winning 34 games and losing 31. His biggest year was 1943 when he won 18 games against 12 losses for the Cubs. Bithorn pitched in the winter league for five years between 1938 and 1943. Luis Olmo, who would play in the PRWL for 16 years, joined the Brooklyn Dodgers in 1943, beginning a six-year major league career. Olmo batted .281 in 1629 at-bats during his career, and hit .273 with a home run in the 1949 World Series. Luis Marquez, a 20-year winter league veteran, played in the majors in 1951 and 1954. Ruben Gomez, who pitched an amazing 29 years in the Puerto Rican Winter League, compiling a record of 174–119, enjoyed a 10-year major league career between 1953 and 1967, primarily with the New York Giants. He won 76 games during his career against 86 losses. His best year was 1954 when he went 17–9 with a 2.88 ERA during the season, and went on to win Game 3 of the World Series by a score of 6–2, as the Giants swept the Cleveland Indians in four.

Juan "Chico" Sanchez was an outfielder, with Santurce, Aguadilla, and Mayaguez-Aguadilla in the 1940s. He was an excellent hitter who hit over .300 most of the time. In addition to playing in his own country, Sanchez played minor league baseball in the United States with New Orleans in the Class AA

Luis "Canena" Marquez batted .300 over a 21-year Puerto Rican Winter League career (courtesy Yuyo Ruiz).

Southern Association. According to Alvelo, Sanchez was a real gentleman and a great clutch hitter. When his team needed a run, Sanchez was there. He was a member of 1940s All-Star team.

"Cherokee Johnny" Davis, an outfielder-pitcher, tossed a no-hitter in 1944, and led the league in home runs with 9 in 256 at-bats in 1951-52. Davis was a double threat in Puerto Rico between 1945 and 1949, averaging more than 20 home runs for every 550 at-bats, and putting together seasons of 7–4, 12–7 and 10–9, on the mound.

In 1945-46, Mayaguez and San Juan captured the split-season titles, and the Senators beat the Indians four games to two in the post-season playoff to determine the league champion. Fernandez Diaz Pedroso, the flashy, Cuban infielder edged Monte Irvin for the batting title by .0007, .3684 to .3677. Pedroso, Irvin, and Sam Bankhead, tied for the lead in home runs with 3. Tomas Quinones of Ponce led all pitchers with 10 victories.

The next year, the Ponce Lions roared back from a second place finish in the first half of the season to capture the second half with a record of 18–12, giving them the best overall record of 38–22, three games better than the Caguas Criollos. And Ponce went on to win the league championship by beating Caguas 4 games to 3 in the post-season playoff. Willard Brown, the 6', 200-pound right-handed slugger, came into his own in 46-47. He led the league in batting with an average of .390, edging Monte Irvin by three points. He also led the league in base hits with 99 and runs batted in with 50. From that point on, Brown would dominate the league's slugging statistics for the next five years. And in 1947-48 he had a career season. He led the league in batting with an average of .432, 22 points higher than Bob Thurman. He also set the pace in runs scored with 79, runs batted in with 86, and home runs with an all-time league record 27. He went on to lead the league in home runs the next two years with 18 and 16 respectively, and in 1949-50 he also led with 117 runs scored, 97 RBIs, and a .353 batting average. The following year he once again led the league in RBIs with 76 while hitting

Willard Brown, the foremost slugger in PRWL history, was fondly known as "Ese Hombre" ("That Man") in Puerto Rico (courtesy Yuyo Ruiz).

.325 with 14 home runs. Willard Brown played in the Puerto Rican Winter League ten years, and still holds two impressive records. He has the highest career batting average at .350, and he has the highest career home run average, with 30 home runs for every 550 at-bats.

Bob Thurman, another of the excellent Negro League players in the Puerto Rican Winter League, played 12 years, with a .313 career batting average. He also has the most career homers with 120 to Brown's 101, averaging 27 homers for every 550 at-bats. And Puerto Rican native "Pancho" Coimbre has the second highest career batting average, .337 for 13 years.

In February 1947, the mighty New York Yankees arrived in Puerto Rico for a series of exhibition games against the Puerto Rican Winter League teams. After defeating the San Juan Senators and the Caguas Criollos, Bucky Harris and his Bronx Bombers traded bats with the Ponce Lions at Charles H. Terry Ballpark in Ponce on February 25. It was not a happy day for New York

Bob Thurman holds the career record for PRWL home runs with 120 over a 14-year career (courtesy Yuyo Ruiz).

as a three-run home run by Fernando Diaz Pedroso off Yankees fireman Joe Page in the sixth inning provided the winning margin in a 12–8 Ponce victory. Raymond Brown started on the hill for the Lions and held the New Yorkers in check until the eighth inning when they tallied four times, helped along by three Ponce errors. Jose "Pantalones" Santiago, who would see limited action with the Cleveland Indians seven years later, set down five Yankees to preserve the victory. The game drew 5,000 spectators and record headlines in the *New York Times* as the proud Bombers weren't used to losing to anybody, let alone a semi-pro team from Puerto Rico. The Yankees went on to split the final two games against a Puerto Rican All-Star team, ending the tour with a 3–2 record.

In league play, the Lions produced the best record, winning 38 games against 22 losses to edge the Caguas Criollos by three games. In the post-season playoff, the Lions, with manager George Scales at the helm, trailed the Criollos three games to none before catching fire. They roared back to sweep a doubleheader from the Criollos on Sunday, March 8, 1947, and repeated the feat against a stunned Caguas team the following Sunday to capture the league championship, four games to three. No other team has ever come back from a 3–0 deficit to win the title. The Ponce fans were particularly proud of their team's achievement because it was accomplished with an all-Puerto Rican roster except for second baseman Fernando Diaz Pedroso and third baseman Howard Easterling. The pitching chores were handled by Jose "Pantalones" Santiago, Tomas "Planchardon" Quinones, and Juan Guilbe, who went a combined 25–10 during the season.

The 1947-48 season saw the result of Jackie Robinson's integration of organized baseball, as white players from the U.S. major league organizations began to filter into the winter league rosters. Two of the first players to winter in Puerto Rico were Ken Sears and Dwayne Sloat, hardly household names, but players from organized ball nevertheless. They were followed by Earl Naylor, Ellis "Cot" Deal, Mike Clark, Pete Wojey, Earl Harrist, Charlie Gorin, Bert Thiel, and Walt Judnich. That would change in a few years, and by the mid–1950s, the Puerto Rican Winter League had gained a reputation as a high quality professional league that could help major league teams develop their talent faster by having them play baseball year-round. Soon, the names of the white players from organized baseball who were refining their skills in Puerto Rico became more easily recognizable. One of the Negro League players who traveled to Puerto Rico in the fall of 1947 was Wilmer Fields, who arrived in San Juan on a Friday and pitched 11 innings in a 4–0 victory over Mayaguez, tripling along the way. The next day, he pitched the final four innings to pick up a save. Lorenzo "Piper" Davis was also in the league that year, playing for Caguas, and the slick second baseman hit .303 with 10 home runs in 188 at-bats, a career number of homers for the singles-hitting infielder. And Negro League right-hander Ford Smith, pitching for Caguas, led the winter league in victories with 13. He would lead the league again the following year, again with 13 victories.

The 1948-49 Mayaguez Indians have been called one of the greatest teams in Puerto Rican Winter League history. Their 51–29 record gave them the pennant by four games over the Ponce Lions. And their victory total was the second highest in league history to the 1950-51 Caguas Criollos' 57 wins. The Indians had an abundance of Negro League talent including Artie Wilson, Luke Easter, Alonzo Perry, Wilmer Fields, and Johnny Davis. Big Luke Easter, a 6', 4", 240-pound powerhouse, coming off a sensational season with the Cleveland Indians where he slugged 28 homers and drove in 107 runs while batting .280, was even more impressive in Puerto Rico as he sparked his team to the pennant. He led the league in batting with an average of .402, and he also showed the way in runs scored with 81 in 80 games, in doubles with 27, and in triples with 9. He was second in RBIs with 80, third in stolen bases with 15, and third in home runs with 14. But Easter was not a one-man team. He had a lot of help. Artie Wilson led the league in base hits with 126, he was third in batting with an average of .373, and third in runs scored with 69. Alonzo Perry was second in runs scored with 76, second in doubles with 24, second in triples with 8, and fourth in stolen bases with 14. The big first baseman also doubled as a pitcher, and ran up a record of 11–4 on the mound to pace the Indians pitching corps. Cefo Conde was 10–6.

Mayaguez also had the benefit of the league's Most Valuable Player, Wilmer Fields, a pitcher-third baseman-outfielder. The 6', 3", 215-pound muscleman was a power pitcher with a live fastball in the 90 mph range, supplemented by a curve and a slider. According to Van Hyning, a player of Field's ability could make $700 a month, possibly more. Wilmer and his wife Audrey flew from New York City to San Juan in a two-engine plane, not expecting the trip to turn into a 15-hour ordeal. The enthusiasm and friendliness that greeted them and stayed with them over the course of Fields' four-year career in

Puerto Rico made up for the trouble in reaching San Juan. In 1947-48 Fields pitched and played third base and the outfield for San Juan, batted .315 and went 6–6 on the mound. In one game he homered twice off Satchel Paige in Sixto Escobar Stadium in San Juan and the fans showered him with money, a common practice in Latin America. Fields pulled $125 through the wire mesh screen behind the plate. As a pitcher, he once pitched two games within 24 hours. The first game, a night game against Mayaguez in 1947-48 when Fields was with San Juan, ended in a 2–2 tie. The next day, he was beaten 2–1 when "Cherokee Johnny" Davis drove in the game-winner in the 11th inning. Fields bemoaned the fact that San Juan was a weak-hitting team that was difficult to pitch for. He was lucky if he got more than two runs a game to work with. That was probably one reason why he signed with the Mayaguez Indians for the 1948-49 season. The Senators finished the season in fourth place in the six-team league with a 26–34 record.

In 1948-49 Wilmer Fields, with Mayaguez, hit .332, led the league with 88 RBIs, and went 10–4 on the mound to help the Indians to the league pennant. He was rewarded with the league's Most Valuable Player trophy in recognition of his outstanding season. In the Caribbean Series, the Indians faced the tough Almendares Scorpians of Cuba with Al Gionfriddo, Monte Irvin, Sam Jethroe, and Chuck Connors. The Scorpians swept the series in six games, but Fields hit the first home run in Caribbean Series history in 1949 in Havana. He was given an electric razor and $50 in cash for the historic feat. Fields hit .326 and went 8–7 on the mound in 1949-50, and a year later, he hit .323 as a full-time outfielder. During his four-year PRWL career, Fields batted a solid .325 with 15 home runs for every 550 at-bats, and went 24–17 on the mound.

A typical game for the 1948-49 winter league champions, played on November 18, 1948, matched the Indians against the Caguas Criollos, a talented team with Tetelo Vargas, Quincy Trouppe, and Gene Baker. Bill Powell, a 6-foot, 2½ inch, 195-pound right-hander, coasted to a 16–6 victory in a game called after six innings. The box score does not agree with the line score for Mayaguez, which was not unusual for the time.

Mayaguez

Name	Pos	AB	R	H
Wilson	SS	3	1	1
Perry	1B	5	0	0
Bernier	RF	5	0	0
Easter	LF	3	3	1
Fields	3B	4	1	3
Villodas	C	3	1	1
Rosas	CF	4	3	3
Polanco	2B	2	3	0
W. Powell	P	4	1	4
Figueroa	P	0	0	0
Totals		33	13	13

Caguas

Name	Pos	AB	R	H
Haddock	3B	2	0	0
Baker	SS	3	0	1
T. Vargas	CF	3	0	0
Davis	2B	3	1	1
Trouppe	C	2	1	0
V. Power	1B	3	1	1
O. Cordero	C	1	0	1
Thon	RF	1	1	1
Alomar	RF	0	0	0
Pena	PH	1	0	1
Albertson	PR	0	0	0
Anglero	LF	2	1	2
Bin. Torres	P	1	0	1
R. Vargas	P	0	0	0
R. Perez	P	0	0	0
Cabezudo	P	0	0	0
R. Lopez	PH	1	0	0
Totals		24	6	8

Mayaguez Indians	2 1 5	0 6 2—16—13—0
Caguas Criollos	0 4 0	2 0 0— 6— 8—3

Doubles: Bernier, Fields, Rosas, Powell.
Winning Pitcher: W. Powell
Losing Pitcher: Bin Torres

By the 1948-49 season, the winter league was playing an 80-game schedule, and new ballparks were being built around the island as reported by Tom Van Hyning: "By 1949-50 several new ballparks had been built, with lights for night games, and attendance had surpassed the 750,000 mark. The new stadiums were Caguas's Sola Morales (6,744 capacity), Mayaguez's Isidoro Garcia (6,718 capacity), and Ponce's Paquito Montaner (9,718 capacity). The novelty of the new lighting systems spurred attendance. Caguas's dedication December 14, 1949, consisted of eight towers and 508 bulbs." The Sixto Escobar Stadium in San Juan, which was built in 1930 with a seating capacity of more than 13,000, was shared by the Senators and the Crabbers. It was replaced by Hiram Bithorn Stadium, with a capacity of 20,000, in 1962-63.

The 1950-51 pennant went to the Caguas Criollos with a record of 57–20. The Santurce Crabbers finished second with a record of 48–30 and they met the Criollos in the finals of the post-season tournament. The seven-game series was tied when the two teams met in the seventh and deciding match in San Juan's Sixto Escobar Stadium on February 16, 1951, with 16,713 screaming fans keeping the air electric. Santurce nursed a 2–1 lead into the late innings when Bus Clarkson homered off Luis Cabrera to deadlock the game. It was still 2–2 when Santurce came to bat in the bottom of the ninth inning. Mike Clark, who had led the league with 14 victories during the season, retired the first two men to face him, the dangerous Willard Brown who had led the league in runs batted in (76), and was second in home runs (14), and Bob Thurman, who finished third in batting (.309), third in runs batted in (66), and third in home runs (13). The next batter was Jose St. Clair, and he put an end to the tension by sending Clark's fastball into orbit. Lew Burdette, who would go on to stardom with the Milwaukee Braves during the 1950s was Mayaguez's top pitcher.

Al Smith, who later became famous when a fan spilled a cup of beer on him while he was positioned in left field during the 1959 World Series, played for Ponce from 1951 to 1954, compiling a batting average of .274 based on 180 base hits in 658 at-bats with 30 doubles, 13 triples, and 18 home runs. He led the league in homers in 1951-52 with 9. Smith batted .272 in a 12-year major league career after hitting .292 in three years in the Negro Leagues. Another Negro League veteran on his way to the major leagues held down the hot corner in Puerto Rico in the early '50s. Chuck Harmon fine-tuned his game with the Ponce Lions during the 1953-54 winter league season, prior to breaking into the Cincinnati Reds lineup. He scorched the ball at a .327 clip in 269 at-bats, against some exceptionally strong pitching. As he told Brent Kelley, "They had a lot of hard throwers down there. Bob Turley and Arnold Portocarrero were down there and Jack Harshman, left-hander for the White Sox, and Karl Spooner, left-hander for the Dodgers. We had Jack Sanford, Steve Ridzik. Howie Judson who pitched for us here pitched for the Reds. It was a really good league and that made it almost sure I was gonna make the Reds."

Tom Van Hyning noted, "Mayaguez sportswriter Rafael Soler Rivas recalls one day [over the winter of 1954-55] when rain was pouring down in Mayaguez and Mays and Thurman challenged Soler Rivas and a partner in dominoes, one of Puerto Rico's favorite pastimes. Rivas remembers Mays jumping up and down after he and Thurman won a hand. 'It was something to see ballplayers like Mays act so spontaneously off the field. They gave it their all on the field, and to see them mingle with us the way they did, was special.'"

Another of the winter league's most outstanding teams took the field in the fall of 1954. The Santurce Crabbers, a formidable blend of Puerto Rican players, Negro Leaguers, and major leaguers, may have been the greatest winter league team ever assembled, although you could get an argument from the fans in Cuba who consider the 1923-24 Santa Clara Leopards to be the greatest ever. But it would be hard to bet against the Crabbers whose roster included two future Cooperstown Hall of Famers and two members of the world champion New York Giants. Roberto Clemente, who was on his way to his rookie season in the National League, held down one of the outfield spots. His fellow gardeners were Bob Thurman, a 37-year-old baseball veteran who was also about to enter the major leagues as a rookie, and Willie Mays, the "Say-Hey Kid," who had led the National League in batting (.345) and triples (13) in 1954. He and Ruben Gomez were also members of the world champion Giants who swept the Cleveland Indians in four straight. Mays became an immediate legend after making the impossible back-to-the-plate catch of a long drive off the bat of Vic Wertz in the eighth inning of Game 1 of the World Series. And Ruben Gomez, a 17-game winner during the regular 1954 National League season, defeated the Cleveland Indians 6-2 in Game 3 of the Series. Other members of the Santurce Crabbers included Bus Clarkson, Don Zimmer, and George Crowe in the infield, Valmy Thomas and Harry Chiti behind the plate, and Sam "Toothpick" Jones on the mound. Crowe would go on to a successful 9-year career as a slugging first baseman for the Milwaukee Braves and Cincinnati Reds, while Sam Jones was about to embark on a 12-year National League career that included a 21–15 record with the San Francisco Giants in 1959.

The Santurce Crabbers won four successive Puerto Rican Winter League pennants between 1954 and 1957, compiling records of 47–25, 43–29, 43–29, and 36–28 respectively. The Crabbers dominated the individual winter league statistics in 1954-55, with Mays capturing the batting championship with an average of .395, and Roberto Clemente finishing fourth with an average of .344. Bus Clarkson led in RBIs with 61, edging out teammate Bob Thurman by one. Clemente led in runs scored with 65 and Willie Mays came in second with 63. Clarkson finished second in home runs with 15 and Bob Thurman was third with 14. Mays showed the way in triples with 7 and was second in doubles with 15. Sam "Toothpick" Jones led all pitchers in victories with 14, in strikeouts with 168, and in ERA with 1.77. Ruben Gomez was second in victories with 13 and second in strikeouts with 107. The Crabbers went on to take the measure of the Caguas Criollos in the post-season playoff series, four games to one.

The Crabbers then capped a perfect season by winning the 1955 Caribbean Series championship in dramatic fashion. Willie Mays, fresh off his National League and World Series achievements, broke out of an 0–12 slump by crushing an 11th inning home run off Ramon Monzant with Roberto Clemente on base to give his Santurce team a 4–2 victory over Magallanes of Venezuela, who were graced with major leaguers "Chico" Carrasquel, Bob Skinner and Jim Lemon.

Magallanes

Name	Pos	AB	R	H
Carrasquel	SS	4	1	2
Lohrke	2B	4	0	0
R. Wilson	RF	3	0	0
Skinner	1B	4	0	0
Lennon	CF	4	0	0
L. Garcia	3B	4	0	0
Finol	LF	4	0	0
Rubinstein	LF	0	0	0
St. Clair	C	3	1	0
Monzant	P	3	0	1
Totals		33	2	3

Santurce

Name	Pos	AB	R	H
Clemente	LF	5	2	2
Zimmer	SS	5	0	1
Mays	CF	5	1	1
Clarkson	3B	4	1	2
Thurman	RF	4	0	1
Crowe	1B	4	0	1
Chiti	C	4	0	0
Sanford	2B	4	0	1
S. Jones	P	3	0	1
		38	4	10

```
Magallanes    1 1 0   0 0 0   0 0 0   0 0—2—3—0
Santurce      1 0 0   1 0 0   0 0 0   0 2—4—10—1
```

Two Base Hits: Zimmer
Three Base Hits: Crowe
Home Runs: Clemente, Mays

Pitcher	IP	W	L	H	SO	BB
Monzant	10	0	1	10	3	1
Sam Jones	11	1	0	3	9	7

Mays went on to hammer 14 base hits in his last 19 at-bats, to spark Mickey Owen's team to the Caribbean World Series championship with a 5-1 record. Shortstop Don Zimmer, known as "El Soldadito" or "The Little Soldier," led the series with 3 home runs, and was voted the Series' Most Valuable Player, the third straight year a Puerto Rican player had received that honor. Rocky Nelson of Cuba's Almendares Club won the batting championship with a .471 batting average. Mays led in RBIs with 9. And Bill Greason of Santurce went 2–0 on the mound.

Willie Mays never returned to Puerto Rico, but Roberto Clemente went on to a brilliant 15-year career in his homeland, capturing the batting title in 1956-57 with an average of .396, and playing on two pennant winners with the San Juan Senators in 1958-59 and 59-60. Bus Clarkson enjoyed an 11-year career in Puerto Rico, compiling a career batting average of .301 with 98 home runs in 2063 at-bats. He led the league with 18 home runs in 261 at-bats in 1950-51. George Crowe played in the PRWL three years, batting a torrid .337. In 1951-52 he hit .335 and led the league in three categories, RBIs with 70, doubles with 23, and home runs with 9.

As the 1950s progressed, the number of white major league prospects who spent their winters in Puerto Rico increased. Dale Long, a hard-hitting major league first baseman during the 1950s got his baptism of fire on the island in 1953-54. Bob Buhl and Karl Spooner pitched there in 1953-54. And Tommy Lasorda, Ed Roebuck, and Sandy Koufax all saw action in the PRWL. Other white players of note who played in the Puerto Rican Winter League during the '50s and '60s included Frank Howard, Sam McDowell, Jim Northrup, Denny McLain, Johnny Bench, and Thurman Munson.

At the same time, the number of Negro League players in Puerto Rico was decreasing, until by the mid–1960s there were no former Negro League players in the winter league. Sadly, the Negro Leagues themselves died about 1960, destroyed by the march of progress and the integration of organized baseball. A way of life was gone and would never return. Bob Thurman played his last PRWL game in 1959-60. Luis Cabrera pitched two games in 1961-62. Jose G. Santiago lost the only game he pitched for Ponce in 1962-63. Dan Bankhead went 3–0 with Ponce and Aguas the same year. Luis "Canena" Marquez finally hung up his spikes after the 1963-64 season. And Lou Johnson, he of Los Angeles Dodgers legend, won the batting championship with Santurce in 1964-65, with a .342 batting average. He may have been the last Negro Leaguer to play in the Puerto Rican Winter League.

The winter leagues around the Western Hemisphere helped pave the way for the integration of organized baseball by exposing the talents of the great Negro League players to a vast audience of baseball fans from Caracas to New York. And the leagues provided one additional advantage that came to light in the early days of integration. When the Brooklyn Dodgers signed Roy Campanella to catch for the Dodgers, their management worried about the ability of a black catcher to handle a white pitching staff. Campy, a veteran of integrated baseball leagues in Venezuela, Cuba, Puerto Rico, and Mexico, put that concern to bed early when he said, "I've been catching white pitchers my whole life."

7

Dominican Republic Adventures

Cuban businessmen fleeing from Spanish oppression in Cuba may have introduced baseball into the Dominican Republic. According to Rob Ruck,

> Two brothers, Ignacio and Ubaldo Aloma, left their home in Cienfuegos, Cuba, and emigrated to Santo Domingo in 1880. As ironworkers, they built balconies and grillworks in Santo Domingo and repaired the bridge over the Ozama River after it was damaged by the hurricane of 1893. In June 1891, they formed the first two clubs to play ball on the island and filled their lineups with Cuban compatriots, a handful of Dominicans, a few North Americans, and a German restaurateur. Dominican baseball would keep such a cosmopolitan cast forever after.
>
> They named one club El Cauto, after the river of that name in Cuba. The other was called Cerveceria, for the beer factory where a number of the players worked. Most fans know them by their colors, as the Azules (Blues) and Rojos (Reds). They played their first game at the Aloma brothers ironworks ... using a ball they got from a sailor aboard a North American brig docked in Santo Domingo.

Other Cuban immigrants, possibly landowners who were threatened by the slave revolt, settled in the fertile coastal plains along the southern coast east of Santo Domingo, and established the country's first ingenios or sugar mills. San Pedro de Macoris became a thriving port city of 80,000 by the end of the 19th century, and it was known as the "Paris of the Caribbean" with an opera hall where Jenny Lind once sang, beautiful homes, and a wide esplanade. Wealthy Cuban businessmen, with knowledge of sugar manufacturing, quickly established estates in the plains around San Pedro. The estates consisted of an ingenio or steam-powered sugar mill and a mill town where the workers lived. The town included a school, a church, a company store, and fields where baseball games could be played. As one resident noted, it was possible to live and work on the estate and never leave your entire life. Most of the laborers in the mill were black immigrants from the West Indies, as the Dominicans considered mill work to be slave labor, and they preferred to farm their own small plots of land. The first sugar estate was Angelina, which was established in 1875. It was quickly followed by Porvenir, Consuelo, Santa Fe, Quisqueya, and Cristobal Colon, all surrounding San Pedro and all located within six miles of the city.

Sugar production involved planting huge fields of cane in the fall, growing the canes during the six month winter period known as the *tiempo muerto* or "dead season," and then harvesting the cane and processing it during the spring and summer months to produce raw sugar, molasses, and refined sugar. This situation was ideal for promoting baseball, as noted in *Beisbol*. "Baseball and sugar production fit perfectly. During the six months it took for the cane to grow, baseball was a cheap and easy diversion for the laborers. The slow pace of the game suited the hot Caribbean days, allowing plenty of rest in the shade and only infrequent bursts of exertion. Bodies made strong by slashing the tough, wiry cane in the harvest were perfectly suited to action at home plate. In addition, the sugar mill owners wanted to field winning teams, so baseball skills brought a premium to workers who possessed them." In effect, baseball was an efficient and economical way for plantation owners to keep their workers busy, out of trouble, and in good physical condition preparatory to cutting the cane during the hot summer months. Conversely, it also afforded owners a way to hire outstanding baseball players by providing them with work in the off-season.

During the 1890s, the Cerveceria and El Cauto clubs played baseball games in and around Santo Domingo. By 1900, most towns and villages, especially the mill towns, in the Dominican Republic had their own teams, and regular tournaments and other competitions were held around the island on Sundays and holidays. Professional baseball teams were first established in 1907 with the formation of the Licey Club of Santo Domingo, followed by the Estrellas Orientales of San Pedro de Macoris, the Aguilas Cibaenas of Santiago, and Escogido also of Santo Domingo. Almost overnight, baseball became the national sport of the country. As early as 1908, ballplayers from other countries were being offered large sums of money to play for teams in the Dominican Republic, and soon tournaments were being held to determine a champion. In 1912, San Pedro de Macoris, the Nuevo Club, and Licey, played the first official national championship series. The Nuevo Club, with the Dominican legend Enrique Hernandez, known as "El Indio Bravo," or the "Brave Indian" after his Taino Indian heritage, on the mound, defeated Licey two games out of three and was crowned as the country's first national champion. In a later series against their eastern rival, Estrelleas Orientales of San Pedro de Macoris, the passion of the fans spilled over, causing an interruption in the play. When Estrellas Orientales won the first two games, the Nuevo players and fans caused such a disturbance that the remaining games were cancelled and the series was forfeited to the San Pedro team.

Two years later, the U.S. cruiser *Washington* visited the country and, while there, a baseball team from the ship challenged the Nuevo Club to a game of baseball. It was the highlight of the year for Dominican fans as Enrique "El Indio Bravo" Hernandez, throwing to his batterymate, Paco Siragusa, embarrassed the haughty Americans by striking out 21 of them on his way to a no-hitter. The crafty right-hander relied almost exclusively on his sharp-breaking curveball to keep opposing batters swinging at nothing but air. Another U.S. warship, the cruiser *Petrel*, played a nine-game series against Licey, with the Tigers winning six games to three for the *Petrel*. Other American ships played a total of eleven games against Dominican teams, and lost them all. The U.S. Marines arrived on the island to maintain order in 1916 and stayed for eight years. They too contributed to the increased interest in the game of baseball, although occasionally it was by sheer chance. According to Alan M. Klein, a newsletter meant for the American forces, but read by many Dominicans, reported that an upcoming baseball game between the Marines and the Licey club wouldn't be much of a contest because the Americans were vastly superior to the Dominicans who "were champions of nothing." That newsletter served as a rallying point for the members of Licey, and they approached the game with an unusual amount of fervor. The game was close throughout, with the Marines holding a narrow 2–1 lead into the bottom of the ninth inning. Then a 19-year-old outfielder by the name of Francisco Rodriguez became an instant national hero by hitting a home run to tie the score at 2–2. The Licey club scored the winning run in the tenth inning, sending the capital city into hysteria. Many games were played between the Marines and local teams between 1916 and 1924, and between the Marines and visiting clubs from Cuba and elsewhere. The Marines were enthusiastic, but their skills at baseball had been greatly overrated and they were frequently defeated. Still, they did their bit for charity, playing the Licey club for the Red Cross, at the same time establishing a rapport with their Dominican opponents. As Rob Ruck reported, "While the marines defended the sugar mills in the east, and went into 'Indian country' to search and destroy, resistance in Santo Domingo took on a more refined cast.... In the east, the guerillas were fighting the marines, but in the capital, we played ball with them. Yes, even here in Santo Domingo, there was some shooting, but there is something about sport that unites people. It makes people forget, or at least attenuates, the anger between them. There is nothing that unites people more than sport."

There were many amateur clubs being formed around the Dominican Republic at this time, including Capital, Santo Domingo, Amor al Progresso, and Gimnasio Escolar. Klein noted, "These teams seem to have been closer to a professional level than amateur teams are now. For instance, the Dominican baseball historians, Vicioso and Alvarez, point out that members of the amateur teams Los Muchachos and Delco Light were among those chosen to make up the professional team, Escogido (the name means 'the chosen' in Spanish), along with members from the recently defunct professional team San Carlos." Most of the players on the early teams were Dominicans from the upper classes, professional people like doctors and businessmen, but that situation didn't last very long. As the game exploded, players emerged from the mill towns to compete for spots on the various teams from Santo Domingo to La Romana. One of the first members of the Escogido team was a young man by the name of Juan Estando "Tetelo" Vargas, who was born in 1906, and who would go on to a memorable baseball career, not only in his own country, but also in Cuba, Panama, Colombia, Puerto Rico, and the American Negro leagues. Vargas, who was known as the "Dominican Deer," may have been the greatest player ever produced by the Dominican Republic. At 5', 10" tall, and weighing 160 pounds, he was an outstanding hitter who struck out less than 30 times for every 550 at-bats, an electrifying base runner, and a sensational center fielder with great range and a strong throwing arm. Vargas began his professional career with Escogido in 1923, playing shortstop on a team that also included his brothers, Guagua and Juan.

Amateur and semi-professional baseball thrived during the '20s and '30s, and one of the men responsible for popularizing the game was Pedro Miguel Caratini, a Puerto Rican emigrant who first visited the island in 1916 as a member of Puerto Rico's Ponce club. Caratini was a long ball hitting shortstop for Ponce and one of his country's early baseball legends. He returned to the Dominican Republic shortly after his visit, as an employee of the American occupiers, and taught mathematics in the local school. He also joined the Licey team as its player-manager, playing shortstop, batting cleanup, and instructing the players in the fine points of the game. During his decade-long tenure in the Republic, the man known as "The Father of Dominican Baseball" built a strong, skillful squad that he eventually took on tour, visiting his homeland and playing exhibition games against the local teams. His contributions to the game earned him a place of honor in the Baseball Hall of Fame in both the Dominican Republic and Puerto Rico.

One of the early Dominican heroes was pitcher Rafael "Fellito" Guerra, who pitched for the Escogido team, and who made a habit of tormenting visiting teams, without partiality. The tall, skinny right-hander defeated an American team, a Cuban team, and tossed an 18-inning shutout at a Puerto Rican team, and when he was asked to join the Negro Leagues, he refused in opposition to the American occupation of his country, making himself a national hero. Guerra's Escogido team was one of the top teams in the country, but they had to share the spotlight with Santo Domingo's other team, Licey. Being so close to each other geographically, it was only natural that a heated rivalry would develop between the players and fans alike. In 1921, Escogido won 31 of 47 games played and met Licey in the championship series. In the opening game of

Pedro Miguel Caratini, one of Puerto Rico's greatest players, has been called "The Father of Dominican Republic baseball" for his outstanding work in that country (courtesy Yuyo Ruiz).

the series, Enrique Hernandez, "El Indio Bravo," bested "Fellito" Guerra by the score of 5–1 in a much-publicized pitching duel. The Licey Tigers made it two in a row when they rallied from a 1–0 deficit on a game-tying home run by Pedro Miguel Caratini in the eighth inning, and a game-winning circuit blast by the same batter in the tenth inning. The series went back and forth over the next two months, finally ending in a 4–4–1 tie. In a second series played in June and July, Licey won four of the seven games played. The batting leaders in the series were:

Name	Team	AB	H	BA
Mateo de la Rosa	Escogido	26	13	.500
Manuel Emilio Castillo	Escogido			.391
Rene Valesquez	Escogido			.384
Enrique "El Indio Bravo" Hernandez	Licey			.333
Vincente Pichardo	Licey			.312
Jose Sabino	Escogido			.310
Armando "Balito" Aquino	Escogido			.296

The following year, they scheduled a 19-game series, to be played between April and September. Escogido presented the following lineup.

Catcher	Guagua Vargas	Shortstop	Rene Velazquez Reyes
Pitcher	"Fellito" Guerra	Third Base	Jose Sabino
	Raul Comme Fernandez	Utility	Pinao Acosta
	Manuel Emilio Castillo	Left Field	Amable Reyes
First Base	Mateo de la Rosa	Center Field	"Balito" Aquino
Second Base	Diogenes Lara	Right Field	Juan "Tetelo" Vargas

Five of the players—Guagua Vargas, Guerra, de la Rosa, Lara, and Tetelo Vargas—are members of the Dominican Republic Baseball Hall of Fame.

The Licey Tigers countered with a lineup that included:

"Fellito" Guerra was one of the Dominican Republic's finest pitchers in the early days of the game (courtesy Cuqui Cordova).

Catcher:	Julio "Burano" Hernandez
Pitcher	Pedro Alejandro San
	Mero Urena
First Base	Luis Tomas Saillant
Second Base	Alvaro Camarena
Shortstop	Pedro Miguel Caratini
Third Base	Ninin Rodriguez
Left Field	Pindu Miranda
Center Field	Rafael "Gugu" Selig
Right Field	Nestor "El Loco" Lambertus

San, Urena, Rodriguez, Miranda, and Caratini also reside in the Dominican Republic Baseball Hall of Fame.

Klein reported on one of the games, played on May 14. The game "came to be known as the 'queen's championship,' because the owner of Licey, convinced of his team's superiority, arranged to have a national beauty queen offer a toast at the game. This was to have the effect of simultaneously impressing and unnerving the opposition." The queen, Senorita Esperanza Pereyra from La Vega, arrived at the game in style, in the owner's car. But the game didn't go as planned. As the ninth inning got underway, Licey was protecting a three-run lead, but Escogido fought back scoring one run and loading the bases, bringing up the dangerous Mateo de la Rosa. The big first baseman sent a screamer to right field that eluded Loco Lambertus, and before he could run the ball down, three runners had crossed the plate, giving Escogido a 6–5 victory, and earning de la Rosa the sobriquet, "the batter who made the queen cry." Escogido went on to win the National Championship by capturing 13 of the 19 games played. Licey's captain and shortstop, Pedro Miguel Caratini, was honored as the league's batting champion, and Diogenes Lara was recognized as the best defensive player in the league.

Baseball was not yet a professional sport in the Dominican Republic, but the 1921 series went a long way toward making it a professional sport. The series realized a profit of $7000, with each team receiving $2000. It was about this time that companies began sponsoring teams and providing them with uniforms and equipment. The game of baseball had spread quickly throughout the Western Hemisphere in the late 19th and early 20th centuries, and was extremely popular, not only in the Dominican Republic, but also in Venezuela, Cuba, Puerto Rico, Panama, and the United States. Teams from all those countries visited each other for tournaments and exhibition series, and talented players were sought by teams throughout the Western Hemisphere ever since the Cuban X-Giants first brought their exciting brand of baseball to Cuba in 1903. Cuban League players as well as the Negro League players were the apostles of baseball during the first 25 years of the 20th century, the unofficial goodwill ambassadors of the game, and their efforts were primarily responsible for the popularity of the game in the above named countries.

A bidding war of sorts became popular in the '20s and '30s, with Dominican star Diogenes Lara joining Humacao in Puerto Rico in 1923 and Tetelo Vargas jumping ship from Escogido and joining the Cuban Stars of the Eastern Colored League in 1927, and then moving on to the Havana Lions of the Cuban League two years later. For the most part, teams in the Dominican Republic, although integrated, preferred to use players from their own country rather than recruit players from other countries.

The Dominican Republic didn't recognize a national champion in 1923 although Escogido finished the season with the best record. In 1924 there was much dissension among the teams and, once gain, no champion was crowned. By 1929, the country had entered the world of professional baseball, and the rosters of all the teams were liberally sprinkled with

Tetelo Vargas, the "Dominican Deer," may have been the Dominican Republic's greatest player during the first half of the twentieth century (courtesy Yuyo Ruiz).

foreigners. "Cocaina" Garcia, who had just completed a rocky season with the Almendares Scorpians in the Cuban League, going 2 and 5, was joined on the Licey Tigers by his Cuban compatriots Alejandro Oms, coming off a .432 season in Cuba that earned him the batting title; Pelayo Chacon, who had hit just .148 in the 1928-29 Cuban League; Pedro Arango; and Ramon Bragana, who had been suspended by his Cuban team for failure to report. Another Cuban legend, and the country's greatest player, Martin Dihigo, who had hit .303 in Cuba, signed with Licey's mortal enemy, the Escogido Lions, who also had the services of Dihigo's catcher, Eustaquio Pedroso, and fellow Cubans Bernardo Baro and Augustin Bejerano, as well as home grown talent like Tetelo Vargas, "Fellito" Guerra, and Pedro Alejandro San. Licey and Escogido were joined in the championship summer series by Sandino from Santiago, but the two Santo Domingo teams dominated the league. In one of the early games, Dihigo tossed a shutout at Licey, blanking the Tigers by a score of 9–0, but that wasn't enough to hold off the powerful Tigers, and Licey captured the first professional Dominican League pennant, with a record of 11–7, edging the Escogido Lions by 1½ games. Escogido finished at 9–8 and Sandino won 3 games and lost 8. The loss by Escogido was particularly shocking because the Lions had a big lead coming down the stretch, but were overtaken by Licey when Cuban pitcher Basilio "El Brujo" Rosell dropped two decisions to the lightly regarded Sandinos.

Although discrimination was not as obvious or as serious in the Dominican Republic as it was in the United States, a "color problem" did exist there, and dictator Rafael Trujillo fueled the flames, as noted by Burgos, who said that

> concerns about race, Haiti's proximity in this case, affected the Dominican Republic's Creole elite thought and influenced their actions. In the 1930s, General Rafael Trujillo consolidated his power and control. Promoting *Hispanidad*, a Dominican identity that stressed Spanish heritage and disassociated itself from African ancestry, Trujillo initiated a State campaign against those noticeably black. Crossing over into Haiti along the mountainous region separating the two nations, the Rio massacre resulted in the death of more than 25,000 black "Haitians." The Dominican state's coding of blacks as "Haitians," and the disassociation with being "Haitian"—that is, having African ancestry, partly explained the absence of Dominicans in the Negro Leagues.

But that's a different story than the one told by Felipe Alou, one of the first generation of Dominican major league players. According to Alou, race was a nonissue in the Dominican Republic during the 1930s.

Baseball fever continued to excite the populace during the decade of the '30s as reported by Klein. "The Dominican press was eager to make a superstar of any Dominican who prevailed over these visitors. Abejita Ruiz, a left-handed pitcher touted as having the best curve ball of his day, was the sort of player the powerful Cuban and Venezuelan teams had to face. On 24 September 1933, he pitched against the highly regarded Ponce team from Puerto Rico, and won, 7 to 2. Six weeks later he beat the Cuban Stars, 6 to 5." The Cubans brought their best players with them, as can be seen by the following lineup.

Cando Lopez	Left Field	Lazaro Salazar	Right Field
Pepin Perez	1st Base	Miguel Solis	2nd Base
Alejandro Oms	Center Field	Jose Maria Fernandez	Catcher
Pedro Arango	3rd Base	Isidro Fabre	Pitcher
Cuco Correa	Shortstop		

7. Dominican Republic Adventures

The Lions countered with:

Titico Guzman	3rd Base	Chaguin Gomez	Shortstop
Miguel Solis	Right Field	Aladino Paez	1st Base
Laitico Mieses	Left Field	Braganita Garcia	2nd Base
Papin Henriquez	Catcher	Livio Guerra	Pitcher
Juan Sonora	Center Field	Abejita Ruiz	Pitcher

Guerra hardly had time to work up a sweat as he was knocked out of the box in the third inning when the Cubans scored three runs to open up a 4–0 lead, but Ruiz came on in relief and held the Cubans to one run and four hits over the last six-plus innings. Escogido, meanwhile, scored three runs of their own in the bottom of the inning, to cut the lead to 4–3 and then, after the Stars had added a run in the top of the sixth, the Lions pushed over the two game-tying runs in the bottom of the seventh inning and scored the winning run against Fabre in the bottom of the ninth. Third baseman Titico Guzman and left fielder Laitico Mieses led the Escogido attack with three hits each, and shortstop Chaguin Gomez and second baseman Braganita Garcia provided brilliant defense. Pedro Arango was the top Cuban hitter with two doubles, while Isidro Fabre took the loss for Cuba.

The following February, the powerful Concordia team from Venezuela, a team considered by many people to be the finest Latin American team of all time, visited the Dominican Republic to lock horns with the impressive Escogido Lions. Concordia had a plethora of talent with such standouts as Tetelo Vargas, Luis Aparicio, Sr., and Josh Gibson. Escogido also presented a strong lineup with Perucho Cepeda from Puerto Rico, the father of the San Francisco Giants' home run slugger, Orlando Cepeda, and "Millito" Navarro. In the opening game, Blanquito Espino stunned the mighty Concordia nine by shutting them out on four hits. His countryman and opponent, Pedro Alejandro San, was relieved after being touched up for two runs in the first three innings. Jose "Ciqui" Lanauze was the batting star of the game, driving in both runs with base hits, one in the first inning and the other in the third inning. Shortstop Chaguin Gomez and Lolo Perez dazzled the noisy crowd with their magic in the field. In the second game, Escogido jumped on Silvino Ruiz for five runs in the opening stanza and coasted to a 6–2 victory as the diminutive southpaw, Abejito Ruiz kept the Concordia sluggers off balance with his pitch selection and his speed changes. Gomez led the Lions' attack with a double and two singles, and Gomez, Perez and "Millito" Navarro all turned in defensive gems.

Concordia

Name	Pos	AB	R	H
Cesar Nieves	2B	4	1	2
"Pollo" Malpica	C	1	0	0
Tetelo Vargas	CF	2	1	1
Rap Dixon	LF	3	0	1
B. Inojosa	RF	4	0	1
F. Quevedo	1B	3	0	0
Luis Jimenez	3B	4	0	0
Luis Aparicio	SS	4	0	1
Silvino Ruiz	P	4	0	0
Josh Gibson	PH-C	2	0	2
Totals		31	2	8

Escogido

Name	Pos	AB	R	H
Laitico Mieses	CF	5	2	2
Checo Delgado	1B	4	1	1
"Ciqui" Lanauze	RF	3	1	1
"Millito" Navaro	LF	4	1	0
P. Cepeda	2B	4	1	2
Lolo Perez	3B	3	0	1
Bobo Benitez	C	3	0	1
C. Gomez	SS	4	0	3
Abejita Ruiz	P	4	0	0
Totals		34	6	11

Concordia	0 0 0	0 1 0	0 1 0—2—8—3	
Escogido	5 0 0	0 0 1	0 0 x—6—11—0	

Two Base Hits: Chaguin Gomez

Pitchers	IP	W	L	H	SO	BB
Silvino Ruiz	8	0	1	11	2	0
Abejita Ruiz	9	1	0	8	1	3

The Concordia team returned to the Dominican Republic in January 1935 looking for revenge, but all they got was more of the same. This time, Yoyo Diaz, a stocky right-hander from Cuba, pitching for Escogido, out-pitched Luis "Lefty" Tiant, the father of the Boston Red Sox pitcher, by a 2–1 count. Interestingly, there were two American Negro League players on the Escogido team, outfielder James "Big Jim" Williams and pitcher Bert Hunter. Williams, a 6', 1", 200-pound right-handed hitting outfielder who may have been the first American Negro Leaguer to play in the Dominican League, enjoyed a 13-year Negro League career, batting .292, while Hunter played in the Negro leagues for six years. Williams was a member of the Homestead Grays in 1937 and, batting behind Josh Gibson and Buck Leonard, he pounded the ball at a .371 clip. Hunter, a noted curveball artist, compiled a brilliant record of 60–22 in the Negro leagues for games that have been recovered, including 18–4 in 1932 and 17–5 in 1933. His Negro League career ended suddenly when, in the middle of the 1936 season, he mysteriously disappeared, later surfacing in the Dominican Republic where he had fled in order to get married and make his home there.

The season batting averages for the top professional hitters in the Dominican Republic for 1935 are listed below.

Name	Team	AB	R	H	BA
Gueba Rodriguez	Licey	2	1	1	.500
Bert Hunter	Licey	8	1	3	.375
Sonlly Alvarado	Licey-Escogido	47	10	17	.362
Lolo Perez	Escogido	17	4	6	.353
Horacio Martinez	Licey-Escogido	51	10	17	.333
Abejita Ruiz	Escogido	3	0	1	.333
Chagun Gomez	Escogido-Licey	22	3	7	.318
James Williams	Escogido-Licey	46	7	14	.304
Enrique Lantigua	Licey	33	6	10	.303

It was becoming increasingly popular now for teams to recruit players from other countries, and some of the Dominican Republic's greatest players took advantage of that situation and left for greener pastures, strutting their stuff in places like Puerto Rico, the American Negro Leagues, and Cuba. Tetelo Vargas played in all those countries, as well in his homeland, between 1923 and 1956; Diogenes Lara, who played for Santo Domingo's Escogido Club, periodically showcased his talents in Puerto Rico and Venezuela; and the three Grillo brothers played for Almendares and Havana in the Cuban League. Some of Cuba's greatest players, like Luis "El Mulo" Padron, Jose Mendez, and Valentin Dreke, found their way into the Negro leagues. Conversely, Negro League greats Dobie Moore, "Bullet Joe" Rogan, and John Henry Lloyd, wintered in Cuba, but strangely enough, the Dominican Republic continued to depend primarily on homegrown talent to staff their teams. When they did recruit outside talent, they usually sought Latino players from Cuba and Puerto Rico, offering $600 and up in salary, a luxury apartment, transportation for the player and his wife, and all expenses paid. The foreign recruits lived like kings, and were treated like heroes.

In 1936 the Estrellas Orientales, with Tetelo Vargas and Cuban imports Ramon Bragana, "Cocaina" Garcia, Pedro Arango, and Javier Perez, finished in first place, followed by Santiago, Licey, and Escogido in that order. One of the more exciting games of the season involved Licey and Escogido. It was played on February 27, 1936, and matched Gustavo Lluberes against Venezuelan ace Narciso "Chingo Canon" Diaz. Both pitchers were in good form, with each pitcher limiting the opposing team to five base hits. The game was tied at 3–3 after six innings, but Escogido pushed over what proved to be the winning run in the top of the seventh inning on hits by right fielder Mariano Defillo and second baseman Braganita Garcia. The lineups were:

Escogido

Name	Pos
Braganita Garcia	2B
Carlos Augusto Fiallo	CF
"Grillo B" (Andres Julio Baez)	LF
Ninin Rodriguez	1B
Lolo Perez	3B
Papin Henriquez	C
Mariano Defillo	RF
Pedrito Alvarez	SS
Narciso Diaz	P

Licey

Name	Pos
Pedro Nina	CF
Enrique Lantigua	1B
Horacio Martinez	SS
Mellizo Puesan	RF
Sonlly Alvarado	LF
Bombolia Medina	2B
Nonito Garcia	C
Enriquito Arias	3B
Gustavo Lluberes	P

```
Escogido    0 2 1    0 0 0    1 0 0—4—5—1
Licey       0 0 2    1 0 0    0 0 0—3—5—4
```

Ramon Bragana was the league's top pitcher with a record of 9–1. Narciso Diaz won four games and Silvino Ruiz won two. Mellizo Pueson of Licey was the batting champion with an average of .409, while Carlos Augusto Fiallo and Ninin Rodriguez of Escogido both hit over .300.

The league turned to the outside world in earnest in 1937, just prior to a presidential election, when the three candidates each subsidized a team in the Dominican League. President Rafael Trujillo backed Los Dragones of Ciudad Trujillo and, to assure his team's victory, he searched the baseball world for the best available players. After deciding the Negro leagues had the most talented players, Trujillo sent his representative, Dr. Jose Enrique Aybar, to Pittsburgh, Pennsylvania, with a suitcase holding $30,000. He gave the money to Satchel Paige, and told him to keep half for himself and use the other half to recruit players for the Dominican League. Satch immediately signed Sammy Bankhead, "Cool Papa" Bell, Leroy Matlock, and Bill Perkins as the nucleus of the team. Trujillo also brought in Lazaro Salazar, Silvio Garcia and Rodolfo Fernandez from Cuba, and Perucho Cepeda from Puerto Rico. El Presidente's team may well have been the strongest professional baseball team in the world in 1937, or at least a close second to the powerful New York Yankees squad of Gehrig, DiMaggio, and Dickey. In fact, after

The famous "Los Dragones" of the 1937 Dominican League: Back (left to right): Josh Gibson, unknown, unknown, Rodolfo Fernandez, unknown, Perucho Cepeda, unknown. Middle (left to right): Lazaro Salazar, Dr. Jose E. Aybar, Satchel Paige. Front (left to right): Tetelo Vargas, Leroy Matlock, unknown, "Cool Papa" Bell, Sam Bankhead, Silvio Garcia, unknown (author's collection).

the Dominican League ended, many of the Dragones played together on other teams, like the powerful La Concordia of Venezuela. Trujillo's Dragones were a fearsome lot, but his political opponents were not sitting around doing nothing. They also brought in hired guns from around the Western Hemisphere. The Estrellas Orientales of San Pedro de Macoris employed their own Tetelo Vargas, as well as George Scales from the U.S. and "Cocaina" Garcia and Ramon Bragana from Cuba, while the Aguilas Cibaenas of Santiago were represented by Martin Dihigo and Luis Tiant, Sr., of Cuba, and Chet Brewer, "Spoony" Palm, and Showboat Thomas of the Negro leagues. The madness was so pervasive that only two native Dominicans played in the league, Tetelo Vargas and infielder Horacio Martinez. The rest of the players were foreign imports.

Chet Brewer faced Satchel Paige early in the season and tossed a no-hitter at his Negro League opponent, winning 4–2, with Los Dragones runs coming on errors. "Spoony" Palm and Santos Amaro each homered for Aguilas Cibaenas. The season, that lasted from March 28 to July 11, did not go well for Trujillo's team in the early going, and the boss began to get impatient. His soldiers were getting impatient too, firing their guns in the air and screaming, "El Presidente doesn't lose." "Cool Papa" Bell wasn't as cool as his name might have implied when he watched the soldiers working themselves into a frenzy. He asked one of the residents of the capital city. "They don't kill people over baseball, do they?" The man nodded matter-of-factly, "Down here they do." Trujillo's players were never without an armed escort throughout the entire season. Soldiers accompanied them everywhere, supposedly to protect them from the president's political opponents. If the players went to the beach, soldiers stood nearby. If they dined in a restaurant, soldiers sat at a nearby table. If they went sightseeing around Ciudad Trujillo, soldiers walked close behind. They even guarded the Hotel Inglata every night, to keep unwanted people out and the ballplayers in.

Josh Gibson did not accompany the team to Ciudad Trujillo. He was busy playing winter baseball in Puerto Rico. But a nervous Satchel Paige contacted him in San Juan, and upped his offer. He needed Josh's big bat to hold off the challenges of the Estrellas Orientales and Aguilas Cibaenas. Josh answered the call, but for the first couple of weeks he was a non-factor in the race. He went 0 for 12 after joining Los Dragones, but he more than made up for it once his bat caught fire. He roared down the stretch with 24 hits in 41 at-bats for a sensational .585 batting average. In one game he hit for the cycle.

The final Dominican League standings reflected the tightness of the race.

	W	L	GA/GB
Los Dragones	18	13	—
Aguilas Cibaenas	15	17	-3½
Estrellas Orientales	14	17	-4

The seven game playoff that followed the regular season matched Los Dragones against Aguilas Cibaenas for the championship of the league, and Aguilas Cibaenas got off the mark quickly, taking Los Dragones to task in the first three games, beating Paige and Matlock in the process. With their backs to the wall, Trujillo's team fought back, winning games four, five, and six, to tie the series at three games apiece. The important seventh game for all the marbles matched Satchel Paige (7–2) against Chet Brewer (2–2). As John Holway reported it, "Just before the big game, Brewer strolled over to visit his buddies on the *Dragones* and found their hotel room deserted. 'Where is everyone?' he asked a kid. 'In the *carcel*,' he replied, jerking his thumb toward the jail. The whole team had been locked up to be sure they were in good shape for the big game. 'You'd have thought we had a secret combination to Fort Knox,'" Satchel said." The game was a classic as it should have been, but the scenario was unlike any other baseball game ever played. Trujillo's soldiers, armed to the teeth, stood at attention down the right-field line, while soldiers representing Trujillo's opponent stood at attention down the left-field line. The grandstands were packed, and guns were fired indiscriminately, by civilians as well as by soldiers. Aguilas took a 5–4 lead into the seventh inning, but then Paige took matters into his own hands, slashing a single to put the tying run on base, and Sammy Bankhead followed with what may have been the most important home run of his life, a drive off Martin Dihigo that carried over the left field wall. Satchel retired the last six men in order, striking out five of them, and Los Dragones walked off the field with the title. Most of the Pittsburgh Crawford players caught the Pan Am Clipper out of the capital early the next morning, happy to escape with their lives. But it was reported that Paige stayed on the island for another two months, writing his memoirs. The last chapter would have made great reading

The Dominican League batting and pitching leaders were as follows:

Josh Gibson led the league with a .453 batting average, on 24 base hits in 53 at-bats, with 4 doubles, 5 triples, and 2 home runs.

Clyde Spearman batted .353.

Martin Dihigo batted .351 with 6 doubles, 2 triples, and 4 home runs in 97 at-bats. He also went 6–4 on the mound.

"Cool Papa" Bell hit .318 and electrified the crowd with his sensational outfield play and daring base running.

Sammy Bankhead hit .309 and crushed the pennant-winning home run in the playoffs.

Silvio Garcia batted .297.

George Scales batted .295.

Satchel Paige led all pitchers with an 8–2 record. He won back-to-back weekend games at least once during the season.

Leroy Matlock compiled a 4–1 record for Los Dragones.

Chet Brewer went 2–3 for Aguilas Cibaenas, and tossed a no-hitter against Satchel Paige and Los Dragones.

Silvio Garcia led the league with 128 at-bats, 38 base hits, and 14 doubles.

Josh Gibson and Lazaro Salazar tied for the lead in triples with 5 each.

Martin Dihigo and Santos Amaro tied for the lead in home runs with 4 each.

The money spent on the 1937 Dominican League by the individual teams depleted the country's finances, and the league was forced to suspend operations indefinitely. Amateur and semi-professional baseball continued to be played in the Dominican Republic, but only on an individual tournament or series basis. Perhaps the most significant change resulting from the termination of professional baseball in the Dominican Republic was the disappearance of foreign players from the country. Negro League players and players from Cuba, Puerto Rico, and elsewhere were strictly professionals, and they followed the moneyed interests around the Western Hemisphere. For the most part, they would not return to the Dominican Republic until professional baseball was resurrected in 1951.

The center of Dominican baseball, outside the capital, was in the sugar-growing region to the east, including San Pedro de Macoris, Consuelo, and Colon. The players all worked in the refineries, and the rivalries between the competing refineries were fierce, and frequently bloody, as told to Alan Klein by Austin Jacobo. "These games (between refineries) were bigger than the World Series to us. When you go to one of these estates baseball was the only thing (diversion) you gonna see. There was no movies. So everybody got into that. They didn't want coffee at the house, everybody was on the field. So when you lose a game, everybody crying or something; fighting or something. If you go to Angelina and they win, they fight you. And if they lose, they fight. It was because they were so excited, you know?" Chico Conton, a player for Consuelo in the 1950s, added, "Oh, we had rivals. Santa Fe and Porvenir were rivals so close to each other. Our rival was Angelina. But those son-of-a-guns, they don't know how to lose (nicely). Each time they'd come over we'd wind up in a fight. Always! Angelinos coming over and we have to prepare for a fight. The fans were always pushing, yelling, and all that.... It would get hot, but not that we would really harm each other. We would fight with fists, not with bats. If anybody grabbed a bat, we wouldn't allow that. We get you off the team. We had disciplined fights."

In 1938, Licey and Escogido met on fifteen occasions with Licey winning eight games and Escogido winning seven. The following year, a tournament was held in Ciudad Trujillo matching Escogido, Licey, and Ponce of Puerto Rico. Licey walked away with the championship trophy and Horacio Martinez was the top hitter in the competition.

The 1940 season saw a remarkable performance by Escogido's ace pitcher, Luis "Nino el Zurdo" Castro who blanked Licey in three consecutive games, on July 14 and 28 and August 4. Castro's first shutout was a four-hitter against Fallon Heureaux, who was knocked around for five runs and eleven base hits. Ninin Rodriguez and Castro led the hit parade with two hits each.

Escogido	1 0 0	3 0 1	0 0 0	—5—11—0
Licey	0 0 0	0 0 0	0 0 0	—0— 4—5

The second meeting between the two teams was a tight pitchers duel between Castro and Heureaux, with Castro coming out on top again, this time by a 2–0 score. Escogido tallied the game winner in the top of the first inning on hits by Pedrito Alvarez and Ninin Rodriguez, and another run in the fifth inning on a hit by "Pepe" Lucas. Guigui Lucas had two hits in the game and the other Lions hits were made by Mellizo Puesan and Castro.

Escogido	1 0 0	0 1 0	0 0 0	—2—7—3
Licey	0 0 0	0 0 0	0 0 0	—0—3—2

The story of game 3 was concentrated in the fifth inning when Escogido bunched five base hits together and Licey contributed two errors to a 6-run uprising. Ninin Rodriguez was the batting star once again with three base hits. "Loro" Escalante and "Pepe" Lucas chipped in with two each, and Guigui Lucas and Mellizo Puesan accounted for the other two. For Licey, Luis Baez "Grillo 'C'", Enrique Veloz, Pedro Nina, Pajarito Perdomo, Roque Holguin, and Papito Vargas had base hits.

Escogido	0 0 0	0 6 0	0 0 0	—6—9—1
Licey	0 0 0	0 0 0	0 0 0	—0—6—4

Licey was overjoyed to hear that Luis Castro would not pitch in their next encounter, on August 12, but their happiness was premature. Ventura "Loro" Escalante took the mound for the Lions and handcuffed the Tigers with just three base hits, and the result was another shutout, this time by an 8–0 score. Escalante also paced the offense with a run scored in the second inning and a two-run home run in the eighth. In the last meeting between the two rivals, the Tigers finally scored a run, but they were still routed, dropping a 6–1 decision. Those victories sparked Escogido to a 9–3 record in the series.

The Dominican Republic joined the *Mundiales*, the World Amateur Championships in 1941, three years after its beginning. Over a period of 33 years, the powerful Cubans captured 11 of the 18 championships played. Competing countries included the United States, Cuba, the Dominican Republic, England, Puerto Rico, Nicaragua, and Venezuela. Rob Ruck reported, "In 1942, the Dominicans went into the ninth game of the twelve game round-robin series tied with the Cubans. They faced a United States team made up primarily of university students. Cuban fans, known for their zealotry throughout the region, shouted the *Yanquis* on to a lead in the game. The scene that day at *Estadio Le Tropical* was more like a madhouse than a ballpark.... The bedlam in the stands soon aggravated play and a hit batsman led to a brawl in the *Yanqui* dugout. Cuban fans began throwing bottles and assorted ballpark comestibles at the Dominican players, and Dominican manager Burrolote Rodriguez flung a bat into the stands in retaliation." Rodriguez was led off to jail, the game resumed, and the Dominicans went down to defeat, finishing in second place in the tournament.

As is obvious from the above game description, international rivalries were heated, and the rivalry with Cuba was particularly intense. Cuba had first introduced the game to the republic, and they flaunted their superiority in every series, giving the Dominicans an extra incentive to beat them. In 1944, the two countries met in the finals of a competition called The Antilles Pearl, and the Dominicans gained sweet revenge for previous defeats at the hands of the Cubans, winning the seven-game series 5 games to 2. In the opener, "Pepe" Lucas, and the youngest of the Grillo brothers, Luis Baez, known as "Grillo 'C'," each pounded out three base hits, and Aquiles Martinez chipped in with two, as the Dominicans romped 8–5. The Cubans bounced back to take the second game, but that only delayed the execution. The boys from the sugar fields captured the third game by a 5–1 count behind the four-hit pitching of Andres Julio Baez, "Grillo 'B'." The following day, "Loro" Escalante, on the mound for the Dominicans, was supported by the big bats of Luis Baez, the batting star of the series, and Elucar Alvarez, both of whom went 4 for 5 in an 8–4 victory. The Dominicans stretched their lead to 4 games to 1 with an 8–3 win in game 5, before the Cubans salvaged their second victory with a 5–2 win behind the pitching of Yoyo O'Reilly. The finale of the series was a hard fought contest as the Cubans battled for respect. Andres Julio Baez toed the rubber for the Dominicans and he edged out Cuban right-hander Moim Garcia 4–3 in the closest game of the series.

There were no organized professional baseball leagues in the country for 14 years, but amateur baseball still thrived. There were a dozen or more teams in and around Ciudad Trujillo and many more teams in the sugar-growing regions to the east. In the 1942-43 season, Santiago routed La Vega to claim the championship of the region. "Pepe" Lucas was the star for Santiago in the final series. In addition to his sparkling defensive play at third base, he was the most consistent hitter of the series, and hit the first home run ever hit over the left field wall at Enriquillo Park in Santiago. "Loro" Escalante of La

Diomedes Olivo was one of the country's greatest pitchers during the 1940s and '50s (courtesy Yuyo Ruiz).

Vega won the batting championship with an average of .373, Andres Julio Baez "Grillo 'B'" was the top pitcher, and Aquiles Martinez of Santiago was the top defensive player.

Diomedes "Guayubin" Olivo, one of the Dominican Republic's greatest pitchers, realized the dream of all pitchers on September 28, 1947, when he threw a no-hitter for the Escogido Lions against their bitter enemies, the Licey Tigers, in Ciudad Trujillo. Olivo, whose baseball career spanned the years from 1940 to 1964, first played amateur ball with a team in Puerto Plata, making a name for himself in international competition during the 1940s. He joined the professional establishment in 1947, at the age of 28, when he became the ace of the Aguadilla team. In September, playing for Escogido, he faced off against Jose "Achin" Matos of Licey in a classic battle, coming away victorious by a 3–0 count. He also contributed to his team's offense by knocking in the winning run in the top of the first inning. Elias Frias drove in the second run and scored the third and final run in the sixth inning.

Escogido

Name	Pos	AB	R	H
Fiallo	RF	5	0	0
M. Perez	1B	4	1	2
L. Escalante	LF	3	0	0
P. Lucas	CF	3	1	1
G. Olivo	P	4	0	1
E. Frias	1B	3	1	2
L. Vinals	C	4	0	0
G. Munoz	2B	4	0	0
B. Delgado	SS	4	0	2
Totals		34	3	8

Licey

Name	Pos	B	R	H
C. Alvarez	CF	3	0	0
A. Martinez	2B	3	0	0
B. Arias	1B	3	0	0
J. Echavarria	RF	3	0	0
M. Abreu	3B	3	0	0
M. T. Tinco	LF	3	0	0
J. Manzueta	C	2	0	0
O. Suarez	SS	2	0	0
A. Matos	P	2	0	0
F. Perez	PH	1	0	0
J. Evins	PH	1	0	0
M. Benzan	PH	1	0	0
Totals		27	0	0

Escogido   1 0 0   0 0 2   0 0 0—3—8—0
Licey   0 0 0   0 0 0   0 0 0—0—0—2

Runs Batted In: Olivo, Frias

Pitcher	IP	W	L	H	SO	BB
G. Olivo	9	1	0	0	8	2
A. Matos	9	0	1	8	4	3

Although Olivo's 11-year Dominican Republic career produced 86 victories against 46 losses, his winter league career, from 1955-56 to 1963-64, showed what a great talent this man was. He was 36 years old when the 1955-56 season began and 44 years old when the 1963-64 season ended, and he still recorded a brilliant 52–32 won-loss record, a winning percentage of .619. On May 22, 1954, with Licey, he hit a ninth inning, two-out pinch-hit single against Negro Leaguer Johnny Wright, breaking up Wright's no-hitter and driving in the winning run to make a winner out of Ewell Blackwell. On the 29th, he tossed his second no-hitter, defeating Escogido, with Bob Thurman and Raymond Dandridge, 3–0. The following year, pitching for the Cibaenas Eagles, he journeyed to Havana, Cuba, to meet the Havana Sugar Kings of the International League in a doubleheader. He pitched and won the morning game by the score of 6–4 when his team rallied for five runs in the bottom of the 7th inning. And Olivo contributed two singles to Cibaenas' 15-hit attack. Emilio "El Indio" Cueche made it a clean sweep for the Eagles by winning the afternoon affair 3–2 on an 8th inning home run by New York Giants slugger, Clint "The Hondo Hurricane" Hartung off Elio Suarez. Olivo finally reached the major leagues in 1960 at the age of 41, helping the Pittsburgh Pirates win the National League pennant with four solid relief appearances down the stretch. His major league career totaled four years and 85 games, with a 5–6 won-loss record.

When the Brooklyn Dodgers held their spring training in Ciudad Trujillo in 1948, the excitement generated by their presence revitalized the people's interest in the game of baseball. The Brooklyn team led by manager Leo Durocher, and featuring former Negro League stars Jackie Robinson and Dan Bankhead, resided at the exclusive Jaragua Hotel during their visit, which covered the period from February 28 until April 1. The Dodgers' top farm club, the Montreal Royals, also trained in the Dominican Republic, 20 miles from the capital. The Royals, with former Negro League all-stars Roy Campanella and Don Newcombe, provided the Dodgers' main opposition during the six-week training camp.

In 1950, during a visit to Managua, Nicaragua, by the Dominican Stars and some of their influential supporters, team members and their fans met to discuss the baseball situation in the republic, and they all agreed that a new professional baseball league should be organized as soon as possible. The Dominican Summer League began operations in 1951 and, four years later, it was converted to a winter league that has since grown into one of the strongest winter leagues in the world. Since it had now been ten years since Jackie Robinson integrated organized baseball, the winter league soon became a popular training ground for major league players and promising minor league players. Foreign players, Negro Leaguers, Cuban Leaguers, etc. once again returned to the Dominican Republic after an absence of fifteen years, but this time they were joined by players, black and white, from organized baseball. Some of the well-known names to grace the 1951 summer league rosters included Luis Villodas from Puerto Rico, Pedro Formental from Cuba, Alonzo Perry and Willard "That Man" Brown from the American Negro leagues, and homegrown Tetelo Vargas.

The integration of organized baseball by Jackie Robinson eventually spelled finis for the Negro leagues, but they managed to stay afloat until 1960. And even in the late '40s and early '50s, some players who would later become Hall-of-Fame major leaguers began their long journey in the Negro Leagues. Ernie Banks, the happy-go-lucky shortstop for the Chicago Cubs, famous for his jovial "Let's play two today" announcement to his teammates upon entering the locker room, played his first professional game with the Kansas City Monarchs in 1950. Willie Mays, the "Say-Hey Kid," covered center field for the Birmingham Black Barons in 1948, at the age of 17. And Hank Aaron, the major league's all-time career home run king, was a member of the Indianapolis Clowns in 1952, smashing 9 home runs 345 at-bats.

The Dominican League, a summer league that put itself into direct competition with the American organized baseball leagues, was staffed by many Dominican players, plus *importados* from Cuba, Puerto Rico, and the slowly dying Negro leagues. The league consisted of four teams, Licey, Escogido, Aguilas, and Estrellas Orientales. The schedule called for a season consisting of two halves, each half to have 27 games per team. There were two divisions of two teams each, with the division leaders playing off after the season ended to determine the league champion. The rosters sounded like a who's who in the United Nations with Tetelo Vargas, "Pepe" Lucas, Diomedes "Guayubin" Olivo, Olmedo Suarez, and Chi Chi Olivo, representing the Dominican Republic, Luis "King Kong" Villodas and Luis Olmo from Puerto Rico, Pedro Formental, Rogelio Crespo, and Alejandro "Filete" Crespo from Cuba, Guillermo Vento and Emilio Cueche, from Venezuela, Garabato Sackie from Panama, Alonzo Perry, Bob Thurman, Terris McDuffie, Ray Dandridge, and Johnny Wright from the Negro leagues, and Pete Burnside, Fred Kipp, Willie Kirkland, Dick Stuart, and Charlie Neal from the U.S. minor leagues. There were usually from 5 to 7 importados on each team, and the quality of play was significantly higher than it had been prior to the integration of organized baseball.

The teams in the Dominican Republic's professional baseball league also had a built-in farm system since amateur leagues still flourished around the country, particularly along the coastal plain to the south and east. Regional leagues were popular around Santiago in the northwest, Santo Domingo (formerly Ciudad Trujillo) in the south, and San Pedro de Macoris in the east, with tournaments deciding a national amateur champion. Tropico, near San Pedro, won five national championships and was competitive in international play. In addition to the city leagues, baseball continued to be a major diversion to the people of the *ingenios*, who dreamed of leaving the estates and joining the professional baseball league in the capital.

The Dominican League, in its inaugural season, crowned the Licey Tigers as the pennant winner, sparked by their native son, "Guayubin" Olivo, who racked up a fine 10–5 record in 16 games. He led the league in victories, strikeouts (65) and earned run average (1.90). The batting champion was Luis "King Kong" Villodas of Aguilas Cibaenas, and Puerto Rico with an average of .346. He also hit the longest home run ever hit in Cabio Park. And the home run champion was Pedro Formental of Aguilas Cibaenas and Cuba with 13. Olivo continued to dominate the league during the remaining three years of its summer existence, going 10–5 in 1952 with a sparkling 1.33 ERA, 6–2 in 1953 with a 2.34 ERA, and 8–2 in 1954 with a 1.86 ERA.

The Aguilas Cibaenas captured the second pennant, led by Negro League veteran Terris "The Great" McDuffie, who won 14 games against just 3 losses, for a .824 winning percentage. Teammate Emilio Cueche, a Venezuelan import, led the league in strikeouts with 101 while posting a 9–9 record. Luis Olmo of the Licey Tigers, a native of Puerto Rico, paced the batters with an average of .344. And Negro League veteran Alonzo Perry, also of the Licey Tigers, was the home run leader with 11.

Licey returned to the winner's circle in 1953, led by the home run champion, Alonzo Perry, who cracked 11 round trippers. Tetelo Vargas of Estrellas Orientales captured the batting title with an average of .355. And Emilio "El Indio" Cueche of Aguilas Cibaenas walked off with most of the pitching honors, as he led the league in complete games (13), innings pitched (161), strikeouts (96), and victories (13). Wilmer "Red" Fields played the outfield and pitched for Estrellas Orientales, batting .395 in 107 at-bats, while recording a 5–2 mark on the mound. Terris McDuffie had another fine season with Aguilas Cibaenas, going 8–4 with a 2.53 ERA. And Bob Thurman batted .288 with Escogido but, surprisingly, was held without a home run in 104 at-bats. Fields, one of the league's most versatile players was paid $2,200 a month plus all expenses. Bill "Ready" Cash remembered the 1953 Dominican Summer League, as he told Kelley. "I was one of the guys in San Diego, Dominican Republic, that hit the ball over the left field wall. There's only two went over there; Alonzo Perry hit one and I hit the other one. The wind was very strong blowing in from left field and unless you hit it on the nose and a line drive—it was about 355 to left field and that's a pretty good poke." Cash hit a torrid .360 that summer. Another Negro Leaguer in the Dominican Republic that year was Curley Williams, an infielder on the Licey team. His contribution to the team's efforts was minimal, however, as he went to the plate just 37 times and hit a barely visible .108.

The 1954 season, the last one to be played in the summer, welcomed Estrellas Orientales, the Eastern Stars, of San Pedro de Macoris, to the winner's circle. Venezuelan Jose "Carrao" Bracho, in his only season of Dominican League baseball, sparked the champions with a league-leading 8 victories and .889 winning percentage. "Guayubin" Olivo of Licey also won 8 games. Alonzo Perry of Licey took his first Dominican League batting title with a .326 average. And Bob Thurman of Escogido, another Negro League veteran, was the home run champion with 11. He also led the league in runs scored (29) and runs batted in (34), while hitting an even .300 in 140 at-bats.

The reputation of the Dominican League grew to the point where it was finally recognized by the American major leagues, and formal ties were established between the two organizations. At that point, in 1955, the Dominican League changed from a summer league to a winter league so it would complement organized baseball's summer leagues instead of competing with them. The Negro League players like Alonzo Perry, Terris McDuffie, and Bob Thurman were a significant factor in the improved quality of play in the Dominican League, that raised it to the level of a AA league, or possibly even a AAA league in the United States. They, along with players from Puerto Rico and Cuba, reinforced the talented Dominican players to produce a professional baseball league that could hold its own with any professional team in the world below the major league level—and they could give a good account of themselves against a major league team as well.

Alonzo Perry, a member of the Dominican Republic Sports Hall of Fame, compiled a career batting average of .305 over nine years, winter and summer (courtesy Yuyo Ruiz).

Organized baseball began

sending some of its most promising major league prospects to the Dominican Winter League in 1955 to gain experience before joining the big team. Some of the early major leaguers who were tutored in the Dominican Winter League during the 1950s included the three Alou brothers, Felipe, Jesus, and Matty; Rico Carty, Juan Marichal, Manny Mota, and Julian Javier, all from the Dominican Republic; Ozzie Virgil from Puerto Rico; and Americans Willie Kirkland, Bill Mazeroski, Charlie Neal, Bob Gibson, Bob Thurman, Dick Stuart, and Stan Williams.

The 1955-56 winter league was a smashing success with Escogido capturing the first winter league championship. Bob Wilson, a Brooklyn Dodgers farmhand who began his professional baseball career with the Newark Eagles in the Negro National League, took the batting title with an average of .333. Willie Kirkland led the home run parade with 9, and Fred Waters, who had just broken in with the Pittsburgh Pirates in 1955, topped the league's pitchers with 11 victories. Wilson played for the Montreal Royals in the AAA International League in 1955, and he led the league with 599 at-bats, 190 base hits, and 41 doubles, while batting .317.

The success of the Dominican entourage like the Alou brothers and Juan Marichal caused the major league teams to sit up and take notice of the quality of baseball that was played in the Dominican Republic and, before long, major league scouts by the dozens were descending on the Caribbean island, looking for other baseball superstars. The quality of play in the Dominican Winter League continued to increase throughout the 1960s as new young prospects arrived every year, and the Dominican players, even after they became major league stars, continued to play in the winter league to show their gratitude to the home fans for their support. As Matty Alou noted, "I played for Escogido every year for twenty-three years. When I was sick, I played, when I won the batting title I played. Didn't miss one." Also, major league salaries were low, about $6000 for a good player, so many of them played ball in the winter to supplement their income.

I attended a baseball game in Ciudad Trujillo between the Dominican All-Stars and the famed Tokyo Giants in March 1955. The Giants were represented by the legendary Tetsuharu Kawakami, 310-game winner Takehiko Bessho, and future Hall-of-Famer Shigeru Chiba. The Dominican All-Stars fielded a team that included Tetelo Vargas, future major leaguer Diomedes Olivo, and Negro League nomad Alonzo Perry. Olivo had compiled an 8–2 record in the 1954 summer season, Vargas hit .292, and Perry, who compiled a .355 career batting average in Mexico and a .316 average in the Negro leagues, hit .336. Kawakami batted .322 in Japan in 1954, Chiba hit .252 and fielded like a demon, and Bessho went 26–12 while pitching 330 innings. The game was a festive occasion attended by a large integrated crowd of noisy fanatics who cheered their heroes at every turn. A tense moment occurred in the middle of the game when a batter fouled a ball straight back, where it became lodged in the screen. A young Spanish-looking girl, about nine years old, jumped from her seat and attempted to pull the ball through the screen, but two big men were right behind her and, in attempting to free the ball, they crushed the young girl into the boards. This brought an immediate reaction from a tall, well-dressed woman, perhaps the girl's sister or mother, who raced to her rescue. Screaming in Spanish, she beat the two men about the shoulders and head with a soda bottle but, before the situation could escalate, cooler heads prevailed. The girl was freed, the woman was returned to her seat, and the two men were escorted from the scene. The Tokyo Giants won the game, but it was a closely contested and skillfully played match, not at the major league level, but at least at a Class AA level. Both leagues have improved considerably since that time, and now perform at a AAA level.

Baseball in the Caribbean basin changed as the 1960s approached. Not better. Just different. Fidel Castro had assumed control of Cuba after years of guerilla warfare, and he immediately withdrew his teams from professional leagues, declaring that all Cuban athletics would be strictly amateur endeavors. Negro League players also disappeared from the winter scene, the victim of integration. But the popularity of winter leagues, particularly in the Dominican Republic and Puerto Rico, would soar to new heights over the last four decades of the 20th century.

The Negro League contribution to the post–1950 Dominican Leagues, summer and winter, included Alphonso Gerrard, Leon Kellman, Honey Lott, Al Pennington, Alonzo Perry, Curt Roberts, Bonnie Serrell, Milt Smith, Earl Taborn, Bob Thurman, Jesse Williams, John Williams, Curley Williams, Silvio Garcia, Willard Brown, Pee Wee Butts, Luis Cabrera, Bill Cash, Alex Crespo, Ray Dandridge, Johnny Davis, Claro Duany, "Red" Fields, Howard Easterling, Tetelo Vargas, Terris McDuffie, and Pedro Formental. Perry, Roberts, Milt Smith, and Vargas played in the winter league. The other players performed in the summer league. The only Negro League player to capture individual honors in the Dominican Winter League, in addition to Bob Wilson, was Alonzo Perry, formerly of the Birmingham Black Barons, who won the batting championship in 1957-58 with an average of .332.

Alonzo Perry was the most prolific Negro League hitter ever to perform in the Dominican Republic. The 6', 3", 200-pound first baseman hit with power from both sides of the plate. He played in the Dominican Summer League from 1951 to 1954, and in the winter league from 1955 to 1958. Along the way, he won two batting titles and two home runs crowns as noted above. In 1951 he put together a 32-consecutive-game hitting streak, and in 1953 he set a league record with 53 runs batted in, and led the league with 16 stolen bases. His career statistics show a .310 batting average with 49 home runs in 1430 at-bats. Perry, the only American-born Negro League player to be elected to the Dominican Republic Baseball Hall of Fame, also starred in Cuba and Mexico.

The last connection between the Negro leagues and the Dominican Winter League may have been severed in the 1963-64 season when Sam "Toothpick" Jones (4–1) and Minnie Minoso participated in the league. Jones, who played for the Homestead Grays in 1946, went on to a successful 12-year major league career that saw him win 102 games against 101 losses, and included a league-leading 21 victories in 1959. Minoso, who played in the Negro leagues from 1945 to 1948, was a major leaguer from 1949 to 1964, and made two promotional appearances in 1976 and 1980, becoming the first man to see action in the major leagues in five decades. One of his final appearances in a Dominican Republic uniform was against La Guaira in Venezuela on December 26, 1963. Juan Marichal, on the mound for Escogido, was KO'd in the 6th inning when La Guaira erupted for five runs triggered by base hits off the bats of Luis Aparicio and "Sweet Lou" Johnson. Both lineups were loaded with major league players including Aparicio, Johnson, Marichal, Minoso, Jesus and Felipe Alou, Dave Roberts, Elio Chacon, J. C. Hartman, and Dale Willis. Lou Johnson and Felipe Alou lit up the evening sky with round trippers, and Aparicio rapped out two base hits and stole a base.

Escogido					La Guaria				
Name	Pos	AB	R	H	Name	Pos	AB	R	H
R. Diaz	SS	4	1	1	J.C. Hartman	3B	5	0	2
F. Santana	2B	4	0	1	E. Chacon	2B	4	0	0
J. Alou	RF	4	0	1	D. Roberts	1B	4	1	0
F. Alou	CF	4	1	1	L. Johnson	LF	5	2	2
A. Martinez	1B	4	0	0	L. Aparicio	SS	5	1	2
O. Minoso	LF	3	0	0	C. W'thersp'n	C	5	1	1
F. Valesquez	C	3	0	1	L. Tovar	RF	2	1	2
F. Fiallo	3B	3	0	0	J. Herrera	RF	0	1	0
J. Marichal	P	2	0	0	A. Bravo	CF	3	2	1
F. Rives	P	0	0	0	E. Thomas	P	3	0	2
R. Rijo	P	0	0	0	D. Willis	P	1	0	0
J. Duran	P	0	0	0					
M. Cartegena	PH	1	0	0					
P. Reynoso	P	0	0	0					
Totals		32	2	5			37	9	12

```
Escogido      0 1 1   0 0 0   0 0 0—2— 5—2
La Guiara     0 0 1   0 1 5   0 2 x—9—12—0
```

Two Base Hits: F. Valesquez
Home Runs: F. Alou, L. Johnson

The first player from the Dominican Republic to enter the major leagues was Ozzie Virgil, who joined the New York Giants in 1956. By 2005, over 400 Dominican natives had played in the major leagues, more than from any other foreign country, and over 40 were still active. There were also 46 active players from Puerto Rico, 38 from Venezuela, 23 from Mexico, 12 from Cuba, more than a dozen from Japan, and smaller contingents from Panama, Colombia, Nicaragua, Hawaii, Canada, Curacao, and South Korea. The major leagues were quickly becoming an international showplace.

8

Far Away in Venezuela

Venezuela is one of the more unstable countries in the Western Hemisphere after being a Spanish colony for almost 300 years, from its discovery by Christopher Columbus in 1498 until its revolution in 1810. Simon Bolivar, the revolutionary leader, won the decisive battle over the Spanish royalist army in 1821 and, since that time, its political history has been one of revolution and counterrevolution, climaxed by the inevitable dictatorship.

Baseball was a late arrival in Venezuela, making landfall during the 1890s. Some sources claim the British introduced the game of rounders to the country when they were building the Venezuelan railroad, and that it soon became the children's favorite street game. Another source claims that Cuba's Emilio Cramer brought an all-star baseball team to the country in 1895, giving exhibitions and conducting clinics, so that by the time Venezuelan students, who had attended American universities, returned home with bats and balls, baseball had already replaced rounders as the street game of choice. The first organized baseball club in Venezuela was the Caracas Base Ball Club, formed in 1895 by students who had learned the game in the United States, and they practiced on a field called the Caracas Baseball Club Exercise Field. The first game was played between two teams from the Caracas BBC, the Blues and the Reds, with the Blues winning by the score of 28–19. Señor Mosquera, the father of one of the Caracas BBC's founders, and the owner of the Caracas Beer Company, built a stadium for the use of the club. It was called Stand del Este, and had grandstands and official distances according to American rules. Caracas played its first game against an outside opponent in Stand del Este on August 5. The game was slow to develop in the South American country that was isolated from the rest of the baseball world by endless miles of ocean and treacherous terrain, but according to Leonte A. Landino, "Hundreds of people went every Sunday to watch a baseball match between Caracas BBC and other new teams like Vargas, Independencia, Los Samanes, San Bernardino, and Magallanes in 1917, which is still alive." *El Tiempo* reported, "It looked like a carnival Sunday, without disguises or flowers or candles or reddish things. The delight of the people was so high that there was not even one complaint about the poverty that existed in the country." As one Venezuelan citizen said, "Our people like to celebrate whenever they can, and they adore noise." On August 15, 1895, the magazine *El Cojo Ilustrado* published the first photos of a baseball game.

According to Krich,

> In 1903, when the U.S. Navy was summoned to break a German blockade of the country, local teams were skilled enough to play a much-publicized doubleheader with the visiting

Seabees. Box scores indicate the locals came back from a first-game pasting to gain sweet revenge in the nightcap. A series of early, barnstorming Cuban clubs—the Caribbean equivalent of the Harlem Globetrotters—helped increase the sport's popularity. Puerto Rico's Borinquen Stars, with Millito Navarro, Marcelino "Moncho Brujo" Blondet, and Tingo Daviu, toured to sell-outs in 1918. Navarro and Blondet would eventually play for Santa Marta seven years later. By the twenties, soccer was the sport identified with foreign elites, while baseball had been established as "native." But baseball had an advantage over soccer in Venezuela in that its slower pace was better suited to the climate of the country, which is hot and humid. Caracas, like most of the inhabitable area of the country, was just 700 miles north of the equator. As a result, the country enjoyed a perpetual summer, with the sun overhead the entire year, and temperatures ranging from the 80s to the high 90s. Most of the population lives along the northern coastal plain, the greatest distance from the equator, with the southern part of the country largely uninhabited. During the rainy season, from May through September, large sections of the country, north of the Orinoco River, are inundated, so the winter league normally operated from mid–October to February.

Newspaper coverage of baseball games was scant in the early part of the century, although there was occasional coverage of important games. One such game was a contest between two popular rivals, Independencia and Los Samanes, in Caracas on September 30, 1917. Hitting took center stage in the game with Independencia racing to a 9–3 lead in the bottom of the first inning and then holding off Samanes for a 10–5 victory. The right fielder for Independencia was Bobby Williams, a native of New Orleans, Louisiana. The tiny 5', 5", 145-pound right-handed hitter, on his way to a 17-year career in the American Negro leagues, was the first Negro League player to play in Venezuela. The competition between the two teams went a long way toward popularizing baseball in Venezuela, especially since Los Samanes was generally recognized as the champion baseball team in the country at the time.

Independencia

Name	Pos	AB	R	H
P. Maury	CF	5	2	1
J. Perez	2B	5	1	0
R. Williams	RF	5	1	0
S. Meneses	SS	5	1	1
A. Brunicardi	1B	4	1	1
R. Escobar	C	4	1	1
L. Ramirez	3B	4	1	0
A. Perez	LF	4	1	0
F.J. Fernandez	P	4	1	3
Totals		40	10	7

Los Samanes

Name	Pos	AB	R	H
R. Carabano	SS	5	2	0
J. A. Perez	P	5	1	0
F. Fuentes	3B	4	1	1
A. Romero	2B	4	0	2
O. Machado	RF	4	0	1
R. Feo	1B	4	0	0
E. Mendez	CF	4	0	0
C. Basso	C	4	1	0
J. Corso	LF	4	0	0
		38	5	4

Independencia   9 0 0   0 0 0   0 1 x—10—7— 9
Los Samanes   3 0 0   1 0 0   0 0 1— 5—4—14

Independencia followed up its victory over Los Samanes with a stirring 4–3 victory over their hated rivals the next year, scoring three runs in the bottom of the 12th inning after Samanes had pushed over two runs in the top of the inning. Scrappy second baseman Bobby Williams drove in the winning run with a two-out line drive down the left field line that was ruled fair by the umpire, setting off a violent argument by Samanes players and fans. Captain F.J. Fernandez of Independencia was the winning pitcher, holding Samanes to six base hits and fanning 15. His opponent, Juan Antonio Perez, pitched an eight-hitter and struck out 9 in losing for the second straight year. An official protest to the president of the Independencia Club from the president of Los Samanes was disallowed, and Samanes subsequently withdrew from the championship series, with Independencia claiming the title.

The game of baseball developed more quickly in cities like Maracaibo and Maracay than it did in Caracas. In Maracaibo, William H. Phelps, an American transplant, organized three teams in the city, the Blues, the Reds, and the Blacks. He outfitted them with equipment he obtained in the United States and held games every weekend in Diamante Veritas. Over the years, Maracaibo grew to become the baseball capital of Venezuela, producing such baseball legends as Luis Aparicio, Sr., and his son, Luis Jr., who became a major league star. By 1920, Maracaibo had 10 baseball stadiums and 30 organized baseball teams. Maracay, the capital of the Aragua State, was the home of the country's president, General Juan Vicente Gomez, and Gomez, a baseball fan, directed the organization of the Maracay BBC. He also pitched for the team that included several of his relatives as well as members of his administration.

Baseball in Venezuela, unlike the situation in the United States, was an integrated sport almost from its beginning. Initially the game was played by members of the aristocracy, many of whom had been educated in the States, but as the game increased in popularity, men of all social classes began to participate. And there was no visible discrimination as far as semi-pro and professional athletics were concerned. Touring integrated baseball teams from Puerto Rico and Cuba were welcomed and the players were idolized and imitated. A majority of the Venezuelan population was mestizo, a mixture of white and Indian, by the beginning of the 20th century, with about 20 percent white, primarily Spanish, 10 percent black, and a small percentage of native Indian, including Arawak and Carib. Government leaders and the major landowners were primarily of Spanish descent, while the mestizos, blacks, and Indians were relegated to the lower levels of the society. Spanish is the official language of the country, as it is with most countries in Central and South America.

In 1922, oil was discovered in the Lake Maracaibo basin in western Venezuela, and the world suddenly became smaller. Oil rose to become the dominant factor in the economy of the country, accounting for up to 95 percent of its exports. And, as usual, American companies, along with Anglo-Persian Oil and British Controlled Oilfields, swooped down on Venezuela and bought most of the oil concessions in the country.

Venezuela's first amateur league was active in the 1920s but, even then, amateurism was a shadowy term. Magallanes, for instance, had hired a Cuban player, Lazaro Quezada, and even he was not the first paid player in the country. Some of the early teams resorted to paying players in order to retain their services, forcing the teams to charge admission to the games to generate the necessary funds. Some players, like Venezuelan natives Balbino Inojosa, and Manuel Malpica, nicknamed "The Chicken," and "Cocaina" Garcia of Cuba, were paid exorbitant salaries of between 50 and 200 Bolivares to play baseball in Venezuela, according to Landino. Malpica, a catcher, and Inojosa, a pitcher, joined the Magallanes Navigators in 1929 and helped the team defeat its hated rival, Royal Criollos, in a three-game series. Malpica, like most of the outstanding baseball players of the period, frequently moved from team to team depending on the incentive offered. During the 1930s, he played for Magallanes (1930–31), Concord (1932–34), Royal Creole (1935), Senators (1936), and Magalanes again (1937–41). Santa Marta of La Guaira, with Puerto Rican imports Menchin Pesante, "Millito" Navarro, and Marcelino "Moncho Brujo" Blondet, the man who introduced the spitball to Venezuela, entered Venezuela's first professional baseball tournament in Caracas in July 1927 along with Maracay, Royal Criollos, and San Martin. In one of the key matchups, Santa Marta, with Blondet tossing a four-hitter, routed Royal Criollos by the count of 7–1. Navarro, who played for the Cuban Stars in the Negro National League, contributed a triple in support of his countryman, who struck out 7 and walked 1.

Santa Marta

Name	Pos	AB	R	H
M. Pesante	SS	2	1	0
Anselmo	CF	4	1	1
M. Navarro	2B	5	1	1
R. Blondet	P	4	0	0
C.M. Perez	LF	4	0	0
J. Perez	RF	4	1	1
Basquin	1B	4	0	0
Coronel	3B	3	1	1
Calderon	C	1	1	1
Torrealba	C	2	1	2
Totals		33	7	7

Royal Criollos

Name	Pos	AB	R	H
Alvarado	RF	4	0	0
Jimenez	SS	4	1	1
Inojosa	P	4	0	1
Arratia	2B	4	0	1
Nieves	1B	3	0	0
Rodriguez	C	4	0	0
Jose Dolores	3B	4	0	0
Borden	CF	3	0	1
Capote	LF	1	0	0
Hernandez	CF	1	0	0
		32	1	4

Santa Marta   1 3 0   0 0 0   3 0 0—7—7—2
Royal Criollos   1 0 0   0 0 0   0 0 0—1—4—5

Two Base Hits: Arratia, Torrealba
Three Base Hit: Navarro

Pitchers	IP	W	L	H	SO	BB
Blondet	9	1	0	4	7	1
Inojosa	9	0	1	7	6	4

Maracay was declared the winner of the tournament, but there was some question about whether or not the president had exerted his influence to guarantee victory for his hometown team. Baseball, by this time, had become a political football, as it had been in Cuba since the 1890s, and General Juan Vicente Gomez, who was an oppressive ruler, banned public congregations in 1928, forcing the cancellation of the amateur baseball season.

But baseball returned again in 1930 and on January 15 of that year the Venezuelan Association of Baseball was formed to promote professional tournaments. This was the beginning of the intense rivalries between two Caracas teams, Magallanes and Royal Criollos, with the Criollos gradually evolving, first into Caracas Cerveceria and finally to the Caracas Lions. The 1930 National Tournament included Magallanes, Royal Criollos, Cincinnati, Santa Marta, and Los Latinos, with Magallanes being crowned the National Champion with a 9–4 record compared to 8–5 for Cincinnati. The following year the Magallanes-Royal Criollos rivalry heated up when they clashed for the National

Championship. The Criollos grabbed the brass ring by defeating the Navigators two out of three. Balbino Inojosa of Royal led the league with 10 victories, 111 innings pitched, 100 strikeouts, and a 0.69 earned run average. The year 1932 brought a mammoth struggle between Concordia and Caribe for the championship. On August 4, "Cocaina" Garcia defeated Royal Criollos, fanning 20 batters in 13 innings. When the season ended on September 19, Caribe and Concordia were tied for first place with 6 wins and 2 losses each. The season came down to one final game that was played on November 20 in the stadium with banners flying, a frenzied crowd straining to see the action, and the country's two top pitchers, Martin Dihigo of Concordia and "Cocaina" Garcia of Caribe, facing each other. The battle raged for 20 innings with neither team gaining an advantage. Over that stretch, Dihigo limited Caribe to just 7 base hits and fanned 11. Garcia held Concordia to 6 hits and fanned 4. The game ended in a dispute with the umpire being accused of favoritism toward Concordia and, when the dust settled, the president of the league awarded the title to Caribe by a forfeit.

It was during this period that the league began to attract ballplayers from all over the Western Hemisphere. Many of the Negro League's greatest players wintered in Venezuela beginning in the early '30s, including Satchel Paige (1932–33), Martin Dihigo (1932–34), Silvio Garcia (1932–1937), "Cocaina" Garcia (1932–37), Pelayo Chacon (1933–34), Josh Gibson (1934), Tetelo Vargas (1934), Ramon Bragana (1934–37), Francisco "Pancho" Coimbre (1935), Ray Dandridge (1938–40), Leon Day (1940), Jose Fernandez, and Alejandro Oms. Dihigo, Cuba's legendary "El Immortal," dazzled Venezuelan fans with his skills, not only on the mound, but also in center field and second base. And he was a .300 hitter who hit with power. In his first year in the country, he tossed a no-hitter, and in his second season, he went through the opposition like Sherman through Georgia, racking up six wins without a loss, and posting an almost invisible 0.15 earned run average. Future Venezuelan Hall of Fame pitcher Daniel Canonico began his career in Caracas in 1934, as an outfielder with the Senators, spending the next year with the Shepherd in Maracaibo before returning to the Senators. In 1936, playing second base for the Senators, he was rated the best second baseman in Caracas, being charged with just one error in 55 chances, a .982 fielding percentage. Cuban pitching sensation Ramon Bragana pitched in the semi-pro winter league in Venezuela during the 1936-37 season, going 8–4 with Gavilanes, and batting .318.

Since the Venezuelan Association of Baseball included only teams from the central region of the country, another league, the Zulian Baseball Association, was formed in the western region of the country, centered in Maracaibo. Lake Stadium was built in Maracaibo in 1933, and an agreement was made with the National League in the United States allowing American players to play with the Maracaibo teams, such as Gavilanes, Pastora, Centauros, Cabimas, and Espadon. The competition between Gavilanes and Pastora became one of the country's most hostile rivalries over the years, with the two teams facing each other countless times between 1931 and 1960. During most of the 1930s, Gavilanes dominated the Zulian League, capturing the championship in 1933, and 1935 through 1940. Pastora nipped Gavilanes 6–5 for the Perrrito Cup on May 1, 1932, behind the pitching of Chucho Hernandez and the potent bat of second baseman G. Cedeno, who lashed out four base hits including a double and a triple. Two years later Pastora was able to wrest the crown from the Gavilanes team again, but except for those two minor bumps in the road, it was all Gavilanes.

8. Far Away in Venezuela

Life was not easy for the foreign players in Venezuela in the early years according to Donn Rogosin: "For the Americans and Cubans, who had the strongest baseball tradition, the most difficult Caribbean country, until the forties, was Venezuela. The money was acceptable, but the forlorn note of Venezuelan isolation was captured in a postcard from Cuban star Pelayo Chacon to his friend Clint Thomas. 'I hope you be well,' he wrote in pidgin English. 'I be well. Thomas, I have been here 14 month, and I am weary. Regards to all boys. Your friend Chacon.' It was sent from La Guaira, Venezuela, dated June 3, 1933."

Satchel Paige was one of the first Negro Leaguers to play baseball in Venezuela. During the winter of 1932-33, he began the year with Tom Wilson's Nashville Elite Giants in the California Winter League but, after compiling a perfect 7–0 record and helping the Giants capture the pennant once again, Satchel packed up his belongings and lit out for more southern climes because, as he told John Holway, "I didn't have a topcoat." His Venezuelan adventures were communicated to David Lipman. Satch said he was playing the outfield one day when the batter hit a ball to the deep recesses of the park, next to what Satch thought was an iron pipe. The pipe turned out to be a snake, and when Satch reached down to pick up the ball, the pipe moved—and so did Satch. He never stopped running until he reached the safety of the dugout. In another game, still fearful of snakes but brave to the last, he roamed the outfield after a fly ball and, just as he caught it, he caught sight of a snake near his feet. Ignoring the runner on first base, Satch picked up a stick and beat the snake to death, while the runner merrily circled the bases with the winning run. At least, that's the way Satch saw it.

Paige related another incident concerning the spicy food that is a main staple in the country. After spending several months in Caracas, he began having stomachaches and, thinking they were being caused by an empty stomach, he would have another hot meal. Finally, the pain became unbearable, and Satch screamed for a doctor. The doctor gave him some medication, but the big stomachache lasted until the season ended and Satch was safely back in the States again. He never ate fried or spicy food again.

The early 1930s also produced what may have been the greatest professional baseball team ever assembled in the Western Hemisphere, and possibly equal to the best the major leagues could offer. The Concordia, composed of the best players in the Western Hemisphere, was a true international conglomeration. It included Marcelino Blondet from Puerto Rico, Martin Dihigo, Francisco Quevedo, and Silvino Ruiz from Cuba, Tetelo Vargas and Pedro San from the Dominican Republic, Josh Gibson and Rap Dixon from the American Negro Leagues, and Balbino Inojosa, Luis Aparicio Sr., Cesar Nieves, Manuel Antonio Alpica, and Luis Jimenez from Venezuela. It even had one major league player. Jimmy Jordan of the Brooklyn Dodgers often wintered in the Caribbean region and played baseball in Venezuela and Puerto Rico. The Concordia team played games against the top amateur clubs in Venezuela, and then took their show on the road, visiting Puerto Rico, the Dominican Republic, and Cuba. They didn't win all their games, but they won most of them.

Ray Dandridge was enticed to go to Venezuela in 1938 for a salary of $350 a month, more than double his Negro League salary of $150 a month. Ray insisted on getting a two-month advance before he would agree to go, and as soon as the money was deposited in his bank account, he withdrew it, according to Jim Riley.

The famous Concordia team of the early 1930s included: Back (left to right): Marcelino Blondet, Tetelo Vargas, Martin Dihigo, Jimmy Jordan, Balbino Inojosa, Francisco Quevedo, Josh Gibson, Arturo Lopez. Front (left to right): Cesar Nieves, Luis Aparacio Sr., Manuel Antonio Malpica, Rap Dixon, Luis Jiminez, Silvino Ruiz, Pedro Alejandro San (courtesy Cuqui Cordova).

When he went to the bank to pick up the money, he stuffed it into both of his front pockets and kept both hands stuck in his pockets to keep from losing it on the subway ride home. He was so concerned with not losing the money that he missed his exchange and had to ride all the way back and start over again. When he finally got home he spread the money all over the bed. "It was more money than I had ever seen in my life," Ray declares. He didn't even know where Venezuela was, but he showed his wife the money and said, "I'm going to play ball there." Ray took $100 for himself, left the rest for his wife, and boarded a boat for South America.

He stayed there for two years, playing alongside other Negro Leaguers like pitcher Leroy Matlock and shortstop Harry Williams. His most vivid memories of Venezuela were "Bad equipment. Bad fields. A living." Venezuela, along with Cuba, the Dominican Republic, and Puerto Rico, would continue to compete for Negro League talent until the integration of organized baseball spelled finis to the popular black leagues.

During Dandridge's first year in Venezuela, he helped the Vargas team to the league title. That same year the league witnessed one of the most incredible pitching duels in baseball history, according to Peter Bjarkman. Andres Julio Baez of the Pastora Club matched pitches with the Cuban superstar Lazaro Salazar, pitching for Gavilanes, in a game that lasted 20 innings. Both pitchers went the distance, with Baez emerging victorious by the score of 1–0. The 6 hour, 30 minute battle saw only five Gavilanes batters reaching first base against Baez, and just seven Pastora batters reaching base against Salazar.

Leon Day left Puerto Rico after his team was eliminated from contention in the 1939-40 winter league, and traveled to Venezuela to play baseball there during the remainder of the winter season. He was joined by Ray Dandridge, and the two of them joined Vargas. Day dominated the Venezuelan Winter League, coasting home with a 12–1 record. Maracaibo, in an effort to slow down the Vargas express, quickly offered Josh Gibson $700 a month, a $1,000 signing bonus, free housing and all expenses paid, to come to Caracas. Josh lived well and enjoyed the nightlife in Caracas for three months, and he hit a torrid .419 in league play. As fate would have it, Leon Day met his old friend and adversary, Bill Byrd, in a key matchup in early April. The game felt like a rematch of the January classic in Puerto Rico, when the two hurlers matched each other pitch for pitch for 18 innings, the game being called on account of darkness with the score tied at 1–1. This encounter was almost as good. After Vargas had gone out in front 1–0, Josh Gibson doubled in the fourth inning and came around to score the tying run. Once again the game went into extra innings, but this time it ended in the 11th when Dandridge smoked a game-winning home run to give Leon Day a well-earned 2–1 victory. The 5', 10", 180-pound right-hander scattered five hits and struck out 11 batters in his gem. Day's year, from May 1939 through April 1940, was one for the books. He went 12–4 with Newark in the Negro National League, 12–11 with Aquadilla in Puerto Rico, and 12–1 for Vargas, for a total record of 36–16.

Venezuela entered the Amateur World Series in October 1940, in El Tropical, Havana, Cuba, their first appearance in the event. They finished in fifth place that year with a 5 and 7 record, trailing the champion Cuban team, who finished at 10 and 2, but they surprised everyone

Leon Day paced Vargas to the pennant in 1939–40 with a 12–1 record (author's collection).

by winning the championship the following year, upsetting the favored Cubans in El Tropical before a packed house of noisy hometown fans. Manuel Malpica managed the victorious Venezuelan team that included the immortal Daniel "Chinese" Canonico, Jose Perez Colmenares, Julio Bracho, Enrique Fonseca, Delmiro Finol, Hector R. Benitez, and Jose Casanova. Canonico, who threw a knuckleball, a fastball, and a deadly change of pace, pitched and won 5 games in the tournament including two games over Cuba. Venezuela, who had dropped a heartbreaking 4–2 decision to the Dominican Republic early in the tournament, bounced back to knock off the favored Cubans 4–1 on October 17 behind Canonico, tying Cuba for first place with 7 wins and 1 loss. That victory forced a championship game to be played on the 22nd. Cuba placed its hopes on 30-year-old right-hander Connie Marrero, who would go on to pitch in the major leagues nine years later. Venezuela countered with its ace, Daniel Canonico, and the 25-year-old pitcher achieved legendary status when he defeated the powerful Cubans by the score of 3–1 before 30,000 screaming fans at El Tropical plus millions more throughout the Caribbean region who followed the game on radio. It was the most famous baseball victory in Venezuelan history, and the players have gone down in baseball lore as "The Heroes of the '41." The game was decided in the opening stanza when Venezuela scored three times on two bases on balls a double by Jesus "Commissioner" Branches and an infield out. Cuba scored its only run in the ninth inning. After the final out was recorded, the huge crowd spilled out onto the field and carried Canonico around on their shoulders. And to prove it wasn't a fluke, Venezuela also won the championship in 1944 and 1945.

Alejandro Oms played in Venezuela in the 1940s and was named the league's best defensive outfielder in 1943. Not bad for an old man of 48. The period from 1942 to 1988 produced the country's second greatest rivalry, Caracas against Magallanes. It also witnessed the country's first professional baseball league that was introduced in 1946 and is still operating today. One year before the inaugural professional baseball season, the Estadio Olimpico in Maracaibo was built, ushering in a new era in Venezuelan baseball. The first game matched Gavilanes against Pastora in one of their many grudge matches. With a crowd of 10,000 baseball fanatics looking on, Rafael Gallis Tello of Gavilanes crushed a home run in the fifth inning to lead his team to a 5–2 victory.

In the fall of 1945, a Negro League All-Star team, known as the American All-Stars, traveled to Caracas, Venezuela, with a lineup that included Roy Campanella, Jackie Robinson, Quincy Trouppe, Buck Leonard, Gene Benson, and Sam Jethroe. Campanella noted the trip in his autobiography. "When the KLM airliner landed at Miami, I went to the back of the four-motor job to sit with Robinson." The two men played poker and "by the time we had passed over the Caribbean and the plane set down in La Guaira, I owed Jackie around ten bucks. We had a real strong team. We played an international series involving Venezuela and Cuba, and the United States. We won eighteen of the twenty games. Robinson played shortstop and I caught and played the outfield. After the exhibitions were over, a good many of the fellows, including Robinson, returned to the States. I stayed down there to play with the local Vargas team. One of the rival clubs was managed by Lefty Gomez, who was a great pitcher with the New York Yankees. We won the pennant, but I played with half a mind on the game, the other half back in the States."

Jackie Robinson also reported on the fall visit in a letter to the *Chicago Defender*, posted in the December 15 edition: "We have played two ball games thus far and I have done fairly well. The first day I had a home run and a single, but the second day I went hitless in three trips. Buck Leonard and Roy Campanella have been doing very well. Buck has two home runs and Campanella has connected for five hits. We won both games, the first 8 to 2, and the second 4 to 3 in ten innings. Felton Snow, manager of the Baltimore Elite Giants, is also managing this team and is doing an excellent job."

Venezuela's baseball skills were still basically undeveloped in 1945, except for an occasional outstanding natural talent like Luis Aparicio Sr., and the Negro Leaguers embarrassed their Venezuelan opponents in head-to-head competition. They used a Wilson 97 ball in the series at the Negro Leaguers' request, because Leonard, Campanella, and company knew the 97 ball was lively and would travel a long distance if hit right. After the All-Star team had won the first 10 or 12 games, the Venezuelan authorities pleaded with them to lose a game, but the Negro Leaguers refused, saying they didn't travel 3000 miles to lose. The Negro Leaguers practically hit the cover off the ball. Buck Leonard led the team with a .425 average, followed by Parnell Woods at .419, Quincy Trouppe at .413, Sam Jethroe at .339, and Jackie Robinson at .281. The 24-year-old Campanella, who was waiting to hear from the Brooklyn Dodgers about joining their organization, hit a mediocre .211. Jethroe, Robinson, and Campanella were on their way to successful major league careers, Jackie having signed a contract with the Brooklyn Dodgers farm team in Montreal, Canada, the day before the team departed for Venezuela. Quincy Trouppe had a cup of coffee in the big time, playing 6 games with the Cleveland Indians in 1952, while Buck Leonard, a 37-year-old graybeard in 1945, had to satisfy himself with a brief appearance in the Piedmont League in 1953, and Parnell Woods reached the Pacific Coast League in 1949, hitting .275 in 40 games. Roy Welmaker, who would go on to a successful minor league career, went a perfect 8–0 on the tour.

Gene Benson talked to Holway in *Black Diamonds* about playing baseball in Venezuela in 1945.

> I played in Puerto Rico, Mexico, Cuba, Panama, South America. Maracaibo, Venezuela: They called it hell. If you played the outfield, the heat burns up through your shoes. You have to keep continually moving. You couldn't play a doubleheader: One game in the morning, go home, then come back and play the second game.
>
> They had an election there, bullets zinging all over the walls. From what I hear, they're still doing it.
>
> That was the first time I was away from home without a round-trip ticket. The guy we were playing for bet all his money on the other team. But we won the game, and before we got back to the hotel, he was dead. Blew his brains out. They were *serious* about baseball.
>
> I said, "We'll go to the American consul," but it didn't do any good, so we decided to go to the inquest. But everybody there was broke too. After that, I made sure I never went anywhere without transportation.

Benson struggled through the winter season in Venezuela that year, batting .271 in 59 at-bats.

Sam Jethroe and Sam Bankhead stayed in Venezuela to play in the 1945-46 winter league that was, at that time, theoretically an amateur league. Both players excelled in the league with Jethroe, who played for the Vargas pennant winners, leading the league with 5 triples and 11 stolen bases, and Bankhead tying for the league lead in home runs with 3.

In December 1945, the Professional Baseball League, the first official professional Venezuelan Winter League was organized with four teams, Cerveceria Caracas, Vargas, Magallanes, and Venezuela. Within a few years, the Cerveceria Caracas team, named after the local brewery, discovered that fans in other towns were not buying Cerveceria beer as a protest against the team. The company eventually sold the team and the new owners changed the name of the team to the Caracas Lions. Initially the league was forced to recruit players from around the Western Hemisphere in order to staff four complete teams. Players were signed from the Dominican Republic, Mexico, Puerto Rico, and Cuba, but by far the largest complement of players came from the American Negro leagues. The inaugural game of the professional Venezuelan Winter League matched Venezuela against the Magallanes Navigators in Cerveceria Caracas Stadium, and Magallanes prevailed by the score of 5–2 behind Alex Carrasquel, a seven-year major league veteran, who won 50 games against 39 losses for the Washington Senators between 1939 and 1945. The 6', 1," 182-pound right-hander, who went 11–7 for Washington in 1953, was the star of the game. He was supported by shortstop Luis Aparicio, the father of the future Chicago White Sox shortstop. Aparicio Sr., who had an opportunity to accompany Carrasquel to the major leagues but turned it down because he didn't like to fly, led off the game with a single and later came around to score the first run in the new professional Venezuelan Winter League, the first of four runs scored in the inning off Negro League right-hander Bill Jefferson.

The second game of the season, on January 13, 1946, saw Vargas defeat Cerveceria Caracas by the score of 12–1, with Negro League pitcher Roy Welmaker on the mound. Vargas, who also had Negro League stars Sam Jethroe, Marvin Williams, and Roy Campanella on their roster, would go on to capture the first Venezuelan Winter League championship.

Sam Jethroe paced Vargas to the pennant in 1945–46, leading the league in triples and stolen bases (author's collection).

Alfonso "Chico" Carrasquel, the nephew of Alex Carrasquel, played shortstop for Cerveceria Caracas in 1946, and he became an instant hero at the age of 17 by hitting a game-winning home run in the 7th inning against Venezuela. The date was January 17, 1946, and it was the first home run hit in the Venezuelan Winter League. Carrasquel went on to enjoy a ten-year stay in the major leagues, primarily with the Chicago White Sox and the Cleveland Indians, leading the league in fielding average three times and hitting .258. Other early Venezuelan pioneers included Jesus Ramos, who joined the Cincinnati Reds in 1944, and Pompeyo "Yo-Yo" Davalillo, who played for Washington in 1953.

Three days after Carrasquel's historic home run, his uncle created a bit of history of his own by pitching his Magallanes team to a tense 3–2, 17-inning victory over Roy Welmaker of Vargas. Both pitchers were still in there at the finish. Magallanes pushed over two runs in the top of the 17th inning to take a 3–1 lead, but Vargas roared back in the bottom half of the inning to score one run and load the bases with two outs. That was all they would get however as Carrasquel settled down and retired Inojosa on a lazy fly ball to Gallis Tello in left field, ending one of the league's classic encounters. Both lineups were loaded with Negro League stars including Sam Jethroe, Carlos Ascanio, Quincy Trouppe, Marvin Williams, Cuco Correa, Roy Campanella, Romando Garcia, Jose Ramos, Vidal Lopez, and Roy Welmaker.

Magallanes

Name	Pos	AB	R	H
L. Aparacio	SS	7	1	2
F. Correa	2B	6	0	1
Q. Trouppe	C	7	0	2
R. Garcia C.	3B	7	1	1
V. Lopez	LF	1	0	0
V. Liendo	1B	2	0	0
A. Carrasquel	P	7	0	0
P. Uzcategui	CF	2	0	0
T. Pinate	CF	4	1	0
D. Barboza	RF	5	0	0
R. Gallis Tello	LF	3	0	1
Totals		57	3	10

Vargas

Name	Pos	AB	R	H
S. Jethroe	CF	7	1	2
C. Ascanio	1B	8	0	3
M. Williams	2B	7	0	0
Campanella	C	7	0	1
B. Inojose	RF	8	0	1
V. Osorio	LF	6	0	3
R. Welmaker	P	6	0	0
L. Rincon	3B	5	0	0
R. Olivares	3B	1	1	1
L. Oliveros	SS	7	0	3
C. Munoz	LF	1	0	0
Totals		62	2	14

Magallanes 0 0 0 0 0 0 0 0 1 0 0 0 0 0 0 0 2—3—10—2
Vargas   1 0 0 0 0 0 0 0 0 0 0 0 0 0 0 0 1—2—14—1

Doubles: J. Ramos, R. Garcia C.
Runs Batted In: Campanella, M. Williams, J. Ramos, Q. Trouppe.

Pitchers	IP	W	L	SO	BB
A. Carrasquel	17	1	0	6	4
R. Welmaker	16⅓	0	1	13	8

Negro League players played a key role in the early Venezuelan Winter League campaigns as can be seen in the above box score. The owners of two of the four teams in the winter league actively recruited the top Negro League players to come to Venezuela over the winter months to play for their team. Team Venezuela had only one Negro League player, Tom Glover, and Cerveceria Caracas relied solely on native players. At least two dozen Negro Leaguers participated in the inaugural season including, in addition to Glover and the players noted above, Parnell Woods, Buck Leonard, Bill Cash, Matty Crue, Oscar Estrada, Raul Espinoza, Silvio Garcia, Manuel Godinez, Bill Jefferson, Rufus Lewis, Henry Miller, Harry "Suitcase" Simpson, Hilton Smith, and Manuel "Cocaina" Garcia.

Campanella, batting in the cleanup spot, knocked in three runs with a single, a double, and a homer, in four at-bats, to spark his Vargas team to a 6–2 win over Magallanes on February 3, immediately endearing himself to the local fans. Four and a half weeks later, Marvin Williams set a batting record that has never been topped. The Vargas second baseman knocked in 8 runs with two home runs and two singles in a 16–9 rout of the Magallanes Navigators. The 6-foot tall, 190-pound second baseman went 4 for 5 on the day, with 4 runs scored. Roy Welmaker was the beneficiary of Williams' outburst, picking up the victory even though he didn't have his best stuff. He did, however, bring his bat to the game, accounting for three base hits including a double and a triple.

Vargas, led by Daniel Canonico, who managed and pitched for the team, won the 1946 Venezuelan Winter League pennant with a record of 18 wins and 12 losses, and Cuban born Pablo Garcia was the first official winter league batting champion. The 22-year-old third baseman batted a stunning .402 with 16 runs batted in, in 77 at-bats. Venezuelan Dalmiro Finol was the home run king with 7, and Marvin Williams was the runs batted in leader with 41, and also led the league in doubles with 14 and in runs scored with 41. Roy Welmaker dominated the pitching statistics. He led the league with 24 games pitched, 20 games started, 17 complete games, 12 victories (against 8 losses), 139 strikeouts (in 193 innings pitched), and a 2.80 earned run average. He also hit a home run. Bill Jefferson of Vargas and Venezuela went 4–2 on the mound.

The Vargas team repeated their success in 1946–47, and Parnell Woods, playing third base for Venezuela, punished opposing pitchers to the tune of .354 to capture the batting championship, while leading the league in doubles with 13, triples with 3, and runs scored with 28 in 36 games and 144 at-bats. He also hit one home run, drove in 17 teammates, and stole 7 bases. Teammate Marvin Williams led the league in doubles for the second consecutive year, this time with 13. Hilton Smith of Vargas went 8–5 on the mound with one home run, and Henry Miller chipped in with a 4–2 mark. Venezuelan native Vidal Lopez of Magallanes was the home run champ with 6, and "Chico" Carrasquel captured RBI honors with 29. Buck Leonard also had a big year in Venezuela in 1946–47, batting a resounding .425 in 47 at-bats. Sam Bankhead was the manager of the team when the season began, according to Bill Cash, but the records don't confirm that. In any case, Bankhead had to leave the team in January as Cash recounted to Brent Kelley. "I was in Caracas, Venezuela, playing with Vargas. Sam Bankhead was the manager. We were in a hotel playing pinochle—Sam Bankhead, Hilton Smith, and Henry Miller—and a guy came in and said, 'Bankhead! Telegram!.' That was the 21st day of January, 1947. Josh (Gibson, Sam Bankhead's godson) died. He died on the twentieth. He (Bankhead) went out that night, got drunk, came in and tore up everything in his room. They had to send him home."

In March 1947, Vargas played a four-game exhibition series against the powerful New York Yankees. Vargas, in addition to their regular players, like Bill Cash, Hilton Smith and Parnell Woods, had Ray Dandridge, Hank Thompson, Lenny Pearson, Ducky Davenport, and Luis Aparicio, Sr. The Yankee lineup included George McQuinn (.304), Snuffy Stirnweiss (.256), Phil Rizzuto (.273), Allie Clark, Aaron Robinson (.252), Tommy Henrich (.287), Yogi Berra (.280), and Charlie "King Kong" Keller (.238). Allie Reynolds (19–8) and Bill Bevens (7–13) pitched. In the opening game of the series, Hilton Smith and Gentry Jessup combined to beat the Bronx Bombers 4–3. Vargas scored two runs in the fourth on a Dandridge triple off Bevens to take a 2–0 lead, but New York, who had been held to one hit in five innings by Hilton Smith, pushed over three markers off Gentry Jessup in the sixth, and carried a 3–2 lead into the bottom of the ninth. Vargas put two men on base against Cuddles Marshall before Ducky Davenport rapped a triple to center field to plate the winning runs. Ray Dandridge singled twice in the next game, a Yankees victory.

New York Yankees					**Vargas**				
Name	*Pos*	*AB*	*R*	*H*	*Name*	*Pos*	*AB*	*R*	*H*
Stirnweiss	2B	3	1	1	Davenport	CF	5	0	1
W. Johnson	3B	4	1	1	Aparicio	SS	2	0	0
Henrich	RF	3	1	0	Thompson	LF	3	0	1
Keller	LF	2	0	0	Pearson	1B	4	1	3
Etten	1B	1	0	0	Williams	2B	4	0	1
Berra	C	2	0	0	Dandridge	3B-SS	4	1	1
Mapes	CF	3	0	0	Contreras	RF	3	0	0
Rizzuto	SS	3	0	1	Cash	C	2	0	0
Bevens	P	1	0	0	Smith	P	1	0	0
D. Johnson	P	0	0	0	L. St. Clair	C	3	1	1
Robinson	C	2	0	1	Jessup	P	1	0	0
Reynolds	P	2	0	1	Bankhead	RF	0	0	0
Mack	2B	1	0	0	Woods	3B	1	0	1
Clark	RF	2	0	2	J. St. Clair	PH	1	1	0
Medwick	LF	1	0	0					
Phillips	1B	1	0	0					
Brown	SS	1	0	0					
Marshall	P	0	0	0					
Houk	C	1	0	0					
Totals		33	3	7			34	4	9

New York Yankees   0 0 0   0 0 3   0 0 0—3—7—1
Vargas   0 0 0   2 0 0   0 0 2—4—9—2

Triples: Dandridge, Davenport

Pitchers	*IP*	*W*	*L*	*SO*	*BB*	*R*
Bevens	3	0	0	0	0	0
D. Johnson	1	0	0	1	0	2
Reynolds	3	0	0	3	1	0
Marshall	1⅓	0	1	0	1	2
H. Smith	5	0	0	1	2	0
Jessup	4	1	0	3	4	3

Cash remembered an incident in one of the other games in the series that he passed on to Brent Kelley. "King Kong Keller was in left, Cliff Mapes in center, and they put Yogi in right. A fly ball went to right field and Yogi was hollering, 'I got it! I got it!' Ball fell 20 feet in back of him. (Laughs). They told (Bill) Dickey, 'Make a catcher out of him.' Yogi could hit. No question about it. (His strike zone was) from his eyes to his toes."

Big Don Newcombe, coming off a brilliant season with Nashua of the New England League, where he led the league with 19 victories against just 6 losses, opened the 1947-48 season for Vargas on October 16 by throwing a 4–0 shutout at Team Venezuela in Caracas. The 6', 4", 220-pound fireballing right-hander fanned 7 and walked 2 in his masterpiece. Luis Aparicio, Sr., paced Vargas with three base hits, two runs scored, and an RBI. Two weeks later, another Negro Leaguer, big Luke Easter, known as "The Dinosaur" in Venezuela, hit a single, double, and home run for his team, Venezuela, but it was not enough to prevent Vargas from capturing the game 9–5. Newcombe, in relief of Johnny Wright, hurled 7⅓ innings of one-run ball to gain the victory. Ascanio, Austin, and Campanella all pounded out three hits to pace the 14-hit attack.

Another slugfest lit up the skies around Caracas on the evening of December 16 when Cerveceria Caracas outlasted Venezuela by the score of 17–16. A total of ten pitchers was unable to stem the tide as the two teams combined for 38 base hits including seven doubles and two homers. Venezuelan native Dalmiro Finol led the attack with four hits including a home run, and drove in seven runs during the pyrotechnics. He also played an outstanding defensive game at second base. The game was a pitchers duel for six innings with Venezuela holding a 3–2 lead, but Caracas opened the floodgates with 3 runs in the seventh inning, 8 in the eighth, and 4 in the ninth. Venezuela countered with 4 runs in the seventh and 9 in the eighth, to take a short-lived 16–13 lead. Then, in the top of the ninth, Finol, known as "The Sheep" in Venezuela, strode to the plate with the bases loaded and uncorked a game-winning grand slam homer. Daniel Canonico pitched the last 1⅔ innings for the victory. Twenty-two-year-old Max Surkont, on his way to the Chicago White Sox, was tagged with the loss after being hammered for 12 runs and 11 base hits in two innings.

Another Venezuelan native set a still-unbroken winter league batting record on November 30, 1947. Guillermo Vento of Cerveceria Caracas went on a six-for-six rampage, with five singles and a double, knocking in three runs in a 12–6 win over the Magallanes Navigators. His teammate, Hector Benitez, rapped three hits including two home runs, good for 4 RBIs. And just 26 days later, on the day after Christmas, Venezuelan ace Luis "Mono" Zuloaga threw a one-hitter at Team Venezuela, winning 5–0 in a game liberally sprinkled with 10 strikeouts. On January 4, 1948, as recounted by Peter Bjarkman,

> One of the most bizarre moments in professional baseball history occurs during a Venezuelan-league game in Caracas when Team Venezuelan pitcher, "Tuerto" Arrieta, yields an eleventh-inning base on balls to Cerveceria Caracas batter Benitez Redondo with the bases filled, yet no run scores. The unprecedented set of circumstances is set in motion when third-base runner Luis Romero delays coming home on the fourth ball, seeing that batter Benitez has not started for first. When Romero finally approaches the plate, he is tagged by catcher Humberto Leal, who completes his clever decoy by shouting "You're out!" The enraged and confused Romero then commits baseball's greatest bonehead play, grabbing the ball from the catcher's mitt and heaving it toward the backstop. Umpire Henry Tatler immediately rules Romero out on perhaps the rarest interference play of all time.

The 1947-48 winter league pennant was won by Cerveceria Caracas with an all-Venezuelan team, including "Chico" Carrasquel, Vento, Romero, Finol, Zuloaga, Benitez, Garcia C., Fonseca, and Machado. Magallanes, in a fruitless attempt to unseat the Lions, brought in some heavy guns from the American Negro Leagues, including Joe Black, Johnny Hayes, Lester Locket, Henry McHenry, Hank Thompson, and Archie Ware. The Vargas team, managed by Roy Campanella, finished second to Caracas, with a record of 24–15. Surprisingly, the stocky backstop led the league with 8 stolen bases. Other Negro League players in the league included Don Newcombe, Johnny Wright, Verdel Mathis, and Luke Easter. Venezuelan born Vidal Lopez was the 1947-48 batting champion with an average of .374 in 139 at-bats. Big Luke Easter of Venezuela was the top home run hitter with 8, and Dalmiro Finol took the RBI crown with 35. Newcombe was the league's best pitcher, leading the league with 25 games pitched, 10 victories, a .768 won-loss percentage, a 2.13 ERA, and 194 strikeouts. Big Newk also led the league in relief appearances and hit 2 home runs to help his own cause. One of the highlights of the season was a rare triple play pulled off by the Magallanes Navigators. Second baseman Cuco Correa was the middle-man in the 6–4–3 gem. Daniel Canonico, who had gone to Maracaibo in 1947, went 10-1 with the Sparrowhawks on the season. He then returned to the winter league in 1947-48 and 1948-49 and pitched for the Cervecerias Caracas.

Representatives of the four Caribbean countries that had professional winter baseball leagues, Venezuela, Cuba, Puerto Rico, and the Dominican Republic, met in Havana in August 1948, to sign an agreement forbidding the signing of each other's players. They also organized a Caribbean World Series that matched the champions from each country's winter league against each other in a six-game tournament to determine the Caribbean area champion. Almendares, Cuba, won the first Caribbean World Series title by posting a perfect 6–0 record. The tournament was held every year from 1949 to 1960, when the league was dissolved after Fidel Castro took control of Cuba and banned all professional sports. A temporary Inter-American Series, with Venezuela, Puerto Rico, Nicaragua, and Panama, operated from 1961 to 1965, but after Panama withdrew because of financial problems the tournament was, once again, put on hold. Finally, in 1970, the three remaining members of the original Caribbean World Series resurrected it, and it has been held every year since.

Cerveceria Caracas repeated as league champions in 1948-49, and "Chico" Carrasquel, just one year away from his major league debut with the Chicago White Sox, took home the batting honors with an average of .373. Negro Leaguer Jim Pendleton made his debut in the league in January and immediately paced the Magallanes Navigators to a 5–3 victory over Venezuela. Batting leadoff, Pendleton went 3 for 4 with a double, 2 home runs, and 2 RBIs. He was lauded by the Venezuelan press, who called him a versatile, aggressive, and spectacular player. And he responded to the plaudits by leading the league with 8 home runs. Pendleton's teammate, Vidal Lopez, was the RBI leader with 29. And once again Negro League star Roy Welmaker set the pace on the pitching mound. The 6' tall, 200-pound, hard throwing southpaw, led the league with 19 games pitched, 14 games started, and 7 complete games, as well as in strikeouts. He had 7 losses for the season, also a league high, but his victory total is not available. Although Welmaker was too old to take his well-earned spot on a major league roster when integration opened the door for black players, he did pitch in the minor leagues for five years, giving a hint of what might have been. He went 22–12 in a league leading 254 innings for Wilkes-Barre in the Eastern League in 1949, and was 16–10 for San Diego in the AAA Pacific Coast League the following year. Another Negro League veteran, Johnny "Hoss" Ritchey, a 5', 9", 180-pound fireplug, playing for Magallanes, led the league with 30 runs scored and 14 doubles.

On November 17, 1949, as the new season got underway, Venezuelan native Luis "Cameleon" Garcia, a 20-year-old third baseman for Magallanes, entered the game in the first inning to replace the regular third baseman, "Pipita" Leal, who took ill. Garcia took advantage of his opportunity and went on to play a Venezuelan Winter League record 732 consecutive games over 14 years before it ended on January 5, 1964. The young infielder got to play on a pennant winner in his rookie season as manager Lazaro Salazar brought his Magallanes Navigators home in first place. Jim Pendleton paced the Navigators to the title, capturing the batting championship with a .387 average, including 12 doubles, 3 triples, 7 home runs, and 24 RBIs, in 155 at-bats. Vidal Lopez won his second home run crown with 9, although he had to share it with Negro Leaguer Howard Easterling of Vargas. Lopez also won the RBI title with 43. Manager Salazar helped his own cause by compiling a 4–2 pitching record, but the ace of the staff was Theolic Smith, who pitched in 17 games with an 8–3 record. He led the league in victories and in winning percentage (.727). Other Magallanes moundsmen included Terris McDuffie who posted a perfect 3–0, record and Bob Griffith, who had a 3–4 record, but did hit a home run. Catcher "Hoss" Ritchey led the league with a .983 fielding percentage. Other Negro Leaguers on the Navigator roster included Bill Cash and Cuco Correa. Ray Neil of Venezuela led the league with 4 triples.

The first of a steady stream of players from organized baseball found their way to Venezuela in 1949, led by former Brooklyn Dodger infielder, Pete Coscarart, who held down second base for Magallanes. The next year, Brooklyn rookie Clem Labine joined the Navigators and immediately made his presence felt. On November 1, 1950, the right-handed sinkerball specialist shut out Vargas 9–0 with a 7-hitter. Minor leaguers Jim Dyck, Clarence Beers, and Frank Mancuso were members of the Vargas team. Labine, who would go on to be one of the National League's top firemen during the 1950s, is best remembered for two games he started for the Dodgers. In the 1951 three-game playoff against the New York Giants, after the Dodgers had lost the opener, Labine took the ball and blanked the New Yorkers 10–0 in game two. Five years later, in the 1956 World Series against the New York Yankees, with the Dodgers trailing three games to two, Labine once again stepped to center stage and shut out the Bronx Bombers 1–0 in ten innings.

On January 14, 1951, future Venezuelan Hall-of-Fame pitcher Jose "Carrao" Bracho of Cerveceria Caracas pitched a one-hitter against Venezuela, winning 10–0. But neither team would win the pennant as Lazaro Salazar brought his Magallanes team home in first place for the second straight year. He also went 2–1 on the mound. Other Navigator hurlers included Terris McDuffie, who was 1–3, and Raul Galata, who was 4–2 with 15 relief appearances. Magallanes' Jim Pendleton, playing shortstop and outfield, led the league in doubles with 18 and triples with 5. Sam Hairston of Vargas took the batting title with an average of .380, and in the process set a record by hitting in 26 consecutive games. Rene Gonzalez of Venezuela and Frank Mancuso of Vargas shared home run honors with 10 each, and Gonzalez, who was coming off a .302 season with the New York Cubans in the Negro American League, was crowned the RBI leader with 56 and the doubles leader with 18, while batting a hefty .358. Mancuso, a native of Houston, Texas, was a former major league player who had played with the St. Louis Browns and Washington Senators for four years. The most explosive batting performance of the year was unleashed by Arthur "Superman" Pennington of Venezuela, who had 5 hits in 5 trips to the plate on December 6, 1950. Thirty-three-year-old catcher Carlos "Charlie" Colas, a native of Havana, rapped a record three triples in the same game, but their team lost to Vargas by a 10–9 score. Two months later, Pennington participated in a 1–5–3–5 triple play.

Negro League players were a critical component in the organization and recognition of the Venezuelan Winter League since 1946, but after the integration of organized baseball, the Negro Leagues went into a slow decline, ending in their eventual disappearance about 1960. Beginning in the early 1950s, major league teams began to realize the value of having their minor league prospects continue to develop their skills during the off-season, and they began sending some of their most promising players to Venezuela to face the high-level competition available there. In addition to the homegrown products like "Chico" Carrasquel and Luis Aparicio, and the Negro Leaguers like Sam Hairston, Wilmer Fields, and Luke Easter, players from organized baseball began making the trip south over the winter. One of the first members of organized baseball to arrive in South America was Pete Coscarart, as noted above. He was followed by major league hopefuls like Mancuso, Labine, Norm Larker, Ed Bailey, Wally Moon, Tommy Byrne, and John Roseboro. Over the next 40 years, the league would help to develop such outstanding baseball talents as Pete Rose, Rico Carty, Rod Carew, Dave Parker, Darryl Strawberry, and Andres Galarraga.

The year 1951 was historic in Venezuelan baseball history for another reason. They hosted the Caribbean World Series tournament, matching their championship team against the championship teams from Cuba, Puerto Rico, and Panama. The city of Caracas was in a holiday mood the entire week, rooting for their heroes, the Magallanes Navigators, to defeat Spur Cola of Panama, the Santurce Crabbers of Puerto Rico, and the Havana Reds from Cuba, with stars like Sandy Amoros, "Chiquitin" Cabrera, and Pedro Formental. But it was Santurce, Puerto Rico, that walked off with the championship, going 5–1 under manager George Scales. Ruben Gomez, who would later enjoy a ten-year major league career, and Jose "Pantalones" Santiago each won two games. Lorenzo "Chiquitin" Cabrera set a series batting record by hitting a cool .619 with 13 base hits in 21 at-bats. Luis Olmo of Santurce led in home runs with 3, and Rene Gonzalez of Magallanes led in RBIs with 11.

The following fall, Lazaro Salazar led his Magallanes Navigators in search of their third consecutive winter league pennant. It was a disappointing search. Cerveceria Caracas, under manager Jose Casanova, got off the mark quickly and never looked back. From late October until mid–November, Caracas went undefeated with 17 victories and one tie, and Casanova's team coasted to the pennant on the clutch hitting of Wilmer "Red" Fields. On January 15, 1952, Fields, a 6', 3", 215-pound slugger known as "The Elephant" in Venezuela, punched out five base hits in five trips to the plate with three RBIs to lead his team to a 9–2 victory over Magallanes.

Cerveceria Caracas

Name	Pos	AB	R	H
Hicks	3B	5	1	1
Carrasquel	SS	5	1	2
Mozzall	1B	5	1	1
Vento	CF	5	2	2
Fields	RF	5	2	5
Finol	LF	5	0	1
Anderson	C	4	0	1
Oliveros	2B	4	1	1
Samson	P	3	1	0
Totals		41	9	14

Magallanes

Name	Pos	AB	R	H
Knoublach	CF	5	1	2
Ramos	1B	4	0	2
Leal	PH	0	0	0
Garcia	3B	5	0	1
Pendleton	SS	3	0	1
Fridley	RF	3	0	1
Trouppe	C	4	0	0
Lopez	LF	4	0	0
Gonzalez	2B	4	1	0
Taylor	P	0	0	0
Butts	P	0	0	0
Barbosa	PH	1	0	1
Berbesis	P	1	0	0
Totals		34	2	8

Cerveceria	3 0 0	5 0 0	0 0 1—9—14—1
Magallanes	1 0 0	1 0 0	0 0 0—2—8—4

Doubles: Vento (2), Anderson, Hicks, Fields, Ramos Pendleton.
Triples: Oliveros
Home Run: Fields
Winning Pitcher: Samson
Losing Pitcher: Taylor

One month later, Caracas was stretched out for 18 innings by Magallanes, the 3-hour, 10-minute game ending in a 3–3 tie. John Hetki, who was on his way to a return trip to the Cincinnati Reds in 1952, pitched the entire game for the Navigators. Fields' two-run homer in the top of the 17th gave his team a 3–1 lead but Jose Bracho was unable to hold it. On the flip side of the coin, Caracas was involved in the shortest game in league history, a 1 hour and 15 minute duel with Venezuela, won by Venezuela 2–1. Wilmer Fields' hot bat raked Venezuelan pitching to the tune of .348 to lead the league. The big outfielder also led the league with 21 doubles, 48 runs scored, and 45 runs batted in, batting in the fifth spot in the Caracas lineup, just behind Willard Brown. Fields played in Venezuela for three years, from 1951 through 1954, and he considered himself to be a pretty good hitter, as he recounted to John Holway. "One time down in Maracaibo, Venezuela, (Terris McDuffie) threw me two balls outside and I hit them for a homer and a single. Then he threw one inside and I doubled. The next Sunday he pitched us all inside. We didn't get but four hits off him and I got three of them. I got me a 34½-inch bat and just waited for those inside pitches. You know, baseball is a lot of guessing. So he woke me up at 6:00 in the morning before he got his plane—he was going back to the States—woke me up and said, 'You can really hit.'" Fields went on to tell Holway, "I had a real good year in Venezuela. I was playing third base. Here's who I was playing beside—"Chico" Carrasquel. You talk about making it rough on a person, he made it rough—playing beside the best fielder in the American League? I had to come up with my hitting. I hit .350 and led the league in home runs and runs batted in. We won 17 straight." Russell Kerns, who had a cup of coffee with the Detroit Tigers in 1945, playing for Venezuela, captured the home run crown with 10, and Jim Pendleton showed the way in stolen bases with 12.

The 52–53 winter league season got off to a rousing start when John Mackinson of the Philadelphia Athletics, pitching for Magallanes, threw 10⅔ innings of no-hit ball in his Venezuelan Winter League debut on October 19 before yielding three hits in the next two innings. His team finally broke through in the top of the 13th, scoring 9 runs, for a 10–1 win. Second baseman Hank Schenz, a former six-year major league player, a member of the Venezuela team, set a new winter league record by hitting in 27 consecutive games, breaking the record previously held by Sam Hairston. Another league record fell on January 8, 1953, when Negro League veteran Quincy Trouppe of the Navigators walked six times in six at-bats against the newly-named Caracas Lions. The Lions, under the direction of Cuban legend Martin Dihigo, captured the pennant, their fourth in eight years. Negro League southpaw Jehosie Heard was the workhorse of the Lions' staff, leading the league with 29 games pitched, 69 strikeouts in 131 innings, and a 3.03 earned run average, but he still could do no better than a 6–7 won-loss record. Hank Schenz of Venezuela batted .355 in 242 at-bats with just 7 extra-base hits. "Cameleon" Garcia of Magallanes was the home run leader with 8 and the RBI leader with 47. Daniel Canonico, the hero of the 1941 World Amateur Championships, pitched in relief for Caracas during the season, and announced his retirement as soon as the season ended.

The Venezuelan Association of Baseball, centered in Caracas, and the Zulian Baseball Association, centered in Maracaibo, finally got together in 1953 and agreed to have the best teams from each league meet in a national championship series called the Rotatory. The first series was held in 1953-54 with Cerveceria Caracas and Magallanes representing the Central League and Gavilanes and Pastora representing the Western League. The pennant went to the Pastora team led by Buster Mills, a 7-year major league outfielder who compiled a .287 batting average in the big show. The road to the pennant wasn't a bed of roses however. On October 14, their pitching staff yielded a record six home runs to Magallanes in Olympic Stadium. Two of the round-trippers were hit by New York Giants players, Foster Castleman and Billy Gardner. Luis Aparicio Jr., who had been playing amateur baseball around his hometown, joined his father's team, the Maracaibo Gavillanes, on November 18 at the age of 19, and collected his first base hit the following night. According to the Oleksaks, "The elder Aparicio gave way to Luis at shortstop, handing his glove over in a special presentation before the game. Aparicio Sr. gave his son a warm hug, sent him out to short, and moved over to first base for a few games before retiring." Luis Jr. would go on to stardom in the major leagues, eventually being elected to the Baseball Hall of Fame in Cooperstown, New York, in 1984. Over an 18-year career, Luis Aparicio Jr. led the American League in stolen bases nine times and fielding percentage eight times, while accumulating 2677 base hits, #57 all-time. When he retired, he led all shortstops in career games played, was number two in assists, and number three in double plays.

Another Negro Leaguer made the headlines on November 22, 1953, when Dave Pope led Gavilanes over Pastora 11–3. The southpaw-swinging outfielder punched out three base hits including a home run to pace his team's 11-hit attack. The lineups of both teams were liberally sprinkled with major league prospects, both black and white. Pope and "Piper" Davis had both moved from the Negro leagues to organized baseball by this time. Other major league hopefuls included Johnny Temple, Wally Moon, and Ed Bailey of Pastora, and Luis Aparicio, Jim Lemon, and Hank Foiles of Gavilanes. Piper Davis added his own star to the Venezuelan hit parade when he lashed out four base hits in four at-bats against the Caracas Lions on January 26, 1954. His barrage included two home runs and 3 RBIs as Gavilanes coasted to a 6–2 win.

The Rotatory lasted only one year. The Western Professional Baseball League was founded in 1954 in Maracaibo, and a new stadium, Olympic Stadium, was built with a seating capacity of 10,000, giving the league the largest stadium in the country. Unfortunately, the league, that featured such teams as Pastora, Gavilanes, Cabimas, Centauros, Rapinos, and Cardinales from Lara State, folded after ten years for economic reasons. In Caracas, in 1964, two new teams were added to the league, the Lara Cardinals and the Aragua Tigers, following the previous additions, Industriales de Valencia, Oriente BBC, and Pampero, which eventually became the La Guaira Sharks.

The 1954-55 pennant was won by Salazar's Magallanes Navigators once again, led by slugger Bob Lennon, who led the league with 9 home runs and 37 RBIs. Harold Bevan of Venezuela was the batting champion with an average of .350. The most heartwarming story of the year belonged to pitcher Tommy Byrne who, at the age of 34, had slumped to a 2 and 5 record with the Chicago White Sox and Washington Senators in 1954. Pitching for Pastora, Byrne tossed consecutive shutouts at Caracas and Magallanes in January, winning by scores of 9–0 and 6–0 respectively. The lanky southpaw went on to lead the Venezuelan Winter League pitchers with a 12–3 record and a .800 winning percentage. That performance brought him a contract from the New York Yankees and he responded by pitching them to the 1955 American League pennant with a 16–5 mark, and a league leading .762 winning percentage.

The most exciting event of the year was not the pennant race however. It was the Caribbean World Series that was hosted by Venezuela. The atmosphere was electric during the weeklong tournament. It was also disappointing. On February 11, 1955, in University Stadium, Caracas, Emilio "The Indian" Cueche of Magallanes matched pitches with former Brooklyn Dodgers southpaw Joe Hatten, of Almendares, Cuba, in one of the most exciting games in series history. Cueche limited the Cuban team to two base hits, but dropped a tough 1–0 decision. The Venezuelan legend had a no-hitter going through six innings before a near riot in the grandstand held the game up for 45 minutes as spectators littered the field with garbage. When the game resumed, Almendares scored the only run of the game on two walks, a single by Rocky Nelson, and a sacrifice fly by Lee Walls. The next night, Magallanes suffered a heartbreaking defeat when Willie Mays hit an 11th inning home run for Santurce to win the game by a 4 to 2 score.

Twenty-four-year-old Ron Mrozinski, a hard-throwing southpaw from White Haven, Pennsylvania, who pitched for the Philadelphia Phillies in 1955, spent the winter of 1955-56 in Venezuela, pitching for Valencia, and dazzled the home fans with a spectacular debut. On October 14, he tossed a shutout against the Caracas Lions. He followed that up with shutout wins over Magallanes and Pampero, giving him a record 27 consecutive scoreless innings. The momentum created by Mrozinski's sensational

Emilio "Indio" Cueche was one of the greatest pitchers in the annals of Venezuelan baseball (author's collection).

pitching carried Valencia to its first Venezuelan Winter League championship. Along the way there were some memorable moments for winter league fans to recall for years to come. On December 8, 1955, 27-year-old southpaw Len Yochim, who had brief trials with the Pittsburgh Pirates in 1951 and '54, threw the first no-hit game in the history of the winter league, sending his Caracas team to a 3–0 victory over the Magallanes Navigators. Just one week later, another major league castoff, Stan Jok, a 6' tall, 190-pound right-handed slugger who had played twelve games for the Phillies and White Sox in 1954 and '55, set a Venezuelan record by smashing three home runs for Caracas against Pampero. His record lasted exactly 24 days before it was broken by minor leaguer Russ Rac of Pastora against Cabimas. And eight days later, shortstop Buddy Hicks, on his way up to the Detroit Tigers, legged out three triples in the same game, tying a winter league record. Norm Larker, playing for Magallanes, led the league in hitting with an average of .340. Stan Jok, thanks to his big day against Caracas, topped the home run brigade with 10 round trippers, and catcher Ed Bailey, who was just beginning a notable 14-year major league career, primarily with the Cincinnati Reds, led the league in RBIs with 40.

The Caracas Lions, led by Clay Bryant, the former manager of the Montreal Royals of the International League and Jackie Robinson's first manager in organized baseball, were the champions of the 1956-57 Venezuelan Winter League. They were led by Negro League graduate Bob Wilson, a Los Angeles Dodgers farmhand who was one of the top minor league players. The 5', 11", 197-pound right-handed hitter had just completed a season with the Montreal Royals of the International League where he batted .306 and led the league with 43 doubles. Wilson, an 11-year AAA veteran with a career batting average of .311, led the winter league with an average of .350. John Roseboro of Caracas, another Dodgers farmhand, who was about to embark on a memorable 14-year major league career, was the home run leader with 10, and Lou Limmer of Pampero knocked in 41 runs to lead the league in that department.

The shortened 1957 winter league season saw Valencia emerge as the pennant winner. Venezuelan native Teolindo Acosta, a left-handed-hitting outfielder, led the league in hitting with an average of .385. John Roseboro won his second consecutive home run title by putting 7 balls into orbit, and minor leaguers Bert Hamric and Mike Goliat shared RBI honors with 28 each. Valencia repeated as pennant winners in 1958-59; 28-year old Rudy Regalado, a Los Angeles native named after Rudolph Valentino, playing for Pampera, won the batting championship with an average of .366; and Allen Jones of Oriente was both the home run king with 8, and the RBI champion with 38. According to Wilmer Fields, Terris McDuffie was still pitching in 1958, and compiled a record of 11–1 that year. There was also a 1959 season that was not completed due to a players strike.

Venezuela hosted its third Caribbean World Series in 1959, and the city of Caracas was once again full of life and excitement. The Oriente Club represented Venezuela in the tournament, competing against the Almendares Club of Cuba, Cocle of Panama, and Santurce of Puerto Rico. Almendares, with a pitching staff that included Camilo Pascual, Orlando Pena, and Mike Cuellar, who would go on to register 415 major league victories between them, won the title with a 5–1 record. Luis "Cameleon" Garcia and Jesus Mora, both with Venezuela's Oriente team, took batting honors with identical .417 averages. Norm Cash of Oriente led the tournament in both home runs (2) and RBIs (8). Babe Birrer of Oriente and Camilo Pascual of Almendares each had 2–0 pitching records.

On December 18, 1960, Jim Pendleton of the Caracas Lions hit three home runs in one game, drove in five runs and scored five times. Several of the players might be familiar to major league fans, in addition to Luis Aparicio and Jim Pendleton, such as winning pitcher Ron Perranoski, Larry Raines, Cesar Tovar, pinch hitters Gary Peters and Ed Rakow, Yo Yo Davalillo, Jim King, Tim Thompson, Mike Roarke, and Joe Morgan. Perranoski went the distance for the victory.

Rapinos

Name	Pos	AB	R	H
L. Aparicio	SS	2	0	0
M. Barboza	P	0	0	0
E. Rakow	PH	1	0	0
R. Castellanos	P	0	0	0
G. Peters	PH	1	0	0
L. Raines	2B-SS	5	0	1
M. Roarke	C	2	0	1
R. Vasquez	C	2	0	0
A. Salvent	LF	4	1	3
J. Morgan	3B	3	0	0
G. Valbuena	3B	1	0	1
P. Romero	RF	4	0	3
M. Martinez	CF	4	0	0
C. Prieto	1B	4	0	0
R. Melendez	P	1	0	0
L. Anez	2B	3	0	0
Totals		37	1	9

Caracas

Name	Pos	AB	R	H
P. Davalillo	3B	5	2	0
J. Pendleton	LF	4	5	3
J. King	CF	6	1	1
F. Koening	1B	5	1	1
A. Gomez	RF	4	3	1
C. Tovar	2B	5	1	3
D. Carrasquel	SS	5	1	2
Ch. Thompson	C	4	1	4
R. Perranoski	P	5	0	1
		43	15	16

Rapinos   0 0 0   0 0 0   0 1 0— 1— 9—4
Caracas   3 3 1   1 0 5   2 0 x—15—16—1

Doubles: A. Salvent, C. Tovar, Romero.
Triples: D. Carrasquel.
Home Runs: J. Pendleton (3).
Winning Pitcher: R. Perranoski
Losing Pitcher: R. Melendez

Four days later, Pendleton hit another home run, giving him four in two games. His career statistics in Venezuela, between 1948 and 1961, included 14 triples and 33 home runs.

As the decade of the '60s got underway, Negro League players were no longer the strength of the league. The baton had been passed to a new generation of players from organized baseball. There were just as many black players in the league as there had been during the 1940s and '50s, but now they were playing under the banner of organized baseball instead of under the banner of the Negro leagues.

The presence of Negro League players in the Venezuelan Winter League that was organized in 1946 gave the league immediate credibility. Players like Buck Leonard, Roy Campanella, Bill "Ready" Cash, and Hilton Smith, put the league on a high professional level, equal to the best minor leagues in the United States. As the integration of organized baseball progressed, the Negro leagues faded into obscurity, but the flow of high level professional baseball players from North America to Venezuela continued, with major league players and minor league players, both black and white, gradually replacing Negro League players throughout the 1950s. The last Negro League player to grace a Venezuelan Winter League roster may have been Bonnie Serrell, who played for Licey in 1965.

A partial directory of Negro League players who helped legitimize the Venezuelan Winter League follows:

Frank Austin, 1947–1948. He played in the Negro leagues for five years, posting a .332 batting average. He also played in Panama and in AAA ball from 1949 to 1956, hitting .268.

Sam Bankhead, 1946–1947. He was a 15-year veteran of the Negro leagues where he starred at shortstop and hit .285 with power. He also played in Mexico, Cuba, Puerto Rico, the Dominican Republic, and one year in organized baseball.

Joe Black, 1947–1948. He pitched in the Negro leagues from 1943 to 1950, and in the major leagues from 1952 to 1957. He was the National League Rookie of the Year with the Brooklyn Dodgers in 1952.

Ramon Bragana, 1936–1937. He pitched in the Negro leagues and in Mexico. He batted .318 in Venezuela.

Luther Branham, 1950–1951. He was an infielder in the Negro leagues in 1949 and 1950.

Ollie Brantley, 1960s. He played in the Negro leagues in 1950.

Jack Brittin, 1952–1953. He played third base in the Negro leagues from 1940 to 1950.

Ray Brown, 1949–1950. He played in the Negro leagues from 1931 to 1945, in Puerto Rico from 1938 to 1945, in Mexico from 1946 to 1949, and in the minor leagues from 1950 to 1953.

Willard Brown, 1951–1952. He played baseball in the Negro leagues between 1935 and 1950, as well as in Puerto Rico and the U.S. minor leagues. He had a cup of coffee with the St. Louis Browns in the American League in 1947.

Harry Butts, 1951–1952. He played in the Negro leagues in 1949 and 1950.

Roy Campanella, 1946–1947. He was an eight-year veteran of the Negro leagues, and a ten-year veteran of the National League. He is a member of the National Baseball Hall of Fame in Cooperstown, New York.

Ray Brown, a 2006 inductee into the National Baseball Hall of Fame in Cooperstown, New York, starred in the Venezuelan Winter League from 1948 to 1950 (courtesy Yuyo Ruiz).

Bill "Ready" Cash, 1946–1950. He played in the Negro leagues from 1943 to 1950 and in the minor leagues in 1951 and 1952.

Jim Cathey, 1948–1949. He pitched in the Negro leagues from 1948 to 1950.

Jim "Fireball" Cohen, 1949–1950. He pitched in the Negro leagues from 1946 to 1950.

Gene Collins, 1958–59. He pitched and played outfield in the Negro leagues from 1947 to 1950 before moving into organized baseball.

Cuco Correa, 1946–1950. He played shortstop in the Negro Leagues from 1926 to 1936.

Martin Crue, 1946–1947. He pitched in the Negro leagues from 1942 to 1947.

Lloyd "Ducky" Davenport, 1949–1950. He played outfield in the Negro leagues from 1935 to 1949. He also played in Cuba where he hit .275 and Mexico where he hit .293.

"Cherokee Johnny" Davis, 1950–1952. He was an 11-year Negro league veteran who also played in the minor leagues.

Martin Dihigo, 1932–1953. He was one of the greatest all-around players in baseball history, along with Babe Ruth. He won more than 300 games pitching, batted over .300, hit the long ball, and was an outstanding defensive second baseman and center fielder, in a playing career that lasted from 1922 to 1947.

Melvin Duncan, 1950–1951. He pitched in the Negro leagues in 1949–1950.

Luke Easter, 1947–1950. He played in the Negro leagues in 1947 and 1948, batting .337 with 33 home runs in 434 at-bats. He then starred for the Cleveland Indians from 1950 to 1954, batting .274 with 93 home runs in 1725 at-bats.

Howard Easterling, 1949–1950. He played third base in the Negro leagues from 1936 to 1949, batting .311.

Raul Espinoza, 1946–1947. He pitched in the Negro leagues in 1947.

Oscar Estrada, 1946–1948. He pitched in the Negro leagues in 1924, 1925, and 1931.

Rudolfo Fernandez, 1959–1966. He pitched in the Negro leagues from 1932 to 1943. He also pitched in Cuba, the Dominican Republic, Mexico, and Canada over a notable 15-year career.

Wilmer "Red" Fields, 1948–1953. He played in the Negro leagues from 1940 to 1950, pitching and playing the outfield and third base. He also played in the Dominican Republic, Mexico, Puerto Rico, and one year in the minor leagues, batting .287 with Toronto in the International League.

Pedro Formental 1952–1956. He played in the Negro leagues from 1947 to 1950, in the Cuban winter league from 1942 to 1954, and in the International League where he hit .293 for Havana.

Jonas Gaines, 1949–1950. He pitched in the Negro leagues from 1937 to 1950.

Raul Galata 1950–1951. He pitched in the Negro leagues in 1949 and 1950.

Manuel "Cocaina" Garcia, 1946–1966. He pitched in the Negro leagues from 1926 to 1936, in Cuba from 1926 to 1948, and in Mexico from 1941 to 1949, with more than 300 total victories. He is a member of both the Cuban and Venezuelan Baseball Halls of Fame.

Silvio Garcia, 1946–1947. He played in the Negro leagues from 1940 to 1947 and in the Cuban League from 1931 to 1954. He was an outstanding shortstop, and a solid .280 hitter with power.

Tom "Lefty" Glover, 1946–1947. He pitched in the Negro leagues from 1934 to 1945.

Manuel Godinez, 1946–1947. He played in the Negro leagues from 1946 to 1949.

Rene Gonzalez, 1950–1951. He played in the Negro leagues in 1950, spending the rest of his career in Mexico.

Whitt Graves, 1950–1951. He pitched in the Negro leagues in 1950, going 7–8 with the Indianapolis Clowns.

Bob Griffith, 1949–1950. He pitched in the Negro leagues from 1933 to 1949.

Sam Hairston, 1949–1953. He played in the Negro leagues from 1944 to 1950, and spent 9 years in the minor leagues.

Jehosie Heard, 1952–1954. He pitched in the Negro leagues for 7 years and in the minor leagues for 6 years.

Dave Hoskins, 1951–1959. He played four years in the Negro leagues, 13 years in the minor leagues, and two years in the major leagues where he hit .227 with Cleveland.

Bill Jefferson, 1946. Jefferson pitched in the Negro leagues from 1937 to 1946, and in the Mexican League for one year.

Sam Jethroe, 1945–1946. "Jet" Jethroe was a seven-year Negro League veteran where he hit .340. He went on to play for four years in the major leagues, hitting .261 and leading the National League in stolen bases in both 1950 and 1951. He also played in Cuba where he hit .290 and Puerto Rico where he hit .340.

Gentry Jessup, 1948–1949. He pitched in the Negro leagues from 1940 to 1949.

Sam "Toothpick" Jones, 1953–1954. He pitched in the Negro leagues for three years before embarking on a notable 12-year major league career that brought him a 102–101 career record. In 1959, he went 21–15 for the San Francisco Giants, leading the National League in victories, shutouts (4), and ERA (2.83).

Buck Leonard, 1946. He was a 15-year Negro League veteran, known as "The Black Lou Gehrig." He played one year in the minor leagues at the end of his career.

Rufus Lewis, 1946–1947. He pitched in the Negro leagues for seven years, in Mexico for four years, and in Cuba for two years.

Lester Lockett, 1947–1948. He was a 14-year veteran of the Negro leagues, and he played three years in the minor leagues.

Terris "The Terrible" McDuffie, 1946–1951. He played in the Negro leagues from 1930 to 1945, winning 43 games and losing 27. He also pitched in Mexico five years, the Dominican Republic three years, Cuba eight years, Puerto Rico one year, and in the Texas League one year

Clyde McNeal, 1949–1950. He played in the Negro Leagues from 1944 to 1950.

Verdel Mathis, 1947–1948. He pitched in the Negro leagues from 1940 to 1950, compiling a record of 56–57.

Henry "Hank" Miller, 1946–1947. He had a ten-year Negro League career where he posted a 25–17 mark for six years. He had a brief tryout with San Diego in the PCL.

Ray Neil, 1949–1950. He played in the Negro leagues from 1942 to 1950.

Don Newcombe, 1947–1948. Big Newk pitched in the Negro leagues for two years, winning nine games and losing seven, and then went on to a sensational career with the Brooklyn Dodgers in the National League, winning as many as 27 games in a season and batting .359 with 7 home runs in 117 at-bats in 1955.

Ray Noble, 1950–1951. He enjoyed a five-year Negro League career where he hit .259, a 12-year minor league career, a three-year stint in the major leagues with the New York Giants where he hit .218, and an 11-year career in Cuba where he hit .272.

Alberto Osorio. The Panamanian pitcher played in Venezuela for six years, with a 27–15 record. He also pitched in the Negro leagues in 1949, logging a 3–7 record, in the minor leagues for ten years, and in the Mexican League for 15 years, compiling a 150–104 record.

Roy Partlow, 1947–1948. He played in the Negro leagues from 1937 to 1948, plus one year in the minor leagues and two years in Canada.

Jim Pendleton, 1948–1952. He was a Negro League veteran who played in the major leagues for 8 years, with Milwaukee, Pittsburgh, Cincinnati, and Houston, hitting .255 in 444 games, although he didn't enter the majors until he was 29 years old.

Arthur "Superman" Pennington, 1950–1951. He was a ten-year Negro League veteran who played seven years in the minor leagues, three years in Mexico, and one year in Puerto Rico.

Dave Pope, 1953–1955. He played one year in the Negro leagues, 12 years in the minor leagues, and four years in the major leagues, hitting .265.

Andrew "Pullman" Porter, 1949–1950. He pitched in the Negro leagues from 1932 to 1950, with short stints in Mexico (49–47) and Cuba (9–9).

Bill Powell, 1953–1954. He was a six-year Negro League veteran who went on to a 14-year minor league career.

Othello Renfroe, 1949–1950. He was a shortstop in the Negro leagues from 1945 to 1950.

Bill Ricks, 1949–1951. He pitched in the Negro leagues from 1944 to 1950.

John "Hoss" Ritchey 1948–1949. He played just one year in the Negro Leagues before going on to a 10-year minor league career, mostly at the AAA level.

Lazaro Salazar, 1949–1957. The native of Havana, Cuba, was an outstanding and versatile athlete who pitched and played second base and outfield in the Negro leagues from 1924 to 1936 (.382 batting average and a 6–8 won-loss record), in Cuba from 1930 to 1948 (.293 batting average and a 35–24 won-loss record), and in Mexico from 1938 to 1952 (.334 batting average and a 112–78 won-loss record). He is a member of both the Cuban and Mexican Baseball Halls of Fame.

Harry "Suitcase" Simpson, 1946–1947. He played in the Negro Leagues for three years, and enjoyed an 8-year major league career where he compiled a .266 batting average.

Hilton Smith, 1946–1947. Smith, better known as Satchel Paige's "relief pitcher," pitched in the Negro leagues from 1932 to 1948, compiling a record of 72–28.

Theolic "Fireball" Smith, 1949–1950. He pitched in the Negro leagues from 1936 to 1951, interrupted by stints in Mexico where he compiled a 121–90 record in eight years. He also pitched in the Pacific Coast League from 1952 to 1955.

Quincy Trouppe, 1941 to 1953. He was a 15-year veteran of the Negro leagues, played eight years in Mexico, and three years each in Puerto Rico and Cuba. He played six games with the Cleveland Indians in 1952.

Orlando Varona, 1949–1950. He played six years in the Negro leagues between 1948 and 1955, four years in Cuba, one year in Mexico, and one year in the minor leagues.

Roy Welmaker, 1946–1952. He was an eight-year veteran of the Negro leagues, pitched two years in Mexico, and five years in the minor leagues including four years in the Pacific Coast League where he compiled a 27–24 mark before he retired at the age of 40.

Marvin Williams, 1946–1947. He played in the Negro leagues from 1943 to 1950, and played 12 years in the minor leagues between 1950 and 1961.

Bob Wilson, 1956–1957. He played three years in the Negro leagues and 11 years in the minor leagues between 1947 and 1960, batting .311. He played three games with the Los Angeles Dodgers in 1958.

John Wright, 1947–1948. His Negro League career covered the years 1937 to 1948. He was the second player signed by Branch Rickey, after Jackie Robinson, and he pitched for the Montreal Royals and Three Rivers in 1946, going 12–8 with Three Rivers, but the pressure associated with integrating organized baseball was too much for the 29-year-old right-hander and he returned to the Negro leagues in 1947.

Some of the more prominent Venezuelan players to play in the winter league between 1946 and 1960 are listed below:

Luis Aparacio, Sr., 1946–1953. The premier shortstop in Venezuela during the 1930s and '40s.

Luis Aparacio, Jr., 1953–1964. Aparacio was one of the best shortstops ever to play major league baseball, starring in the big show from 1956 to 1973. He was an outstanding defensive shortstop, and also an offensive threat. He played for the Go-Go Chicago White Sox for ten years, and paced them to the 1959 American League pennant. Aparacio led the American League in stolen bases his first nine years in the league, and led in fielding percentage eight times. He was elected to the National Baseball Hall of Fame in Cooperstown, New York, in 1984.

Jose "Carrao" Bracho, 1946–1965. Bracho led all pitchers in victories four times during his Venezuelan Winter League career. He also holds the record for most victories in a season with 15, and most years pitched with 23, as well as the career records for games started with 192, most complete games with 93, most innings pitched with 1758, and most victories with 110. His 100th victory, on January 6, 1964, was a 5–0, 3-hitter for Orientales over La Guaira.

Alejandro "Alex" Carrasquel, 1946–1947. Alex Carrasquel pitched in the major leagues, primarily for the Washington Senators, from 1939 to 1949, compiling a record of 50–39. His best season was 1943 when he went 11–7.

Alfonso "Chico" Carrasquel, 1946–1982. "Chico" Carrasquel played in the winter league for many years and also managed in the league. He led the league in batting in 1948-49 with an average of .373, and in home runs in 1959 with 5. Later, he managed the Caracas Lions to the Caribbean Series championship in 1982. "Chico" was an outstanding defensive shortstop in the major leagues from 1950 to 1959, and led the league in fielding average three times while batting .258.

Daniel "Chinese" Canonico, 1934 to 1953. Canonico was the hero of the 1941 World Amateur Championships, winning 5 games including the championship game. He later managed Vargas to two winter league pennants.

Emilio "El Indio" Cueche, 1947–1962. Emilio Cueche also pitched in the Dominican Summer League in 1952 and 1953. The 26-year-old right-hander led the Dominican League with 13 victories in 1953. His two-year totals were 22 wins against 18 losses. He also pitched in Mexico from 1960 to 1962, winning 4 games and losing 9. And he pitched for the Havana Sugar Kings in the International League in 1957. His Venezuelan Winter League statistics follow:

Years	Wins	Losses	Innings Pitched	Strikeouts	Walks	ERA
16	80	64	1217.2	640	408	3.43

Luis "Cameleon" Garcia, 1949–1970. Luis Garcia played infield for Magallanes for many years. He led the league in batting in 1964-65 with an average of .394. He also led the league home runs in 1952-53 with 8, and in RBIs with 47 in 1952-53 and 31 in 1960-61. His career statistics include 22 seasons played with 959 games played, 3564 at-bats, 1058 base hits, a .299 batting average, 183 doubles, 43 home runs, a league record 516 RBIs and 307 runs scored. He set the record, since broken, of 732 consecutive games played. Garcia also played third base in Mexico between 1956 and 1965, batting .322 with 1348 base hits in 4181 at-bats.

Vidal Lopez, 1946–1955. Lopez pitched in the Negro leagues between 1923 and 1939. His Venezuelan Winter League statistics as an outfielder show 910 at-bats and 279 base hits, for a .307 batting average. He was considered to be one of the most complete players in Venezuelan baseball history, pitching in addition to playing the outfield, but he was considered too dark-skinned to play in the major leagues. He also played in Mexico from 1943 to 1945, hitting .291 and going 29–27 on the mound. He also played in Cuba, and Puerto Rico, once hitting two home runs in a Puerto Rican Winter League game.

Manuel Malpica, known as "Pollo" or "The Chicken," was one of Venezuela's first paid professional baseball players, earning up to 200 Bolivares to play for the Magallanes Navigators beginning in 1929. He was an outstanding catcher who also played for Concord, Royal Criollos, Senators, and Venezuela during the 1930s, and he managed the Venezuelan team to its glorious victory over Cuba in the 1941 World Amateur Championships.

Ramon Monzant, 1953–1958. Monzant is remembered for yielding the famous 11th inning home run to Willie Mays in the 1955 Caribbean World Series, but he was one of Venezuela's best pitchers during the 1950s, leading the league in strikeouts four times. He pitched in the major leagues with the New York–San Francisco Giants from 1954 to 1960, winning 16 games against 21 losses. His best year was 1958 when he went 8–11 in 43 games with 16 starts.

Jesus "Chucho" Ramos, 1946–1952. "Chucho" Ramos played infield and outfield in the Venezuelan Winter League for many seasons. He had a cup of coffee with the Cincinnati Reds in 1944, playing four games and batting .500 with five hits in ten at-bats.

The Venezuelan Sports Hall of Fame includes the following players:

Luis Aparicio, Sr.	SS
Luis Aparicio, Jr.	SS (major leagues—1956 to 1973)
Jose "Carrao" Bracho	P
Daniel Canonico	P
Alejandro Carrasquel	P (major leagues—1939 to 1949)
Alfonso Carrasquel	SS (major leagues—1950 to 1959)
David Concepcion	SS (major leagues—1970 to 1988)
Emilio Cueche	P
Baudillo "Bo" Diaz	C (major leagues—1977 to 1989)
Martin Dihigo*	P-Mgr.
Victor Davalillo	OF-IF (major leagues—1963 to 1980)
Luis "Cameleon" Garcia	IF
Manuel "Cocaina" Garcia*	P-OF

Vidal Lopez*	P-OF
Ramon Monzant	P (major leagues—1954 to 1960)
Andres Quintero	IF-OF
Jesus "Chucho" Ramos	IF-OF (major leagues—1944)
Benito "Juey" Torrens	IF-OF
Cesar Tovar	IF-OF (major leagues—1965 to 1976)

*–Player also played in the Negro leagues.

9

Other Venues

Panama

Panama was first visited by a European explorer in 1501 when Rodrigo de Galvan Bastidas established a Spanish presence in the area. It soon became a Spanish colony and remained so for the next 300 years. In 1821 Panama declared its independence from Spain, eventually becoming a democracy. The United States obtained the rights to build a canal across the country in 1903, paying Panama $10,000,000 plus an additional sum annually, to cover the 10-mile-wide strip of land. Baseball was a late arrival in the Central American country, being introduced to the population by American laborers working on the canal. According to Rod Carew, Panama's most famous baseball player, as reported by the Oleksaks,

> The Canal Zone was segregated. When the Canal was built, starting in the late 1800s, a lot of whites from the southern states in America came down as organizers and laborers. They brought some of their racial attitudes with them. Workers were also recruited from the black populations in the West Indies—my grandparents included. Living quarters, schools, even toilet facilities, were separate. To this day, white people live in one section, blacks in another. The commissary was where most of the people in Gamboa did their shopping. A partition divided it in half, and the whites shopped on one side, the blacks on the other.... I can't recall ever being called a racial name in Panama. But we knew enough to stay out of the white area.

The first organized baseball league was established in 1912, with teams representing Mateo Iturralde, Tigrillo Tosania, Walk Over, and El Palais Royal. Two years later, the Canal Zone Winter League was formed, operating from December to April. According to the Oleksaks, "Canal Zone ballparks in Colon, Pedro Miguel, and Balboa were outfitted with grandstands for 2,500 to 3,000 spectators with the help of a $19,000 government appropriation. The league got underway when President Porras threw out the first pitch."

Panama's love of baseball grew slowly but steadily over the years. Ten years after the formation of the first Canal Zone League, a baseball team from the University of Havana, Equipo Caribe, visited the country to play exhibition games against Panama's best. Although Panama lost the series two games to one, they thrilled the fans with their superb play. In 1935, after supporting amateur leagues for several decades, the country entered a team in the American and Caribbean Games in El Salvador, finishing second to Cuba. Their success encouraged them to send a baseball team to the 1936 Olympic Games in Berlin, where baseball was scheduled as an exhibition event. Their search for a qualified coach ended when they hired 33-year-old shortstop Bill Yancey of the Negro League Brooklyn Eagles, a sparkplug infielder who was an outstanding defensive player with a strong arm, a speedy base runner, and a strong hitter. Yancey immediately formed two teams, the Atlantic Side and the Pacific Side, to seek a nucleus for his Olympic team. The Berlin experience created a baseball firestorm, as reported by Donn Rogosin. "Panamanian baseball caught on with such intensity, that almost a dozen Panamanians entered the Negro leagues, including Pat Scantlebury—proud possessor of one of the most feared spitballs in the league. Bob Feller, who barnstormed against Scantlebury, described his spitter as looking like 'a pigeon coming out of a barn.'"

An official professional baseball league, the Panama Winter League was formed in 1946, providing Negro League veterans with another option for a winter sojourn. The league included five teams, all sponsored by local industries. Chesterfield was sponsored by the cigarette company, Cerveceria Balboa was sponsored by the beer company, Spur Cola was sponsored by the soft drink company, Carta Viejo was sponsored by the rum manufacturer, and General Electric was sponsored by the transformer giant. One of the Negro League's best pitchers, Chet Brewer, pitched in the Panama Winter League for several years in the late '40s. Black players were treated like heroes south of the border in those days, but they had to be constantly on the lookout for the unexpected in the hot-blooded Latin countries, according to Rogosin. "One day while [Brewer] was pitching—his leg cocked high at the top of his windup—he heard a rat-a-tat-tat of machine gun fire. 'You talk about getting prone right now,' he exclaimed, 'It was those college students raising Cain.' That too was part of the Caribbean baseball."

In 1948, baseball representatives from Cuba, Panama, Venezuela, and Puerto Rico met in Havana and organized the Caribbean World Series, matching the professional champion from each country in a tournament to determine the best baseball team in the Western

Chet Brewer pitched his Carta Viejo team first to the 1949–50 league pennant, and then to the Caribbean Series championship (author's collection).

Hemisphere, outside the major leagues. The first Series was played in Havana, Cuba, in 1949, and the hometown Almendares Club won the first championship by sweeping all six games. In 1950, Brewer and Scantlebury anchored a Carta Viejo pitching staff that won the Panama Winter League championship, and went on to capture the Caribbean World Series, held in San Juan, Puerto Rico. It was Panama's second year of competition in the Series, the 1949 league champion Spur Cola having gone down to defeat. The four-team tournament that included Cuba, Venezuela, and Puerto Rico, found Panama and Puerto Rico tied with 4–2 records after six games. Brewer was tabbed by his manager, Wayne Blackburn, to pitch the championship game against Puerto Rico's Dan Bankhead, who had just completed a 9–4 season with the major league Brooklyn Dodgers. Panama drove the big Dodgers right-hander to cover with a six-run uprising in the third inning and coasted to a 9–3 victory. As Brewer told Rogosin, "We were the poorest country of all of them. The other players laughed at us when they had the pregame ceremony, and lined the players up from home to first, first to second, second to third, and third to home. They looked resplendent in their fine uniforms. We looked like boys in knickers. But we had some real ballplayers." Joe Tuminelli of Carta Vieja, who led the tournament with 2 home runs and 6 runs batted in, was voted the Most Valuable Player in the tournament. When they returned home to Panama victorious, parades and parties broke out all over Panama City. "We were some kind of heroes," acknowledged Brewer.

Panama was a participant in the Caribbean World Series from 1949 to 1960, and then in the Inter-American Series from 1961 to 1964, after which they withdrew from the competition because of financial problems. The 1950 Caribbean Series Championship was their only title, but they hosted the Caribbean World Series in 1952, 1956 and again in 1960, crowning the Havana Reds the champion in '52, and Cienfuegos, Cuba, the champion the other two years. During the 1952 Series in Panama City, Tommy Fine of Havana tossed a 1–0 no-hitter at Cerveceria Caracas of Venezuela. Panama did take home some honors, however. Elias Osorio won the home run crown in 1956 with 3 round-trippers, and Hector Lopez won the crown in 1960, also with 3. Stan Palys won the RBI title in 1960 with 12. Victor Strizka of Carta Vieja was the top pitcher in the 1954 classic, finishing with a 2–0 record, Winston Brown of Balboa was the top pitcher in the 1957 Series with a 2–0 record, and Humberto Robinson won the honor in 1958 with a 2–0 record. His record for the entire 12-year series was 4–4. Pat Scantlebury's Caribbean Series career record was 2–3 and Alberto Osorio's was 1–3.

The 1959 Caribbean World Series, held in Caracas, Venezuela, ended in another championship for Almendares, Cuba, but Norm Cash, a big left-handed hitting first baseman who was on his way to a memorable 17-year career with the Detroit Tigers, was the big story of the tournament. The 24-year-old slugger, representing Oriente of Venezuela, led all players in home runs with 2 and RBIs with 8. His biggest game came against the Cocle Club of Panama on February 14, 1959. He sparked his team to a 14–5 rout of Cocle by banging out four singles in five at-bats, and driving in 6 runs. The rosters of both teams were dotted with major league hopefuls and Negro League graduates. The future major leaguers were Rod Graber, Jerry Snyder, Norm Cash, Ken Hunt, and Gail Henley, while the Negro Leagues were represented by Dave Hoskins, Frank Austin, and Granville Gladstone.

Oriente, Venezuela

Name	Pos	AB	R	H
T. Obregon	SS	6	3	3
R. Graber	CF	4	3	2
G. Snyder	2B	6	2	4
N. Cash	RF	5	1	4
J. R. Oscanio	1B	6	0	0
A. Jones	C	5	2	2
D. Hoskins	P	5	0	2
L. Garcia	3B	4	1	3
P. Espinosa	3B	1	0	0
J. More	LF	5	2	2
V. Cler	P	1	0	0
S. Arthurs	P	0	0	0
R. Alston	PH	1	1	1
Totals		**47**	**14**	**22**

Cocle, Panama

Name	Pos	AB	R	H
F. Austin	2B	5	1	2
E. Green	SS	5	1	3
K. Hunt	LF	4	1	2
E. Osorio	1B	5	0	0
L. Peden	C	4	1	2
G. Henley	CF	4	0	0
G. Keron	3B	4	0	2
G. Gladstone	RF	4	0	1
D. Donnelly	P	0	0	0
W. Slack	P	2	0	0
Totals		**39**	**5**	**13**

```
Oriente    4 1 0   0 6 0   2 0 1—14—22—2
Cocle      0 1 3   0 0 0   0 0 1— 5—13—1
```

Doubles: Garcia (2), Jones, Hunt, Alston, Keron
Triples: Garcia.
Home Run: K. Hunt
Winning Pitcher: Dave Hoskins
Losing Pitcher: D. Donnelly

The first era of the Caribbean World Series came to an end in 1960 when Cuba's new dictator, Fidel Castro, eliminated professional baseball in his country. During the 12-year run of the Series, Cuba won seven titles, Puerto Rico took three, and Panama won one. Venezuela came up empty. The won-loss records of the teams from 1949 to 1960 follow.

Team	Wins	Losses	Percentage
Cuba	51	20	.718
Puerto Rico	38	34	.528
Panama	29	44	.397
Venezuela	26	46	.361

An alternative series, the Inter-American Series, matched teams from Panama, Puerto Rico, and Venezuela, beginning in 1961. Nicaragua joined the tournament in 1963, but the tournament lasted only four years, partly because fan interest in Panama was on the decline, making it economically unfeasible to continue to participate in international tournaments. During the four-year existence of the tournament, each team won one championship. Panama's Chiriqui-Bocas team was crowned champion in 1963, in Panama City, led by former Negro League pitchers "Webbo" Clarke and Al Osorio. The country's baseball fortunes continued on a downhill trend during the 1960s however, and in 1966 the Panama Winter League was dissolved. The Caribbean World Series was reinstituted in 1970, but without Panama. Puerto Rico was joined by the Dominican Republic, Venezuela, and Mexico, beginning a competition that is still active in 2006.

The political turmoil in Panama has been an ongoing adventure for the past one hundred years, and the chaos created by this situation has had an adverse effect on baseball in the country. Still the game has survived and prospered, with dozens of talented Panamanian players succeeding in the major leagues. Players from the American Negro leagues played a significant part in that progression, including Panamanian natives Frank Austin, Granville Gladstone, Al Osorio, Pat Scantlebury, Pablo Bernard, Alonzo Braithwaite, Vibert "Webbo" Clarke, Jonathan Parris, and Leon Kellman, and Americans Chet Brewer, Dave Hoskins, Bill Yancey, Sam Bankhead, Wilmer Fields, "Pumpsie" Green, Lou Johnson—the hero of the Los Angeles Dodgers 1965 World Series triumph over the Minnesota Twins—Jim Pendleton, Curt Roberts, Milt Smith, Al "Slick" Surratt, Joe Taylor, Charlie White, Wilmer Harris, and Connie Johnson. And there are dozens more whose names have not been found in the scanty records that have thus far been located.

The four senior members of the Negro League winter contingent were all Panamanian citizens, led by Jonathan Parris who played winter ball in the Central American country for 13 years. He was a hard-hitting third baseman for five different teams from 1945 through 1960. He was a .318 career batter who led the league with a .434 average in 1959-60 while playing with Comercios. During his career, the 5', 8", 170-pound right-handed hitter averaged 25 doubles, 5 triples, and 19 home runs for every 550 at-bats. Parris also played four years in the Negro leagues and ten years in the minor leagues where he hit .298 with 18 home runs a year. Frank "Pee Wee" Austin, a diminutive 5', 7" dynamo, played baseball in the Panama Winter League for ten years beginning with General Electric in 1945-46, and continuing with Chesterfield from 1946 through 1955. He held down the shortstop position during the 40-game per season playing schedule, while compiling a .309 batting average with 455 base hits in 1471 at-bats, including a league-leading .331 average in his final season. Austin enjoyed a 19 game hitting streak while with Chesterfield, lasting from late December 1946 until January 14, 1947. In addition to his exploits in Panama, Austin led the Negro National League in hitting with an average of .390 in 1944 at the age of 22, on his way to a five-year career Negro League average of .332. He went on to compile a .268 batting average in AAA minor league ball, primarily in the Pacific Coast League, but never made an appearance in a major league game. Alonzo "Archie" Braithwaite played in the Panama Winter League for eleven years, while compiling a .307 batting average with 29 doubles, 4 triples, and 6 home runs for every 550 at-bats. He played in the Negro leagues from 1944 to 1948, and then spent nine years in the minor leagues. Leon Kellman, another of the lightweight Panamanians, played third base, primarily for Spur Cola, from 1945 to 1955. He, like his fellow countrymen, was a good hitter, averaging .297 in 1109 at-bats, with 36 doubles, 7 triples, and 11 home runs for every 550 at-bats. Kellman played in the Negro leagues for seven years and the Mexican League for seven years, batting .297 and .309 respectively. The available batting and pitching statistics for the Negro League players who toiled in Panama can be found in the appendix.

Panama's baseball fortunes were limited to games and tournaments in the Caribbean basin and to participation in the American Negro leagues until after the color barrier was broken in 1946. Even then, with their winter league underway, it was eight more years before a native of Panama broke into the big time. But the country had a ringside seat to the integration of organized baseball when the Brooklyn Dodgers and their top farm club, the Montreal Royals, both of whom were conducting their spring training programs in Havana, Cuba, visited Panama City in late March 1947 for games against local clubs. It was less than one month before Jackie Robinson would integrate the major league sanctuary and his performance in the spring training games was being viewed closely. In one of the early exhibition games, Panama's all-black General Electric team defeated the Dodgers, but the Royals, with Robinson in tow, gained a measure of revenge on Tuesday March 18, when they routed Negro League ace George Jefferson and his GE team by the score of 8–5. Other Negro Leaguers on the GE team were Frank Austin and Bud Barbee. Two days later Brooklyn faced their Montreal minor league team in the final exhibition game in Panama and easily outdistanced them by a score of 10–3, much to the delight of the Panama City fans. But it was Jackie Robinson who gave the big leaguers a lesson in how the game should be played. He collected three base hits in four trips to the plate, two of them on well-placed bunts, the first of which caught the Dodgers' third baseman, Arky Vaughan, by surprise, and the second of which startled second baseman Eddie Stanky, who was so embarrassed by the play that he threw the ball over the grandstand onto the street after first calling time out. Robinson's third hit was a sizzler down the third base line that Vaughan managed to knock down but was unable to make a throw. His only out was the result of an outstanding play by Dodgers shortstop Pee Wee Reese who ranged far to his right for his hard hit ground ball, and then made a perfect throw from the hole to erase the Royals star. As the *Pittsburgh Courier* reported, "Both of these bunts were accomplished so deftly that the crowd rose as one and gave Jackie a great ovation. When crowds start giving demonstrations for bunting it must mean that the man they are saluting is more than just an ordinary ballplayer. In this particular contest—strange as it may seem—not a single throw was made to first base to nip Robinson after Reese threw him out in the first inning."

A new era dawned in organized baseball in 1947 thanks to Jackie Robinson, and baseball players formerly barred from the arena began to enjoy the fruits of their labor. The major league doors finally swung open for Panamanians in 1955 and three of them marched in, Humberto Robinson, Hector Lopez, and Vibert "Webbo" Clarke. Clarke was the only one of the three who had played baseball in the Negro leagues. His eight-year Negro League career showed a 36–31 slate with Cleveland and Louisville in the Negro American League. He also played organized baseball with Charlotte in the South Atlantic League, and he pitched in seven games with the Washington Senators in 1955 with no record. The 6', 170-pound southpaw pitched in the Panamanian Winter League between 1945 and 1954 compiling records of 4–3, 3–6, 6–5, 7–5, 9–5, 14–4 with a 2.87 ERA, 5–6, 7–8, 6–8, and 1–9. He came back in 1963 to pitch two more years, posting records of 2–2 and 4–2, giving him career totals of 68 wins against 63 losses. Humberto Robinson pitched five years in the major leagues with an 8–13 record, and Hector Lopez, the only position player of the group, enjoyed a solid 12-year major league career with the Kansas City Athletics and the New York Yankees. The 5', 10", 182-pound outfielder batted .269 during the regular season with 136 home runs and .286 with one homer in four World Series.

Over the past fifty years, there have been 40 Panama-born baseball players in the major leagues, beginning with Humberto Robinson in 1955. Some of the more notable Panamanian major leaguers include Hector Lopez, Rod Carew, Manny Sanguillen, Ben Oglivie, and Roberto Kelly. Carew, one of baseball's greatest hitters and a member of the National Baseball Hall of Fame, batted .328 (number 30 all-time) over a memorable

19-year major league career with a high of .388 in 1977, and with 3053 base hits (number 20 all-time). He led the league in batting seven times, second only to Ty Cobb's twelve titles. Sanguillen was an outstanding catcher with a .296 batting average, from 1967 to 1980. Oglivie, who played in the majors for 18 years, was a dangerous hitter who compiled a .273 batting average with 235 home runs. He led the league with 41 homers in 1980. Kelly, a 14-year major leaguer, hit .290 with 124 home runs.

As of 2005, there are seven natives of Panama still active in the major leagues—Bruce Chen, Einar Diaz, Carlos Lee, Jose Macias, Ramiro Mendoza, Mariano Rivera, and Olmedo Saenz. Lee, a seven-year veteran, now with the Milwaukee Brewers, is a powerful right-handed batter who has crushed 94 home runs over the past three years, with 326 runs batted in, while batting .286. And Mariano Rivera, who is an eleven-year veteran with the New York Yankees, may be Panama's most famous export since Carew. He is on his way to establishing himself as baseball's all-time greatest closer. He has recorded 379 saves through 2005 and, at 36 years of age, is in position to break Lee Smith's career mark of 478 saves.

Nicaragua

Nicaragua, like most of the countries in Central and South America, was a Spanish colony for 300 years, from the arrival of Gil Gonzalez Davila in 1522 until the country's declaration of independence in 1821. Black slaves were brought to the country in the 19th century to replace the Indian slaves who had died from disease or mistreatment. Internal strife followed the separation from Spain as Liberals and Conservatives battled for control of the country. Finally, in 1893, Jose Santos Zelaya, the Liberal leader, assumed the presidency, although his position was not universally accepted by the populace. And such has been the case for the last 100 years.

U.S. troops invaded Nicaragua in 1912 at the request of President Adolfo Diaz, after an unsuccessful revolt to depose him. The Marines occupied the country until 1933, following which Anastasio Somoza, a commander in the Venezuelan National Guard, staged a coup d'etat in 1936, establishing a dictatorship that lasted until 1979 when his son, Anastasio Jr., was deposed by the Sandinista Front for National Liberation. The first Anastasio Somoza had been assassinated in 1956, but while he was in power, he was a strong supporter of baseball as a result of his having been a student in the United States as a young man. He had attended the Pierce School of Business Administration in Philadelphia and was a Philadelphia Athletics fan.

Baseball was introduced in Nicaragua in the 1850s when gold prospectors, on their way to the California gold fields, traveled across the country to reach the west coast. These fortune hunters, en route to San Francisco, normally booked passage on a steamship down the eastern seaboard to Nicaragua or Panama, Costa Rica being too mountainous to cross. They then crossed Central America by wagon, before catching another steamship for the final leg of the journey up the west coast to northern California. During their stay in Nicaragua, the prospectors, most of them from the northeast section of the United States where baseball was rapidly becoming the National Game, passed the time by playing the game. But, as there were both American and British companies vying for control of the cross-country transportation rights, the natives were also introduced to cricket by British businessmen. The period from 1850 to the end of the 19th century was a hectic time in

Nicaragua. In 1887, two baseball teams, Southern and Four Roses, were formed, and baseball thrived in the area known as the Mosquito Coast after the Indian tribes, or Miskitos, that inhabited the Atlantic coast of Nicaragua and Honduras. Two years later, the U.S. consul sponsored the first official baseball game in the country, between Managua and Grenada, in the town of Bluefields, on the Atlantic coast. The popularity of the game was enhanced by the experience of several Nicaraguan young men who had studied at universities in the United States, and had then returned home with bats and balls to teach the game to their neighbors. The U.S. Navy supposedly built the first baseball field on their base at Puerto Cabezas, north of Bluefields, in 1902. Gradually the game took root in Nicaragua, and in 1904 the first organized baseball team, the Boer Club of Managua, was organized by U.S. Consul Carter Donaldson. Curiously, as noted on the Internet, it was a custom in Nicaragua at the time to name teams after warring groups or countries, so the Boer Club was named for the natives of South Africa who fought against the British in 1899. Other teams were subsequently named Russia and Japan after the combatants in the 1904 Russo-Japanese War. Eight years later, the first national tournament was held, matching Boer, Chinandega, and Leon, with Boer being crowned the first national champion. After a two-year hiatus, Managua took the title away from Boer in a six-team tournament with Masaya, Leon, Chinandega, and Grenada. Shortly thereafter, the U.S. Navy team traveled to the Pacific Coast of Nicaragua for a series of exhibition games, and returned home triumphantly with a 40–3 record. One reporter noted that the athleticism of the Navy team was so amazing the fans accused them of witchcraft.

Although Nicaragua did not have a professional baseball league until 1946, there were amateur leagues operating around the country almost continuously after 1912. Between that year and 1945, Managua won nine National Championships, including seven in a row from 1920 to 1931. Boer won seven championships, and General Somoza won three. The country participated in the Central American Games as early as 1935, when they battled Cuba and Panama for the amateur baseball supremacy of the Caribbean region. Cuba captured the title with a record of 8 and 1, followed by Panama at 5 and 3, and Nicaragua at 4 and 4. Other countries competing in the tournament held in El Salvador included El Salvador, Guatemala, and Honduras. Mexico withdrew its team when it was discovered that its roster included many professional players like Martin Dihigo, Luis Tiant, and Ramon Bragana.

Shortly after Anastasio Somoza became dictator in 1936, he declared baseball to be the national sport, beginning a period of baseball growth in the country. According to *Beisbol*, Manuel Cueto, a talented Cuban baseball player, brought a Cuban all-star team to Nicaragua to play against the locals. The Cubans won 24 of 25 games, but it spurred Nicaraguan interest in the game and, with Somoza's support, Nicaragua formed a national team to compete in international competition. In 1935, the national team traveled to Panama where they won 18 of 19 games. They then traveled to El Salvador where they competed in the third Central American and Caribbean Games, finishing third after a playoff with Panama and Cuba. They participated in other international tournaments over the years, including the Amateur Baseball Championships, which they supported from 1939 to 1964. Somoza took a personal interest in the sport himself. So much so in fact, that in one international competition, he fired the manager and managed the team himself.

The first Amateur World Series was held in London, England, in August 1938, with both the American and British teams made up entirely of American players. The team representing Great Britain won the tournament four games to one. The second Amateur World Series, the first genuine World Series, was held at La Tropical in Havana, Cuba, in August 1939. Cuba raced to the championship with Nicaragua finishing second. The following year, it was the same story, with Nicaragua coming in behind the Cubans. Gonzalez Echevarria reported, "Nicaragua, managed by Cuban Ramoncito Mendez, brought a strong team led by J.S. 'Chino' Melendez, a veteran pitcher who could also hit, Jonathan Robinson, another hard-hitting pitcher, slugger Stanley Cayasso, and Sam Garth, who was the 'Series' batting champion with nine hits in eighteen at-bats. Robinson and Cayasso hit the only homers of the tournament. Melendez, most likely a professional, held Cuba without hits in the first game until the fifth inning, only to lose 4–3, in ten innings against Pedro 'Natilla' Jimenez." In 1940, Nicaragua tied for second with the United States, each team finishing with 9 and 3 records, losing again to Cuba who went 10 and 2. Nicaragua, according to Echeverria, "brought Melendez, Robinson, and Cayasso, as well as J.M. Vallecillo, who hit four doubles; Carlos 'Pichon' Navas, a hard-hitting shortstop, and star catcher, Julio 'Canana' Sandoval. Robinson was the batting champion at .444. He hit the only homer and scored the most runs. Vallecillo led in runs batted in, Cayasso led in hits with nineteen, and Melendez, who won three and lost none, was the champion pitcher." The 11th annual Amateur World Series took place in Managua in 1950 with twelve countries participating, including Cuba, Mexico, El Salvador, Puerto Rico, the Dominican Republic, Panama, and Colombia. Puerto Rico was initially crowned champion but the title was taken away from them the following year at an Extraordinary Congress that was held in Mexico City when it was determined that Puerto Rico had used professional players when they defeated Cuba. Cuba was then named champion.

Since 1946, many teams have raised the Nicaraguan National Professional Championship flag over their stadium. The first national champion in 1946 was Cinco Estrellas, or Five Stars, and they went on to capture the first four pennants and eight of the first ten. San Felipe won five National Championships during the 1960s, Chinandega won three flags during the '70s, Leon won four pennants during the '80s, and Leon and Boer each won three titles during the '90s, showing how well distributed the talent has been over the years.

Nicaraguan baseball teams and leagues were integrated from the very beginning because the population of the country was a melting pot of races. Up to 69 percent of the people were mestizo, or mixed Amerindian and white, by the middle of the 20th century. The remainder of the population was composed of 17 percent white, 9 percent black, and 5 percent Amerindian. Since the country was located in the Torrid Zone, with the sun hovering overhead the entire year, and the average temperature in the 80s, with highs in the 90s most days, baseball, with its slower pace compared to sports like soccer, was an ideal national sport. Even though the game was popular in Nicaragua, the political climate of the country over the past 100 years discouraged players from North America, Puerto Rico, the Dominican Republic, and Cuba from participating in the Nicaraguan baseball leagues. An article on Library.thinkquest.org notes, "Nicaragua's history has been characterized by two things—instability and oppression. Ruthless dictators, corruption, and turmoil have been the norm. In addition to wars and rebellions, natural disasters have led to the destruction of the capital city of Managua twice in the last century, a tsunami plundered two Pacific cities, and the Juana hurricane recently devastated the Atlantic coast."

In 1956, Nicaragua began operation of a winter league, composed of four teams, El Boer, Leon, Oriental, and Cinco Estrellas. Originally, Cinco Estrellas was supported by Somoza so, as one fan noted, if you were opposed to Somoza, you always rooted for the other team. But that situation ended in short order with Somoza's assassination. The winter league operated for eleven years and participated in the Inter-American Series against Venezuela, Puerto Rico, and Panama in 1963 and 1964. The tournament matching the champions of each competing country's winter league, in a round-robin competition, began in 1961 with just three competing countries. Nicaragua was the fourth country and, in 1963 they competed in Panama. The following year, as the host country, Nicaragua's winter league champion, Cinco Estrellas, won the tournament. But that was the last tournament held as interest in it waned in both Panama and Nicaragua. In fact, the Nicaraguan Winter League folded in 1967 after Anastasio Somoza Jr. withdrew government financial support from the leagues.

During the existence of the Nicaraguan Winter League, many major league players and Negro League players traveled south to participate in the league between October and February. The major league contingent included Cuban-born Luis Tiant, Jr., who enjoyed a 19-year big league career while compiling a won-loss record of 229–172; Ferguson Jenkins, another 19-year veteran who won 284 major league games against 226 losses; Jim Kaat, who won 283 games and lost 237 from 1959 to 1983; Zoilo Versalles, an outstanding shortstop with a .242 batting average over a 12-year career; George Scott, whose 14-year major league career resulted in 271 home runs and a .268 batting average; Bert Campaneris, another excellent shortstop, who hit .259 over a 19-year career while sparking the Oakland Athletics to three consecutive world championships; and Lou Pinella, a hard-hitting outfielder for the New York Yankees, who batted .291 over 18 years, and helped the Bronx Bombers win three American League pennants and two world championships.

The Negro League members included Silvio Garcia, Claro Duany, "Chiquitin" Cabrera, Alejandro Crespo, Carlos Colas, Pedro Naranjo, Pedro Pages, Rene Gonzalez, Sam "Toothpick" Jones, Fernando Diaz Pedroso, Curt Roberts, and Harry "Suitcase" Simpson. Gonzalez, who played for the New York Cubans in 1950, was a member of the Oriental Club during the 1957-58 season, and led the league with 18 doubles, 10 home runs and 56 runs batted in. Pedroso, an outfielder with the New York Cubans from 1945 to 1952, also played for Oriental in 1957-58, hitting .292 in 178 at-bats. Roberts, like many of the Negro League players, was a baseball nomad who played in no less than eleven professional leagues from California to Nicaragua during his 18-year career. The 5', 8", 165-pound second baseman played for the Leon Lions during the 1963-64 season, batting .283 in 233 at-bats. Roberts also spent parts of three seasons with the Pittsburgh Pirates, batting .223 in 575 at-bats. Suitcase Simpson played in the Negro leagues from 1946 through 1948 with a .244 batting average, and in the major leagues, primarily with the Cleveland Indians, for eight years between 1951 and 1959, hitting .266 in 2829 at-bats. He played in Nicaragua during 1963-64, batting .302 in 202 at-bats. Sam "Toothpick" Jones went 13–10 in the Negro leagues from 1946 to 1948. He then pitched in the major leagues from 1951 to 1964, winning 102 games against 101 losses. His best year was

1959 when he led the National League in victories with 21, shutouts with 4, and earned run average with 2.83. He pitched for Boer in the Nicaraguan Winter League in 1964-65, going 2–0 with a 3.60 ERA. Ollie Brantley pitched in Nicaragua during the 1960s but his records have not been located.

Nicaragua returned to a period of amateur baseball after 1967, and produced many strong teams that fared well in international competition. In 1972, with future major league pitchers Dennis Martinez and Nestor Chavez on the mound, Nicaragua finished second in the World Amateur Baseball Championships held in Managua. That same year, a hurricane devastated the country, causing more than one billion dollars in property damage and killing more than 10,000 people. It also destroyed Estadio Somoza, Managua's most modern baseball stadium. Martinez was the first ballplayer of Nicaraguan descent to enter the major leagues when he joined the Baltimore Orioles in 1976. He was followed to the major leagues by Chavez in 1977 and Albert Williams in 1980. Martinez, who is known as "El Presidente" in his hometown of Grenada, is undoubtedly the country's greatest major league player. He enjoyed a notable 23-year career in the major leagues, winning 245 games, the most by any Latin American pitcher, against 193 losses. He led the league in victories during the strike-shortened 1981 season with 14. He also led the league in games started (39), complete games (18), and innings pitched (292) in 1979, and in complete games (9), shutouts (5) and ERA (2.39) in 1991. And he appeared in two World Series with a 0–1 record. Chavez pitched in just four games for the Baltimore Orioles in 1977. Through 2005, a total of eight Nicaraguan natives have played major league baseball, and two of them, Oswaldo Mairena and Vincent Padilla, are still active.

Nicaragua continued to field an amateur league throughout the '70s, with Grenada, El Boer, Leon, Chinandega, Esteli, Cinco Estrellas, and Managua. On July 19, 1979, Anastasio Somoza Jr. was deposed by the Sandinista Front for National Liberation, and soon went into exile. The Sandinistas, like Somoza Sr. and Fidel Castro in Cuba, realized the importance of maintaining a strong baseball presence in the country, so they subsidized an amateur league of ten teams that included El Boer, Nicaragua's first organized team; Los Dantos, a former military team; and Bluefields, an all-black team. The league schedule ran from December through May, including playoffs. According to *Beisbol*,

> There was also a government-sponsored youth federation of four leagues for 22,000 players on over 1,000 teams.
>
> In March 1980, before the Sandinistas fully embraced Castro, they encouraged the Baltimore Orioles to send local hero Dennis Martinez and a team of reserves for a two-game series against a local amateur All-Star team. The local All-Stars won one game and tied the other.
>
> The national champion coming out of the Nicaraguan Winter League does not participate in the Caribbean World Series, which is for professionals only. However, the Nicaraguans frequently send teams to the amateur international competitions, including the World Amateur Championships, the Pan American Games, and the Olympics.

Mexico

Baseball was first brought to Mexico by laborers from the United States who were building a railroad from the northwestern part of the country to Mexico City. According to *Beisbol,* "The northern railroaders brought more than sledge hammers, spikes, and railroad expertise with them. They also brought bats, balls, and baseball strategy. So it was that in the late 1870s in Nuevo Laredo, one of the first Mexican baseball games was played under the watchful eye of railroad construction supervisor Johnny Tayson.

"Sailors also helped turn Mexico into a baseball country. In the port city of Guaymas, which lies along the western coast, sailors from the U.S. ships *Montana* and *Newborne* taught local workers the game in 1877. Within ten years, baseball had spread to the capital, where the Mexico Club was formed as weekend recreation."

Baseball also invaded the east coast of the country in the 1890s when refugees from the Cuban War of Independence fled to the Yucatan Peninsula. The game was soon taught to the children around the capital city of Merida, and within two decades an intense baseball rivalry grew between the people of the Yucatan Peninsula and visitors from Cuba.

Some of the early Mexican baseball pioneers included Lucas "El Indio" Juarez, Antonio Delfin, Julio "El Diamante Blanco" Molina, Leonardo "Najo" Alanis, and Fernando Barradas. Juarez was an exceptional pitcher and catcher from 1900 to 1918. He was Mexico's greatest pitcher of the early years. As with many of the baseball pioneers in other countries, "El Indio" was a versatile player, who could play several positions with great skill and was also one of the most powerful hitters in the game.

Antonio Delfin was considered to be one of the most complete players of the early years, pitching and playing several other positions between 1914 and 1932. He played in his home state of Veracruz, where he was a local hero, and in Mexico City, where he was a noted hitter. Delfin is best remembered for pitching a no-hitter for Aguila against Mexico in 1922.

Julio "El Diamante Blanco" Molina was another legendary right-handed pitcher from the Yucatan Peninsula whose career lasted from 1910 to 1925. He was one of the participants in the most sensational pitching duel ever witnessed in the Yucatan Peninsula. In 1910, he faced off against Cuban ace Camilo Pujadas, with both pitchers throwing goose eggs at the opposing team until darkness forced an end to the scoreless game after 16 innings.

Leonardo "Najo" Alanis was an outstanding defensive center fielder, a superb batter, and a fast base runner. He starred in the Class C Western Association between 1925 and 1932, and he led the league in home runs in 1925 with 34, and in runs scored with 195 in 151 games. His contract was acquired by the Chicago White Sox in 1926, but he broke his leg before the season began, ending his dream of a major league career.

Fernando "Cocuite" Barradas was an outstanding southpaw pitcher for Mexico from 1925 to 1937, excelling in games against Cuba. He won a celebrated victory over the Cuban team in Havana in 1930 by the score of 2–1, helping his own cause with three base hits. During his pitching career, he threw three no-hitters. In his later years, from 1937 to 1944, he played first base for Agrario and Veracruz in the Mexican League, compiling a career batting average of .290.

Mexico participated in the Central American Games and the Amateur World Series during the 1920s and '30s, hosting the Central American Games in 1926 that matched Mexico against Cuba and Guatemala. Cuba dominated the tournament, blanking Mexico 12–0 in the opening game, en route to the championship. The next tournament, held in Havana's new La Tropical Stadium in 1930, welcomed five teams, Cuba, Mexico, El

Salvador, Guatemala, and Panama. Cuba, to no one's surprise, won the tournament, but not without a fight. Narciso Picazo of Cuba, who won two games in the tournament, was out-pitched by Fernando Barradas of Mexico by the score of 2–1 in the tournament's most exciting game. Mexico routed El Salvador 26–0 in one game, but eventually finished second with a 4–2 record to Cuba's 5–1 mark. Mexico had to withdraw its team from the 1934 competition because many of its players, such as Martin Dihigo, Luis Tiant Sr., and Ramon Bragana, were deemed ineligible because of their professional status.

In October 1932, the first recorded visit to Mexico by Negro League players showcased the talents of Willie Wells, "Cool Papa" Bell, Newt Allen, Chet Brewer, and other members of the Kansas City Monarchs who toured the country, meeting the best teams in Mexico, notably the Aztecas, renowned for their superior pitching staff, and the Gallos, noted for their hitting and defense, on the field of battle. Two other American teams, one a major league all-star team and the other the Chattanooga Lookouts, were both drubbed by Mexico's finest just weeks earlier. The Monarchs lost their first game as they were still becoming acclimated to the 6000-foot altitude. But from then on, it was all Kansas City. They roared through their next ten games, winning nine. They lost one game each to the Aztecas and Gallos. The Mexico City newspapers called the Monarchs the greatest baseball team ever to invade Mexico. As Q. J. Gilmore reported in the *Chicago*

Willie "El Diablo" Wells was a hero in Mexico for his sensational shortstop play (courtesy John B. Holway).

Defender, "The Aztecas have never been shut out before, and the Monarchs gave them the worst drubbing they have ever had when they lost to the Monarchs by the score of 17–0. The American colony in the City of Mexico are really happy since the Monarchs arrived. The American clubs from the States have suffered so many defeats at the hands of the Mexico City clubs that the Americans have been afraid to go out to the baseball parks. Since we have been here, the Americans are having their day. The Americans come around to our hotel every morning to tell us to keep on winning."

Four years later, the Negro League All-Stars returned to Mexico, assuming they were to match bats with local teams again. But they were surprised to learn their opponents would be a major league all-star team led by Rogers Hornsby, and including Jimmie Foxx, Heinie Manush, and Doc Cramer. In game one, the Negro Leaguers took a 6–4 lead into the ninth inning when the roof caved in. Manush singled and Foxx hit one into the center field bleachers to tie the game at 6–6. That's the way the game ended as the umpire called it a few minutes later. The major leaguers won games 2 and 3, sending the Negro League players home winless.

Willie Wells became infatuated with Mexico during his two early visits to the country, and he returned later in the decade to play in their summer league, earning the moniker "El Diablo," "The Devil," for his aggressive play. It became common practice for the fans to shout to the opposing batters, "Don't hit it to shortstop. The Devil plays out there." Wells liked playing baseball in Mexico because he didn't have to face the racial segregation he suffered in the United States. He said in Mexico, he was more than a baseball player. He was treated like a hero. He could live in the best hotels, eat in the best restaurants, and go anywhere he wanted to go. Wells also said the playing conditions were equal to major league conditions. The team traveled first class and stayed in first class hotels. Willie Wells also made more money in Mexico than he could have made in the Negro leagues. And most important, as he said more than once, "Here they treat me like a man."

Willie Wells played in the Mexican League in 1940, 1941, 1943, and 1944. The 1941 Veracruz team may have been the greatest team in Mexican baseball history. They won the league by a whopping 13½ games, finishing with a record of 67–35. Josh Gibson destroyed Mexican pitching, hitting a blistering .374 and leading the league with 33 home runs and 124 RBIs in just 358 at-bats. Ray Dandridge hit .367, Wells hit .347, and Lazaro Salazar hit .336. On the mound, Barney Brown went 16–5, Ramon Bragana went 13–8, Ray Taylor went 13–10, and Lazaro Salazar went 7–3. Dandridge played second base in Mexico, and teamed with Wells to give the Mexicans the flashiest double play combination they had ever seen. Dandridge liked Mexico so much he played there for eight years between 1940 and 1948. In 1944, he played in the Negro leagues. Playing baseball in the summer in Veracruz was a challenge, however, as Wells found out. He told Jim Riley, "And down in Veracruz it's so hot and all that water and stuff down there. And those mosquitoes. We had to sleep in nets. But, that's the only way to sleep down there in Veracruz. If you don't sleep under those nets, you were in trouble, partner. I would wake up in the morning and the nets would be clogged with big mosquitoes, you know. After one year playing in Veracruz, our team moved to Mexico City. Mexico City was different."

Ray Dandridge had an interesting experience in Mexico in 1945. Jorge Pasquel, the most powerful man in Mexico, the owner of more than 80 newspapers throughout the country, the president of the Mexican League, and the owner of the Mexico City Reds, was trying to recruit major league players to jump ship and come to Mexico. He was offering bonuses of $5,000 to $10,000 to any player who would join his team. Several players like Sal Maglie and Max Lanier took Pasquel up on his offer. Dandridge, who was earning $350 a month in Mexico, went to Pasquel looking for more money. When the owner refused to give him more money, Dandridge made plans to return to the United States. On the day of his departure, as he stood on the train platform waiting to board the train, a group of armed soldiers surrounded him, preventing him from boarding. Pasquel's secretary, who was with the soldiers, told Dandridge that he wouldn't be allowed to leave the country until he had spoken to Pasquel. With that, Dandridge accompanied the secretary to a waiting limousine and returned to Pasquel's office. When the two men met again, negotiations went much smoother. Ray got a raise to $10,000 for the season, all expenses paid, and a bigger apartment with a maid for him and his family. And Ray was particularly happy because he loved Mexico. He thought it was the best place to play in the Western Hemisphere. He told John Holway, "I set some records down there. I played me some baseball."

Winter baseball was played in Mexico throughout the 20th century, but the leagues were not well organized and the records are difficult to find or, in some cases, are non-existent. The Mexican Pacific League, a winter league, was formed in the late 1940s. It is still operating, and has been called Mexico's most prestigious baseball league. The league is composed of teams from the northern Pacific coast, where baseball is close to being a religion. The season runs from October to January to attract players from organized baseball in the United States, including major league players of Mexican descent. The weather in the northwest part of the country is conducive to playing baseball during the winter season with the daytime

Ray Dandridge played for Obregon in the Mexican Winter League in 1948–49, batting .317 in 47 games (courtesy James A. Riley).

temperature a comfortable 60 degrees, with a maximum temperature in the low 70s and an evening low in the upper 40s. One of the first Negro League players to join the league was Thomas "High Pockets" Turner, who journeyed to Hermosillo after his discharge from the U.S. Army after World War II. He told Brent Kelley about it.

> First year I was there, we played in the Pacific Coast League; that was the winter league. Bob Lemon managed our team—Hermosillo. Herman Breech from Minneapolis, he played. And I forget this guy's name—he was Chicago Cubs shortstop, he played on the team. And when spring training came, they had to leave.
>
> The winter league consisted of four cities: Hermosillo, Guaymas, Culiacan, and Mazatlan. Bill Wright played with Mazatlan. I played against him; I was very anxious to see him. Bill was an excellent hitter. Bill was a long ball hitter and to me, when he did hit the ball, it looked like it would just suddenly disappear like a rocket. It would be gone! Over the fence, in the stands, wherever. He was a good outfielder; he had a good arm. He was a big man. He was an exceptionally nice person and he still is.

Turner enjoyed playing baseball in Mexico, particularly because of the racial freedom the players experienced there, probably due to the racial makeup that was approximately 60 percent mestizo, a mixture of Amerindian and Spanish, 30 percent Amerindian, 9 percent white, and 1 percent other. Turner told Kelley:

> You would never believe the enthusiasm that baseball created in the country of Mexico during those days. You'd have to see it to believe it. I would go to the post office from my hotel, which was about six blocks. It would take me half a day to go from my hotel to the post office 'cause I would get stopped by everyone and everyone in every one of those stores and they wanted to talk to me. And they made me speak Spanish; they wouldn't let me speak English. They made me learn it. They would pick me up in their automobiles and ride me to the park; it wasn't that far—you could walk—but they'd come by the hotel and pick me up in a car and ride me. They paid me $700 a month, they paid for my laundry, they paid for my food, and they paid for everything. Only thing that I could spend money for was just for my personal effects. I couldn't spend money in a restaurant; I could go to the restaurant to eat and they wouldn't take my money. They were just that nice to me.
>
> They wanted to give me a home and they would furnish it for me if I would stay down there. I had married down there and my wife was pregnant with my first child. Well, I wanted my kid to be born in the States, so I left there in early '47.

Ray Dandridge, who had had a problem in Cuba during the 1947-48 season, joined the Mexican Pacific League the next year. He had jumped from his Cuban League team to an outlaw league and, after the league folded, Dandridge and the other outlaws were banned from playing in the Cuban League for one year. So Ray went to Mexico for the 1948-49 season, and played with Obregon along the Pacific coast, about 270 miles south of the Arizona border. He batted .317 in 47 games, with 11 doubles, 3 triples, and 6 stolen bases, in 189 at-bats. He was named to the All-Star team that winter along with a 20-year-old southpaw pitcher named Edward "Whitey" Ford. According to Dave Barnhill, Dandridge hit Ford like he owned him. Dandridge told John Holway, "I made an appearance on the *Good Morning America* show. [The announcer] said, 'You know Whitey Ford had a good curve ball.' I told him, 'I know Whitey had one of the best curve balls. But I had one of the best bats.'" Ford's teammate, Don Larsen, the only pitcher to throw a perfect game in the World Series, a feat he accomplished in 1956, also pitched in the Mexican Winter League for many years, with mixed results.

Willie "The Devil" Wells spent five winters playing baseball in the Mexican Pacific League according to Jim Riley, probably near the end of his career, in the late '40s or early '50s, but his records have not yet been found. Al "Slick" Surratt, a diminutive outfielder who played in the Mexican winter league in the 1950s, told Brent Kelley, "I didn't make a lotta money but I had a lotta fun. I loved to play. From a kid growin' up in a little ol' town, that was a thrill to me just to play because I loved the game."

Other Negro League veterans to display their wares in the Mexican Pacific League were "Cool Papa" Bell, Dave Barnhill, Ramon Bragana, Bill Cash, Sam Hairston, Edward Locke, Bonnie Serrell, Marvin Williams, Art "Superman" Pennington, Minnie Minoso, and Lino Donoso. Jim Riley said that "[Bragana] preferred playing in the Latin Leagues to the Negro Leagues because he was treated better there than in the States. He is ranked with Dihigo and Luque as the three greatest Cuban pitchers ever." Dave Barnhill was a 5', 7", 145-pound right-handed pitcher with a blazing fastball. He was one of the top pitchers in the Negro Leagues, in the 1940s. Playing for the New York Cubans, Barnhill posted a 13–8 record in 1941 and 12–4 two years later. Overall, between 1941 and 1946, he won 50 games against 28 losses for a .641 winning percentage. He played three years with the Minneapolis Millers in the American Association between 1948 and 1951, going 7–10, 11–3, and 6–5. Sam Hairston played for Puebla in 1956–57, batting .362 with 6 home runs and 60 RBIs in 318 at-bats. Edward Locke went 18–6 in 1956–57, pitching 194 innings. The following year, he led the league in innings pitched with 221 and in victories with 19, against just 7 losses. He led the Mexican Summer League in victories twice, with 18 in 1957 and 19 in 1958. He also led in ERA in 1957 with 3.30 and in innings pitched in 1958 with 267. And in 1959 he was 21–14. Bonnie Serrell, a talented second baseman, played in the Negro leagues for eight years between 1941 and 1951, batting a comfortable .309. The tall, slender, infielder known as "Grillo" (or the "Vacuum Cleaner") in Mexico, was a superb defensive player with outstanding range and the strong throwing arm. He played in the Mexican Pacific League in 1957-58, stroking the ball at a .265 clip. The 35-year-old left-handed hitter had 40 base hits in 151 at-bats with 5 home runs and 19 runs batted in. He also played in the Mexican summer league for ten

Ramon Bragana pitched in Mexico for 18 years, compiling a 211–162 win-loss record (courtesy Yuyo Ruiz).

years between 1945 and 1957, hitting .311 in 863 games. And ancient Minnie Minoso, who played baseball year-round in Mexico between 1965 and 1973, and who would eventually play major league baseball in five different decades, won the batting championship in the Mexican Pacific League in 1969-70 with an average of .359. He was 47 years old.

Art "Superman" Pennington played in Mexico winter and summer for at least three years as he related to Brent Kelley.

> When I left the United States, I never had so much freedom in all my life because you could eat anywhere and they got the finest restaurants, the beautifulest women—all colors, don't make no difference—and they're crazy about athletes. They got dance halls and I used to love to dance. I just told my mother, I said, "Mom, you should see this country. It's beautiful. Mexico City and Monterrey and Acapulco. Everybody swimmin' together." I went right from summer to winter ball and I was gonna stay in Mexico. I was gonna live there 'cause I married a Spanish girl down there. My mother and dad, they had a fit to think I would live in Mexico and not come back to the United States but I just told 'em, I said, "The things the way it is in the United States"—it was so prejudiced—"Mexico is freedom. They don't think about no color." This Spanish girl I married down there was white so I tried to explain to 'em but my mother didn't see it, so I stayed down there, I think, three or four years playin' winter and summer ball, then she got so that I come back to the United States.

Pennington also noted, "I hit a grand slam to open a ballpark in Culiacan, Mexico. They got my name on the ballpark down there." Marvin Williams held down second base for Veracruz in 1957-58, batting .332 with 11 home runs and 57 RBIs in 232 at-bats. "Wild Bill" Wright's winter league records are not available, but he liked Mexico so much, he played baseball there winter and summer for almost 20 years. He moved to Mexico permanently during the 1940s, making his home in Aguascalientes. And after his retirement from baseball, he opened a restaurant there called Bill Wright's Dugout that became a popular eatery.

Negro Leaguers presently residing in the Mexican Baseball Hall of Fame include Ray Dandridge, Martin Dihigo, Lazaro Salazar, "Cool Papa" Bell, Ramon Bragana, Roy Campanella, Josh Gibson, Monte Irvin, Alfred Pinkston, "Wild Bill" Wright, Adolfo Luque, and Minnie Minoso. Minoso, who led the Mexican Pacific League in batting in 1969-70 with an average of .359, was the last Negro Leaguer to play in that league.

Two of Mexico's most famous baseball players, although not Negro Leaguers, should be mentioned. Hector Espino, Mexico's most famous home run hitter, enjoyed a 25-year professional baseball career from 1960 to 1984, most of it in his home country. He made one venture into the United States in 1954 to play with Jacksonville, Florida, in the International League, but after just 32 games, the homesick first baseman went home, never to return. He had demonstrated his authority with the bat while he was in Florida, batting .300 in 100 at-bats with 3 home runs, but try as they might, the St. Louis Cardinals, who owned the rights to Espino, could never convince him to travel north of the border again. His Mexican League career included a .335 batting average, 2752 base hits, and 453 home runs, 29 home runs for every 550 at-bats. Espino also played winter baseball with the Hermosillo Orangemen in the Mexican Pacific League, where he batted .329 and hit another 299 home runs, giving him a grand total of 752 career home runs, trailing only Sadaharu Oh, who hit 868 home runs in the Japanese League, and Hank Aaron, who hit 755. During his year-round career, Espino won 11 home run titles and 18 batting championships. He also starred for Mexico in the Caribbean World Series, appearing in seven series, batting .297 with 6 home runs in 155 at-bats. His complete winter league statistics follow.

Dates	Years	AB	H	D	T	HR	BB	RBI	BA
1960–1985	26	5544	1824	259	13	299	940	1097	.329

As Espino's sensational baseball career was winding down in 1981-82, a young left-handed pitcher by the name of Fernando Valenzuela was breaking in with Navajoa in the Mexican Pacific League. Eleven years later, he pitched for Navajoa again, going 7–4 with a 2.95 ERA. Over the winter of 1981-82, the National League's Rookie of the Year and Cy Young Award winner pitched for Navajoa during the regular winter league season, and then was asked to join the league champion, Hermosilla, for the Caribbean World Series against the champions of Puerto Rico, the Dominican Republic, and Venezuela. Fernando started Mexico's first game against Ponce of Puerto Rico, in Hector Espino Stadium in Mexico City, and won in a romp, 14–0. He also pitched Mexico's last game, leaving in the 8th inning with the score tied at 1–1, but Mexico eventually lost 7–2. The Caracas Lions of Venezuela won the championship.

Colombia

Wilmer Fields played in Colombia in 1954-55 and 1955-56. He batted .330 in 1954-55, and .319 in 1955-56 where he won another MVP award, to go along with similar awards in Puerto Rico and Venezuela. Ollie Brantley, another Negro Leaguer, played winter baseball in Colombia during the 1960s, but his records are not available.

The Baltimore Orioles had a number of players in Colombia in 1955-56, including Brooks Robinson and Jim Gentile. According to Fields, Robinson, who was a .219 hitting part-time player for the Orioles at the time, practiced hitting the ball to the opposite field all season. He never pulled a single ball, but still hit .319. And he fielded like a demon. Fields said, "He could pick up dust." Gentile, who would develop into one of the American League's top sluggers over the next four years, was just breaking in with Baltimore after spending two years with the Brooklyn–Los Angeles Dodgers.

Luis "Jud" Castro, a diminutive, 5', 7", 145-pound second baseman, was Columbia's first major league player. He was a member of the Philadelphia Athletics in 1902, batting just .245 in 43 games. Bryan Oelkers pitched in 45 major league games between 1983 and 1986 with a 3–8 record. And Alberto Pardo played in 53 major league games between 1985 and 1989, batting .132. Other Colombian natives presently playing in the major leagues as of 2006 include Jolbert Cabrera, who is beginning his ninth year in the big show; Orlando Cabrera, entering his 10th year; and Edgar Renteria, entering his 11th season.

10

Looking Back

During the first half of the 20th century, Negro League baseball players, like their counterparts in the major leagues, were forced to seek employment year-round. Their baseball salaries, unlike today's inflated salaries, were only slightly higher than the typical working-man's wage, forcing them to work during the off-season. Many of the players took jobs outside baseball, as construction workers, insurance salesmen, and waiters, but many more sought jobs within their profession as pitchers, catchers, and outfielders. These men plied their trade in Florida and California in the U.S., and in other countries like Mexico, Puerto Rico, the Dominican Republic, Cuba, and Venezuela. They also barnstormed around the country in October and November, playing a tough exhibition schedule against major league all-star teams. Their efforts in many of these competitions helped to hasten the integration of organized baseball by providing the black players with a stage where fans and baseball executives throughout the Western Hemisphere could witness first hand the comparative skills of the Negro League players and players from the major leagues and the high minor leagues. These winter excursions to such places as Cuba, Puerto Rico, and the Dominican Republic were pleasant interludes for the Negro League players and their wives. They were treated as equals and were held in high regard in the community for their outstanding skills on the baseball field.

Baseball executives in the United States were well familiar with the skills of the black players through their efforts in the Negro League games that were played in many of the major league stadiums such as Yankee Stadium, Griffith Stadium, and Forbes Field. But these games pitted black against black and didn't give the major league owners any indication of how the black players would perform against the stiff competition offered by the white major league players. Several of the winter leagues, however, including the California Winter League, the Cuban Winter League, and the Puerto Rican Winter League, helped to dispel the owners' doubts about the skills of the black players, and advanced the integration of organized baseball. In California, from 1920 to the beginning of World War II, a Negro League team competed against several all-white teams composed of major league players, former major league players, future major league players, and Pacific Coast League players, from October to February each year. Frequently, the players faced each other in one-on-one matchups, with Bob Meusel of the New York Yankees stepping in against "Bullet Joe" Rogan, Dobie Moore facing Specs Meadows of the Philadelphia Phillies, or Satchel Paige going head to head with the Washington Senators' Buck Newsom. Word of mouth is a great communicator, and word of the tremendous skills of the Negro League players was a popular topic of conversation in baseball circles from coast to coast during the 1920s and '30s. Paige embarrassed his white opponents in California, fanning an average of 12 batters a game while running up a record of 56–7 against them. "Bullet Joe" Rogan went 42–14 and Chet Brewer was 43–13. At the same time, the big Negro League hitters feasted on big league pitching with Mule Suttles batting .326 with 13 home runs in just 121 at-bats against active major league pitchers like Newsom and Larry French, Dobie Moore scorching the ball at a .362 clip, and "Wild Bill" Wright hitting .361.

The Cuban Winter League added an extra dimension to the reputation of the black players. In the island nation south of Florida, one of the highest rated professional winter leagues operated from the late 1800s until Fidel Castro eliminated professional sports in the country in 1960. Almost from the beginning, black players competed with and against white players in league play, and on integrated Cuban teams in exhibition games against touring major league teams like John McGraw's New York Giants, Connie Mack's Philadelphia Athletics, and Ty Cobb's Detroit Tigers. And the Cuban teams more than held their own against their big league opponents, winning more than they lost and on one occasion stopping the Tigers with an 11-inning no-hitter. Word of the sensational play of the integrated Cuban teams made headlines in the United States and led to the commissioner of baseball banning exhibition games between major league teams and teams with black players. Major league players seeking winter employment, however, made the sojourn to Cuba from the beginning of the 20th century right up to the integration of organized baseball. During the 1920s, the Cuban Winter League was reported to be one of the strongest professional baseball leagues in the Western Hemisphere including the major leagues, if not the best. The league employed some of Cuba's greatest players, such as Cristobal Torriente, Martin "El Immortal" Dihigo, and Alejandro Oms, legendary Negro League players like Oscar Charleston, John Henry Lloyd, and Dobie Moore, and major leaguers such as Eddie Brown, a career .303 hitter with the Brooklyn Dodgers, Charlie Dressen of the Cincinnati Reds, and Jesse Petty. Adolfo Luque, another Cuban legend, starred in both the Cuban League and the major leagues, compiling a record of 106–71 in his home country, and 194–179 in the major leagues including a brilliant 27–8 record in 1923 in which he led the National League in victories, winning percentage (.771), shutouts (6), and earned run average (1.93).

In Puerto Rico, blacks and whites played on the same team as a matter of routine from the inception of the sport on the island.

Barnstorming exhibitions against major league all-star teams strengthened the reputation of the Negro League players, from the "Cyclone Joe" Williams era to the Satchel Paige era. In the early days, the Negro Leaguers enjoyed great success against such teams as Connie Mack's powerful Philadelphia Athletics with Chief Bender and Eddie Collins, and against his later team that included Lefty Grove and Jimmie Foxx. They continued their friendly competition into the 1930s and '40s, particularly when Satchel Paige toured the country against all-star teams headed by Dizzy Dean and Bob Feller.

Other venues made lesser contributions toward the final solution, including the Dominican Republic Winter League, the Venezuelan Winter League, the Panama Winter League, the Nicaraguan Winter League, the Colombian Winter League, and military teams like the 25th Infantry Regiment Baseball Team. Most players on the Dominican Republic baseball teams of the 1920s, '30s, and '40s were Dominican natives. Very few of them played in the Negro leagues, and very few Negro League players from the United States played in the Dominican Republic until after the integration of organized baseball.

Most players on the Venezuelan baseball teams of the 1920s, '30s, and '40s were Venezuelan natives, and very few of them played in the Negro leagues, but the influx of Negro League players from the United States had a significant effect on the progress of professional baseball in the country. The presence of Negro Leaguers like Roy Campanella, Buck Leonard, and Hilton Smith in the Venezuelan Winter League in 1946 gave the league immediate credibility, and the league has gone on to become one of the strongest winter leagues in the Western Hemisphere.

The Florida Hotel League was an all-black league that did not have a significant effect on the integration of organized baseball although it did educate many of the influential citizens of the northeast and central sectors of the country, such as the Rockefellers, Vanderbilts, Cabots, Lodges, and Flaglers, about the considerable skills of the black baseball players.

The immense talent of the Negro League players is reflected in the fact that almost 100 of them have been honored in the Baseball Halls of Fame of at least six countries in the Western Hemisphere, including the United States.

United States

Martin Dihigo	Josh Gibson	Buck Leonard
Judy Johnson	Ray Dandridge	Hilton Smith
Wilbur "Bullet Joe" Rogan	Satchel Paige	Turkey Stearnes
Monte Irvin	Roy Campanella	Jackie Robinson
Willie Mays	Ernie Banks	Willie Foster
Leon Day	"Smokey Joe" Williams	"Cool Papa" Bell
Willie Wells	John Henry Lloyd	Oscar Charleston
Ray Brown	Willard Brown	Andy Cooper
Biz Mackey	Mule Suttles	Cristobal Torriente
Jud Wilson	Frank Grant	Pete Hill
Jose Mendez	Louis Santop	Ben Taylor
Rube Foster		

Mexico

Martin Dihigo	Josh Gibson	Ray Dandridge
Lazaro Salazar	Roy Campanella	Monte Irvin
Ramon Bragana	Al Pinkston	Bill Wright

Puerto Rico

Ray Brown	Bus Clarkson	"Pancho" Coimbre
Leon Day	Josh Gibson	Satchel Paige
George Scales	Bob Thurman	Tetelo Vargas
Artie Wilson	Luis Villodas	"Millito" Navarro
Carlos Santiago		

Dominican Republic

Tetelo Vargas	Alonzo Perry	Horacio Martinez
Enrique Lantgua	Pedro San	

Cuba

Martin Dihigo
Adolfo Luque
Antonio Garcia
Julian Castillo
Alejandro Oms
Pelayo Chacon
Isidro Fabre
Ramon Bragana
Sandy Amoros
Rodolfo Fernandez
Yo Yo Diaz

Strike Gonzalez
Cristobal Torriente
Regino Garcia
Bernardo Baro
Jacinto Calvo
Bienvenido Jimenez
Emilio Palomino
"Cocaina" Garcia
Minnie Minoso
Luis Tiant, Sr.
Pedro Formental

Mike Gonzalez
Luis Padron
Valentin Dreke
Pablo Mesa
Jose Rodriguez
Lazaro Salazar
Silvio Garcia
Alejandro Crespo
Eustaquio Pedroso
Jose Maria Fernandez

Venezuela

Martin Dihigo

"Cocaina" Garcia

Vidal Lopez

Appendix:
Negro League Player Statistics

Key: AB—At Bats; R—Runs; H—Hits; D—Doubles; T—Triples; HR—Home Runs; BA—Batting Average; G—Games; CG—Complete Games; W—Wins; L—Losses; IP—Innings Pitched; SO—Strikeouts; BB—Bases On Balls; SH—Shutouts; S—Summer League; W—Winter League; ( )—Estimated Number Based On Partial Statistics; *Season Record; †California Winter League Record

Table I:
Comparison of Professional Leagues

League	AB	H	D	T	HR	BA
Major Leagues	550	143	25	6	19	.260
Cuban League—1930 to 1960	550	152	—	—	14	.276
Puerto Rican Winter League—1958 to 1994	550	152	—	—	15	.276
Dominican Winter League—1955 to 1997	550	155	—	—	16	.281
Cuban League—1920 to 1960	550	158	—	—	12	.284
AAA Minor Leagues	550	159	26	6	20	.287
Puerto Rican Winter League—1938 to 1957	550	161	—	—	16	.293
AA Minor Leagues	550	168	—	—	29	.306
Negro Leagues—1930 to 1950	550	169	24	8	15	.308
Mexican League—1938 to 1997	550	167	—	—	20	.310
Panama Winter League—1940 to 1959	550	181	—	—	24	.329
California Winter League—1920 to 1947	550	185	—	—	25	.336
Venezuelan Winter League—1930 to 1959	550	201	—	—	23	.365
Florida Hotel League—1896 to 1932						

Table II: Florida Hotel League (Coconut League)—
Negro League Player Statistics, Batting and Pitching

Batting

Name	Years	G	AB	H	D	T	HR	BA
Todd Allen	1916–1926	22	61	15	0	0	0	.234
Jess Barbour	1914–1921	34	111	23	2	0	0	.207
Pelayo Chacon	1918	11	41	8	2	0	0	.195
Oscar Charleston	1917	11	39	6	0	0	0	.154
Bingo DeMoss	1918–1921	17	57	8	1	0	0	.140
Pete Duncan	1910–1918	27	97	31	3	1	1	.320*
Brodie Francis	1911–1930	48	154	29	2	0	1	.188

Name	Years	G	AB	H	D	T	HR	BA
Jude Gans	1912–1918	25	87	15	2	1	0	.172
Leroy Grant	1911–1921	52	166	33	3	2	0	.199
Blainey Hall	1916–1921	35	117	33	0	3	0	.282
Bill Handy	1911–1917	37	121	24	3	0	1	.198
Nate Harris	1906	—	—	—	—	—	—	—
Vic Harris	1926–1927	9	36	15	1	0	1	.417
Pete Hill	1910–1918	39	131	29	7	0	0	.214
John Henry Lloyd	1908–1921	59	123	38	5	1	0	.309
Dick Lundy	1918–1923	14	52	10	3	0	0	.192
Jimmie Lyons	1913–1921	26	83	15	2	3	1	.181
Jap Payne	1907–1914	7	23	2	0	0	0	.154
Bill Pettus	1914–1917	27	88	18	1	0	1	.205
Bruce Petway	1907–1918	31	94	15	0	1	0	.160
"Spot" Poles	1914–1917	37	137	39	3	0	0	.285
Wes Pryor	1910–1927	15	49	14	0	1	1	.286
Al Robinson	1909–1910	—	—	—	—	—	—	—
Louis Santop	1914–1921	46	147	34	5	0	0	.231
Ben Taylor	1915–1916	13	45	16	1	1	1	.356
Jules Thomas	1912–1928	66	233	48	5	1	1	.206
Dick Wallace	1913–1917	27	82	10	0	1	0	.122
Jap Washington	1926–1928	14	54	20	0	2	3	.375
Pearl Webster	1909–1917	26	84	18	2	1	0	.214
"Smokey Joe" Williams	1914–1931	51	129	24	1	1	0	.186

Pitching

Name	Years	G	CG	W	L	IP	SO	BB	SH
Walter Ball	1912–1913	8	4	4	1	60	—	—	2
Phil Cockrell	1918–1921	9	2	4	3	48	—	—	1+
Dizzy Dismukes	1913–1916	16	13	9	6	—	—	—	—
John Donaldson	1916	6	5	1	5	45	—	—	—
Frank Earle	1907–1915	13	12	9	3	118	—	—	1+
Rube Foster	1904–1911	8	6	5	0	46	—	—	1+
Bill Gatewood	1907–1914	8	7	1	5	64	—	—	—
Ad Langford	1915–1916	8	5	6	2	67	—	—	—
Dan McClellan	1904–1913	9	6	4	3	64	—	—	—
Juan Luis Padron	1917–1918	18	10	6	5	127	—	—	3
Dick Redding	1915–1918	13	5	5	5	84	—	—	1+
Lee Wade	1912–1916	12	7	4	7	86	—	—	2+
Frank Wickware	1910–1918	16	8	3	7	113	—	—	—
Joe Williams	1914–1931	57	39	26	14	428	—	—	8
Dick Whitworth	1918	7	4	5	0	43	—	—	1

Table III: Cuban League—Negro League Player Statistics, Batting and Pitching

Batting

Name	Years	AB	R	H	D	T	HR	BA
Newt Allen	1924–1938	223	29	62	5	3	1	.278
Sam Bankhead	1937–1941	802	139	238	24	10	10	.297
Jess Barbour	1910–1916	179	15	40	5	1	0	.223
"Cool Papa" Bell	1928–1941	569	131	166	30	16	10	.292

Negro League Player Statistics

Name	Years	AB	R	H	D	T	HR	BA
Gene Benson	1947–1948	239	22	57	9	2	1	.238
Charles Blackwell	1920–1923	95	11	30	2	4	0	.316
Bob Boyd	1949–1957	647	85	194	21	6	9	.300
Phil Bradley	1908–1909	70	8	16	0	2	0	.257
Roy Campanella	1943–1944	128	15	34	9	3	0	.266
Larry Brown	1924–1930	500	62	126	12	10	0	.252
Walter Cannady	1926–1940	142	17	32	6	1	0	.225
George "Tank" Carr	1926–1927	(125)	(21)	(52)	—	—	—	.416
Oscar Charleston	1920–1930	999	219	360	(61)	(27)	(26)	.360
Ray Dandridge	1937–1953	2128	269	601	(75)	(15)	(11)	.282
Ducky Davenport	1943–1948	907	113	249	34	12	1	.275
Rap Dixon	1929–1930	175	38	46	10	6	5	.263
Frank Duncan	1923–1938	604	83	164	(24)	(16)	(1)	.272
Billy Francis	1908–1913	123	12	17	1	1	0	.138
Jude Gans	1913–1916	186	40	62	6	4	0	.333
Jelly Gardner	1924–1925	118	22	34	0	1	0	.288
Josh Gibson	1937–1939	224	61	79	10	5	14	.353
Pete Hill	1907–1916	661	158	203	9	16	2	.307
Crush Holloway	1924–1929	252	44	73	10	6	1	.290
Monte Irvin	1947–1949	358	66	95	16	7	11	.266
Sam Jethroe	1947–1955	663	126	192	22	17	10	.290
Chappie Johnson	1907	99	10	19	0	0	1	.192
Grant Johnson	1907–1912	549	116	175	11	8	4	.319
Judy Johnson	1926–1930	386	55	129	(23)	(7)	(3)	.334
Newt Joseph	1928–1929	110	16	30	3	1	3	.273
Henry Kimbro	1939–1949	942	184	276	23	13	1	.293
Buck Leonard	1936–1949	236	35	67	7	1	3	.284
John Henry Lloyd	1908–1930	1327	210	436	(49)	(36)	(5)	.329
Dick Lundy	1920–1930	876	146	299	(39)	(13)	(8)	.341
Jimmie Lyons	1912	(118)	19	34	5	(4)	0	.288
Biz Mackey	1924–1925	152	29	47	11	5	0	.309
Oliver Marcelle	1922–1930	957	148	292	(30)	(15)	(7)	.305
Bill Monroe	1907–1908	123	3	41	2	2	1	.333
Dobie Moore	1923–1924	283	38	100	(14)	(9)	(2)	.353
Lennie Pearson	1946–1951	1299	160	341	54	5	28	.263
Jim Pendleton	1952–1953	227	33	66	9	3	6	.291
Bill Perkins	1935–1941	902	146	260	25	10	9	.288
Bruce Petway	1908–1916	385	43	81	7	0	0	.210
"Spot" Poles	1910–1915	383	79	122	9	12	1	.319
Bill Riggins	1924–1930	266	40	80	7	10	1	.301
Curt Roberts	1955–1957	560	74	143	17	6	7	.255
George Scales	1927–1930	375	63	112	12	8	3	.299
Bonnie Serrell	1945–1947	338	44	91	(19)	(4)	(3)	.269
Chino Smith	1926–1930	565	83	189	(44)	(17)	(4)	.335
Milt Smith	1955–1959	705	108	189	27	11	11	.268
Clyde Spearman	1936–1940	774	121	211	20	4	4	.273
Ed Stone	1937–1948	352	52	93	19	4	4	.264
Mule Suttles	1928–1940	460	65	128	14	5	12	.278
Clint Thomas	1923–1930	697	135	216	(19)	(16)	(8)	.310
Hank Thompson	1946–1949	789	148	252	31	24	12	.319
Frank Warfield	1922–1930	583	123	177	(21)	(10)	(5)	.304
Willie Wells	1928–1940	1099	189	352	47	20	16	.320
Chaney White	1927–1930	37	59	117	6	6	2	.347
Jud Wilson	1925–1936	769	165	286	38	27	18	.372

Pitching

Name	Years	G	CG	W	L	IP	SO	BB	SH
Walter Ball	1908–1911	27	20	9	16	—	—	—	—
Dave Barnhill	1947–1950	54	30	23	19	384	211	127	—
Joe Black	1950–1952	43	17	20	13	255	119	97	—
Barney Brown	1935–1940	59	21	16	23	—	—	—	—
Dave Brown	1922–1925	31	15	17	12	—	—	—	—
Raymond Brown	1936–1948	89	57	46	20	—	—	—	—
Andy Cooper	1923–1929	37	13	1	17	—	—	—	—
Rube Currie	1923–1924	11	6	10	5	—	—	—	—
Rube Foster	1907–1916	33	24	18	11	—	—	—	—
Willie Foster	1927–1928	16	8	6	8	—	—	—	—
"Cocaina" Garcia	1926–1948	222	93	85	61	—	—	—	—
Bob Griffith	1937–1939	35	18	16	11	—	—	—	—
Bill Holland	1922–1939	50	23	27	22	—	—	—	—
Connie Johnson	1954–1955	32	11	12	11	(175)	(123)	(84)	—
Rufus Lewis	1947–1949	55	15	19	11	274	139	136	—
Max Manning	1945–1948	88	26	27	33	519	167	217	—
Booker McDaniels	1945–1948	49	10	15	14	—	—	—	—
Terris McDuffie	1937–1953	135	38	37	43	—	—	—	—
Satchel Paige	1929–1930	15	8	6	5	—	—	—	—
"Pullman" Porter	1939–1941	23	11	9	9	—	—	—	—
Ted Radclife	1938–1940	35	12	12	11	—	—	—	—
Dick Redding	1912–1923	62	32	18	23	—	—	—	—
Joe Rogan	1924–1925	18	5	9	4	—	—	—	—
Red Ryan	1920–1927	39	12	12	10	—	—	—	—
Hilton Smith	1937–1940	23	9	1	5	—	—	—	—
Theolic Smith	1938–1948	19	8	5	9	—	—	—	—
Sam Streeter	1924–1930	39	11	10	10	—	—	—	—
Ted Trent	1928–1930	23	9	6	10	—	—	—	—
Joe Williams	1912–1916	48	26	22	15	—	—	—	—
Nip Winters	1923–1926	27	8	4	12	—	—	—	—

Table IV: 25th Infantry Regiment Baseball Team— Negro League Player Statistics, Batting and Pitching

Batting

Name	Years	AB	R	H	D	T	HR	BA
Joe Rogan	1914–1920	30	—	13	1	2	2	.433
Dobie Moore	1916–1920	24	—	7	0	1	1	.292
"Heavy" Johnson	1916–1920	18	—	6	0	1	1	.333
Lem Hawkins	1914–1920	23	—	6	0	0	0	.260
Bob Fagin	1916–1920	23	—	10	2	0	0	.435
Fred Goliath	1916–1920	25	—	10	2	0	2	.500

Pitching

Name	Years	G	CG	W	L	IP	SO	BB	SH
Chief Waterhouse	1914–1920	3	2	2	0	23	17	0	0
Jacques Jasper	1914–1920	4	3	4	0	31	32	1	0
Joe Rogan	1914–1920	3	3	3	0	27	38	1	0
Semaphore Morgan	1916–1920	1	1	1	0	9	—	0	0

Table V: California Winter League—Negro League Player Statistics, Batting and Pitching

Batting

Name	Years	AB	R	H	D	T	HR	BA
Newt Allen	1925–1931	552	—	179	35	6	4	.324
Sam Bankhead	1932–1945	276	—	96	16	9	8	.351
John Beckwith	1927–1929	172	—	71	13	1	19	.413
"Cool Papa" Bell	1922–1945	596	—	219	31	12	16	.368
Henry Blackman	1920–1924	207	—	72	6	8	6	.348
Willie Bobo	1924–1931	252	—	78	9	8	6	.310
Spencer Butcher	1920–1928	491	—	122	15	6	3	.248
George "Tank" Carr	1915–1931	715	—	240	52	17†	27	.336
Dewey Creacy	1924–1932	268	—	83	13	10	1	.310
Connie Day	1922–1929	532	—	139	24	6	13	.261
Rap Dixon	1925–1931	479	—	156	33	7	18	.326
Tommy Dukes	1932–1934	236	—	81	17	3	14	.343
Jake Dunn	1930–1944	328	—	110	20	7	13	.335
Bob Fagan	1920–1926	480	—	129	16	3	2	.269
Lem Hawkins	1908–1925	529	—	154	24	7	0	.291
Crush Holloway	1922–1930	476	—	144	21	5	7	.303
Sammy T. Hughes	1934–1942	294	—	113	17	5	17	.384
Newt Joseph	1926–1930	193	—	55	17	1	9	.285
Biz Mackey	1920–1945	957†	—	350†	62†	17†	28	.366
Hurley McNair	1920–1925	314	—	101	21	12	5	.322
Jose Mendez	1917–1923	140	—	35	4	3	2	.250
Dobie Moore	1920–1925	377	—	145	28	13	13	.385†
Dink Mothel	1926–1930	381	—	114	12	2	4	.299
Bill Pettus	1909–1921	149	—	51	8	9	3	.342
Neal Pullen	1920–1931	437	—	137	21	5	11	.314
John Reese	1924–1925	103	—	26	7	1	0	.252
Bill Riggins	1922–1931	271	—	87	14	4	6	.321
"Bullet Joe" Rogan	1917–1930	434	—	157	25	5	15	.362
Felton Snow	1933–1941	395	—	126	21	5	14	.319
Turkey Stearnes	1922–1936	754	—	281	39	16	56	.373
Mule Suttles	1930–1940	450	—	170	29	0	64†	.378
Jesse Walker	1931–1947	254	—	83	14	5	5	.328
Pinky Ward	1920–1925	308	—	86	4	5	1	.279
Willie Wells	1924–1945	528	—	159	40	6	11	.301
"Wild Bill" Wright	1933–1945	416	—	156	26	11	15	.375

Pitching

Name	Years	G	CG	W	L	IP	SO	BB	SH
"Cherry" Bell	1924–1932	28	18	14	8	201	127	69	3
Chet Brewer	1926–1946	72	42	43	13	445	211+	—	6
Andy Cooper	1922–1931	43	22	22	6	260	—	—	4
Rube Currie	1920–1926	61	35	26	19†	402	162	94	4
"Plunk" Drake	1924–1925	20	17	11	5	155	70	54	1
Willie Foster	1926–1932	(28)	(22)	24	1	(185)	(159)	(57)	4
Ping Gardner	1920–1929	19	13	12	3	131	73	61	2
Robert Griffith	1934–1939	29	22	20	2	214	228	(59)	0
Jess Hubbard	1920–1928	15	11	11	4	112	(77)	(42)	3

Name	Years	G	CG	W	L	IP	SO	BB	SH
Satchel Paige	1931–1947	80†	47	56†	7	572†	770	(175)†	17†
"Pullman" Porter	1932–1945	35	25	23	6	224	—	—	4
"Bullet Joe" Rogan	1917–1930	64	52†	42	14	516	351	189	5
William Ross	1924–1931	21	17	1	5	166	96	47	1
James Willis	1930–1935	68	47	41	10	397	(288)	(91)	8

Table VI: Puerto Rican Winter League—Negro League Player Statistics, Batting and Pitching

Batting

Name	Years	AB	R	H	D	T	HR	BA
Hank Aaron	1953–1954	274	37	84	16	3	9*	.307
Joseph Atkins	1948–1949	120	25	39	7	—	6	.325
Gene Baker	1952–1954	487	—	140	—	—	6	.287
Dan Bankhead	1941–1963	844	(109)	238	(45)	(19)	(7)	.282
Sam Bankhead	1941–1947	701	120	218	(14)	(5)	(14)	.311
Bob Boyd	1951–1953	598	101	196	28	8	8	.331
Willard Brown	1941–1957	1940	378	679	135	27	101	.350
Jose Burgos	1944–1955	1886	270	408	(50)	(19)	3	.245
Roy Campanella	1940–1947	457	86	126	(28)	(6)	11	.276
Bus Clarkson	1940–1956	2063	448	621	109	15	98	.301
Gene Collins	1948–1950	—	—	—	—	—	—	—
"Pancho" Coimbre	1938–1951	1915	370	646	135	17	24	.337
George Crowe	1950–1955	467	(121)	179	(59)	(11)	20	.383
Ray Dandridge	1953–1954	228	22	53	—	—	1	.232
Johnny Davis	1947–1949	—	—	—	—	—	—	—
"Piper" Davis	1947–1952	492	(82)	146	19	12	13	.297
Leon Day	1939–1950	177	27	48	8	5	3	.271
Larry Doby	1946–1947	152	27	53	—	—	12	.349
Luke Easter	1948–1956	440	112	158	34	10	31	.359
Wilmer Fields	1947–1952	1067	—	347	—	—	(30)	.325
Silvio Garcia	1939–1940	124	17	37	8	3	1	.298
Alphonso Gerrard	1944–1958	2288	365	693	88	24	6	.303
Josh Gibson	1939–1945	389	—	138	(31)	(10)	19	.355
Alphonso Gerrard	1944–1958	503	—	159	—	—	—	.316
George Giles	1936	—	—	—	—	—	—	—
Junior Gilliam	1951–1953	328	—	118	—	—	3	.278
Charles Harmon	1953–1956	547	—	170	(10)	(14)	6	.311
William Harrell	1956–1958	484	—	141	(18)	(13)	8	.291
Johnny Hayes	1939–1940	—	—	—	—	—	—	.273
Elston Howard	1954–1955	121	—	45	—	—	7	.372
Monte Irvin	1940–1947	722	(145)	259	(67)	(18)	(24)	.359
Sam Jethroe	1944–1947	200	—	68	—	(9)	1	.340
Lou Johnson	1964–1965	237	—	81	—	—	6	.342*
Buck Leonard	1940–1941	118	45	46	17*	0	8*	.390
Louis Louden	1947–1948	168	32	51	9	3	2	.304
"Canena" Marquez	1944–1964	4018	768	1206	235	66	97	.300
Willie Mays	1954–1955	172	63	68	15	7*	12	.395*
Roy Partlow	1939–1947	463	(84)	169	(24)	(8)	1	.365
Lennie Pearson	1939–1942	—	—	—	—	—	—	—
Fernando Pedroso	1945–1950	1080	(221)	350	(64)	(24)	(41)	.324
David Pope	1951–1953	129	—	38	—	—	2	.295

Name	Years	AB	R	H	D	T	HR	BA
Neil Robinson	1940–1941	—	—	—	—	—	—	—
Bonnie Serrell	1949–1950	294	51	85	11	9	1	.289
Harry "Suitcase" Simpson	1948–1949	109	—	35	—	—	2	.331
Al Smith	1951–1954	658	134	180	30	13	18	.274
Gene Smith	1940s	—	—	—	—	—	—	—
Herbert Souell	1947–1948	252	44	87	11	0	3	.345
Lonnie Summers	1949–1950	67	10	17	2	1	0	.254
Joseph Taylor	1953–1955	262	—	60	—	—	11	.229
Bob Thurman	1947–1960	2978	527	931	149	61	120	.313
Quincy Trouppe	1941–1950	—	—	—	—	—	—	—
"Tetelo" Vargas	1938–1963	2821	606	906	119	56	23	.321
Luis Villodas	1954–1956	156	—	40	1	0	4	.256
Willie Wells	1941–1942	106	—	40	—	—	—	.378
Chester Williams	1941–1942	—	—	—	—	—	—	—
Jesse Williams	1948–1949	92	—	19	—	—	—	.207
Marvin Williams	1944–1950	273	48	78	(12)	1	3	.286
Artie Wilson	1947–1950	852	187	315	—	—	(8)	.370
Jud Wilson	1944	52	—	21	—	—	—	.404
Parnell Woods	1939–1940	—	—	—	—	—	—	.269

Pitching

Name	Years	G	CG	W	L	IP	SO	BB
Dan Bankhead	1941–1963	—	—	48	33	—	565	—
Frank Barnes	1956–1957	—	—	6	2	80	53	50
Dave Barnhill	1940–1941	—	—	—	—	—	193	—
Chet Brewer	1947–1948	—	—	7	6	—	—	—
Barney Brown	1946–1948	—	—	34	15	408	—	—
Ray Brown	1938–1945	—	—	40	20	496	—	—
Luis Cabrera	1939–1962	219	—	105	99	1378	704	462
Leon Day	1939–1950	—	—	35	28	571	518	—
"Rocky" Ellis	1930s	—	—	—	—	—	—	—
Wilmer "Red" Fields	1947–1950	—	—	24	17	—	—	—
Silvio Garcia	1939–1940	16	—	10	6	150	98	48
Bill Greason	1953–1958	—	—	46	31	701	372	—
Bob Griffith	1946–1947	—	—	3	4	—	—	—
Bill Harvey	1930s	—	—	—	—	—	—	—
Juan Guilbe	1938–1949	128	—	58	37	833	263	217
Jay Heard	1949–1950	—	—	0	1	4	1	2
Sam "Toothpick" Jones	1951–1952	—	—	27	9	325	311	(182)
Cecil Kaiser	1949–1950	—	—	13	2	—	—	—
Lefty LeMarque	1948–1949	—	—	—	—	—	—	—
Max Manning	1938–1939	—	—	—	—	—	—	—
Booker McDaniels	1949–1950	—	—	2	5	52	24	15
Lazarus Medina	1940s	—	—	—	—	—	—	—
Rafaelito Ortiz	1938–1953	182	—	85	51	875	344	357
Satchel Paige	1939–1948	(40)	—	23	11	(318)	304	(87)
Roy Partlow	1939–1946	—	—	34	22	553	450	—
Tomas Quinones	1940–1953	151	—	82	39	1028	233	232
Wilfredo Salas	1940–1941	—	—	1	4	—	—	—
Pedro San	1926–1928	—	—	—	—	—	—	—
Jose G. Santiago	1946–1963	277	—	107	97	1690	976	544
Pat Scantlebury	1946–1947	—	—	—	—	—	—	—
John F. Smith	1947–1949	—	—	26	—	—	—	—

Name	Years	G	CG	W	L	IP	SO	BB
Bob Thurman	1949–1960	—	—	5	3	—	—	—
Roberto Vargas	1947–1960	—	—	(51)	(24)	—	—	—
Roy Welmaker	1939–1940	—	—	8	2	—	—	—
Johnny Williams	1947–1948	—	—	0	2	16	5	5
Johnny Wright	1946–1947	—	—	8	5	—	—	—

Table VII: Dominican Republic Leagues—Negro League Player Statistics, Batting and Pitching

Batting

Name	Years	AB	R	H	D	T	HR	BA
Sam Bankhead	1937 (S)	68	—	21	—	—	—	.309
"Cool Papa" Bell	1937 (S)	66	—	21	—	—	—	.318
Ramon Bragana	1937 (S)	74	—	23	—	—	—	.311
Pee Wee Butts	1954 (S)	132	12	28	—	0	—	.212
Bill "Ready" Cash	1953–1954 (S)	197	31	65	—	—	0	.330
"Pancho" Coimbre	1930s	—	—	—	—	—	—	—
Alex Crespo	1952–1954 (S)	585	92	178	—	—	—	.304
Raymond Dandridge	1954	—	—	—	—	—	—	—
"Piper" Davis	1956–1957 (W)	—	—	—	—	—	—	—
Martin Dihigo	1937 (S)	97	—	34	6	2	4*	.357
Wilmer "Red" Fields	1953	107	15	42	—	—	0	.393
Pedro Formental	1951–1953	382	76	112	(70)	(20)	17	.293
"Cocaina" Garcia	1937 (S)	—	—	—	—	—	—	.254
Silvio Garcia	1937 (S)	128	—	38*	14*	—	—	.297
	1952–1953	142	24	52	—	—	—	.356
Josh Gibson	1937 (S)	53	—	24	4	5*	2	.453
Bert Hunter	1935	8	1	3	—	—	—	.375
Cando Lopez	1937 (S)	—	—	—	—	—	—	.283
Alejandro Oms	1937 (S)	99	—	23	—	—	—	.232
"Spoony" Palm	1937 (S)	71	—	16	—	—	—	.254
Pat Patterson	1937 (S)	—	—	—	—	—	—	.319
Bill Perkins	1937 (S)	99	—	25	—	—	—	.253
Alonzo Perry	1951–1959 (S&W)	1430	218	443	72	18	49	.310
Alonzo Perry	1955–1959 (W)	803	93	238	37	11	10	.296
Lazaro Salazar	1937 (S)	120	—	35	—	5*	—	.292
Milt Smith	1959–1960 (W)	230	—	66	—	—	1	.287
Bob Thurman	1953–1954 (S)	244	53	72	(10)	(3)	20	.295
"Tetelo" Vargas	1921–1956 (S&W)	662	144	213	35	7	2	.322
Harry Williams	1937 (S)	—	—	—	—	—	—	.227
James Williams	1935	46	7	14	—	—	—	.304
Jesse Williams	1954 (S)	67	16	18	—	—	—	.269
Willie "Curley" Williams	1953	37	7	4	—	—	0	.108

Pitching

Name	Years	G	CG	W	L	IP	SO	BB
Ramon Bragana	1936, 1937 (S)	—	—	13	8	—	—	—
Chet Brewer	1937 (S)	—	—	2	3	—	—	—
Barney Brown	1954 (S)	4	—	0	1	13	—	—
Harry T. Butts	1951 (S)	11	—	4	1	66	—	—
Luis Cabrera	1951 (S)	5	—	1	3	20	—	—

Name	Years	G	CG	W	L	IP	SO	BB
Gene Collins	1953 (S)	4	—	0	2	13	—	—
Johnny Davis	1952–1954 (S)	5	—	3	2	28	—	—
Martin Dihigo	1937 (S)	—	—	6	4	—	—	—
"Rocky" Ellis	1930s	—	—	—	—	—	—	—
Rodolfo Fernandez	1937 (S)	—	—	4	5	—	—	—
"Red" Fields	1953 (S)	11	—	2	7	67	—	—
"Cocaina" Garcia	1936, 1937 (S)	—	—	5	3	—	—	—
Silvio Garcia	1937 (S)	—	—	0	2	—	—	—
Bob Griffith	1937 (S)	—	—	2	1	—	—	—
Bert Hunter	1935, 1937 (S)	—	—	4	5	—	—	—
Sam "Toothpick" Jones	1963–1964 (W)	16	0	4	1	34	33	15
Cecil Kaiser	1940s	—	—	—	—	—	—	—
Max Manning	1940	—	—	—	—	—	—	—
Leroy Matlock	1937 (S)	—	—	4	1	—	—	—
Terris McDuffie	1952–1954 (S)	40	8+	23	9	290	(106)	(42)
Jimmy Newberry	1951 (S)	2	—	0	1	—	—	—
Satchel Paige	1937 (S)	—	—	8	2	—	—	—
Roy Partlow	1951 (S)	5	—	5	0	47	—	—
Alonzo Perry	1951 (S)	2	—	0	1	4	—	—
Al Preston	1951 (S)	3	—	1	2	17	—	—
Wilfredo Salas	1952 (S)	5	—	2	2	26	—	—
Lazaro Salazar	1937 (S)	—	—	0	2	—	—	—
Jose G. Santiago	1954 (S)	8	—	3	3	59	—	—
John F. Smith	1954 (S)	2	—	0	0	15	—	—
Bob Thurman	1953 (S)	5	—	1	1	31	—	—
Luis Tiant, Sr.	1937 (S)	—	—	1	3	—	—	—
Jim Tugerson	1952 (S)	9	—	3	4	52	—	—
Samuel C. Williams	1952 (S)	13	—	1	6	52	—	—
Sam Woods	1951 (S)	11	—	5	5	66	—	—
John Wright, Sr.	1952–1954 (S)	23	—	4	16	122	—	—

Table VIII: Venezuelan Winter League—Negro League Player Statistics, Batting and Pitching

Batting

Name	Years	AB	R	H	D	T	HR	BA
Frank Austin	1947–1948	—	—	—	—	—	—	—
Sam Bankhead	1946–1947	—	—	—	—	—	—	—
Gene Benson	1945	—	—	—	—	—	—	—
Ramon Bragana	1936–1937	44	—	14	—	—	—	.318
Luther Branham	1950–1951	—	—	—	—	—	—	—
Ameal Brooks	1930s–'40s	—	—	—	—	—	—	—
Harry Butts	1951–1952	—	—	—	—	—	—	—
Roy Campanella	1946–1948	—	—	—	—	—	—	—
Bill Cash	1946–1950	—	—	—	—	—	—	—
William Cathy	1948–1949	—	—	—	—	—	—	—
Pelayo Chacon	1930–1935	—	—	—	—	—	—	—
Jimmy Cohen	1949–1950	—	—	—	—	—	—	—
"Pancho" Coimbre	1930s	—	—	—	—	—	—	—
Gene Collins	1950–1959	104	9	37	9	2	0	.356
Cuco Correa	1946–1950	—	—	—	—	—	—	—
Alex Crespo	1950	—	—	—	—	—	—	—
Martin Crue	1946–1947	—	—	—	—	—	—	—

Appendix

Name	Years	AB	R	H	D	T	HR	BA
Ray Dandridge	1938–1949	—	—	—	—	—	—	—
Lloyd Davenport	1949–1950	—	—	—	—	—	—	—
Johnny Davis	1950–1952	—	—	—	—	—	—	—
"Piper" Davis	1953–1956	—	—	—	—	—	—	—
Martin Dihigo	1932–1934	—	—	—	—	—	—	—
Claro Duany	1950	—	—	—	—	—	—	—
Marvin Duncan	1950–1951	—	—	—	—	—	—	—
Luke Easter	1947–1950	—	—	—	—	—	8*	.302
Howard Easterling	1949–1950	—	—	—	16*	—	9*	—
Raul Espinosa	1946–1947	—	—	—	—	—	—	—
Oscar Estrada	1946–1951	—	—	—	—	—	—	—
Wilmer "Red" Fields	1950–1953	207	48*	72	21*	2	8	.348*
Pedro Formenthal	1954–1956	—	—	—	—	—	—	—
Jonas Gaines	1949–1950	—	—	—	—	—	—	—
Raul Galata	1950–1951	—	—	—	—	—	—	—
Silvio Garcia	1932–1947	—	—	—	—	—	—	—
Josh Gibson	1939–1940	—	—	—	—	—	—	—
Manuel Godinez	1946–1947	—	—	—	—	—	—	—
Rene Gonzalez	1950–1951	(202)	57	(71)	18*	(2)	10*	.358
Sam Hairston	1949–1953	163	29	62	15	1	0	.380*
Johnny Hayes	1947–1948	—	—	—	—	—	—	—
David Hoskins	1955–1959	(96)	—	(31)	—	—	—	.323
Gentry Jessup	1948–1949	—	—	—	—	—	—	—
Sam Jethroe	1945–1946	—	—	—	—	5*	—	—
Leon Kellman	1944–1945	—	—	—	—	—	—	—
Buck Leonard	1946–1947	47	20	—	—	—	—	.425
Rufus Lewis	1946–1947	—	—	—	—	—	—	—
Lester Lockett	1947–1948	—	—	—	—	—	—	—
"Rabbit" Martinez	1935–1946	—	—	—	—	—	—	—
Henry McHenry	1947–1948	—	—	—	—	—	—	—
Clyde McNeal	1949–1950	—	—	—	—	—	—	—
Henry Miller	1946–1947	—	—	—	—	—	—	—
Ray Neil	1949–1950	—	—	—	—	—	—	—
Ray Noble	1950–1951	—	—	—	—	—	—	—
Pedro Pages	1950	—	—	—	—	—	—	—
Clyde Parris	1944–1945	—	—	—	—	—	—	—
Jim Pendleton	1948–1961	155+	47+	60+	30	14	33	.387
Art "Superman" Pennington	1950–1951	—	—	—	—	—	—	—
David Pope	1953–1955	446	89	150	(35)	12	14	.336
Bill Powell	1953–1954	—	—	—	—	—	—	—
Othello Renfroe	1949–1950	—	—	—	—	—	—	—
John "Hoss" Ritchey	1948–1949	—	30	—	14	—	—	—
Harry "Suitcase" Simpson	1947–1948	—	—	—	—	—	—	—
Lonnie Summers	1950	—	—	—	—	—	—	—
Frank Thompson	1947–1948	—	—	—	—	—	—	—
Quincy Trouppe	1946–1953	—	—	—	—	—	—	—
Orlando Varona	1949–1950	—	—	—	—	4*	—	—
Archie Ware	1947–1948	—	—	—	—	—	—	—
Marvin Williams	1946–1947	—	29*	—	13*	—	—	—
Bob Wilson	1956–1957	180	27	63	14	2	4	.250*
Parnell Woods	1946–1947	144	28	51	13*	3	1	.354

Pitching

Name	Years	G	CG	W	L	IP	SO	BB
Joe Black	1947–1948	—	—	—	—	—	—	—
Ramon Bragana	1936–1937	—	—	8	4	—	—	—
Ollie Brantley	1960s	—	—	—	—	—	—	—
Jack Brittin	1952–1953	—	—	—	—	—	—	—
Raymond Brown	1948–1950	—	—	—	—	—	—	—
Bill Byrd	1940	—	—	—	—	—	—	—
Gene Collins	1958–1959	—	—	—	—	—	—	—
Johnny Davis	1950	—	—	—	—	—	—	—
Leon Day	1939–1940	—	—	12	1	—	—	—
Martin Dihigo	1932–1934	—	—	6	0	—	—	—
Lino Donoso	1948–1949	—	—	—	—	—	—	—
Rodolfo Fernandez	1938–1966	—	—	—	—	—	—	—
Raul Galata	1950–1951	—	—	—	—	—	—	—
"Cocaina" Garcia	1932–1937	—	—	—	—	—	—	—
Tom Glover	1946–1947	—	—	0	0	—	—	—
Whitt Graves	1950–1951	—	—	—	—	—	—	—
Bob Griffith	1949–1950	—	—	3	4	—	—	—
Wilmer Harris	1949	—	—	—	—	—	—	—
Jay Heard	1952–1954	—	—	—	—	—	—	—
David Hoskins	1955–1959	—	—	(26)	(12)	(325)	(193)	—
Bill Jefferson	1946	—	—	4	2	—	—	—
Sam "Toothpick" Jones	1953–1954	—	—	—	—	—	—	—
Max Manning	1950	—	—	—	—	—	—	—
Verdel Mathis	1947–1948	—	—	—	—	—	—	—
Leroy Matlock	1939–1940	—	—	—	—	—	—	—
Terris McDuffie	1949–1951	—	—	4	3	—	—	—
Don Newcombe	1947–1948	25*	10	10*	3	137	(?)*	—
Alberto Osorio	1950s ??	—	—	27	15	—	—	—
Roy Partlow	1947–1948	—	—	—	—	—	—	—
Andrew "Pullman" Porter	1949–1950	—	—	—	—	—	—	—
Bill Ricks	1949–1951	—	—	—	—	—	—	—
Wilfredo Salas	1950	—	—	—	—	—	—	—
Lazaro Salazar	1949–1957	—	—	5	3	—	—	—
Pedro San	1926–1928	—	—	—	—	—	—	—
Hilton Smith	1946–1947	—	—	8	5	—	—	—
Theolic Smith	1949–1950	—	—	—	—	—	—	—
Roy Welmaker	1946–1952	(33)	(24)	(12)	15	(193)	(139)	(61)
John Wright, Sr.	1947–1949	—	—	—	—	—	—	—

Table IX: Panamanian Winter League—Negro League Player Statistics, Batting and Pitching

Batting

Name	Years Played	AB	R	H	D	T	HR	BA
Frank Austin	1945–1955	1471	255	455	72	16	7	.309
Sam Bankhead	1947–1948	—	—	—	—	—	—	—
Pablo Bernard	1957–1961	484	—	127	—	—	(4)	.262
Alonzo Braithwaite	1945–1958	1457	219	447	71	10	14	.307
Granville Gladstone	1953–1959	253	—	73	—	—	5	.289
"Pumpsie" Green	1959+							

Name	Years Played	AB	R	H	D	T	HR	BA
Lou Johnson	1963–1965	342	—	112	—	—	9	.327
Leon Kellman	1945–1955	1109	194	329	71	14	21	.297
Lester Lockett	1948	—	—	—	—	—	—	—
Jonathan Parris	1953–1960	1647	216	524	(99)	(19)	56	.318
Curt Roberts	1960–1961	140	—	38	—	—	1	.271
Milt Smith	1960–1961	136	—	38	—	—	1	.279
Al Surratt	1950s	—	—	—	—	—	—	—
Joe Taylor	1953–1954	113	—	43	—	—	7	.381
Charlie White	1960–1961	128	—	40	—	—	1	.313

Pitching

Name	Years	G	CH	W	L	IP	SO	BB
Chet Brewer	1948–1950	—	—	—	—	—	—	—
Vibert "Webbo" Clarke	1945–1964	—	—	68	63	—	—	—
Rodolfo Fernandez	1940s	—	—	—	—	—	—	—
Wilmer Harris	1945	—	—	—	—	—	—	—
Connie Johnson	1950–1951	—	—	—	—	—	—	—
Cecil Kaiser	1940s	—	—	—	—	—	—	—
Lazarus Medina	1943	—	—	—	—	—	—	—
James Newberry	1947–1948	—	—	—	—	—	—	—
Al Osorio	1956–1967	—	—	30	22	462	(205)	—
Pat Scantlebury	1946–1947	—	—	(6)	(1)	—	—	—
Al Wilmore	1948–1949	—	—	—	—	—	—	—

Table X: Nicaraguan Winter League—Negro League Player Statistics, Batting and Pitching

Batting

Name	Years	AB	R	H	D	T	HR	BA
"Chiquitin" Cabrera	1940s	—	—	—	—	—	—	—
Carlos Colas	1940s	—	—	—	—	—	—	—
Alejandro Crespo	1930s	—	—	—	—	—	—	—
Claro Duany	1940s	—	—	—	—	—	—	—
Silvio Garcia	1940s	—	—	—	—	—	—	—
Rene Gonzalez	1957–1958	159	—	54	—	—	6	.340
Pedro Pages	1940s	—	—	—	—	—	—	—
Fernando Pedroso	1957–1958	178	—	52	—	—	2	.292
Curt Roberts	1963–1964	233	34	66	—	—	—	.283
Harry "Suitcase" Simpson	1963–1964	202	35	61	—	—	—	.302

Pitching

Name	Years	G	CG	W	L	IP	SO	BB
Ollie Brantley	1960s	—	—	—	—	—	—	—
Rodolfo Fernandez	1946–1947 (manager)	—	—	—	—	—	—	—
Sam "Toothpick" Jones	1964–1965	—	—	2	6	45	46	—

Table XI: Mexican Winter League—Negro League Player Statistics, Batting and Pitching

Batting

Name	Years	AB	R	H	D	T	HR	BA
"Cool Papa" Bell	????	—	—	—	—	—	—	—
	1938–1941 (S)	1189	310	436	72	38	27	.367
Johnny Britton	1945	—	—	—	—	—	—	—
Bill "Ready" Cash	1940s	—	—	—	—	—	—	—
Francisco "Pancho" Coimbre	1945 (S)	356	55	123	26	6	5	.346
Ray Dandridge	1939–1949	189	21	60	11	3	0	.317
"Piper" Davis	1956–1957	—	—	—	—	—	—	—
Josh Gibson	1940–1941 (S)	450	132	177	38	7	44	393
George Giles	1932	—	—	—	—	—	—	—
Joe Filmore	1940s	—	—	—	—	—	—	—
Pedro Formental	1940s	—	—	—	—	—	—	—
	1943–1946 (S)	1091	246	376	79	30	19	.345
Sam Hairston	1956–1957	318	—	115	—	—	6	.362
Doc Horn	1953	—	—	—	—	—	—	—
"Rabbit" Martinez	1930s-40s	—	—	—	—	—	—	—
Art Pennington	1947–1951	—	—	—	—	—	—	—
Alonzo Perry	1955–1963	3122	648	1107	202	58	138	.355
Bonnie Serrell	1956–1958	151	—	40	—	—	5	.265
Tom Turner	1945–1947	—	—	—	—	—	—	—
	1954 (S)	24	3	5	1	0	1	.208
Willie Wells	1940–1944 (S)	1354	301	437	87	15	26	.323
	1940–1945 (W)	—	—	—	—	—	—	—
Marvin Williams	1957–1958	232	—	77	—	—	11	.332
"Wild Bill" Wright	1940–1951 (S)	2891	549	969	175	52	67	.335
	1940–1956 (W)	—	—	—	—	—	—	—

Pitching

Name	Years	G	CG	W	L	IP	SO	BB
Ramon Bragana	1953–1954	24	—	7	6	108	37	63
Lino Donoso	1957–1958	—	—	4	7	101	—	—
Rodolfo Fernandez	1941 (S)	—	—	4	5	—	—	—
Willie Greason	1949–1950 (S)	—	—	11	5	—	—	—
Bill Harvey	1930s	—	—	—	—	—	—	—
Willie Jefferson	1944	—	—	—	—	—	—	—
Edward Locke	1956–1958	—	—	37	13	415	—	—
Verdell Mathis	1940s	—	—	—	—	—	—	—
Roy Welmaker	1940s	—	—	—	—	—	—	—

Table XII: Colombian Winter League—Negro League Player Statistics, Batting and Pitching

Batting

Name	Years	AB	H	D	T	HR	BA
Wilmer Fields	1954–1956	—	—	—	—	—	.325
Quincy Trouppe	1953–1954	—	—	—	—	—	—

Pitching

Name	Years	G	CG	W	L	IP	SO	BB
Ollie Brantley	1960s	—	—	—	—	—	—	—

Major League Player Statistics

Name	Years	AB	H	D	T	HR	BA
Jim Gentile	1955–1956	—	—	—	—	—	—
Brooks Robinson	1955–1956	—	—	—	—	—	.319

Bibliography

Alvelo, Luis. Personal correspondence, 1996–2005.
_____. "The Golden Age of Puerto Rican Ball." In *National Pastime 11*. Cleveland: Society for American Baseball Research, 1992.
Anonymous. *They Were Giants: Negro League Baseball in Florida, 1920's & 1930's*. N.p., n.d.
Bak, Richard. *Turkey Stearnes and the Detroit Stars*. Detroit: Great Lakes Books, 1994.
Bankes, James. *The Pittsburgh Crawfords*. Dubuque, IA: Brown, 1991.
Beck, Warren, and David A. Williams. *California: A History of the Golden State*: Garden City, NY: Doubleday, 1972.
Benitez, Jose A. Crescioni. *El Beisbol Profesional Boricua*, San Juan, PR: Aurora Comunicacion Integral, 1997.
Bjarkman, Peter C. *Baseball with a Latin Beat*. Jefferson, NC: McFarland, 1994.
Bruce, Janet. *The Kansas City Monarchs*. Lawrence: University Press of Kansas, 1985.
Burgos, Adrian, Jr. "Caribbean Players in the Negro Leagues, 1910–1950." *CENTRO: Journal of the Center for Puerto Rican Studies* 8 (1, 2): 1996.
California Eagle. Los Angeles, CA. 1898–1948.
Campanella, Roy. *It's Good to Be Alive*. New York: New American Library, 1959.
Chadwick, Bruce. *When the Game was Black and White*. New York: Abbeville Press, 1992.
Chicago Defender. Chicago, IL. 1898–1948.
Cisneros, Pedro Treto, ed. *Enciclopedia del Beisbol Mexicano*. Mexico City: Revistas Deportivas, 1996.
Clark, Dick, and Larry Lester, eds. *The Negro Leagues Book*. Cleveland: Society for American Baseball Research, 1994.
Cordova, Cuqui. *Historia de los Leones Rojos Del Escogido*. Herrera, Dominican Republic: Editorial Cañabrava, 1999.
Dixon, Phil S. *The Monarchs: 1920-1938*. Rapid City, SD: Mariah Press, 2002.
Dixon, Phil, with Patrick J. Hannigan. *The Negro Baseball Leagues*. Mattituck, NY: Amereon House, 1992.
Dixon, Phil S. *The Ultimate Kansas City Baseball Trivia Quiz Book*. Shawnee, KS: Bon A Tirer Publishing, 1992.
Figueredo, Jorge S. *Cuban Baseball*. Jefferson, NC: McFarland, 2003.
_____. *Who's Who in Cuban Baseball*. Jefferson, NC: McFarland, 2003.
Graham, Frank. *McGraw of the Giants*. New York: Putnam, 1947.
Hoie, Bob, and Carlos Bauer, comps. *The Historical Register*. San Diego: Baseball Press Books, 1998.
Holway, John. "Spottswood Poles." In *Baseball Research Journal*. Washington, DC: Society for American Baseball Research, 1975.
_____. *The Complete Book of Baseball's Negro Leagues: The Other Half of Baseball History*. Fern Park, FL: Hastings House, 2001.
_____. *Voices from the Great Black Baseball Leagues*. New York: Da Capo Press, 1992.
Holway, John B. *Blackball Stars*. Westport, CT: Meckler Books, 1988.
_____. *Black Diamonds*. New York: Stadium Books, 1991.
_____. *Josh and Satch*. New York: Carroll and Graf, 1991.
Jimenez, Jose de Jesus. "Alonso Perry in the Dominican Republic." In *Baseball Research Journal 23*. Cleveland: Society for American Baseball Research, 1994.
_____. "The Great Dominican, Diomedes Olivo." In *Baseball Research Journal 20*. Cleveland: Society for American Baseball Research, 1991.
Kelley, Brent. *Voices from the Negro Leagues*. Jefferson, NC: McFarland, 1998.
Klein, Alan M. *Sugarball*. New Haven, CT: Yale University Press, 1991.
Kleinknecht, Merl. *Register of Negro Leaguers in the Winter Leagues*. Galion, OH; Society for American Baseball Research.
Krich, John. *El Beisbol*. New York: Prentice Hall Press, 1989.
Landino, Leonte A. *Baseball Around the World—Venezuela*. iml.jou.ufl.edu/projects/Fall02/Landino/index.html.

Lavender, David. *California: A Bicentennial History.* New York: Norton, 1976.

Leonard, Buck, with James A. Riley. *Buck Leonard: The Black Lou Gehrig.* New York: Carroll and Graf, 1995.

Lester, Larry. Personal communications, 2000.

Los Angeles Examiner. Los Angeles, CA. 1900–1947.

Los Angeles Times. Los Angeles, CA. 1900–1948.

McCarthy, Kevin. *Baseball in Florida.* Sarasota: Pineapple Press, 1996.

McIver, Stuart. "Cooks to Catchers, Bellhops to Batters." *Sunshine Magazine,* 1993.

McKissack, Patricia C., and Frederick McKissack, Jr. *Black Diamond.* New York: Scholastic, 1994

McNary, Kyle P. *Ted "Double Duty" Radcliffe.* St. Louis Park, MN: McNary, 1994.

McNeil, William F. *Baseball's Other All-Stars.* Jefferson, NC: McFarland, 2000.

_____. *The California Winter League.* Jefferson, NC: McFarland, 2002.

Malloy, Jerry. *The 25th Infantry Regiment Takes the Field. National Pastime.* Cleveland: Society for American Baseball Research, 1995.

Martin, Sidney Walter. *Florida's Flagler.* Athens: University of Georgia Press, 1949.

Minoso, Minnie, with Herb Fagen. *Just Call Me Minnie.* Champaign, IL: Sagamore, 1994.

Nankivell, John H. *Buffalo Soldier Regiment: History of the Twenty-Fifth United States Infantry, 1869–1926.* Lincoln: University of Nebraska Press, 2001.

Navarro, Victor, and Angel Armada. *The Book of the 14 & Other 33 Ways to Enter in Puerto Rican Professional Baseball.* Aguadilla, PR: Inter-Island Spring, 1995.

Oleksak, Michael M., and Mary Adams Oleksak. *Beisbol: Latin Americans and the Great Old Game.* Indianapolis: Masters Press, 1996.

O'Neil, Buck, with Steve Wulf and David Conrads. *I Was Right on Time.* New York: Fireside, 1996.

Paige, LeRoy "Satchel," as told to David Lipman. *Maybe I'll Pitch Forever.* Lincoln: University of Nebraska Press, 1993.

Palm Beach Daily News. Palm Beach, FL. 1898–1919.

Palm Beach Life. Palm Beach, FL. 1905–1915.

Palmer, Pete, and Gary Gillette, eds. *The Baseball Encyclopedia.* New York: Barnes & Noble Books, 2004.

La Pelota Nuestra. Osvaldo Rodriguez Suncar, ed. Santo Domingo, D.R., 1994.

Peterson, Robert. *Only the Ball Was White.* New York: McGraw-Hill, 1970.

Pittsburgh Courier. Pittsburgh, PA. 1921–1948.

Ribowski, Mark. *The Power and the Darkness.* New York: Simon & Schuster, 1996,

Riley, James A. *Dandy, Day, and the Devil.* Cocoa, FL: TK Publishers, 1987.

_____. *The Biographical Encyclopedia of the Negro Baseball Leagues.* New York: Carroll and Graf, 1994.

Robinson, Jackie, as told to Alfred Duckett. *I Never Had It Made.* Hopewell, NJ: The Ecco Press, 1995.

Rogosin, Donn. *Invisible Men.* New York: Atheneum, 1983.

Royal Poinciana Daily Program. Palm Beach, FL. 1905–1919.

Rucker, Mark, and Peter C. Bjarkman. *Smoke: The Romance and Lore of Cuban Baseball.* Kingston, NY: Total Sports, 1999.

Ruck, Rob. *The Tropic of Baseball.* Westport, CT: Meckler, 1991.

Ruiz, Yuyo. *The Bambino Visits Cuba, 1920: Unedited Notes Regarding the Visit of Babe Ruth to Cuba in 1920.* San Juan, PR: La Esquina Del Left Field, 1990.

Salas, Alexis H. *Los Eternos Rivales, Caracas-Magallanes, Pastora-Gavilanes, 1908–1988.* Caracas: Grupo Editorial, 1988.

_____. *Momentos Involvidables del Beisbol Profesional Venezolano, 1946–1984.* Caracas: Miguel Angel Garcia, 1985.

San Diego Union. San Diego, CA. 1912–1946.

Sayama, Kazuo. "Their Throws Were Like Arrows"—How a Black Team Spurred Pro Ball in Japan." In *Baseball Research Journal.* Manhattan, KS: Society for American Baseball Research, 1987.

Sol White's History of Colored Base Ball, with Other Documents on the Early Black Game 1886–1936. Compiled and Introduced by Jerry Malloy. Lincoln: University of Nebraska Press, 1995.

Spalding, John E. *Always on Sunday.* Manhattan, KS: Ag Press, 1992.

Thorn, John, Pete Palmer, Michael Gershman, and David Pietrusza, eds. *Total Baseball.* New York: Viking Penguin, 1997.

Torres, Angel, *La Leyenda del Beisbol Cubano.* Miami: Review Printers, 1996.

The Universal Standard Encyclopedia, Vols. 1–25. Joseph Laffan Morse, editor in chief. New York: Unicorn, 1956.

Van Hyning, Thomas E. *Puerto Rico's Winter League.* Jefferson, NC: McFarland, 1995.

Wilson, Lyle K., esq. Personal communications, 2000.

Zuckerman, Larry. Personal communications, 2000.

Index

Aaron, Hank 150, 203, 214
Abreu, J. 46
Abreu, Mangolo 149
Acosta, Pinao 138
Acosta, Teolindo 177
Alanis, Leonardo "Najo" 197
Albertson 129
Alexander, Grover Cleveland 95
Alfonso, A. 42
Allen (bandleader) 9
Allen, Johnny 40
Allen, Newt 75, 87, 99, 101, 103, 198, 210, 213
Allen, Todd 25, 209
Almada, Mel 76
Almeida, Rafael 38
Aloma, Ignacio 134
Aloma, Ubaldo 134
Alomar 129
Alou, Felipe 140, 153–155
Alou, Jesus 153–155
Alou, Matty 153
Alpica, Manuel Antonio 161
Alston, R. 189
Alvarado 159
Alvarado, Sonlly 142, 143
Alvarez 136
Alvarez, Chino 149
Alvarez, Elucar 148
Alvarez, Pedrito 147
Alvelo, Luis 112, 115, 121–123, 126, 223
Amaro, Santos 48, 49, 144
Amoros, Sandy 173, 208
Anderson, Doc 69, 71, 86
Anderson, Ferrell 173, 174
Andrews, Ed 6
Andrews, Pop 14, 16
Anez, L. 178
Anglero 129
Anselmo 159
Antonello, Bill 50
Aparicio, Luis, Jr. 154, 155, 158, 173, 175, 178, 183, 184
Aparicio, Luis, Sr. 3, 141, 158, 161, 162, 165–169, 175, 183, 184
Applegate, Fred 13
Aquino, Armando "Balito" 137
Arango, Pedro 44, 140, 141, 143
Arcano, Alfredo 32, 34
Archer, Jimmy 90
Arias, Bell 149

Arias, Enriquito 143
Arlington 78
Armada, Angel 224
Armstrong, Neil 104
Arratia 159
Arrieta, "Tuerto" 170
Arthurs, S. 189
Ascanio, Carlos 167, 170
Atkins, Joseph 214
Austin, Frank "Pee Wee" 170, 179, 188–191, 217, 219
Avila, Roberto 49
Aybar, Dr. Jose Enrique 143, 144

Babich, Johnny 101
Bachant 74
Baez, Andres Julio "Grillo B" 142, 143, 148, 162, 163
Baez, Luis "Grillo C" 142, 147, 148
Baez, Maximo Gomez y 32
Bailey, Ed 173, 175, 177
Bak, Richard 223
Baker 70
Baker, Gene 129, 214
Ball, George 90
Ball, Rosetta 16
Ball, Walter 16, 38, 67, 210, 212
Bancroft, Dave 43
Bankes, James 223
Bankhead, Dan 122, 133, 150, 188, 214
Bankhead, Sam 46, 101, 122, 124, 126, 143–146, 165, 168, 169, 179, 190, 210, 213–217, 219
Banks, Ernie 150, 207
Barbee, Bud 191
Barber (Barbour), Jesse 18, 21–24, 38, 68, 209, 210
Barbosa 173
Barbour, Jesse see Barber, Jesse
Barboza, D. 167
Barboza, M. 178
Barnes, Frank 215
Barnes, John "Tubby" 99
Barnhill, Dave 121, 125, 201, 202, 212, 215
Baro, A. 34
Baro, Bernardo 40, 140, 208
Barradas, Fernando "Cocuite" 46, 197, 198
Barrett, Red 105

Barry, Shad 35
Bartell, "Rowdy Dick" 101
Barton 80
Basquin 159
Bassler, Johnny 71, 73
Basso, C. 157
Bastidas, Rodrigo de Galvan 186
Bauer, Carlos 223
Baum, Allen T. 68
Baumann 13
Beck, Warren 64, 223
Beckwith, John 23, 75, 87, 92–94, 213
Beers, Clarence 172
Bejerano, Augustin 42, 46, 140
Bell, Clara 42
Bell, Clifford "Cherry" 42, 213
Bell, Fern 78
Bell, Fred 42
Bell, James "Cool Papa" 1, 2, 42, 43, 71, 73–76, 78–80, 82, 87, 88, 96–98, 101, 110, 143, 144, 146, 198, 202, 203, 207, 210, 213, 216, 221
Bell, V. 77
Bell, William, Sr. 100
Bellan, Estaban 30, 32
Bench, Johnny 132
Bender, Chief 95, 206
Benevides, P. 34
Benitez, Bobo 141
Benitez, Hector R. 164, 170
Benitez, Jose A. Crescioni 111, 223
Bennett 16
Benson, Gene 106, 120, 121, 164, 165, 211, 217
Benzan, Manuel 149
Berardino, Johnny 106
Berbesis 173
Bergen 114
Berkowitz 78
Bernard, Curt 66
Bernard, Pablo 190, 219
Bernier, Carlos 129, 130
Berra, Yogi 168, 169
Berry 28
Bessho, Takehiko 153
Bevan, Harold 175
Bevens, Bill 168, 169
Bianchi 114
Biggs, Peter 63

Index

Binga, William 10
Birrer, Babe 177
Bithorn, Hi 116, 117, 125, 130
Bjarkman, Peter 38, 162, 170, 223, 224
Black, Joe 170, 179, 212
Blackburn, Wayne 188
Blackman, Henry 71–73, 213
Blackwell, Charlie 91, 211
Blackwell, Ewell 149
Blake, Frank "Big Red" 113, 114
Blanco, Carlos 44, 46
Blondet, Marcelino "Moncho Brujo" 157, 161, 162
Blondet, Ramon "Moncho El Brujo" 112, 159
Blue, Lu 70–73, 91
Boada 40, 41
Bobo, Willie 213
Bodie, Ping 74
Boeckel, Tony 70, 71, 73
Bolden, Edward 114
Bolivar, Simon 156
Bonura, Zeke 104
Booker, Pete 10, 13, 90
Borden 159
Bowman, Emmet "Scotty" 7, 8, 10, 11, 35
Boyd, Bob 211, 214
Bracho, Jose "Carrao" 152, 172, 174, 183, 184
Bracho, Julio 164
Bradley, Phil 9–11, 14, 211
Bragana, Ramon 43, 113, 140, 143, 144, 160, 179, 193, 198, 199, 202, 203, 207, 208, 216, 217, 219, 221
Braithwaite, Alonzo "Archie" 190, 219
Branca, Ralph 105
Branches, Jesus "Commissioner" 164
Branham, Luther 179, 217
Brantley, Ollie 179, 196, 204, 219, 220, 222
Brashear, Ray 66
Bravo, A. 155
Breech, Herman 201
Brewer, Chet 41, 75, 79, 80, 83, 85, 87, 100, 104, 106, 108, 109, 124, 144–146, 187, 188, 190, 198, 206, 213, 215, 216, 220
Briggs, Otto 92, 93
Bright, John 12
Britt, Chippy 25
Britton, John "Johnny" "Jack" 179, 219, 221
Brooks, Ameal 217
Brooks, Beattie 22
Brooks, Chester 23
Brown 10, 74
Brown, B. 46
Brown, Barney 122–124, 199, 212, 215, 216
Brown, Bobby 169
Brown, Dave 23, 24, 212
Brown, Eddie 2, 40, 41, 206
Brown, George 16

Brown, Jim 23, 98
Brown, Larry 77, 78, 211
Brown, Mike 25
Brown, Mordecai "Three-Finger" 1, 89, 90
Brown, Raymond 44–47, 50, 115, 116, 118–122, 124, 127, 179, 207, 212, 215, 219
Brown, Willard 2, 80, 115, 122, 123, 126, 127, 130, 150, 154, 174, 179, 207, 214
Brown, Winston 188
Bruce, Janet 223
Brunicardi, A. 157
Bryant, Clay 177
Buck 28
Buckner, Harry 11–13, 16, 35, 36
Buhl, Bob 132
Burdette, Lew 130
Burgos, Adrian, Jr. 39, 140, 223
Burgos, Jose 214
Burnett, Peter H. 64
Burnett, Tex 29, 114
Burns, George 92
Burnside, Pete 151
Burt, Col. Andrew S. 52
Burton, W. 26–28
Bush, Joe "Bullet" 95
Bush, Ownie 91
Butcher, Spencer 74, 213
Butler, John 13
Butts, Pee Wee 154, 173, 179, 216, 217
Byrd, Bill 105, 120–123, 163, 219
Byrd, Sammy 116
Byrne, Tommy 173, 175, 176

Cabezudo 129
Cabots 207
Cabrera, Jolbert 204
Cabrera, Lorenzo "Chiquitin" 173, 195, 220
Cabrera, Luis 122, 130, 133, 154, 215, 216
Cabrera, Orlando 204
Cadore, Leon 111, 112
Calderon 159
Calvo, Jacinto 208
Calzadilla, R. 34
Camarena, Alvaro 138
Campanella, Roy 3, 105, 121–124, 133, 150, 164–168, 170, 178, 179, 203, 207, 211, 214, 217, 223
Campaneris, Bert 195
Campbell, Archie 83
Campbell, Gilly 116
Canizares, Avelino 48
Cannady, Rev. 91, 94, 114, 211
Canonico, Daniel "Chinese" 160, 164, 168, 171, 175, 183, 184
Capers, "Lefty" 114
Capote 159
Carabano, R. 157
Caratini, Pedro Miguel 112, 136–139
Carew, Rod 173, 186, 191, 192
Carey, Max 70, 99

Carillo, Bernardo 35
Carlyle, Cleo 76
Carr, George "Tank" 26, 27, 68–73, 82, 87, 92, 93, 107, 108, 114, 115, 211, 213
Carrasquel, Alejandro "Alex" 48, 166, 167, 183, 184
Carrasquel, Alfonso "Chico" 48, 132, 166–168, 170, 171, 173, 174, 178, 183, 184
Cartegena, M. 155
Carter, Charles "Kid" 7
Carter, Ernest "Spoon" 76, 77
Carty, Rico 153, 173
Casanova, Jose 164
Cash, Bill "Ready" 48, 151, 152, 154, 167–169, 172, 178, 180, 202, 216, 217, 221
Cash, Norm 177, 188, 189
Cason, John 25
Castellanos, R. 178
Castener, J. 34
Castillo, Julian 33, 34, 208
Castillo, Manuel Emilio 137, 138
Castleman, Foster 175
Castro, Fidel 50, 51, 154, 171, 189, 196, 206
Castro, Luis "Jud" 204
Castro, Luis "Nino El Zurdo" 147
Cathey, Jim 180
Cathy, William 217
Cavet, Pug 74
Cayasso, Stanley 194
Cedeno, G. 160
Celada 42
Cepeda, Orlando 3, 118, 124, 141
Cepeda, Perucho 2, 118, 119, 121, 122, 125, 141, 143, 144
Cespedes, Carlos Manuel de 31
Chacon, Elio 154, 155
Chacon, Pelayo 22, 140, 160, 161, 208, 209, 217
Chadwick, Bruce 36, 48, 223
Chambers, Rube 27
Chance, Frank 112
Chandler, A.B. "Happy" 4, 81
Chandler, Spud 105, 106
Chapman, Ben 106
Chapman, Calvin 116
Charleston, Oscar 2, 40, 41, 43, 54, 55, 71–73, 75, 83, 87, 91–93, 98, 100, 103, 110, 206, 207, 209, 211
Chavez, Nestor 196
Chen, Bruce 192
Chiba, Shigeru 153
Chiti, Harry 131, 132
Ciqui 111
Cisneros, Pedro Treto 223
Clark, Allie 168, 169
Clark, Del 20
Clark, Dick 12, 223
Clark, Mike 128, 130
Clark, Specs 26, 27
Clarke, Vibert "Webbo" 189–191, 220
Clarkson, Bus 50, 115, 119, 121–124, 130–132, 207, 214

Index

Clemente, Roberto 118, 123, 131, 132
Cler, V. 189
Cobb, Ty 91, 109, 192, 206
Cockrell, Phil 23–26, 92, 210
Cohen, Andy 98
Cohen, Jim "Fireball" 180, 217
Coimbre, Francisco "Frank," "Pancho" 113, 115, 118, 119, 122, 124, 125, 127, 160, 207, 214, 216, 217, 221
Colas, Carlos "Charlie" 172, 195, 220
Colburn 78
Collins, Eddie 206
Collins, Gene 180, 214, 217, 219
Collins, Sgt. 54
Colmenares, Jose Perez 164
Columbus, Christopher 156
Comellas, Jorge 48
Comiskey, Charles 3, 4
Concepcion, David 184
Concepcion, Monchile 112, 113
Conde, Cefo 118, 119, 121, 122, 124, 125, 128
Connors, Chuck 50, 129
Conrads, David 224
Conton, Chico 146
Contreras 169
Cooper, Andy 53, 55, 108, 207, 212, 213
Cooper, Mort 103
Cordero, O. 129
Cordova, Cuqui 138, 162, 223
Coronel 159
Correa, Cuco 140, 171, 172, 180, 217
Correa, F. 46, 167
Corso, J. 157
Cortez, A. 42
Cortez, Hernando 62
Coscarart, Pete 172, 173
Cotter, Hooks 92
Courtney, Clint 48
Crafton 54, 58, 60, 61
Cramer, Doc 100, 199
Cramer, Emilio 156
Cravath, Gavvy 67
Crawford, Sam 16
Creacy, Dewey 99, 213
Crespi, Juan, Father 62
Crespo, Alejandro "Filete" 48, 151, 195, 208, 220
Crespo, Alex 154, 216, 217
Crespo, Rogelio 151
Crowe, George 131, 132, 214
Crue, Martin "Matty" 167, 180, 217
Crutchfield, Jimmy 117
Cueche, Emilio "El Indio" 51, 150, 151, 176, 183, 184
Cuellar, Mike 177
Cueto, Manuel 193
Cummings, Chance 26, 27, 29
Currie, Rube 40, 41, 70, 212, 213
Cutshaw, George 91
Cuyler, Kiki 115, 116

Dahlgren, Babe 80
Dandridge, Ray 44–47, 50, 75, 80, 113, 115, 116, 122–124, 149, 151, 154, 160–163, 168, 169, 199–201, 203, 207, 211, 214, 216, 218, 221, 224
Dauss, Hooks 92
Davalillo, Pompeyo "Yo-Yo" 166, 178
Davalillo, Victor 184
Davenport, Ducky 48, 168, 169, 180, 211, 218
Davila, Gil Gonzalez 192
Davis, "Cherokee Johnny" 105, 106, 126, 128, 129, 154, 180, 214, 217–219
Davis, George 35
Davis, Lorenzo "Piper" 128, 129, 175, 214, 216, 218, 221
Davis, Walter "Steel Arm" 96, 98
Daviu, Tingo 112, 157
Day, Connie 213
Day, Leon 46, 113, 115, 116, 120, 122–124, 160, 163, 207, 214, 215, 219, 224
Deal, Ellis "Cot" 128
Dean, Dizzy 1, 79, 89, 101–104, 109, 206
Dean, Paul 101–103
Defillo, Mariano 143
Delahanty, Jim 13
Delfin, Antonio 197
Delgado, Birrito 149
Delgado, Checo 141
Dell, Wheezer 83
Demaree, Frank 76
DeMoss, Bingo 21–23, 91, 209
Derringer, Paul 115, 116
Diaz, Adolfo, President 192
Diaz, Baudillo "Bo" 184
Diaz, Einar 192
Diaz, Narciso "Chingo Canon" 143
Diaz, R. 155
Diaz, Yoyo 142, 208
Dickey, Bill 143, 169
Dihigo, Martin 2, 3, 31, 39, 42, 43, 45–48, 94, 112–115, 140, 144–146, 160–162, 174, 180, 184, 193, 198, 202, 203, 206–208, 216–219
Dillon, Pop 66
DiMaggio, Joe 1, 101, 143
Dismukes, Dizzy 17–20, 29, 210
Dixon, Paul 114
Dixon, Phil S. 57, 223
Dixon, Rap 3, 23, 24, 75, 94, 98, 115, 141, 161, 162, 211, 213
Dixon, Tom 114
Doby, Larry 214
Dolores, Jose 159
Donald 10
Donaldson 60
Donaldson, Carter 193
Donaldson, John 20, 68, 210
Donlon, "Turkey Mike" 90
Donnelly, D. 189
Donoso, Lino 202, 219, 221

Doran, Tom 9, 10
Dorr 78
Dougherty, Pat 14, 16, 37, 89
Douglas, Eddie 23, 40
Downs, Bunny 25
Drake, William "Plunk" 213
Dreke, Valentin 31, 40, 142, 208
Dressen, Charlie "Chuck" 2, 40, 41, 105, 115, 206
Duany, Claro 154, 195, 218, 220
Duckett, Alfred 224
Dugan, E. 13
Duggan 10, 11
Dukes, Tommy 213
Dunbar, Ashby 20
Duncan, Frank 42, 46, 115–117, 211
Duncan, Marvin 218
Duncan, Melvin 180
Duncan, Pete 14, 21, 22, 29, 209
Dunlap, Bill 47
Dunn, Jake 213
Dunn, Joe 114
Duran, J. 155
Durocher, Leo 150
Duval, Clarence 65
Dyck, Jim 172
Dykes, Jimmy 92

Earle, Frank 9–14, 16, 19, 29, 210
Eason, Malcolm "Kid" 9
Easter, Luke 128, 129, 170, 171, 173, 180, 214, 218
Easterling, Howard 80, 106, 124, 128, 154, 172, 180, 218
Echevarria, Gonzalez 194
Echevarria, J. 149
Eddington 70
Edwards, J. Francis 114
Eggleston, Macajah Marchand "Mack" 25
Ehmke, Howard 91
Elliott 70
Ellis, "Rube," "Rocky" 66, 114, 215, 217
Engle, Clyde 9–11
English, Woody 80, 100
Ens, Jewel 43
Erskine, Carl 48
Escalante, Ventura "Loro" 147–149
Escobar, R. 157
Escobar, Sixto 130
Espino, Blanquito 141
Espino, Hector 203, 204
Espinosa, P. 189
Espinoza, Raul 167, 180, 218
Estalella, Roberto 46
Estrada, Oscar 167, 180, 218
Etheridge 14
Etten, Nick 169
Evans 18, 74
Evans, Bill 98
Evers, Johnny 112
Evins, Jovito 149
Ewing, William "Buck" 94

Index

Fabre, Isidro 140, 141, 208
Fagan, Bob 53–61, 70, 73, 74, 212, 213
Fagen, Herb 224
Farbell, Fabito 111
Farrell, Luther 28, 114
Feller, Bob 1, 71, 89, 103–107, 109, 187, 206
Feo, R. 157
Fernandez, Carmelito 118
Fernandez, F.J. 157, 158
Fernandez, Jose Maria 140, 160, 208
Fernandez, Raul Comme 138
Fernandez, Rodolfo 47, 113, 116, 143, 144, 180, 208, 217, 219–221
Fiallo, Carlos Augusto 143, 149
Fiallo, F. 155
Fields, Audrey 128
Fields, Wilmer "Red" 115, 128–130, 151, 154, 173, 174, 177, 180, 190, 204, 214–218, 221
Figueredo, Jorge S. 39, 223
Figueroa 129
Filmore, Joe 221
Fine, Tommy 188
Finol, Delmiro 132, 164, 168, 170, 171, 173
Fisher, Gus 58
Flagler, Henry Morrison 5, 6, 224
Flaglers 207
Fleetwood 60
Fleitas, Angel 48
Fleitas, C. Andres 49
Flournoy, Pud 25, 28, 29, 95
Foiles, Hank 175
Fonseca, Enrique 164, 170
Fontanalis, E. 34
Foote 74
Forbes, Joe 27
Ford, Edward "Whitey" 201
Formental, Pedro 51, 150, 151, 154, 173, 180, 208, 216, 218, 221
Foster, Rube 7–9, 13, 14, 21, 23–25, 29, 35–37, 66–68, 90, 92, 207, 210, 212
Foster, Willie 75, 85–87, 98, 99, 207, 212, 213
Foxx, Jimmie 1, 94, 100, 199, 206
Francis, Brodie, Billy 11, 18, 21–23, 29, 209, 211
Frankhouse, Fred 100
Frederick, Johnny 100
French, Larry 2, 43, 71, 78, 84, 85, 100, 206
Frias, Elias 149
Fridley 173
Fuentes, F. 157
Fullis, Chick 100
Furillo, Carl 89

Gaines, Jonas 180, 218
Galan, Augie 101
Galarraga, Andres 173
Galata, Raul 172, 180, 218, 219
Galloway 29

Gans, Jude 16, 18, 22, 210, 211
Garcia, Antonio "El Ingles" 32, 208
Garcia, Braganita 141, 143
Garcia, Cholo 111
Garcia, Isodoro 130
Garcia, Luis "Cameleon" 132, 171, 172–175, 177, 184, 189
Garcia, Manolo 123
Garcia, Manuel "Cocaina" 2, 46, 47, 49, 113, 140, 143, 144, 158, 160, 167, 180, 184, 208, 212, 216, 217, 219
Garcia, Miguel Angel 224
Garcia, Moim 148
Garcia, Nonito 143
Garcia, Pablo 168
Garcia, Regino 208
Garcia, Silvio 2, 45, 46, 120, 143, 144, 146, 154, 160, 167, 180, 195, 208, 214–218, 220
Garcia C., R. 167, 170
Gardella, Danny 48, 50
Gardner, Billy 175
Gardner, Jelly 42, 94, 96, 98, 211
Gardner, Ping 23, 25–27, 29, 213
Garland, Lou 77
Garth, Sam 194
Gatewood, Bill 9–11, 36, 67, 210
Gatewood, Ernest 25
Gay, W. 28
Gehrig, Lou 98, 108, 121, 143
Gehringer, Charlie 96, 98, 103
Gentile, Jim 204, 222
Gerrard, Alphonso 154, 214
Gershman, Michael 224
Gibson, Bob 153
Gibson, Josh 1–4, 44, 46, 48, 84, 87, 98, 100, 103, 110, 113–115, 117, 120–124, 141, 142, 144–146, 160–163, 168, 203, 207, 211, 214, 216, 218, 221
Giesentaner, Lefty 27
Giles, George 99, 103, 214, 221
Gillette, Gary 224
Gilliam, Junior 214
Gilmore, Q.J. 198, 199
Gionfriddo, Al 129
Gisentaner, Willie "Lefty" 100
Gladstone, Granville 188, 189, 219
Gladu, Roland 48
Glover, Tom "Lefty" 29, 167, 180, 219
Godinez, Manuel 167, 181, 218
Goliat, Mike 177
Goliath, Fred 55, 58–61, 212
Gomez, A. 178
Gomez, Chaguin 141, 142
Gomez, Gen. Juan Vincente 158, 159
Gomez, Lefty 108, 109, 164
Gomez, Ruben 125, 131, 173
Gonzalez 22
Gonzalez, Mike A. 42, 208
Gonzalez, Rene 172, 173, 181, 195, 218, 220
Gonzalez, Roberto 33

Gonzalez, Strike 112, 208
Gonzalez, V. 34
Gorin, Charlie 128
Graber, Rod 188, 189
Graham, Dennis 94
Graham, Frank 5, 34, 38, 39, 223
Grant, Charlie "Tokahoma" 3, 7–9, 35, 36
Grant, Frank 5, 207
Grant, Leroy 18–20, 22, 23, 210
Graves, Whitt 181, 219
Gray, Dolly 66
Greason, Bill 132, 215, 221
Green, Dalbert P., M.Sgt 52, 53
Green, Elijah "Pumpsie" 189, 190, 219
Greenlee, Gus 3, 77
Grey, H. 28
Griffin, "Big Boy" 82
Griffith, Bob 172, 181, 212, 213, 215, 217, 219
Griffith, Clark 3, 4
Griggs, Art 71
Grillo see Baez
Grove, Lefty 1, 92, 103, 109, 206
Guerra, Livio 141
Guerra, Rafael "Fellito" 46, 137, 138, 140
Guilbe, Juan 124, 125, 128, 215
Guillo, Nemsiso 30
Gullic 80
Guzman, Titico 141
Guzman, William 111

Haddock 129
Hafey, Chick 101
Hairston, Sam 172–174, 181, 202, 218, 221
Haley 70
Hall, Blainey 20–24, 29, 210
Hamric, Bert 177
Handy, Bill 14, 16, 18, 20, 210
Haney, Fred 75, 76, 91
Hannah, Truck 70
Hannigan, Patrick J. 223
Harbold, R.P. 54
Harmon, Charles "Chuck" 130, 214
Harney, George 92, 98
Harrell, William 214
Harris, Bucky 127
Harris, Nate 90, 210
Harris, Vic 25–28, 94, 103, 115, 116, 210
Harris, Wilmer 190, 219, 220
Harrist, Earl 128
Harshman, Jack 130
Hartman, J.C. 154, 155
Hartung, Clint "The Hondo Hurricane" 51, 150
Harvey, Bill 215, 221
Harvey, Frank 18
Hassler, Joe 94
Hatten, Joe 176
Hausmann, George 48
Hawkins, Lem 53–61, 70, 72–74, 212, 213
Hayes, Frank 106, 109

Hayes, John 114, 116, 170, 214, 218
Heard, Jehosie "Jay" 174, 181, 215, 219
Heath, Jeff 106
Hegan, Jim 106
Heilmann, Harry "The Horse" 94, 96
Heimach, Fred 92
Heintzelman, Ken 104
Henley, Gail 188, 189
Henrich, Tommy 168, 169
Henriquez, Papin 141, 143
Henry 40, 41
Henry, Dutch 98
Heredia 48
Herman, Babe 2, 71, 74, 75, 99
Hermann, Garry 38
Hernandez 159
Hernandez, Chucho 160
Hernandez, Enrique "El Indio Bravo" 135, 137
Hernandez, Jacinto "Jayase" 112, 113
Hernandez, Julio "Burano" 138
Herrera, J. 155
Herrera, Ramon 40, 42, 43
Herrmann, Leroy 117
Hetki, John 174
Heureaux, Fallon 147
Hewitt, Joe 20, 21, 91
Hickman, Jimmy 95
Hicks, Buddy 173, 174, 177
Higbee 58
Higgins, Pinky 100
Hill, John 7-9
Hill, Pete 7, 8, 10, 13, 17, 18, 22, 29, 35, 36, 38, 68, 90, 207, 210, 211
Hockette, George 114
Hoey, Jack 13
Hogan, Dr. Lawrence D. 84, 116
Hogan, Willie "Happy" 56
Hoie, Bob 223
Holguin, Roque 147
Holland, Bill 36, 41, 98, 114, 212
Hollocher, Charlie 58
Holloway, Crush 114, 211, 213
Holmes, Ducky 90
Holmes, Tommy 105
Holsey, Frog 98
Holway, John 28, 40, 41, 54, 58, 61, 72, 77, 86, 94, 103, 109, 119, 145, 161, 165, 174, 198, 201, 223
Hooker, Lennie 105
Horn, Doc 221
Hornsby, Rogers 103, 199
Hoskins, Dave 181, 188-190, 218, 219
Houk, Ralph 169
Howard, Del 90
Howard, Elston 214
Howard, Frank 132
Howard, Janet 77
Hubbard, Jesse 114, 213
Hubbell, Carl 43, 102
Hudlin, Willis 96
Huggins, Miller 9, 37

Hughes, Sammy T. 46, 76, 78, 79, 213
Hunt 117
Hunt, Ken 188, 189
Hunter, Bert 142, 216, 217
Hyde, Cowan "Bubba" 80

Inojosa, Balbino 141, 159-162, 167
Irvin, Monte 105, 121-124, 126, 129, 203, 207, 211, 214

Jackman, Will 27
Jackson 114
Jacobo, Austin 146
Jacobson, "Baby Doll" 98
James 10, 18
Jasper, Sgt. Jacques 54, 57, 59, 61, 212
Javier, Julian 153
Jefferson, "Bill" "Willie" 166-168, 181, 219, 221
Jeffries, Jim 71-73
Jenkins, Ferguson 195
Jessup, Gentry 106, 168, 169, 181, 218
Jethroe, Sam 3, 105, 106, 129, 164-167, 181, 211, 214, 218
Jimenez 159
Jimenez, Bienvenido 208
Jimenez, Jose de Jesus 223
Jimenez, Luis 141, 161, 162
Jimenez, Pedro "Natilla" 194
Jimenez, S. 34
Johns 60
Johnson, Ban 39
Johnson, Bill "Big C" 29, 54, 55, 61
Johnson, Billy 169
Johnson, Cecil 29, 92
Johnson, Chappie 11, 16, 36, 67, 211
Johnson, Connie 190, 212, 220
Johnson, Dicta 67
Johnson, Don 169
Johnson, George Washington 24
Johnson, Grant "Home Run" 7-10, 35, 36, 38, 211
Johnson, John B. 114
Johnson, Judy 28, 207, 211
Johnson, Lou "Sweet Lou" 133, 154, 155, 190, 214, 220
Johnson, Oscar "Heavy" 53-61, 212
Johnson, Syl 78
Johnson, Tom 68
Johnson, Walter 65, 67, 95
Johnston (Johnson), Wade 25
Jok, Stan 177
Jones 27
Jones, Allen 177, 189
Jones, Bob 91
Jones, C. 28
Jones, Hattie 114
Jones, Lefty 114
Jones, Sam "Toothpick" 131, 132, 154, 181, 195, 196, 215, 217, 219, 220
Jones, Slim 115, 116

Jones, Yunk 29
Jordan, Adolf "Dutch" 35
Jordan, Jimmy 3, 161, 162
Joseph, Newt 42, 99, 211, 213
Juarez, Lucas "El Indio" 197
Judnich, Walt 128
Judson, Howie 130

Kaat, Jim 195
Kaiser, Cecil 215, 217, 220
Kampouris, Alex 117
Kawakami, Tetsuharu 153
Keating, Ray 83
Keller, Charlie "King Kong" 105, 106, 168
Kelley, Brent 130, 151, 169, 201-203, 223
Kellman, Leon 154, 190, 218, 220
Kelly, George 98
Kelly, Roberto 191
Keltner, Ken 105, 106
Kennard, Dan 91
Kennedy, Bill "Brickyard" 95
Kennon, Col. Lyman W.V. 54
Kenyon, Harry 25
Kerns, Russell 174
Keron, G. 189
Kerr, Buddy 105
Kimball, Newt 80
Kimbro, Henry 47, 211
King, Jim 178
Kipp, Fred 151
Kirkland, Willie 151, 153
Klein, Alan M. 135, 136, 138, 140, 146, 223
Klein, Lou 49
Kleinknecht, Merl 223
Kluttz, Clyde 105
Knickerbocker, Bill 77
Knoublach 173
Koening, F. 178
Koufax, Sandy 132
Koupal, Lou 82, 83, 85
Kress 80
Krich, John 223
Krueger, Ernie 40, 41
Kuhel, Joe 99
Kurowski, Whitey 105
Kyle, A. 70
Kyle, W. 70

Labine, Clem 172, 173
Lambertus, Nestor "El Loco" 138
Lanauze, Jose "Ciqui" 141
Landino, Leonte A. 223
Landis, Kenesaw Mountain 75, 80, 81, 93, 106
Langford, Ad 20, 67, 210
Lanier, Max 50, 200
Lantigua, Enrique 142, 143, 207
Lapan, Pete 74
Lara, Diogenes 138, 139, 142
Larker, Norm 173, 177
Larsen, Don 201
Lasorda, Tommy 132
Lavender, David 224
Lawson, Al 5, 34
Leafwich 105

Index

Leal, "Pipita" 171, 173
Lee 25
Lee, Carlos 192
LeMarque, Lefty 215
Lemon, Bob 201
Lemon, Jim 175
Lennon, Bob 105, 132, 175
Leonard, Buck 3, 43–46, 79, 80, 89, 102, 104, 113, 115–117, 119, 121, 122, 142, 164, 165, 167, 168, 178, 181, 207, 211, 214, 218, 224
Lester, Larry 223, 224
Levis, O. 42, 43
Lewis, Buddy 104
Lewis, Joseph "Sleepy" 25
Lewis, Phil 9, 10
Lewis, Rufus 116, 167, 181, 212, 218
Liendo, V. 167
Likins 60
Limmer, Lou 177
Linares, R. 46
Lind, Jenny 134
Lindell, Johnny 80, 81
Lindsay, Bill 14, 67, 68
Lipman, David 161, 224
Lipon, Johnny 51
Little, Stephen D. 60
Lloyd, John Henry 1, 4, 11, 13, 17–21, 23, 24, 29, 36–38, 40, 43, 68, 75, 84, 90, 98, 142, 206, 207, 210, 211
Lluberes, Gustavo 143
Locke, Edward 202, 21
Lockett, Lester 170, 181, 218, 220
Lockhart, Hubert 25
Lodges 207
Lohrke, Lucky 132
Long, Dale 132
Lopez, Arturo 162
Lopez, Cando 140, 216
Lopez, Hector 188, 191
Lopez, M. 34
Lopez, Rafaelito 129
Lopez, Vidal 167, 168, 170–173, 184, 185, 208
Lott, Honey 154
Louden, Louis 214
Lowrey, Peanuts 79, 80
Lucas, Guigui 147
Lucas, Papito "Pepe" 147–149, 151
Lujan, Adolfo 32
Lundy, Dick "King Richard" 22, 24, 40, 41, 43, 84, 114, 210, 211
Luque, Adolfo 40, 41, 44, 48, 50, 112, 202, 203, 206, 208
Lyons, Jimmie 23, 29, 210, 211
Lyons, Ted 100

Machado, O. 157, 170
Macias, Jose 192
Mack, Connie 3, 4, 38, 206
Mack, Earl 92
Mack, Ray 169
Mackey, Biz 41, 71–73, 75, 79, 80, 82, 87, 92, 105, 107, 108, 125, 207, 211, 213
Mackinson, John 174

Maduro, Bobby 47
Maglie, Sal 50, 200
Mails, Duster 70, 83
Mairena, Oswaldo 196
Malarcher, Dave 23, 69
Malloy, Jerry 53, 61, 224
Maloney, Billy 9
Malpica, "Pollo" 141, 158, 159, 162, 184
Mancuso, Frank 172, 173
Manion, Clyde 91
Manley, Abe 115
Manning, Max 48, 212, 215, 217, 219
Manush, Heinie 71, 92, 96, 98, 100, 199
Manzueta, Julio 149
Mapes, Cliff 169
Marcelle, Oliver "The Ghost" 40, 41, 211
Marichal, Juan 153–155
Markham, John 80
Marquard, Rube 95
Marquez, Luis "Canena" 125, 133, 214
Marrero, Connie 164
Marsans, Armando 38
Marshall, Cuddles 169
Marshall, Jack 23, 24
Martin 108
Martin, Sidney Walter 224
Martin, Speed 70
Martinez, Aquiles 148, 149, 155
Martinez, Dennis 196
Martinez, Horacio "Rabbit" 142–144, 207, 218, 221
Martinez, M. 178
Mason 24
Mathewson, Christy 38
Mathis, Verdell 170, 181, 219, 221
Matlock, Leroy 47, 143–146, 162, 217, 219
Matos, Jose "Achin" 149
Maury, P. 157
Mayor, Agapito 49
Mays, Willie 77, 83, 123, 131, 132, 150, 176, 184, 207, 214
Mazeroski, Bill 153
McAdoo, Dudley "Tully" 91
McCann, Emmett 92
McCarthy, Kevin 5, 9, 224
McClain, Joe 18
McClellan, Dan 7, 9, 11–14, 16, 35, 36, 210
McClure, Bob 24
McCormick, Frank 105
McCredie, Walter 68
McCuller, George 32
McDaniels, Booker 80, 212, 215
McDonald 77, 78
McDonald, Webster 98
McDowell, Sam 132
McDuffie, Terris 50, 116, 122, 151, 152, 154, 172, 174, 177, 181, 212, 217, 219
McGraw 74
McGraw, John 3–6, 8, 34, 38, 39, 57, 206, 223

McHenry, Henry 170, 218
McIntyre, Matty 13
McIver, Stuart 6, 27, 224
McKissicks, Frederick 42, 224
McKissicks, Patricia 42, 224
McLain, Denny 132
McMullen 77, 78
McNair, Hurley 53, 55, 56, 61, 69, 70, 72–74, 213
McNary, Kyle P. 224
McNeal, Clyde 181, 218
McNeil, William F. 224
McQuinn, George 113, 115, 116, 168
Meadows, Specs 70, 205
Medina, Bambolio 143
Medina, Lazarus 215, 220
Medio, Quince y 32
Medwick, Joe 169
Meine, Heinie 99
Melendez, J.S. "Chino" 194
Melendez, R. 178
Mendez, E. 157
Mendez, Jose 31, 36–38, 40, 41, 69, 72, 73, 75, 112, 142, 207, 213
Mendez, Ramoncito 194
Mendoza, Ramiro 192
Meneses, S. 157
Mesa, Andres 48
Mesa, Pablo "Champion" 40, 208
Metkovich, George "Catfish" 79, 80
Meusel, Bob 2, 70–73, 75, 205
Meusel, Emil "Irish" 2, 70, 71, 73, 75
Meyers, Chief 67
Meyers, George "Deacon" 91
Mieses, Laitico 141
Miller 10, 60
Miller, Bing 92, 94
Miller, Henry "Hank" 167, 168, 181, 218
Miller, Lee 23
Mills, Buster 175
Minoso, Minnie 31, 154, 155, 202, 203, 208, 224
Mirabel, Juanelo 24
Miranda, Pindu 138
Mitchell, Alonzo 26, 28
Mitchell, Fred 12, 13
Mitchell, Mike 12
Mize, Johnny 103, 113, 114
Molina, Augustin "Tinti" 33
Molina, Julio "El Diamante Blanco" 197
Monfort, Charles 39
Mongin, Sam 12, 14
Monroe, Bill 7–9, 11, 12, 14, 36, 37, 68, 211
Montalvo, Esteban 40, 41
Montaner, Paquito 130
Monzant, Ramon 132, 184, 185
Moon, Wally 173, 175
Moore 60, 73
Moore, Dobie 2, 3, 40, 41, 53, 55–61, 69–72, 75, 82–84, 87, 142, 205, 206, 211–213

Moore, Lefty 60
Moore, Mike "Daddy" 7, 10, 67
Moore, Roy 91
Mora, Jesus 177
Mora, Ricardo 30
Morales, Solar 130
Moran, Carlos 34
Moran, F. 34
Moran, Pat 90
More, J. 189
Morgan, Joe 178
Morgan, Semaphore 212
Morse, Joseph Laffan 224
Moses, Wally 113
Mosquera, Senor 156
Mota, Manny 153
Mothell, Dink 43, 99, 213
Mozzall 173
Mrozinski, Ron 176, 177
Mulkern 60
Munion 74
Munoz, C. 167
Munoz, Gallego 149
Munoz, Jose 35–37
Munoz, Luis 35–37
Munson, Thurman 132
Murphy, Dod 73
Murphy, Johnny 98
Musial, Stan 105
Mutis, Manuel 111
Myers, Billy 116, 117

Nankivell 54, 56, 224
Naranjo, Pedro 195
Navarro, Emilio "Millito" 112, 113, 121, 141, 157, 159, 207
Navarro, Victor 224
Navas, Carlos "Pichon" 194
Naylor, Earl 128
Neal, Charlie 151, 153
Needham, Tom 9, 10, 13
Neil, Ray 172, 181, 218
Nelson, Billy 93
Nelson, Rocky 132, 176
Neve, Felip de 62
Newberry, Jimmy 217, 220
Newcombe, Don 105, 150, 169–171, 181, 219
Newsom, Buck, Bobo 2, 71, 76, 79, 80, 82, 84, 85, 109, 205, 206
Newsome, Skeeter 80
Nieves, Cesar 141, 159, 161, 162
Nina, Pedro 143, 147
Noble, Ray 48, 181, 218
Northrup, Jim 132
Novikoff, Lou 80

Obregon, T. 189
O'Brien, Dink 58
O'Connor, Leslie M. 81
Oelkers, Bryan 204
Oglesby, Jim 77
Oglivie, Ben 191, 192
Ograin 78
Oh, Sadaharu 203
Oldham, Johnny "Red" 70, 82
Oleksaks, Mary Adams 186, 224
Oleksaks, Michael M. 186, 224

Oliva, Tony 123
Olivares, J. 42
Olivares, R. 167
Oliver, L.E. 28
Oliveros 167
Oliveros, L. 167, 173, 174
Olivo, Chi Chi 151
Olivo, Diomedes "Guayubin" 148–153
Olmo, Luis 118, 122, 125, 151, 173
Oms, Alejandro 2, 40–42, 112, 113, 118, 119, 121, 140, 160, 164, 206, 208, 216
O'Neil, Buck 105, 106, 224
O'Neil, Steve 94, 98
O'Reilly, Yoyo 148
Orndorff, Jess 66
Ortiz, David 34
Ortiz, Rafaelito 118, 119, 121, 122, 124, 215
Ortiz, Roberto 48, 49
Oscanio, J.R. 189
Osorio, Alberto 182, 188–190, 219, 220
Osorio, Elias 188, 189
Osorio, V. 167
Outland, John 77
Owen, Mickey 132
Owens (umpire) 39

Pace 28
Padden, Tom 100
Padget, Ernie 92
Padilla, Vincent 196
Padron, Luis "El Mulo" 20, 21, 29, 34, 35, 111, 112, 142, 208, 210
Paez, Aladino 141
Pafko, Andy 79, 80
Page, Joe 127
Page, Ted 3, 98, 100, 103
Pages, Pedro 48, 49, 195, 218, 220
Paige, Satchel 1–3, 71, 75–83, 85–89, 98, 100, 101, 103–107, 113, 117, 119, 121, 129, 143–146, 160, 161, 182, 205–207, 212, 214, 215, 217, 224
Palm, Clarence "Spoony" 120, 121, 144, 216
Palmer, Pete 224
Palomino, Emilio 34, 208
Panier 26
Pardo, Alberto 204
Parker, Dave 173
Parmelee, Roy 95, 100
Parris, Jonathan Clyde 190, 218, 220
Partee, Roy 80
Partlow, Roy 105, 120, 121, 182, 214, 215, 217, 219
Pascual, Camilo 177
Pascual, Carlos 51
Pasquel, Jorge 199, 200
Pastoriza, Juan 32
Patterson, Pat 216
Payne, Jap 16, 18, 90, 210
Peacock, Johnny 116, 117
Pearson, Lennie 49, 121, 122, 168, 169, 211, 214

Peden, L. 189
Pedroso, Eustaquio "Bombin" 37, 112, 208
Pedroso, Fernandez Diaz 126–128, 195, 214, 220
Pena 129
Pena, Orlando 177
Pendleton, Jim 171–174, 178, 182, 190, 211, 218
Penner, K. 58
Pennington, Al see Pennington, Arthur
Pennington, Arthur "Superman" 154, 172, 182, 202, 203, 218, 221
Perdomo, Pajarito 147
Pereyra, Esperanza, Senorita 138
Perez, A. 157
Perez, Azucena 46
Perez, C.M. 159
Perez, Conrado 48
Perez, Federico 149
Perez, J. 46, 159
Perez, Javier 108, 143
Perez, Juan Antonio 157, 158
Perez, Lolo 141–143
Perez, Marinito 149
Perez, Pepin 140
Perez, R. 129
Perkins, Bill 100, 120, 143, 211, 216
Perkins, Cy 92
Perranoski, Ron 178
Perritt, Pol 95
Perry, Alonzo 128, 129, 150–154, 207, 216, 217, 221, 223
Perry, Carl 26, 27
Pertica, Bill 71, 73
Pesante, Menchin 159
Peters 99
Peters, Gary 178
Peterson, Robert W. 37, 55, 56, 224
Pettus, Bill 17, 18, 67, 210, 213
Petty, Jesse 40, 41, 206
Petway, Bruce 9–13, 17, 18, 22, 35, 38, 68, 210, 211
Phelps, William H. 158
Philips, Jack 169
Picazo, Narciso 198
Pichardo, Vincente 137
Pierce, Bill 14, 20
Piercy, Bill 83
Pietrusza, David 224
Pillette, Herm "Old Folks" 92
Pinate, T. 167
Pinella, Lou 195
Pinelli, Babe 58
Pinkston, Alfred 203, 207
Pirrone, Joe 2, 69–71, 73–76, 79, 81, 86
Pirrone, John 69, 75
Plaker 58
Plant, Morton F. 20
Polanco 129
Poles, Reid N. 19
Poles, Spottswood "Spot" 1, 17–21, 29, 38, 90, 210, 211
Pope, Dave 175, 182, 214, 218
Porras, President 186

Porter, Andrew "Pullman" 78, 103, 104, 182, 212, 214, 219
Portocarerro, Arnold 130
Posey, Cum 68
Powell, Bill 129, 130, 182, 218
Power, Vic 129
Powers 78
Poyo, Jose 33
Preston, Al 217
Priddy, Jerry 79
Prieto, C. 178
Pryor, Anderson 26, 27
Pryor, Wes 16, 18, 210
Puesan, Melizzo 143, 147
Pujadas, Camilo 197
Pullen, Sgt.-Maj. Frank W. 52
Pullen, Neal 73, 74, 213
Purse, Edward 65

Quevedo, Francisco 141, 161, 162
Quezada, Lazaro 158
Quiesser 10, 11
Quinones, Tomas "Planchardon" 124, 126, 128, 215
Quintero, Andres 185

Rac, Russ 177
Radcliffe, Ted "Double Duty" 47, 50, 80, 100, 212, 224
Raffensberger, Ken 51
Raggs, Harry (aka Harry Roberts) 24
Raines, Larry 178
Rakow, Ed 178
Ramirez, L. 157
Ramos 173, 174
Ramos, Jesus "Chucho" 166, 184, 185
Rawlings, Johnny 71, 73
Rector, Connie 114
Redding, Dick "Cannonball" 19–22, 25, 29, 90, 112, 210, 212
Redondo, Benitez 170
Redus, Frog 99
Reel, Jimmy 26
Reese, John 25, 213
Reese, Pee Wee 191
Regalado, Rudy 177
Renfroe, Othello 182, 218
Renteria, Edgar 204
Reyes, Amable 138
Reyes, Rene Velasquez 138
Reynolds, Allie 168, 169
Reynoso, P. 155
Ribowski, Mark 224
Richards, Paul 113
Richardson, Harry 113
Rickey, Branch 4, 183
Ricks, Bill 182, 219
Ridzik, Steve 130
Riggins, Orville 91, 98, 211, 213
Riggs, Lew 116
Rigney, Topper 91
Rijo, R. 155
Rile, Huck 96
Riley, James A. "Jim" 26, 50, 54, 85, 102, 103, 124, 161, 199, 200, 202, 224

Rincon, L. 167
Ritchey, Johnny "Hoss" 171, 172, 182, 218
Ritchie, O. 13
Rivas, F. 155
Rivas, Rafael Soler 130, 131
Rivera, Mariano 192
Rizzuto, Phil 105, 106, 168, 169
Roach 114
Roarke, Mike 178
Roberts, Curt 154, 190, 195, 211, 220
Roberts, Dave 154, 155
Roberts, Harry *see* Raggs, Harry
Roberts, Roy 23, 24, 26
Robinson 64
Robinson, Aaron 168, 169
Robinson, Al 10–12, 14, 16, 210
Robinson, Bojangles 77
Robinson, Brooks 204, 222
Robinson, Humberto 188, 191
Robinson, Jackie 2, 4, 49, 81, 105, 122, 128, 150, 164, 165, 177, 183, 191, 207, 224
Robinson, Jonathan 194
Robinson, Ken 28
Robinson, Neil 215
Robinson, Wilbert 43
Rockefeller, John D. 5
Rodgers, Bill 58
Rodriguez 48, 159
Rodriguez, Burrolote 148
Rodriguez, Francisco 136
Rodriguez, Gerardo 18
Rodriguez, Gueba 142
Rodriguez, Jose 208
Rodriguez, Ninin 138, 143, 147
Roebuck, Ed 132
Rogan, "Bullet Joe" 1, 2, 3, 41, 53–61, 69–71, 75, 82, 83, 87, 92, 110, 142, 205–207, 212–214
Rogers, Nat 99
Rogosin, Donn 115, 161, 187, 188, 224
Rojo, Julio 40–42
Romero, A. 157
Romero, Luis 170
Romero, P. 178
Roosevelt, Teddy 53
Root, Charlie 83
Rosa, Mateo de la 137–139
Rosario, Luis, Jr. 121, 124
Rosas 129, 130
Rose 70
Rose, Pete 173
Roseboro, Johnny 173, 177
Rosell, Basilio "El Brujo" 140
Ross, William 108, 214
Royer, Carlos "Bebe" 34
Rubenstein 132
Ruck, Rob 136, 147, 148, 224
Rucker, Mark 224
Ruether, Dutch 81
Ruiz, Abejita 140–142
Ruiz, Silvino 46, 141–143, 161, 162
Ruiz, Yuyo 33, 47, 119, 125–127, 137, 139, 148, 152, 179, 202, 224

Russell, Branch 42, 91
Russell, Rip 79
Ruth, Babe 2, 12, 16, 84, 108, 112, 115, 122, 180, 224
Ryan, Red 27, 28, 212
Ryba, Mike 103, 104

Sabino, Jose 137, 138
Sabourin, Emilio 32
Sackie, Garabato 151
Sadler, Bill 116
Saenz, Olmedo 192
Saillant, Luis Tomas 138
Sain, Johnny 105, 106
St. Clair, Jose 130, 132, 169
St. Clair, L. 169
Salas, Alexis H. 224
Salas, Wilfredo 215, 217, 219
Salazar, Lazaro 46–48, 113, 140, 144, 162, 163, 172, 173, 182, 199, 203, 207, 208, 216, 217, 219
Salmon, Harry 113
Salvent, A. 178
Sampson, Tommy 79, 80
Samson 173, 174
Sanchez, Juan "Chico" 125, 126
Sandoval, Julio "Canana" 194
Sanford, Jack 130, 132
Sanford, Jay 8, 43
Sanguillen, Manny 191
San, Pedro Alejandro 138, 140, 141, 161, 162, 207, 215, 219
Santaella, Tacho 46
Santana, F. 155
Santana, Jose "Pepe" 112, 113
Santiago, Carlos 207
Santiago, Jose G. 133, 215, 217
Santiago, Jose "Pantalones" 124, 127, 128, 173
Santop, Louis 17–19, 21–24, 29, 112, 207, 210
Sarnis 70
Saunders, Bob 26
Saunders, Lt. O.H. 54
Savage 74
Sawyer, Carl 73, 74, 78, 81, 82
Sayama, Kazuo 224
Scales, George 25, 113, 114, 117, 124, 127, 144, 146, 173, 207, 211
Scantlebury, Pat 187, 188, 190, 215, 220
Scarcia 117
Schacht, Al 90, 95
Schang, Wally 92, 96
Schatzlein 58
Schenz, Hank 174
Schirm 10
Schott, Gene 117
Schulde 60
Schulte, Frank 90
Schultz, Toots 69
Schulz, Al 95
Schulze 60
Scott, Bob 25
Scott, George 195
Scott, Jim "Death Valley" 56
Seay, Dick 115–118
Seimer 99

Seldon, William 5
Selig, Rafael "Gugu" 138
Serrell, Bonnie 154, 179, 202, 203, 211, 215, 221
Sewell, Joe 91
Shafer, Tillie 67
Sheckard, Jimmy 90
Shellenback, Frank 70
Shires, Art "The Great" 96, 98
Shorrs 70
Shrouds, Ida Alice 5
Silveiro, P. 34
Simmons, Al 108
Simpson, Harry "Suitcase" 167, 182, 195, 215, 218, 220
Siragusa, Paco 135
Skiff, Bill 98
Skinner, Bob 132
Slack, W. 189
Sloat, Dwayne 128
Smith 74
Smith, Al 130, 215
Smith "Big Bill" 7, 11, 14
Smith, Bob 43
Smith, Chino 42–44, 211
Smith, Cleveland "Cleo" 25, 58–61
Smith, Ford 128
Smith, Gene 215
Smith, Harry 11
Smith, Hilton 44, 46, 103–105, 167–169, 178, 182, 207, 212, 219
Smith, John F. 215, 217
Smith, Jud 66
Smith, Lee 192
Smith, Milt 154, 190, 211, 216, 220
Smith, "Shine" 114
Smith, Theolic "Fireball" 47, 172, 182, 212, 219
Snodgrass, Fred 67
Snow, Felton 46, 76–78, 82, 101, 165, 213
Snyder, Jerry 188, 189
Solis, Miguel 140, 141
Soloso, Severino T. 32
Somoza, Anastasio, Jr. 192
Somoza, Anastasio, Sr. 192, 193, 196
Sonora, Juan 141
Souell, Herbert 215
Spalding, Albert G. 5, 30, 65
Spalding, John E. 64, 224
Spearman, Charles 26, 27
Spearman, Clyde 46, 80, 114, 146, 211
Spooner, Karl 130, 132
Stanky, Eddie 105, 191
Stanley, Joe 90
Stanley, John "Neck" 106, 113
Stark, Jim
Starks, Otis 25, 117
Statz, Jigger 75
Stearnes, Turkey 2, 42, 75–78, 83, 101, 207, 213
Stengel, Casey 3, 61
Stephens, Vern 80
Stine, Lee 77, 82, 117

Stirnweiss, Snuffy 168, 169
Stone, Ed 29, 46, 105, 115–118, 120, 211
Stoneham, Charles A. 38
Stovall, George 66
Stovey, George 5
Strange 77
Strawberry, Darryl 173
Streeter, Sam 26, 27, 98, 212
Streuss 98
Strizka, Victor
Strothers, Timothy "Sam" 90
Stuart, Dick 151, 153
Stumph, Bill 58
Styne see Stine
Suarez, Elio 150
Suarez, Miguel 47
Suarez, Olmedo 149, 151
Suhr, Gus 101
Summers, Lonnie 215, 218
Suncar, Osvaldo Rodriguez 224
Surkont, Max 170
Surratt, Al "Slick" 190, 202, 220
Susce, George 103
Suttles, Mule 2, 43, 71, 75–79, 82, 84, 96, 98, 99, 101, 206, 207, 211, 213
Sweeney, Bill 94, 98
Swift, Bill 100
Swinton, Sgt. 54, 58–61

Taborn, Earl 154
Tatler, Henry 170
Taylor, Ben 19, 20, 72, 207, 210
Taylor, C.I. 72
Taylor, "Candy Jim" 20, 68, 72, 91
Taylor, Danny 100
Taylor, Harry 50
Taylor, John 47, 71–73
Taylor, Johnny "Schoolboy" 173, 174
Taylor, Joseph "Joe" 54, 190, 215, 220
Taylor, Ray 199
Tello, Rafael Gallis 164, 167
Temple, Johnny 175
Terry, Bill 99
Terry, Charles H. 127
Tesreau, Jeff 95
Thiel, Bert 128
Thomas, Clint 29, 92, 114, 161, 211
Thomas, David "Dave," "Showboat" 114, 144
Thomas, E. 155
Thomas, Earl 14
Thomas, Frank 34
Thomas, Jules 17, 18, 20, 22–25, 210
Thomas, Valmy 131
Thompson (umpire) 59
Thompson, Charles "Tim" 178
Thompson, Frank 218
Thompson, Hank 49, 105, 106, 168–170, 211
Thon, Dickie 129
Thorn, John 224

Thurman, Bob 115, 126, 127, 130–133, 149, 151–154, 207, 215–217
Thurston, Sloppy 2, 82, 85
Tiant, Luis, Jr. 142, 195
Tiant, Luis, Sr. 42, 44, 48, 142, 144, 193, 198, 208, 217
Tierney, Cot 99
Tincannon 100
Tinco, Miguel Tiant 149
Tinker, Joe 89, 90
Tirado, Jorge 122, 125
Todd, Al 100
Torrens, Benito "Juey" 112, 185
Torres, Angel 224
Torres, Bin. 129, 130
Torriente, Cristobal 2, 39–41, 206–208
Tovar, Cesar 178, 185
Tovar, L. 155
Travis, Cecil 104
Trent, Ted 28, 99, 114, 212
Trouppe, Quincy 105, 106, 122–124, 129, 164, 165, 167, 173, 174, 182, 215, 218, 221
Trucks, Virgil "Fire" 105
Trujillo, Rafael, General 113, 140, 143–145
Tuminelli, Joe 188
Turgerson, Jim 217
Turley, Bob 130
Turner, Terry 13
Turner, Thomas "High Pockets" 201, 221

Uhle, George 91, 92, 94, 98
Ulloa, Francisco de 62
Urena, Mero 138
Uzcategui, P. 167

Valbuena, G. 178
Valdes, R. 34
Valentino, Rudolph 177
Valenzuela, Fernando 204
Valero, Eduardo 113
Valesquez, F. 155
Valesquez, Rene 137
Vallecillo, J.M. 194
Van Cuyk, Chris 50
Van Cuyk, Johnny 50
Vanderbilts 207
Van Hyning, Tom 115, 121, 123, 128, 130, 224
Vargas, Guagua 136, 138
Vargas, Juan 136
Vargas, Juan Estando "Tetelo" 3, 113, 116, 118, 119, 121, 129, 136, 139–144, 150, 151, 153, 154, 160–163, 207, 215, 216
Vargas, Papito 147
Vargas, Roberto 129, 216
Varona, Orlando 182, 218
Vasquez, R. 178
Vaughan, Arky 191
Vaughn, Ray "Slim" 26, 27, 29
Veach 116, 117
Veach, Bobby 91
Vega, Chechon 112
Veloz, Enrique 147

Index

Venema 60
Vento, Guillermo 151, 170, 173, 174
Vernon, Mickey 105, 106
Versalles, Zoilo 195
Vicioso 136
Villard, George 112
Villodas, Luis "King Kong" 129, 150, 151, 207, 215
Vinals, Luis 149
Virgil, Ozzie 153, 155
Vizcaino, Sebastian 62

Wade, Lee 16, 18, 210
Wagner, Honus 38
Walberg, Rube 94, 95
Walker 99
Walker, Jesse 80, 213
Wallace, Dick 210
Wallace, Felix 20, 21, 90
Wallace, Jack 26
Walls, Lee 176
Waner, Lloyd 99
Waner, Paul 99
Ward, Pinky 213
Ware, Archie 170, 218
Warfield, Frank 23, 40, 91, 92, 94, 211
Warstler, Rabbit 100
Washington, George 57
Washington, Jap 25–28, 94, 210
Washington, John 47
Waterhouse, Chief 59–61, 212
Waters, Fred 153
Weaver, Buck 93, 94
Webster, Pearl 210
Webster, Specks 16, 18, 20
Wells, Willie 42–44, 46, 47, 50, 71, 74–76, 78, 84, 85, 87, 96, 98, 99, 101, 102, 105, 122–124, 198, 199, 202, 211, 213, 215, 221, 224
Welmaker, Roy 165–168, 171, 182, 216, 219, 221
Wertz, Vic
Westerzil 70
Wheat, Zack 92
White, Burlin 25–27, 29
White, Chaney 25, 27, 28, 42, 211

White, Charlie 190, 220
White, Sol 7–9, 35, 224
Whitehill, Earl 98
Whitworth, Richard "Big" 22, 210
Wickware, Frank "The Red Ant" 13, 16–19, 22, 29, 210
Wiley, Doc 22
Wilie *see* Willie
Wilkinson, J.L. 59, 61
Williams, Albert 196
Williams, Andrew "Stringbean" 21
Williams, Bobby 22, 23, 27, 76, 77, 157
Williams, Charles "Lefty" 28, 42, 43, 94
Williams, Chester 114, 215
Williams, Clarence 5, 7, 11, 35, 38
Williams, Curley *see* Williams, Willie C.
Williams, David A. 64, 223
Williams, Dib 99
Williams, Gloomy Gus 58
Williams, Harry 162, 216
Williams, James "Big Jim" 142, 216
Williams, Jesse 154, 215, 216
Williams, John 154
Williams, Johnny "Honolulu" 59, 216
Williams, Ken 73
Williams, Marvin 166–169, 183, 202, 203, 215, 218, 221
Williams, Samuel C. 217
Williams, "Smokey Joe," "Cyclone Joe" 1, 4, 16–26, 28, 29, 67, 68, 75, 83, 87, 94–96, 100, 110, 206, 207, 210, 212
Williams, Stan 153
Williams, Ted 1, 88
Williams, Tom 21, 23, 24, 92
Williams, Willie C. "Curley" 152, 154, 216
Willie D. (Wilie) 58
Willis, Cpl. 56, 57
Willis, Dale 154, 155
Willis, Jim "Cannonball" 101, 214

Wilmore, Al 220
Wilson, Artie 106, 128, 129, 207, 215
Wilson, Bob 132, 153, 154, 177, 183, 218
Wilson, George 35
Wilson, Hack 100
Wilson, Jud 2, 40, 42, 43, 75, 83, 87, 94, 100, 207, 211, 215
Wilson, Lyle K. 76, 224
Wilson, Ray 36
Wilson, Tom 75–77, 100, 161
Winston, Bobby 10, 67
Winters, Nip 25, 40, 92, 93, 212
Witherspoon, C. 155
Wojey, Pete 128
Wolfer 58
Wood 69
Woodall, Larry 91, 94
Woods 70
Woods, Parnell 165, 167–169, 215, 218
Woods, Sam 217
Wright, George 12, 16, 67, 90
Wright, John, Sr. "Johnny" 149, 151, 170, 183, 216, 217, 219
Wright, "Wild Bill" 76, 78, 79, 85, 88, 101, 122–124, 201, 203, 206, 207, 213, 221
Wulf, Steve 224
Wynn, Early 47

Yancey, Bill 98, 186, 187, 190
Yochim, Len 177
Young, Cy 204
Young, Ted 121
Young, Tom 99

Zabala, Adrian 47, 48
Zarilla, Al 79
Zelaya, Jose Santos 192
Zitland 60
Zimmer, Don 131, 132
Zimmerman, Heinie 90, 112
Zomphier, Charles "Zomp" 99
Zoumps *see* Zomphier
Zubillaga, J. 34
Zuckerman, Larry 64, 224
Zuloaga, Luis "Mono" 170

www.ingramcontent.com/pod-product-compliance
Lightning Source LLC
Chambersburg PA
CBHW081158230426
43666CB00016B/2858